Theory into Practice

Theory into Practice

An Introduction to Literary Criticism

THIRD EDITION

ANN B. DOBIE
Professor Emerita, University of Louisiana at Lafayette

CENGAGE Learning®

Andover • Melbourne • Mexico City • Stamford, CT • Toronto • Hong Kong • New Delhi • Seoul • Singapore • Tokyo

Theory into Practice: An Introduction to Literary Criticism
Ann B. Dobie

ISBN-13: 978-81-315-1740-6
ISBN-10: 81-315-1740-3

Cengage Learning India Private Limited
418, F.I.E., Patparganj
Delhi 110092
India

Tel: 91-11-43641111
Fax: 91-11-43641100
Email: asia.infoindia@cengage.com

Cengage Learning is a leading provider of customized learning solutions with office locations around the globe, including Andover, Melbourne, Mexico City, Stamford (CT), Toronto, Hong Kong, New Delhi, Seoul, Singapore, and Tokyo. Locate your local office at: www.cengage.com/global

Cengage Learning Products are represented in Canada by Nelson Education, Ltd.

For product information, visit our website at **www.cengage.co.in**

Printed in India
First Indian Reprint 2012

Contents

Preface

PURPOSE OF *THEORY INTO PRACTICE*

Practicing literary criticism used to be easier. Not too many years ago it involved working from three or four established perspectives, all of them well within a student's (and a teacher's) intellectual comfort zone. Then the ground shifted, and one difficult to grasp literary theory followed another in quick succession, each one demanding difficult mental gymnastics and many of them seeming to be only vaguely related to literature as readers had known it. When it became clear that the emerging theories were here to stay and the literary world was not going to return to its traditional ways of reading and understanding, it also became evident that students were going to need some strong support in learning how to use the new ideas. That recognition led to the appearance of the first edition of *Theory into Practice*. Its purpose was to provide clear explanations of complex theoretical material in a manner that did not corrupt the original ideas by over simplifying them. It tried to honor the principles of each critical theory while making it possible for novice critics to understand and use them.

Subsequent editions of *Theory into Practice* have continued to honor that original intent, at the same time taking note of newly emerging theories and expanding discussions that have proved to be of particular interest to students and teachers. The current edition, for example, features a new chapter on one of literary criticism's newest approaches: ecocriticism. It also features a greatly expanded general glossary and extended attention to some figures who were noted but less than fully developed in the second edition.

ORGANIZATION

The presentation of material in *Theory into Practice* moves from the simple to the complex. That is, it begins with critical approaches that are relatively well known and easily practiced, then introduces more complex, less familiar perspectives. In each case the historical background is explained, special terms are defined, and principles are exemplified by reference to one of the fifteen literary selections included in the text. A student essay serves as a model of how an analysis should appear. Such support allows students to grow more confident in their ability to understand and use new ways of reading and understanding poems and stories. To further reduce their anxieties, the language of the text is relatively informal and engaging. In short, the presentation is designed to be user-friendly.

PEDAGOGICAL AIDS AND FEATURES

From the beginning, this book has been a "teaching text." That is, it has included numerous pedagogical aids. The third edition expands those features in an effort to facilitate student use. The following assistance is provided for each school of criticism:

- Concise historical literary background
- Guidelines for reading as a critic
- Guidelines for writing each stage of a critical analysis
- A list of helpful suggested readings
- Access to a comprehensive list of Web sites
- At least one model student essay
- Lists of questions to assist student thinking

In addition, several more comprehensive pedagogical aids follow the explanatory chapters. They include the following:

- Fifteen literary selections for quick and easy reference
- A comprehensive, fully articulated glossary of critical terms
- Information at a Glance, a succinct summary of the purposes, assumptions, strategies, strengths and weaknesses of each approach

NEW TO THIS EDITION

The third edition of *Theory into Practice* includes several significant additions and expansions. The following are of particular interest:

- A new chapter on one of the newest critical perspectives. Called "Literature Goes Green," it addresses the emerging field of ecocriticism. More specifically, it includes historical background to the movement, explains its purpose and principles, offers suggestions for how to read and write as an ecocritic, provides a glossary of common terms, and supplies a model student ecocritical essay of a literary work.

- A substantially expanded glossary. In place of the succinct glossaries that have heretofore been included in each chapter, this edition will offer a comprehensive glossary for the field of criticism that not only defines an increased number of terms but also offers more probing discussions for students who want greater depth of examination.
- An extended exploration of structuralism. Chapter 8 now carries new discussion of the ideas and work of Claude Lévi-Strauss, Roland Barthes, Vladimir Propp, and Jonathan Culler that helps make the principles of deconstruction more approachable.
- A new section on Mikhail Bakhtin. Although Bakhtin was mentioned in the second edition, his place in literary criticism was not thoroughly examined. In the current edition, some of his major principles, such as dialogism, heteroglossia, and polyphony are explored in depth in Chapter 3.
- Four new model student essays. New analyses for the psychological, mythological, new historicist, and ecocritical approaches have been included. They offer exemplary guidance to students who will write their own essays.
- Additional expansions and clarifications. For example, the place of the Russian formalists in literary criticism is examined in greater detail. Also, the principles of Lacanian psychology have been updated.

Acknowledgments

I am fortunate to have had help from many quarters in writing this book. Chief among them are my students, for whom and from whom I have learned more than I can measure. They have always been some of my most effective teachers. I am also grateful for the honest and helpful responses of my colleagues to what and how I wrote. In particular, I thank Judy Gentry, Duane Blumberg, Patricia Rickels, and Mary Ann Wilson for reading parts of the text and advising me on matters about which they know far more than I. Reviewers of the second edition also helped to shape much of what appears here: Jolanta Wawrzycka, Radford University; Lisa Schwerdt, California University of Pennsylvania; Steve Holder, Central Michigan University; and Tracie Church Guzzio, SUNY Plattsburgh. Their experience in using the book in their own classrooms allowed them to make constructive suggestions that led to a richer, more comprehensive version of the text. The Wadsworth staff assured that the production process went smoothly. I am especially indebted to my editor, Jill D'Urso, who has been of incalculable assistance at every step of revision. Finally, to my friends, who have listened patiently to accounts of the progress of my writing, I owe hours of reciprocal listening. And to my husband I give thanks for his unflagging encouragement and support.

To The Student: An Introduction to *Theory into Practice*

If you are a person who reads on your own for pleasure or for information, you probably are in the habit of talking with other readers about what you find interesting. You share the questions a book raised for you, compare it with other works by the same writer, and reminisce about what it made you recall from your own experience. The discussion is probably informal, spontaneous, and momentary. You may not even remember it a couple of days later.

Theory into Practice: An Introduction to Literary Criticism invites you to join a similar conversation, the main difference being that it will be more thoughtful, prepared, and memorable than the casual one just described. If those seem like intimidating terms, a look at the table of contents will reassure you that this work begins with critical approaches that are not far removed from the friendly conversation mentioned earlier. The first few chapters ask you to engage in forms of literary talk with which you are probably already comfortable. As your critical skills improve, you will be introduced to newer, and probably less familiar, schools of criticism.

The new approaches have appeared as part of a dramatic shift that has taken place in literary criticism over the past several decades. In a college literature class not too long ago, you would probably have been expected to read with either a biographical, historical, or formalist approach—the critical perspectives covered in the opening chapters of *Theory into Practice*—but the situation is dramatically different today. The forms of criticism available to (and expected of) a good reader have grown more complex, and sometimes a bit troubling. They have certainly grown more numerous. Some fundamental assumptions and practices regarding the reader's role have changed with them, making your job as student and critic less easily defined and prescribed than it once was. Consider how the following changes have redefined your responsibilities.

The literary canon, once accepted as a fixed cultural heritage to be passed down from one generation to another, is no longer a stable body of texts that all readers agree upon. Instead, it is now a conflicted, disputed set of materials that stay in flux. The "masterworks" have been challenged by others drawn from popular culture, and serious attention is paid to materials that once were not deemed worthy of study in higher education. Now that the canon of masterworks is no longer accepted as such, it is up to you to decide what a masterful text is after all and to which ones you would award that label.

Teachers, too, have changed, or at least some of them have. Once regarded as dispensers of knowledge and wisdom through the medium of the class lecture, they relieved the student of having to do much more than take down what was said, remember it, and demonstrate on occasion an understanding of it. The premise was that the teacher had the answer, and the student would learn it. Many effective classrooms operated under that system, for decades producing well-educated people who were good critical readers. Some still do, but today, most teachers acknowledge that with the multiplicity of readings provided by the numerous critical approaches, no single interpretation will suffice. Competing systems of inquiry create differing and sometimes conflicting understandings of any given work, and those disagreements, as Gerald Graff argued in *Beyond the Culture Wars,* can provide healthy debate that makes us better readers and critics. In short, in many of today's classrooms, you are not expected to be the passive receptor of information or experience. Instead, you are required to assume the role of coparticipant in the making of a text. As a good reader, you cannot remain a silent partner in the conversation about a text, because what you have to say about it helps to create it.

Another influence on current literary criticism is the sheer volume of information that is readily available on any subject. The amount of data that can be found on the Internet alone is almost overwhelming. Its effects on literary study are apparent in critics' frequent use of material that is drawn from nonliterary sources. In many of the newer approaches, it is not enough to identify metaphors or rhyme schemes in a poem. Now you may be expected to use ideas from anthropology, sociology, or economics to explain what it means. The cross-disciplinary demands of today's critical approaches ask you to use everything you know—and more.

Perhaps the most demanding aspect of the reader's new role, but also probably the most important, is that you are put in the position of questioning basic assumptions about everything, not just literature. You may find that task to be a disquieting one, because reading to affirm what we already know and accept is certainly a more comfortable position to be in. However, much of the vitality of the new approaches comes from the fact that they closely connect literature with our lives. They do so by making us look hard at what we often take for granted to see if it is valid, justifiable, and true. They make us examine values and practices that are so much a part of our lives that they exist, most of the time, beyond our questioning and evaluation.

Such practices are not universally accepted or approved. There have been some powerful voices raised in opposition. Allan Bloom in *The Closing of the American Mind,* for example, argued strongly against changes in the traditional curriculum, objecting to the inclusion of studies of popular culture and its products, which he saw as a less rigorous and significant body of subject matter than that which has been the staple of college curricula for several decades. Other detractors have objected to the political edge that many of the current critical perspectives have developed. Those who make such protests deny the validity of treating poetry or fiction as political documents that critique the complex relations among people living in society, examine social power and leadership, reveal the shortcomings of a society, promote the agendas of reformists, or serve to publicize an ignored minority. They ask, "Whatever happened to literature as art, aesthetics, timeless beauty? Doesn't looking at a text from a political point of view demean its existence? Doesn't literature transcend the transience of political concerns?"

Two counterarguments are commonly used to justify the political aspect of today's literary criticism. Those critics who espouse the first agree with George Orwell's assertion that "no book is genuinely free from political bias. The opinion that art should have nothing to do with politics is itself a political attitude." Simply put, there is no escaping politics. It is present in every assumption made about the social order, even when nothing explicitly labeled as political is being addressed.

The second justification points out that our culture is not a homogeneous one and that numerous minorities are no longer willing to pretend that it is. Previously silent voices are now calling for new definitions of cultural identity, celebrating their uniqueness and refusing to deny their own backgrounds by blending in with the rest. Their efforts are as influential in literature as in life; in both arenas, they have ramifications that are political in nature. In the case of literature, their stand has led to new readings of both contemporary and traditional works and to recognition of previously overlooked writers.

Clearly the conversation about literature to which this book invites you is not a simple one. It is fraught with conflicts and disagreement. It questions traditional assumptions and practices. It requires you to evaluate what is and to reflect on what you think should be. You will not agree with everything that is said in the discussions; you will not agree on all points with fellow students or even your instructor. The resulting dissonance is expected and justifiable because intellectual engagement, not consensus, is the purpose. Your responsibility is to try out the techniques presented here so that you can make your own informed judgments about literature, literary criticism, and the world beyond them.

To play a competent part in any conversation requires being able to use the language in which it occurs with skill and effectiveness. To talk about literature means knowing the language of criticism. *Theory into Practice* is designed to help you understand that language, or languages, because each critical perspective has its own manner of speaking and writing. This text is, then, more than simply an invitation. It is a guide that will help you move from familiar conversations to others that may challenge your traditional ways of thinking. For each approach, it will give you historical background, explanations of basic principles, extensive examples, suggestions for writing your analysis, a model student essay, and lists for further reading. A collection of well-known poems and stories, even a memoir and part of a famous correspondence, is included for your reading pleasure, as well as to serve as objects of analysis. Every analytical essay in *Theory into Practice* addresses a literary work that appears in it, making it simple for you to refer to the literary work as you read an analysis. Several of the works are analyzed from more than a single perspective, thereby demonstrating how differing critical approaches influence the work's effect on the reader. At the end, in "Information at a Glance," you will find brief statements about purposes, assumptions, strategies, strengths, and weaknesses of each approach. A glossary of literary terms is also included at the back of the book, for your reference.

As you make your way through the schools of criticism discussed here, you will be dealing with complex ways of reading, analyzing, and interpreting literature that ask you to think long and deeply. If you approach them with a willingness to master their basic principles, to apply their strategies, and to make informed choices about their validity and effectiveness, they will help you discover the inexhaustible richness of reading critically. You are urged to make use of all the help *Theory into Practice* offers as you join the critical conversation.

1

The Relationship of Reading and Writing

Reading is to the mind what exercise is to the body.
SIR RICHARD STEELE, IRISH ESSAYIST AND POLITICIAN

How can I know what I think till I see what I say?
E. M. FORSTER, ENGLISH NOVELIST AND ESSAYIST

READING AND WRITING IN COLLEGE

Reading and writing seem to be inseparable acts, rather like two sides of the same coin. Sometimes we even say the three words as if they were only one: reading-and-writing. Their connections are echoed in the advice every successful writer gives fledgling ones to "read, read, read." So, too, we know that good readers grow more perceptive and insightful if they "write, write, write."

It all sounds so easy and natural. When we encounter a book that touches our emotions or disturbs our assumptions, for example, we want to share our reactions with someone else. We may call a friend to talk about it, or if there is nobody to listen, we may turn to writing to explain what we think and feel about what we have read. It is then we all too often discover that putting what we think about a novel or a poem down on paper in a form that someone else will find interesting (and intelligible) is not so simple. In school, where reading and writing are assigned, the problem can be more serious. Students sometimes struggle not only with expressing their opinions but also with finding them. When reading works that someone else has chosen for them, students may have trouble identifying something to write about. In the worst case scenario, they may not even understand very well what they've read.

Academic survival depends on developing skills that will allow you to explore the meaning, aesthetics, or craft of a text and then write about the insights you've discovered. They are the skills of a literary critic, a person who examines how a piece of writing works, what it has to say about the culture or author that produced it or about human nature in general, why it was written, in what ways it is similar to other works, and how it ranks in comparison with them. In short, to be a successful critic, you need to be a resourceful reader, one who can utilize the principles of more than a single school of literary analysis and who can write with insight and understanding, as well as clarity and grace.

The writing you are asked to do in literature classes can take many forms, from marginal notes to quick journal entries and free writing sessions, perhaps eventually going through many drafts to become a full-blown piece of academic discourse. Or it may take final form as a letter to a friend, a poem for your eyes only, or the answer to an essay question on an examination. The purpose and audience for your writing will determine how your critical pieces take shape and what that shape is. What does not change is that the reading–writing connection can be a valuable one for you—by writing responses to what you read, you are likely to understand it better, remember it longer, relate it to other experiences more often (both those you have and those you read about), and use it more effectively.

We read and respond, then talk and write. The text we ultimately publish, whether as rough notes, a reading log, a creative effort, examination questions, or a research report, is literary criticism, an effort to share our experiences with someone else.

ENGAGING THE TEXT

Regardless of the assignment you are given, practicing literary criticism requires more than a single effort or skill. Even answering a question in class requires that you think about your response before speaking. Written criticism requires still more care. Whether you are dealing with a long research paper or an essay question on an exam that has a time limit, the job calls on you to carry out several complex tasks, and the process can be overwhelming if you try to think about the various steps all at once. As a result, the hard part for many people is getting started, as where to begin isn't always obvious. To gain some control over the process, you can use several fairly simple techniques to help make your initial approach. They take little time but can pay big dividends later.

The techniques suggested as starting points here involve connecting reading and writing so that you can discover what you have to say. They include making marginal notations, keeping a reading log, and using prewriting strategies. As you learn about all the different critical perspectives in Chapters 2–10, you should return to these strategies as you begin to read more deeply and with more understanding. In a sense, all the chapters in this book work together, presenting ways to approach a text that complement and supplement one another.

It is likely that some techniques for engaging the text will work better for you than others. For example, some readers find that making entries in a log disrupts their enjoyment of a text, whereas others make it a regular part of their reading process. You will have to be the judge of which strategies are most effective for you and which you find to be unproductive. The important step is to incorporate those that help into your own reading-writing process. Here are some methods that you may want to make a routine part of your approach to engaging a text.

Adding Marginal Notations

One reason that reading and writing seem to be two parts of a whole is that they sometimes take place at the same time. During the first reading of a work, for example, you may find yourself underlining sentences, putting question marks or checks in the margins, highlighting passages, or circling words that you don't understand. You may not think of such cryptic markings as writing at all, but they are, in fact, representations of what you think and feel as you go through a text. And because nobody completely takes in a work the first time through, these markings can serve as starting points for the next reading. They will help you find those passages and ideas that you wanted to think about some more or perhaps didn't understand at all. You will be glad when you return to a work to find that you left some footprints to follow. Look at how a first-time reader responded to Robert Frost's poem "Nothing Gold Can Stay."

NOTHING GOLD CAN STAY

Nature's first green is gold, → *How can green be gold?*
Her hardest hue to hold.
Her early leaf's a flower; *Lots of rhyme in this poem!*
Something "subsides" to itself? But only so an hour.
Then leaf subsides to leaf.
So (Eden) sank to grief,
What does Eden have to do w/ nature? So dawn goes down to day. *Opening sounds get repeated, too.*
Nothing gold can stay.

The advantage of marginal notations is that they don't interrupt your reading very much. They are, however, usually too terse and superficial to serve as the basis of a full-scale analysis. Several other techniques that will connect your reading with your writing in more substantive ways include keeping a reading log and using prewriting strategies, sometimes referred to as heuristics.

Keeping a Reading Log

If you do make marginal and textual notes while you read, you will have the rough beginnings of a reading log. A log amplifies the process and thus requires a separate notebook for your comments. You may even want to skip the marginal markings and use the notebook from the beginning.

Several kinds of information, depending in part on how familiar you are with a work, will be appropriate for your reading log. When you read something for the first time, you are likely to make notes about relatively basic information. If you are reading a narrative, for example, you may want to answer such questions as the following:

- Where is the action happening?
- What are the relationships of the characters?
- Which character(s) do I find to be the most interesting?
- Which one(s) do I care for most?
- Which one(s) do I dislike the most?

You might even want to pause in the middle of your reading to speculate about the following:

- What do I want to happen?
- What am I afraid will happen? What do I think will happen?
- What have I read that prompted the answers to these questions?

If you are reading a poem, you may want to record answers to questions like these:

- Who is the speaker of the poem? (Remember, the speaker is not necessarily the poet.)
- What do I know about him or her?
- What is his or her occasion for saying it?
- Where does the poem take place?
- Who is listening?
- Which lines seem to be the most important?
- Which words resonate powerfully with me?
- Do they give me insight into the poem as a whole?

Another way of beginning to think about a work is to jot down questions, memories it has called up, arguments with the ideas, or speculations about how the author came to write it. These considerations will help you connect with what you have read, not simply focus your attention on the text itself. They will make it more meaningful to you as an individual. It is often in personal interaction with a work that you begin to make meaning as a writer-critic.

When you are more familiar with the work, you will want to address more complex issues in your reading log or journal. You have several different models to follow, including the following:

- Use it as a learning log (sometimes called a double-entry log or a dialectical log): Divide a page into vertical halves, noting page numbers, phrases, or words from the text on one side and your own response on the other. On your side of the page, you may express confusion, record definitions of words you don't know, question connotations, argue with the text, note the recurrence of an image—whatever you think you should return to later.

- Use it as a dialogue journal: This uses the same format as a learning log, except you devote one side of the page to your comments and leave the other half for comments from another reader (student, friend, teacher, etc.).
- Use it as a "what if" journal in which you respond to hypothetical questions such as these: If you could talk to the author (or one of the characters or the narrator), what questions would you ask? What objections would you raise?
- Use it as a vocabulary journal in which you record all the words with which you are unfamiliar.
- Use it as a personal writing journal. Include informal freewrites on a passage or a scene; a descriptive paragraph, poem, or short narrative about an experience the text brings to mind; or an imagined conversation between two characters.

When you have finished reading a text, recording a summary paragraph about your reactions on your half of the double-entry log will help you pull together what you think about the work. A word of caution: Don't let too much time pass between reading a work and writing your summary paragraph. Responses fade quickly, and the longer you wait to set down your feelings and ideas, the less pointed and vibrant they will be.

Using Heuristics

Sometimes the notes you made in your reading log are an end to the process. Perhaps you do not need or want to do anything more with the work in question, and so you leave it to go on to other texts. However, if you have been assigned a class paper dealing with a particular poem or have an upcoming examination on a given novel, you will want to continue your study.

One way to find out more about your responses to the reading is to use prewriting strategies, the same discovery processes you have most likely used in other writing situations. The notes you took in your reading log can serve as starting places to stimulate further thinking. You might, for instance, have identified in your notes a recurring image that could be at the center of a clustering exercise. Or maybe a question you jotted down about the text could launch a 10-minute freewriting exercise. Other popular techniques include listing, making analogies, and looping. There are many ways to begin; you should use the techniques that are helpful and productive for you. If you want to know more about how these techniques work, you can find explanations in most writing handbooks and rhetoric texts, such as those you may have used in composition courses.

SHAPING A RESPONSE

Up to this point, you have mainly been gathering your responses and ideas, thinking through the work and your involvement in it. At some point—and you will have to be the judge of when—you will want to share your ideas with someone else. Whether you simply talk about a work with a friend, make an oral class presentation, or prepare a fully developed written text, you will need to make some decisions about how to present your opinions and ideas. To do so, you will want to be aware of the context of your presentation: its purpose, audience, and voice.

Determining a Purpose and Understanding Forms of Response

As noted earlier, marginal notations and log entries are often made without any purpose beyond serving as a starting point for your next reading. However, independent presentations usually require a specific approach, one that determines how you proceed. For example, your reason for writing might be to compare and contrast two characters in a novel, in which case you might write a relatively short analytical essay. Your purpose at other times could be to examine the issues treated in the work—the controversies and ideas it presents—a purpose that often yields a longer paper. You might examine characters in a narrative or describe and analyze the structure of a work. More closely focused still are papers about imagery, symbolism, prosody, or point of view. There is, obviously, no shortage of possible topics. Two of the most troublesome (and critical) forms in which you are likely to be asked to write are those of examinations and research papers. The remaining chapters in this book discuss making literary analyses and composing extended papers that report them from a wide variety of perspectives. Following are some suggestions for how to understand and respond to the purposes behind essay exams and research papers.

Answering Essay Questions Assuming that you have carefully prepared for an exam, you have several strategies to help ensure that you write effective answers to the exam's essay questions. First, recognize the intent behind the questions. Some are designed simply to assess whether you have read assignments or whether you have ingested specific information. On the other hand, sometimes an instructor expects you to demonstrate that you have done more than memorize material—that you can draw inferences from it, relate it to other information, evaluate it, agree or disagree with it. In short, you may be asked to show that you can think critically about a subject. Finally, on some rare occasions, you may be expected to be creative. A question such as "If you could invite any three authors whose work you have studied to a party, whom would you invite, and what do you think they would talk about?" asks for more than data or even inferences. It expects you to be inventive and imaginative.

A second consideration involves how extensive the answer should be. If the directions ask for "brief identifications," you should be highly specific and to the point, reserving valuable time for the rest of the examination. If, on the other hand, you are directed to "discuss thoroughly," you will need to begin with a broad statement of fact or opinion and then move onto its explanation by citing causes, comparisons, examples, or other more specific proof and logic.

Finally, an important point to keep in mind when composing any answer is that you must address the question that is asked. Probably the biggest cause of low scores on essay examinations is that students do not keep to the topic or follow directions. All too often they stray off into discussing a related topic—for example, giving a plot summary instead of making a comparison of two characters. One way to stay on task is to begin a discursive answer by partially restating the question. For example, if your test question reads, "How does the imagery found in the poems of Robert Frost reflect his own life?" try turning the question into a statement that begins your response. In this example, you might say something like, "Robert Frost's life is reflected in his poems in images such as birch trees, stone walls, and snowy evenings, which are typical of New England, where he lived."

Writing Research Papers A research paper differs from other papers that deal with literary topics in two ways. First, its purpose is not simply to convey your interpretation of the work but also to present ideas and data from others. (This material is called a *secondary source.*) Second, because it will be presented as academic discourse, the style will be more formal than that of some other work you have done.

Many of the conventions that you follow will depend on your instructor. Although some general guidelines almost always apply, be sure that you understand and use those provided for your particular assignment. The guidelines may vary somewhat from the suggestions that follow.

- You will enjoy the project more if you choose a topic that interests you. Because you will be spending many hours working with it, you will not want to suffer through dealing with a subject you find boring or irrelevant.
- Keep a reputable writers' handbook at your side. Many helpful books offer step-by-step guides for finding materials you need in the library, taking relevant notes, and documenting sources. If your instructor has suggested or required a particular handbook, be sure to get it and use it.
- Start early. Good research cannot be done quickly. You will need time not only to write the paper but also—even before composing a draft—to consider the various data and opinions that you read in order to come up with your own ideas.
- With all the work you put into a research paper, it should be more than a scrapbook of other people's ideas. It should reflect your own thinking. If you begin to feel that you have nothing to contribute to the rich critical dialogue that has preceded your study, you can use several strategies to find your own opinions. First, remember that you can argue with other critics. If you disagree with the conclusions drawn by one of your secondary sources, you have the basis for critical argument. Another way to find your own point of view is to look at a work from a perspective that has not been traditionally used. For example, feminist critics are providing some surprising new readings of well-known texts by looking at them (for the first time) through women's eyes. Finally, you can interact with the work

on a personal level by asking yourself early on how you respond to it and why. Some brainstorming on this topic may lead you to ideas that you can then investigate and test by examining the ideas of other critics.

- Your paper will probably run between five and fifteen pages, although length is one of those matters that instructors often stipulate. Regardless of its length, in its final form it should have an introduction, a well-developed discussion section, a conclusion, and a list of sources cited. Not only should the introduction announce the topic to be discussed, and perhaps your particular focus, but it should also provide an attractive, inviting beginning. The discussion section—the heart of your explanation or argument—should follow a clear plan of development, using examples from the work itself and references to secondary sources to strengthen your case. The conclusion need not be long if you have been clear in the preceding sections. It should simply provide a satisfying sense of completion to the paper.

Knowing Your Audience

Just as your purpose will affect what you write and how you write it, the audience (your reader) will also influence both the information you include and the form and style you use to communicate it. Imagine, for example, that as a result of driving too fast on a rain-slick street, you were responsible for sliding into the back of another car. How would you write an account of the accident for the police report? To your parents? In a letter to a friend who habitually drives too fast? In each case, the basic facts would be the same, but the details would vary. The language would change, because different readers provide different obligations and opportunities. The same situation is true for writing literary criticism.

When you make notes in a reading log, the primary audience is yourself. Consequently, you are not likely to worry about writing in complete sentences or editing for correctness. You may have even developed a personal shorthand to save time. When you use those notes as the basis of a commentary to be shared with a writing group, however, you will need to revise them so that they are more easily understood by others; that is, you will move to standard forms of expression.

The research paper is likely to be the most formal assignment you are asked to carry out. It is written in academic prose, a relatively impersonal, formal, tightly organized type of discussion that is addressed to a well-informed and intelligent audience that you may not know personally. Traditionally this situation has meant that the writer avoids all colloquialisms, slang, abbreviations, or references to the self; probably includes some technical terms and headings for the different sections; and always documents references to other scholars' work. Currently some of this impersonal formality seems to be receding, with more acceptance of the use of the first-person personal pronoun, *I*. However, readers of research reports retain a strong preference for formal academic prose, which you will probably want to honor.

Choosing A Voice

Your writer's "voice" changes just as your audible one does in different situations. As the audience grows more distant and unknown, your writing continues to become more formal and impersonal. When, for example, you write an answer to an essay question on an examination, you are hoping to assure an instructor, who may or may not know you well, that you have mastered a body of material or a set of skills or that you have the ability to think critically. The expression will, of necessity, differ significantly from the short notes you made for yourself in your log.

One reason that the audience affects the form and language of your writing—your voice—is that you change roles as you deal with different people. Remember the car accident you hypothetically had on the slick street? When writing to the police and to your parents, you were dealing with authority figures, people you were expected to treat with deference and respect. When you composed the accident report, you were acting as a responsible citizen trying to get the facts down as clearly as possible. With your parents, you were probably acting as a defendant, trying to explain that it wasn't entirely your fault. In the letter to your friend, on the other hand, you were writing as an equal, making remarks that were half-informative and half-entertaining. Your personality changed with the audience, thereby causing your written voice, the representation of who you were in that piece, to change as well.

When you write literary criticism, your voice will differ, depending not only on the audience but also on the purpose of your piece. Short, personal questions and reminders are basically starting points for more serious thinking later. Reading logs are ruminative in nature; they explore ideas and possibilities for dialogues with others. You take examinations to exhibit what you know and can do. The purpose of the research report is to explore a topic in depth, possibly turning up new and interesting perspectives in the process. Basically you are moving through several roles, from novice to questioner, authority figure, researcher, and critical thinker. As your persona changes in each case, your voice will change as well, adjusting to the role you have assumed.

HELPING THE PROCESS

In writing classes, you have probably already been introduced to the process by which a piece moves from a rough draft (based on exploratory beginnings, discussed earlier) to a final, polished document that is ready to be shared with readers. Keep in mind that the process is not a lockstep affair. Instead of a sequence of separate stages, each one completed before the next is begun, it is a fairly jumbled procedure in which you move forward and then go back to change what you have already done, thereby necessitating changes in what follows. The main point to remember is that effective writing is usually the result of numerous false starts, multiple versions, a substantial number of small changes, and maybe even some big ones.

The chapters that follow provide you with ample suggestions for prewriting, creating a draft from a particular critical perspective, and revising it. They also include lists of printed sources that can help you find information about the approach you are using to analyze a poem or a piece of fiction. You can also set up some collaborative efforts of your own, as well as refer to additional electronic and printed aids that can help you with just about everything from comma splices to the composing process in general. Here are some suggestions for both collaboration and more impersonal assistance.

Collaboration

One myth about writing is that it is a solitary activity. We have all seen cartoons of the lonely poet waiting for inspiration by the light of a flickering candle. Real writers, however, know they are not alone at all. They are heavily dependent on an audience that responds to what they've written. Only by getting reactions from other readers can a writer know if the work has succeeded or, if it hasn't, where it has missed the mark. A beginning writer also profits from working with supportive peers who can sense strengths and weaknesses that he or she is unaware of. In the end, although the piece of writing belongs to the person who wrote it, a little help from one's friends along the way can be invaluable.

Collaboration can begin simply by sharing initial reactions to a work. A brief reading of the comments and questions recorded in a reading log, for example, can form the basis for discussion of any aspect of a story or poem. If everyone agrees, then everyone can feel validated; if opinions vary widely, which is more likely, there is much to be examined and discussed.

Although the instructor is responsible for arranging shared sessions in class, you can also do much on your own. This may mean making arrangements to meet outside of class, but the rewards can be worth the trouble. If you want the support and suggestions of your friends and colleagues, you can do with them much of what a teacher would ask you to do in a workshop situation. Consider trying the following suggestions.

If you are ready for more extended sharing than has been described so far, brief freewriting of 5 to 10 minutes, or perhaps some clustering or listing of your ideas can provide material for discussion. If you do not feel comfortable working with a group, you may find it more productive at this stage to be paired with another person. The two of you can simply read one another's informal responses and react to them, or you can be more organized about the process by consciously finding one thing to agree with or to compliment. Later, when you feel ready, your pair can be combined with another to form a group of four to continue discussions and sharing. If you have more than one such group, you can hold a larger session in which each quartet selects its strongest piece to share with everyone.

Sometimes you will want or need to share something longer than the short pieces of freewriting or journal entries. One way to generate a more extended discourse is to try what Richard Adler calls "answering the unanswered question"; that is, ask yourself what you do not understand or where you wish you had more information. Another possibility is to use David Bleich's technique of first asking yourself what you think is the most important word in the work, then the most important passage, and, finally, the most important feature. For each answer, specify why you find it to be the most important. Your answers will reflect you as an individual with a unique perspective on the text. Your experiences and opinions will lead you to shape a response that is different from those of your colleagues. You will have a unique response to share with them. (Incidentally, these are also good methods for making sure you have something to contribute to class discussion of a piece of literature.)

When you share a more fully developed piece of writing, you will probably need to follow a more formal process. Several models of collaborative revising are helpful. The element common to all of them is their positive nature. Collaboration is most productive when it takes place in an atmosphere of support and affirmation, not one steeped in negative criticism. The point is to help one another achieve more effective writing by making helpful comments.

One popular model of a writing group involves having the writer read a piece to the entire group, not stopping until he or she reaches the end, then pausing briefly for the group to write brief responses to the piece. Another uses a series of questions about each writer's paper that the group responds to. The questions can be formulated to suit the needs of the occasion, but they usually involve questions such as the following:

- What is the main idea of this paper?
- Did the opening sentence make you want to hear the rest? Why or why not?
- Were there enough examples to make the major points clear?
- Were the examples interesting, appropriate, and vivid?
- Did you have a satisfying sense of closure at the end?

Whatever approach your group chooses, remember that, as the writer, you have the final say in what happens in your paper. You are free to implement or reject the suggestions you receive. Most of the time, however, it is a good idea to pay attention to what your audience says.

On some occasions, you may find it impossible to assemble a writing group to help you shape or polish a piece of writing. However, there are a few strategies you can use when working alone to help distance yourself from your work so that you are more likely to see and hear it as another reader might. You can, for example, read the piece aloud. Your ear will pick up problem areas (wrong words, missing punctuation, even underdeveloped points) that your eye has missed. Listen as a stranger to the language and ask yourself what is lacking, what is unclear. It is easier to remove yourself from the author's seat if you allow yourself time to forget what you have written. That is, if you can put a piece away for several days without reading it or even thinking much about it, when you take it out again, it will sound as if someone else has composed it. You may be surprised at the awkward passages you discover but equally surprised at the improvements you are able to make to those passages when you come back to a text with fresh eyes (and ears).

Reference Materials

In addition to the assistance that critical friends can provide, you will also find it helpful to keep a good reference book or two by your side while you write. Handbooks, dictionaries, and rhetoric texts are all helpful when you compose, revise, and edit your manuscript.

Today the solitary writer can also benefit from technological assistance. The computer is no substitute for a human reader (yet), but it does an excellent job of finding misspelled words and is (sometimes) helpful in identifying ungrammatical constructions. Even highly skilled writers use such devices to create final copy that is as close to being error-free as possible. In addition, the opportunities that computers provide for producing visually attractive copy have made it mandatory that the papers you produce have a professional look to them. No excuses will justify a sloppy presentation. Any reader expects a clean, well-designed format that invites attention.

Technology can also help you find material that will enrich your reading. As you no doubt recognize, the information available on the Internet is increasing at an astonishing rate that shows no signs of slowing down. Information from the Internet has many advantages for the user, not the least of which is its easy accessibility. However, anyone who uses the Internet should be aware of some of its shortcomings. Simply put, online material is not always reliable. First of all, because of the easy access, anyone can create a Web site or post comments to various groups. The result is that not all information on the Internet can be trusted. You must always question the source of material that you find. Even addresses that end in *.edu,* which some people tend to assume are reputable because they are located at universities, can pose problems. As students come and go and courses change, such sites are very likely to move or disappear without warning.

SUMMING UP

As you have seen in this chapter, the reading–writing relationship is not a simple one. Making analyses and writing papers that explain those analyses are made manageable, however, by adopting a method that does not require you to work on all aspects at once but instead allows you to concentrate on one or two tasks at a time. Engaging a text, shaping a response, and finally sharing it with other readers is demanding but satisfying, because it not only leads to new insights about yourself and your world but also puts you in touch with a community of thinking people.

SUGGESTED READING

Abrams, M. H. *A Glossary of Literary Terms.* 8th ed. Boston: Thomson, Wadsworth, 2005.

Adams, Hazard, and Leroy Searle, eds. *Critical Theory since 1965.* Tallahassee: Florida State University Press, 1986.

———. *Critical Theory since Plato*. Boston: Thomson, Wadsworth, 2005.

Bressler, Charles. *Literary Criticism: An Introduction to Theory and Practice*. 4th ed. Upper Saddle River, NJ: Prentice Hall, 2007.

Carpenter, Scott. *Reading Lessons: An Introduction to Theory*. Upper Saddle River, NJ: Prentice Hall, 2000.

Cuddon, J. A., and Claire Preston. *Penguin Dictionary of Literary Terms and Literary Theory*. London: Penguin, 2000.

Eagleton, Terry. *Literary Theory*. Minneapolis: University of Minnesota Press, 1996.

Foster, Thomas C. *How to Read Literature Like a Professor: A Lively and Entertaining Guide to Reading between the Lines*. New York: Quill, 2003.

Groden, Michael. *The Johns Hopkins Guide to Literary Theory and Criticism*. Baltimore: The Johns Hopkins University Press, 2005.

Harkin, Patricia. *Acts of Reading*. Upper Saddle River, NJ: Prentice Hall, 1999.

Harmon, William. *Handbook to Literature*. 10th ed. Upper Saddle River, NJ: Prentice Hall, 2006.

Heilker, Paul, and Peter Vandenberg. *Keywords in Composition Studies*. Portsmouth, NH: Heinemann, 1996.

Kaplan, Charles, and William Anderson, eds. *Criticism: Major Statements*. 4th ed. Boston: Bedford/St. Martin's Press, 2000.

Keesey, Donald. *Contexts for Criticism*. 4th ed. Boston: McGraw-Hill, 2003.

Lentricchia, Frank. *Critical Terms for Literary Study*. 2nd ed. Chicago: University of Chicago Press, 1995.

Rivkin, Julie, and Michael Ryan. *Literary Theory: An Anthology*. Malden, MA: Blackwell, 2004.

Selden, Raman, Peter Widdowson, and Peter Brooker. *A Reader's Guide to Contemporary Literary Theory*. 5th ed. New York: Pearson Longman, 2005.

Staton, Shirley F., ed. *Literary Theories in Praxis*. Philadelphia: University of Pennsylvania Press, 1987.

Storey, John. *An Introductory Guide to Cultural Theory and Popular Culture*. Athens: University of Georgia Press, 1993.

Tyson, Lois. *Critical Theory Today: A User-Friendly Guide*. 2nd ed. New York: Routledge, 2006.

For up-to-date information on the many Web sites addressing literary theory, including those that present primary sources, definitions of terms, bibliographies, and further discussion of individual schools of criticism, visit www.cengagebrain.com.

2

Familiar Approaches

> Almost every literary work is attended by a host of outside circumstances which, once we expose and explore them, suffuse it with additional meaning.
>
> RICHARD D. ALTICK, *The Art of Literary Research*

CONVENTIONAL WAYS OF READING LITERATURE

Taking a course in literary criticism is an exercise in discovering how many different ways you can read a single text. Some approaches will be familiar—so familiar that they may seem to be not so much special strategies for dealing with a work but simply the natural way to read. Others may seem more bizarre and complex, at least at first. You will likely recognize the perspectives discussed in this chapter, because they have probably served as the organizing bases for courses you have taken or assignments you have been given. They include approaching a text from a social viewpoint, which involves history and biography; seeing it as representative of a particular genre; fitting it into the whole body of a writer's work; or applying particular ways of thinking to it, such as comparison and contrast or cause and effect. These "tried and true" methods continue to be helpful to understanding literature.

A Social Perspective

To understand the discussion that follows, you should read the short story "Barn Burning," by William Faulkner, which begins on page 268.

Nobody lives a completely isolated existence. Each of us is a product of more biological, intellectual, emotional, and spiritual influences than we can recognize, much less name. The reverse is true as well: To some degree, each human being affects the world he or she lives in—some in monumental ways; some in quiet, unnoticed ones; some leave the world better for their having lived in it; some seem bent on destruction.

When we apply this assertion to works of literature, we can say that they are products of a time, a place, a culture, and an individual and that they have the capacity to affect, and perhaps even change, the world into which they are introduced. The French critic Hippolyte Taine (1828–1893) was one of the earliest theorists to explore this idea. Hoping to establish a scientific basis for literary criticism, he tried to make interpretations by applying the methods of biological science to literature. He looked at the historically verifiable causes of a text. He wanted the facts. Three major factors, he announced, determine a work of art's unique character: ***race***, ***milieu***, *and* ***moment***. By the term *race,* Taine referred to national characteristics that are typically found in works of art produced by the creative artists of a given country. His meaning is close to what is today called *culture.* Consider the music of Duke Ellington or George Gershwin. Could a listener ever think it was by a Russian composer? What is it that makes "Rhapsody in Blue" peculiarly American? The answer, Taine would say, is its "racial" characteristics. When Taine spoke of milieu (his term), he was referring to the artist's environment, the sum total of the artist's experience. This includes family background, education, travel, marriages and love affairs, income—all those forces that combine to create the individual as a unique human being. *Moment* refers to the less personal influences in a writer's life, to those things that govern not the individual but the age. It points to the major intellectual currents of a period, its governing ideas and assumptions. Taine's idea is reflected in the categories into which literature is sorted: classical, romantic, absurdist, and so on. Such labels are a way of referring to a group of identifiable characteristics that held sway at a particular literary period.

A more contemporary statement of the social approach comes from René Wellek and Austin Warren. In their *Theory of Literature,* they name three areas that are of interest to the social critic. First, they note the importance of the writer's heredity and environment, which help explain social attitudes and opinions that appear in the work. In the short story "Barn Burning," for example, we find evidence of William Faulkner's own family background. Born in 1897 near Oxford, Mississippi, into a society that still had vivid memories of the Civil War, Faulkner grew up in a family with roots buried deep in the state's history. His great-grandfather had been a colonel in the war, as well as a prominent figure in the postwar South as it struggled to rebuild its society. In that era, he played numerous roles, including lawyer, politician, financier, railroad builder, and general public figure. His end was a violent one, at the hands of a business rival. Faulkner's grandfather continued the family businesses, and his maternal grandmother lived with Faulkner's family for a number of years until her death in 1907. His father, a man who preferred hunting and fishing to "polite society," worked at one time for the railroad but later became business manager of the University of Mississippi. Faulkner's mother was an early literary influence on the writer-to-be. Although Faulkner left Oxford before completing high school, he returned in 1919 after having served as a member of the British Royal Flying Corps during World War I. Back in his native state, he spent time reading and writing but expressed no particular professional ambition. After publishing a volume of poetry, *The Marble Faun* (1924), he moved to New Orleans, where he met Sherwood Anderson and other writers who encouraged him to write about his native region. In 1929, he returned again to Oxford, where he married his high school sweetheart. He lived there until his death in 1962.

The family lore, the identification with place, the knowledge of people and events of the Civil War, and the war's lasting effects on the defeated South are all evident in "Barn Burning." The characters, drawn from more than a single social class, are typical of those Faulkner would have known or heard about. The conflicts among the tenant family, the town merchants, and the landed gentry were drawn from firsthand experience or local legend. The effect is a sense of depth of awareness and understanding that cannot come from simply reading about a place and its people or even from observing it as an outsider, for that matter.

Wellek and Warren go on to call attention to the world that is presented in the work itself. What culture and society are being depicted? How does the fictive (or poetic) world reflect its outer world? Faulkner's created place, Yoknapatawpha County, Mississippi, which critic Malcolm Cowley called "Faulkner's mythical kingdom," has become almost synonymous with the one in which he lived. It has a physical presence with dimensions (2,400 square miles lying between the hills of north Mississippi and the black bottomlands), population (15,611 people of all classes and types), and a history (beginning with the story of the nephew of a Chickasaw chief and moving forward to narratives in which the old order meets the modern world). Faulkner's works can be described as sociological studies of all classes of people, from the aristocratic old families and county-seat lawyers to the tenant farmers and bootleggers. All are defined by speech, attitudes, food, and houses that are true to their status and background. In "Barn Burning," for example, Major de Spain's world, briefly glimpsed by Sarty through the opened front door as "a suave turn of carpeted stair and a pendant glitter of chandeliers and a mute gleam of gold frames," is a far cry from that of the unlettered, uncultured Abner Snopes, but both are a part of the time and place that Faulkner knew firsthand. Cowley saw the story of Yoknapatawpha finally as the story of the South in general, a region settled by aristocrats and ambitious people who took the land from the Indians with the idea of founding an enduring and civil society. Their efforts were corrupted, however, by slavery, interrupted by the Civil War, and ultimately defeated by people like the Snopeses, who were unprincipled and exploitative.

Finally, Wellek and Warren turn their focus on the world that the work entered—that is, the audience for which it was intended. What kind of impact did it have on its readers? How was it critically received? This last area of interest has more recently been the concern of a group of critics known as the receptionists, about whom you will learn more in Chapter 7. These critics are interested in how the reading public in different periods responded to a given work. In Faulkner's case, the news was not always good. In the early 1930s, he had a hard time making a living. His fiction, which was difficult and experimental, did not have a ready audience. Neither *The Sound and the Fury* nor *As I Lay Dying,* complex because of their multiple narrators and interior monologues, was a popular success. Faulkner tried to support himself by selling short stories to national magazines, but his earnings did not meet his needs. After publishing *Sanctuary,* a sensational (sometimes called sordid) work to produce income, he found a more durable means of earning money by writing for the movies while he continued to produce his novels. His last major novelistic effort was a series about the rise of the Snopeses and the decline of the old-line families. Using some of the characters introduced in "Barn Burning," he extended their stories through *The Hamlet* (1940), *The Town* (1957), and *The Mansion* (1959). His acceptance as a major fiction writer of the twentieth century was signaled by his being awarded the Nobel Prize in 1949.

Several schools of criticism that have recently adapted and applied a social perspective in ways that go beyond traditional approaches have grown powerful enough to warrant separate study. The receptionists, for example, are discussed in Chapter 7, "Reader-Response Criticism." Even more distinctive are the Marxists, treated in Chapter 5, whose approach was widely practiced in the 1930s by such luminaries as Granville Hicks, Cecil Day-Lewis, Archibald MacLeish, and others. More recently, critics using the principles and techniques of the new historicism, covered in Chapter 9, have challenged basic premises and goals of traditional historical literary study. They reject, for example, the assumption that one can know with any certainty what actually happened in any particular event, or that a period can be understood by determining its defining spirit, or that history unfolds in a sequence of causes and effects that is positive and progressive. To make their case, they do not limit their focus to literature; rather, in their effort to understand a period in all its dimensions, they turn also to nonliterary documents and information usually left to sociologists and anthropologists.

For several reasons, the social approach, as traditionally practiced, has waned in importance over recent years. Certainly the influence of the New Critics diminished its role (see Chapter 3). The reluctance of readers to judge the worth of a work by its social relevance, their desire to value it for its aesthetic qualities, and their aversion to studying society rather than literature caused people to turn away from the social perspective to others that serve them in different ways. Nevertheless, history and biography, once the principal means of approaching a literary text, are still in widespread use, though contemporary critics seldom make them their entire, or even their central, focus. Although some readers find that such approaches offer less opportunity for creative reading, and others object that connecting a work to an author's life or times provides little opportunity for considering how, or how well, a poem or piece of fiction works, and still others protest that the reader's attention is directed to nonliterary and even nonaesthetic matters that are of only peripheral concern to the work itself, many people still find history and biography to be helpful means of extending the understanding of a story, a poem, or a play.

One of the most important reasons that history and biography are helpful is that knowledge of the past gives readers a way to understand more deeply and clearly the language, ideas, and purposes of literature. (The reverse is also true: As artifacts produced in a certain period, works of literature give historians a way to see the past.) For example, such knowledge can make a reader aware of social trends and conventions that would have influenced a writer's attitudes and tastes. It can clarify allusions to local and historical events and explain special uses of individual words and expressions. A case in point is *The Annotated Pride and Prejudice,* edited by David M. Shapard (2007), which has a page of explanatory notes for every page of Austen's novel. The notes include clarifications regarding eighteenth-century meanings of words, as well as explanations of proper etiquette, legal and economic realities, clothing fashions, leisure activities, and class differences of that time. The more than 2,300 annotations sometimes surprise the contemporary reader, who may not know, for example, that being seated at the foot of the dining table is not an insult but an honor or that to be "condescending" is to be polite to inferiors.

Knowing something of history and biography can explain the origins of a specific work, clarify the source of the author's convictions, and reveal his or her deep concerns and conflicts. In short, it can show us why certain artists wrote as they did. It can even identify differences between contemporaries. Of course, matters can get complex when the biographical information (or what we know about an author's values) is contradictory to what a story implies, and such conflicts need to be resolved. Sometimes it is simply a matter of recognizing that the content of a work and the author's life are never the same; on other occasions, however, sorting out fact from fiction involves the skills and resources of a trained researcher. For most readers and students, historical and biographical information won't make a bad story good or a good story better, but it can draw attention to literary qualities that might be missed by a reader from another period.

In the classroom, history and biography are certainly alive and well, often serving as the basis of lectures and writing assignments—even providing the organizing principle of many survey courses. Part of the appeal for teachers and students is that history and biography furnish background against which a text can be more readily understood. By providing the reader with a sense of the world in which a writer lived and worked, these two subjects can enhance and clarify the meaning of a text. Such knowledge can also aid interpretation by preventing gross misreadings. In short, even if you do not choose to make history and biography your only analytical strategies, you can use them to supplement, complement, and support other, more complex ones.

Several characteristics distinguish historical and biographical studies. For one, they are primarily descriptive, rather than analytical or evaluative, in nature. In addition, they tend to be lengthy, because the background to a work has to be described, and the work has to be shown to fit the description. Some critics think history and biography are more appropriate for fiction (especially the novel) than for lyric poetry, but others have applied them effectively to poems. Obviously, a historical novel that recounts real events of great consequence lends itself easily and naturally to an examination of the real world outside the fictive one; a novel written as social protest or calling for reform can easily be studied for its impact on the situation it depicts. Poetry, too, however, can be examined from this perspective. Marxist critics, for example, have repeatedly managed to demonstrate that poems reflect class struggle or the writer's own background, and F. W. Bateson, in *English Poetry: A Critical Introduction,* goes so far as to organize literary history into six chronological schools, assign a social order to each, then show how individual poems reflect the writer's response to his or her social world.

Today most readers who use biographical and historical information to complement other methods of analysis turn to more than a simple recitation of the facts of an author's life or of the publication of the text. They search out the social and intellectual concerns of both the writer and his or her society. They look for other works of the same period with which they can draw comparisons regarding themes, style, and genre. Sometimes they make comparisons between a specific work and others by the same author.

Whether you are using a historical-biographical approach as your sole perspective or using it to complement another means of analysis, you will find the following questions to be helpful aids to thinking and organizing your ideas.

- Where does this work fit into the chronology of the author's published works?
- Are the events of the plot based on the author's own experiences?
- How old was the author when the text was written?
- Is the setting (time and place) one in which the author lived? If not, how did he or she become knowledgeable about it? Through travel? Reading? Research?
- Are any of the characters based on people the author knew?
- Is one of the characters based on the author him- or herself?
- How do the issues addressed (or conflicts depicted) reflect controversies, questions, and problems of the author's day?
- How does this work exemplify the definition of the intellectual or literary period in which it was produced—for example, classicism or romanticism?
- What are the author's attitudes, either implied or explicit, about the central concerns of the text? Why does he or she have them?
- Does the language include words with archaic meanings? If so, what did they mean when the author used them?
- What writers and texts can be said to have influenced the writing of the work under consideration?

The Effects of Genre

To understand the discussion that follows, you should read the short story "Barn Burning," by William Faulkner, which begins on page 268.

Another traditional approach, the study of **genre**, represents some of the earliest literary criticism we have, going all the way back to Aristotle's classification of forms in his *Poetics* (fourth century BC). Viewing poetic art as an imitation or representation of reality, he grouped literary works according to the **means**,

objects, and **manner** of the imitations. The term *means* refers to the medium of the work—for example, music, prose, or verse; *objects* refers to the nature of the situation or characters being imitated; and *manner* is the point of view, which can be the voice of a character, the author's own voice, or the voice of an actor. Recall, for example, that Aristotle defined tragedy as dealing with noble actions of great magnitude (objects), in artistically enhanced language (means), and presented in a dramatic, not narrative, form (manner).

Throughout much of literary history, readers have found it helpful to be able to approach a new work with certain preconceived notions about what would be found there and what would be expected of the person who chose to read it. By knowing the elements commonly found in a story or poem or what shape it is likely to take, a reader can come to it with certain expectations and, hence, ways of understanding it. Conversely, to mistake the category into which a work fits can result in serious misreading. For example, to expect a lyric poem to have the sweep and grandeur of an epic would stand in the way of enjoying the lyric poem's personal and musical qualities.

Genre criticism, which was somewhat less powerful in the nineteenth century, had a small renaissance in the 1940s, when a group known as the Chicago School (because many of the early members were at the University of Chicago) called for an approach to criticism that was less narrowly focused than that of the New Critics (see Chapter 3). They found in Aristotle the foundations of a system that could be extended in ways that would provide a broader and more comprehensive approach to literature. R. S. Crane, for example, argued in *Critics and Criticism* (1952) for the need to determine the kind of artistic object an author intended to produce before considering other elements of the work: "To what extent, and with what degree of artistic compulsion any of the particular things the writer has done at the various levels of his writing, down to the details of his imagery and language, can be seen to follow from the special requirements or opportunities which the kind of whole he is making presents to him." Another way of approaching the study of genre was advanced by Northrop Frye in his *Anatomy of Criticism* (1957). He reserved the term *genre* for distinctions based on what he called the "radical of presentation," the relationship between an artist and the audience in the presentation of the work. He saw four such relationships and thus four major genres: *epos,* in which the poet speaks or recites to an audience; *drama,* in which the artist's words are enacted by characters before an audience; *lyric,* in which the audience seems to be overhearing a poetic speaker who does not direct the work to them; and *fiction,* in which the artist writes to a reading audience.

Genre studies take a number of different forms, but they usually have several basic aspects in common. Initially they attempt to determine the genre of any given work. The issue is more important than it might seem; sometimes readers of the same text disagree about what kind of work they are reading, causing them to approach it with different expectations and, afterward, to judge it by different criteria. When we pick up a new novel, for example, our experience with other novels causes us to look for similar elements and strategies of development and to evaluate the new one by how well those elements and strategies are used. Our assumptions about fiction mean that we expect to meet interesting characters, listen to a narrator who may or may not be someone in the story, and find descriptive passages and perhaps even some philosophical commentary. We hope to enjoy a compelling plot, complete with conflict and resolution; a setting that logically contains the characters and maybe even extends our understanding of them; and symbols that become meaningful because they properly belong in the world of the story. With poetry, on the other hand, we expect to hear music in its sounds and rhythms, see images, recognize patterns, and savor ambiguity and figurative language. Similarly, we approach drama knowing that it will work out its narrative through dialogue, monologue, soliloquy, and action, because it does not have the luxury of authorial description or commentary.

Subcategories have additional distinctions. For example, lyric poetry is vastly different from epic poetry, and we do not expect of the latter the brevity and subjectivity we have come to expect of the former. The popular forms of certain periods of literary history set up their own special presumptions. A Wordsworthian sonnet will not read like Walt Whitman's free verse, but both are poetry. Certainly we read (or see) *Oedipus Rex* with a mind-set that is different from the one we bring to *The Sunshine Boys,* but both belong to the genre known as drama. If for some reason we mistake the genre of a text, we are likely to be disappointed and confused. To take Jonathan Swift's essay "A Modest Proposal" as a straightforward suggestion for curing the social ills of eighteenth-century Ireland by selling children for food, instead of as the ironic satire that it really is, would lead the reader to assume that the author was a sadistic monster. In short, whether dealing with major or minor categories of genres, our expectations partly shape how we receive the text.

A question that sometimes affects genre is, What is the authentic text? That, too, is a more complicated matter than it seems because writers sometimes publish different versions of the same work. Charles Dickens wrote an unhappy ending to his novel *Great Expectations,* but when the reading public objected, he published a more pleasing one. Which is the authentic one? Further complicating the situation is that printing errors are likely to be repeated and finally accepted as the correct text. James Joyce's *Ulysses,* written in English that is characterized by original and daring wordplay and that was first typeset by French printers, still leaves readers wondering what was an intentional break with convention and what was accidental. To make such determinations, scholars who practice **textual criticism** usually need access to manuscripts and other hard-to-find documents. Such study also requires knowledge of linguistics, literary history, and other even more specialized fields. As a result, textual criticism is a field of study in itself that is difficult for anyone but trained researchers to pursue. Nevertheless, all readers should at least be sure they are dealing with a standard edition and be aware of any disputed words or passages. To identify a genre with any certainty, a reader must have a stable text.

Once the text has been identified and the genre determined, a genre study examines how a text complies with, varies, or deviates from other works of its kind. We can ask, then, what makes "Barn Burning" a story? The answer is that it *acts* like one. It has what we expect a story to have—a narrator, in this case a third-person, omniscient one; characters who outwardly engage in dialogue and action but whose inner souls we grow to know as well; a plot that begins with exposition, quickly moves to develop a conflict that rises to a climax, and, at the end, comes to a close with a denouement. The narrator describes the country store that has been turned into a makeshift courthouse in such a way that we know its smells and its hard nail kegs that serve as seats. He tells us about the grandeur of Major de Spain's home and, by contrast, the harsh circumstances in which Sarty's family lives. On some level, we begin to notice the recurrence of images of fire—candles burning, the small fire of the Snopeses' camp, the large one that consumes Major de Spain's barn. Point of view, developed characters, an ordered plot, description, and motifs and symbols make "Barn Burning" a story.

Certainly we recognize its ways of proceeding as those typically found in of short fiction, but if "Barn Burning" were totally consonant with our expectations, we might easily grow bored. When the characters are stereotypes, the causality of the plot forced, or the dialogue mundane, a text is likely to become too predictable and will thereby lose our interest. That makes a second question necessary: How does "Barn Burning" employ the conventions of the short story so that it holds our attention? For one thing, it is grounded in characters who sound real and true. They speak in ways that define them as people of a particular place and time, of certain economic and educational levels. We believe they exist. Their problems are also of interest to us. We ache for Sarty's desperate need to respect his father even as it conflicts with his innate understanding of the mean, destructive nature of his father's acts. The increasing viciousness of Abner is balanced against Sarty's hope, carrying us forward to his ultimate decision to betray his father to Major de Spain.

We are more likely to stay focused on a story that not only uses the techniques of fiction in highly competent, even artistic ways but also surprises us by deviating from them from time to time. This leads to a third question: How does "Barn Burning" break the rules to create its own presentation? One element that makes this story distinctive is Faulkner's prose style. It is easily recognized because it has certain characteristics that are not commonly found in the style of other fiction writers. (At least they were not highly evident in writers who preceded Faulkner, though he has often been imitated and even parodied since his work went into publication.) He makes sentences, for instance, that we do not expect. We hear something new and interesting, for example, in his account of Sarty's running away from Major de Spain's house toward his unknown future. Listen to the complexity—and the music—of this one sentence:

> He could not hear either: the galloping mare was almost upon him before he heard her, and even then he held his course, as if the very urgency of his wild grief and need must in a moment more find him wings, waiting until the ultimate instant to hurl himself aside and into the weed-choked roadside ditch as the horse thundered past and on, for an instant in furious silhouette against the stars, the tranquil early summer night sky which, even before the shape of the horse and rider vanished, stained abruptly and violently upward: a long, swirling roar incredible and soundless, blotting the stars, and he springing up and into

> the road again, running again, knowing it was too late yet still running even after he heard the shot and, an instant later, two shots, pausing now without knowing he had ceased to run, crying "Pap! Pap!", running again before he knew he had begun to run, stumbling, tripping over something and scrabbling up again without ceasing to run, looking backward over his shoulder at the glare as he got up, running on among the invisible trees, panting, sobbing, "Father! Father!"

As readers, we are caught up in the power of this very long sentence that quickens its pace and increases its intensity as it goes on. The story rushes forward on its back. Such complexity could easily spin out of control, and it is interesting to consider how Faulkner manages to keep it going. A close look reveals that it is actually several utterances in one. That is, the sentence breaks down into units—some long, some short—that are set off from those next to it by commas and colons. For example, the unit that reads "knowing it was too late yet still running even after he heard the shot and, an instant later," eighteen words, is followed by the staccato two-word unit that reads "two shots," then by the nine-word unit "pausing now without knowing he had ceased to run." The pauses between units of unequal length, not always coming where the reader would expect them, provide a rhythm that both controls the speed of the sentence and calls attention to important narrative elements, such as the firing of the shots. The images, too, are rich and exotic, filled with the sound of the galloping horse, the sight of the early night sky that silhouettes the action, and the kinesthetic appeal of the boy's running and falling and running again. Though Faulkner's sentences, such as this one, may not be thought of as a deviation from traditional storytelling, their daring complexity gives his fiction its own personality; they make it anything but predictable or boring.

CONVENTIONAL WAYS OF WRITING ABOUT LITERATURE

Sometimes you will receive an assignment that is based less on specific subject matter than on a way of thinking about a text. It might be an approach that could be applied to many texts, not just the one assigned for study. For example, instead of asking you to use historical background to explain the role Abner Snopes played in the Civil War, your instructor might assign an essay that analyzes the motives of Snopes or that compares and contrasts Sarty with the character of another boy depicted in a story about coming of age in difficult circumstances. Such assignments ask you to use a specific thinking technique, which has its own rules of governance, instead of looking for a body of information that may be ordered in numerous ways. Some of the more common assignments that take this form include making an explication, doing an analysis, comparing and contrasting, and studying the works of a single author. Each requires that you formulate a response, your own argument about the topic. The statement of that position is commonly referred to as your thesis statement.

Explication

An explication, sometimes called by its French name, ***explication de texte***, usually examines a fairly brief work or sometimes a single passage from a larger one. In it, you are expected to present an interpretation of the work, explain its meaning, or show how the writer achieves a particular effect. To do so you make a close reading, noting all the nuances of the language and style and then assessing how they fit together to create the whole. Explication was a mainstay of the New Critics (Chapter 3).

It is important to remember that an explication is not a summary. That is, it is not a brief recitation of plot, which can result from following the chronological sequence of events, nor is it a paraphrase of a poem, which comes from examining the poem line by line or stanza by stanza. Instead, you should think about the work or passage in terms of significant literary elements, such as symbols, motifs, or figurative language, and then point out the meanings and effects they have.

Analysis

An analysis of anything involves dividing it into its parts, then noting how they relate to or create the whole. Analysis is a traditional assignment popular with teachers of literature, because it can be applied to the study of characters, plot structure, or imagery—a wide variety of literary elements. For example, if you were asked to analyze the character of Sarty in "Barn Burning," you would think about various aspects of his being, such as his family background, societal pressures, education, and experiences. How do these things work together so that in the end he runs away from his childhood into adulthood?

Sometimes an analysis traces the stages of development of an event. In the case of Sarty's final act, for example, you would look for signs of his evolving decision or for formative events that change the way he sees his life—and that of his father. Analysis is a process, not a single unchanging entity. In an analysis, you will not be able to discuss every aspect of a work, nor do you need to. Instead, you restrict your concern to those issues that are pertinent to the character or another literary element that you are analyzing.

Comparison and Contrast

Essay questions on examinations often take the form of comparison and contrast because the form allows an instructor to assess your knowledge about more than one topic in a single question. It also makes evident your ability to think critically, as it asks you to assess the similarities and differences of two persons or things, usually with a view to evaluating their worth relative to one another.

When you meet such an assignment, you would do well to begin with a simple list of how your two topics are similar and different in significant ways. If you are comparing two works, they should have some meaningful point of commonality—for example, the subject, author, or setting. The word *significant* is important here, because you cannot draw meaningful inferences from your study if you are dealing with trivial instances of comparison. In the end, you will want to draw conclusions about which is better, stronger, more important, longer-lasting, or more desirable. Without such a central idea, an organizing focus, your information will remain disconnected bits of data that mean nothing.

There are several different ways to present your conclusions, but two basic organizational patterns are always available. Say you are comparing "Barn Burning" with "Spotted Horses," another short story by Faulkner. Using the first pattern described above, you can present your discussion of "Barn Burning" in the first half of your paper, then turn your attention to "Spotted Horses," noting where the two stories share meaningful similarities but also where they diverge in other important ways. The second pattern presents one piece of information at a time about each story. For example, you might discuss the setting of each story, then the symbolism, followed by the theme. (Of course, there should be strong connections among the elements you choose to examine.) Both models call for a conclusion in which you make inferences and generalizations about the essential sameness, difference, or relative worth of the two texts.

Study of a Single Author's Works

An analysis of several works by the same author takes the basic techniques of comparison and contrast one step further, for it continues to search for characteristics that recur from one work to another, albeit sometimes with variations and changes. You are trying to find the artist's creative fingerprints—what makes him or her unique and, thereby, recognizable.

Regardless of how many works by a single author you choose to consider in your analysis, you should prepare yourself by reading as many as possible. The more you have read of a single writer's work, the easier it will be for you to identify typical attitudes, concerns, and strategies. You will know that you are ready to discuss significant characteristics when you can recognize a poem or story as probably having been written by a particular person, even when the authorship was not disclosed.

Topics that grow out of such studies are numerous. For example, you can focus your attention on a given theme or issue, the recurring treatment of certain social values, repeated stylistic characteristics, or reflections of the author's own experiences. In all cases, you will want to trace the appearance of whatever you are examining through several works of the same author.

SUMMING UP

The approaches to reading texts and writing literary analyses that are explained in this chapter are probably not new to you, given that they have been standard classroom methods of teaching for many years. That they have been popular with teachers for decades is evidence of their usefulness. They will provide a good starting place for you to begin your literary explorations, and later they can be valid means of extending other approaches.

SUGGESTED READING

Abrams, M. H. *A Glossary of Literary Terms.* 8th ed. Boston: Wadsworth Cengage Learning, 2009.

Adler, Mortimer, and Charles Van Doren. *How to Read a Book.* New York: Simon & Schuster, 1972.

Bateson, F. W. *English Poetry: A Critical Introduction.* 2nd ed. Westport, CT: Greenwood Press, 1978.

Crane, R. S. *Critics and Criticism, Ancient and Modern.* Chicago: University of Chicago Press, 1952.

Dictionary of Literary Biography. Detroit, MI: Gale Research Series, Cengage Gale, 1978–2000.

Frye, Northrop. *Anatomy of Criticism: Four Essays.* ed. Robert D. Denham. Buffalo, NY: University of Toronto Press, 2006.

Harmon, William. *Handbook to Literature.* 10th ed. Upper Saddle River, NJ: Pearson/ Prentice Hall, 2009.

Warren, Austin, and René Wellek. *Theory of Literature.* 3rd [revised] ed. Harmondsworth, UK: Penguin, 1973.

For up-to-date information on the many Web sites addressing historical-biographical critical approaches, visit www.cengagebrain.com.

Model Student Analysis

Between Gloom and Splendor: A Historical Analysis of Hawthorne's "Young Goodman Brown"

MEGHAN HARMON

Wo to the Inhabitants of the Earth, and of the Sea; for the Devil is come down to you, having great Wrath; because he knoweth, that he hath but a short time.

REVELATION 12:12 (QTD. IN MATHER 34)

Hawthorne's young Goodman Brown first entered the dark woods surrounding Salem in the spring of 1835, and readers have been puzzling over his questionable experience ever since. Critics have often, and aptly, interpreted the happenings in the story as an allegory for man's internal struggles with the loss of faith. The point of puzzlement for readers, however, rests somewhere upon the blurred borderline between reality and fiction. Did Brown actually witness a communion of witches? Hawthorne's text goes so far as to question reality at its close: "Had Goodman Brown fallen asleep in the forest and only dreamed a wild dream of a witch-meeting?" Hawthorne then quickly counters his previous inquiry with the statement, "Be it so if you will; but alas! It was a dream of evil omen for young Goodman Brown." With this comment, the author draws attention not to the possibility of the event but to the very real psychological repercussions on Brown. This analysis intends to examine the connections between Brown and Hawthorne as another example of fiction woven from real-life experiences and the necessity for the two (fiction and fact) to exist at once. Examination of Hawthorne's ancestral past may prove Hawthorne's history to be rooted as deeply in darkness as the fictional history of Goodman Brown.

When he wrote "Young Goodman Brown," Hawthorne drew the details from the history of Salem, Massachusetts—his birthplace and home to the infamous Salem witch trials. The local lore surrounding seventeenth-century witchcraft episodes became inspiration for the meeting that Goodman Brown witnesses in the woods. To evoke a sense of historical accuracy in Brown's fantasy-like world, Hawthorne uses the actual names of individuals of Salem's past, such as Goody Cloyse and Goody Cory. In the story, Brown watches in horror as Goody Cloyse, the woman who taught him catechism, speaks to his guide in a friendly and familiar way. Cloyse asks of her "old gossip," "But—would your worship believe it?—my broomstick hath strangely disappeared, stolen, as I suspect, by that unhanged witch, Goody Cory, and that, too, when I was all anointed with the juice of smallage, and cinquefoil, and wolf's bane—." Cloyse, it seems, is completely comfortable accusing Cory of witchery even while Cloyse was consumed in making quite the fiendish brew herself.

The exchange between Brown's guide and Goody Cloyse serves as Hawthorne's commentary on what he likely read when studying what happened in Salem 150 years before he wrote "Young Goodman Brown" (Turner 64). The names of Cloyse and Cory (in various spellings) appear throughout the historical records and often in connection with each other. In the case of *Ephraim Sheldon v. Martha Corey,* a woman "in one of her fits" cried out the name of Goodwife Cloyse. The testimony reads: "When [the afflicted woman] came to herself [and] she was asked who she saw, she answered that she saw nobody, they demanded of her whether or no she did not see Goodwife Nurse or Goodwife Cloyce, or Goodwife Cory she answered she saw no body" (*Records* 55). Despite the fact that the names of Cloyse and Cory are evoked several times and in several cases [including a case in which Cloyse was called an "old witch" (*Records* 65)], most frequently it is Goody Cory whom charges are brought against. Hawthorne and his audience would not have been present at the time of the trials. For this reason, it became important for Hawthorne to create a fictional explanation for the behavior and actions documented in the record books. Hawthorne entertains the idea that these women who had once been accomplices have now resorted to childish accusations and finger-pointing (i.e., "She stole my broomstick!"). By manufacturing the relationship between Cory and Cloyse, Hawthorne cements the relationship between fact and fiction by supporting the details of a fictional story with actual history.

In addition to using the names associated with the trials, Hawthorne includes elements from the prevailing belief system (Puritanism) very much at the core of what occurred in Salem years earlier. Examples of how definitive Puritans believed their faith to be can be garnered from the words of the Puritan minister Cotton Mather, who wrote texts concerning what he firmly believed to be the devil's work in Salem. In his book *Wonders of the Invisible World,* Mather calls New Englanders "a people of God settled in those, which were once the Devil's Territories" (14). Of course, the previous inhabitants of the territories were Native Americans, not devils. Hawthorne teases out the xenophobic implications Mather makes when he has Brown observe, "There may be a devilish Indian behind every tree" and the minister and deacon say that Indian powwows know "almost as much deviltry as the best of us." Mather rationalizes that Satan was angry at the people of Salem for taking his land and had thus tied "a dreadful Knot of Witches in the Country" (16).

Mather, like many other Puritans, believed firmly in the realm of angels and demons. It was in Salem, however, that the appearance of witches served as a bridge from the invisible world to the visible one. Mather said it was "as if the

Invisible world were becoming Incarnate" (67). In "Young Goodman Brown," Hawthorne expands upon Mather's ideas by incorporating fantastic elements into something that might have been nothing more than a walk in the woods. From his research, Hawthorne knew that once the witch paranoia began, there was no one out of suspicion's reach. Mather's language further propagates this feeling among the New Englanders when he tells them, "Daemons might Impose the Shapes of Innocent Persons in their Spectral Exhibitions upon the Sufferers" (Mather 15). Now everyone, including those thought to be people of God, could be the devil in disguise. Mather later describes occurrences similar to those found in "Young Goodman Brown," further highlighting Hawthorne's use of Mather as a source text. The hellish rendezvous that Brown attends resembles the one that Mather describes here:

> The Devil, Exhibiting himself ordinarily as a small Black man, has decoy'd a fearful knot of proud, froward, ignorant, envious and malicious creatures, to lift themselves in his horrid Service, by entring their Names in a Book by him tendred unto them. These Witches, whereof above a Score have now Confessed, and shown their Deeds, and some are now tormented by the Devils, for Confessing, have met in Hellish Randezvouzes, wherein the Confessors do say, they have had their Diabolical Sacraments, imitating the Baptism and Supper of our Lord, In these hellish meetings, these Monsters have associated themselves to do no less a thing than, To destroy the Kingdom of our Lord Jesus Christ. (Mather 67– 8)

Mather's language conveys what he views to be factual information, citing a number of confessors and even a book as evidence. Brown's guide mentions, "The deacons of many a church have drunk the communion wine with me," and Goody Cloyse says, "They tell me there is a nice young man to be taken into communion tonight." And later, deep in the woods, the "shape of evil dip[s] his hand and prepare[s] to lay the mark of baptism upon their foreheads." Hawthorne includes both of the diabolical sacraments mentioned in Mather's writing to further emphasize to his readers that evil exists in everyone—even clergy members.

The intermingling of Christian practices with Satanic ritual in "Young Goodman Brown" reflects Hawthorne's own skepticism about the Puritan faith. Hawthorne imparts the message of evil's existence in everyone—even in those whom we would least expect. Of Cloyse, Brown says, "That old woman taught me my catechism," and the narrator observes, "There was a world of meaning in this simple comment." This "world of meaning" comes to fruition for Brown during the climactic scene in which his guide forces Brown to take note of those in attendance:

> "There," resumed the sable form, "are all whom ye have reverenced from youth. Ye deemed them holier than yourself, and shrank from your own sin, contrasting it with their lives of righteousness and prayerful aspirations heavenward. Yet here are they all in my worshipping assembly."

The presence of clergy and other people of faith destroys Brown's previously held beliefs. Brown's realization of humanity's inherent sin causes the dramatic shift in Brown displayed at the text's close. Brown loses all faith he had in goodness and purity and is transformed into "[a] stern, a sad, a darkly meditative, a distrustful, if not a desperate man." In *Hawthorne's Historical Allegory*, John E. Becker explains how this shift explains Hawthorne's outlook on Puritanism: "In [Goodman Brown] we see the helplessness of Puritan faith to deal successfully with the universality of evil. What Hawthorne is saying is that to those who insist, as do the Puritans that the world be seen as black and white, blackness is the vision that will prevail. The fault is with the Puritan view of life, not with the strength of the hero" (19). All, from whores to the holy, have the mark of sin upon them.

Once Brown becomes aware of this all-encompassing sin, there will be nothing but blackness, for now nothing can ever be completely pure. Brown realizes that people he thought were upstanding have chosen to take a walk with his menacing tour guide. Through the character of the guide, Hawthorne demonstrates humankind's inseparable link with evil by making evil a relative. Hawthorne masterfully weaves connections between Satan and young Goodman Brown into the character of Brown's guide through the woods. Brown himself does not seem to recognize the man, but acknowledges a strange family resemblance:

> As nearly as could be discerned, the second traveler was about fifty years old, apparently in the same rank of life as Goodman Brown, and bearing a considerable resemblance to him, though perhaps more in expression than features. Still they might have been taken for father and son.

Later, at the fire in the woods, Brown "could have well-nigh sworn that the shape of his own dead father beckoned him to advance." While these clues point to Brown and the man being of the same bloodline, others hint at the possibility that this man could be the devil, or "he of the serpent," himself. The man's staff bears "the likeness of a great black snake, so curiously wrought that it might almost be seen to twist and wriggle itself like a living serpent," and he had "an indescribable air of one who knew the world"—perhaps like one who has eaten from the Tree of Knowledge? Hawthorne uses Goody Cloyse's character to support the idea that the man represents both the devil and a relative of Brown. She identifies him when she screams, "The devil!" and then explains that he is "the very image of [her] old gossip, Goodman Brown, the grandfather of the silly fellow that now is."

Why would the author place such importance on the evil remnants of Brown's ancestry? Hawthorne's ties to the religious fanaticism of our young nation are thicker than merely growing up in Salem could produce; Hawthorne's ties are in blood. Brown states, "My father never went into the woods on such an errand, nor his father before him. We have been a race of honest men and good Christians since the days of the martyrs." Nevertheless, his companion asserts otherwise. Goodman Brown's guide through the wilderness assures the doubtful Brown that he has been well acquainted with long-passed members of Brown's family. The man says, "I helped your grandfather, the constable, when he lashed the Quaker woman so smartly through the streets of Salem." Here, Hawthorne refers to the history of his own family, as his ancestor, William Hathorne did this very thing.

William Hathorne whipped not just one Quaker woman through the streets of Salem but *four* (Turner 61). Soon thereafter, Hathorne's son John became a magistrate in the witch hearings at Salem and provided a great deal of inspiration for Hawthorne throughout his work. Biographers of Hawthorne tend to have different interpretations on how he may have felt about a member of his family having played so prominent a role in the trials. In *A Reader's Guide to the Short Stories of Nathaniel Hawthorne,* Lea Newman writes, "Those readers who believe Hawthorne meant his portrayal of Puritans to be self-incriminating relate all his Puritan stories to the guilt he felt over his ancestors' part in the persecutions recorded during the early history of Puritan New England" (339). Today, it is a common belief that Hawthorne added the "w" to his surname in order to distance himself from his ancestors out of shame.

Yet Hawthorne also commented on the remarkable achievements of both John and William Hathorne in many of his works. The records Hawthorne reviewed on Salem history were "for the most part interpretative rather than documentary" (Turner 64). Some accounts depict John Hathorne "more like a prosecuting attorney than a magistrate, assuming the guilt of the person under examination and trying to force a confession with bullying questions" (Hansen 59). Others view Hathorne "seemingly without the harshness of the judges before whom the accused were later tried" and "as a faithful public servant" (Turner 65–66). Biographers of Hawthorne often cite the trial of Rebecca Nurse to be a case in which Magistrate Hathorne admits uncertainty over the validity of witchcraft claims and shows sympathy toward the accused. He displays doubt over the likelihood that he can determine whether or not Nurse perpetrated any crime. He says to Nurse, "Glory to God I pray God clear you, if you be innocent, and if you be Guilty discover you" (*Records* 85). John Hathorne, like Goodman Brown, distresses himself over the idea of Christians being involved in witchcraft. During the trial of Nurse, he says, "What a sad thing it is that a church member here and now another of Salem, should be thus accused and charged" (*Records* 85). Here, Hathorne's comment resonates with as much sorrow as Brown's does when he recognizes the good old woman who taught him his catechism. It cannot be forgotten, however, that Magistrate Hathorne had a responsibility to be stern and rid his community of an evil that appeared to him as real as the flesh on his bones.

The divided opinions on John Hathorne's character and the trials themselves are all rooted in different versions (or perspectives) of truth. Hawthorne would likely find redeeming qualities in the words of his ancestor. Yet, looking back at the witch trials and the skewed history surrounding them, Hawthorne was aware of the disastrous consequences and stain forever placed upon Salem. Writing "Young Goodman Brown" led Hawthorne to see this wonderful combination of fiction in reality and reality in fiction. As mentioned in this essay's introduction, the psychological repercussions on Brown exist regardless of whether he attended a witch meeting or dreamed one. The realization of the "instinct that guides mortal man to evil" and the proclamation from Brown's guide that "Evil is the nature of mankind" leave Brown in complete darkness. Hawthorne draws from a very Puritan idea here, as Mather writes that if the devil "fetches up the Dirt which before lay still at the bottom of our sinful Hearts. If we allow the Mad Dogs of Hell to poyson us by biting us, we shall imagine that we see nothing but such things about us, and like such things fly upon all that we see" (Mather 21). Black is all that Brown can see, and so his story will end without promise: "They carved no hopeful verse upon [Brown's] tombstone, for his dying hour was gloom."

Examining the binaries of fact/fiction and good/evil provides an exceptional opportunity for understanding the motivations Hawthorne had for writing "Young Goodman Brown." Through historicizing fiction, Hawthorne may have been working to cope with his own demons, the sins of his forefathers, and the struggle to find that middle ground "between gloom and splendor"—separate from a Puritan view of history—as *nothing* can truly exist solely in Puritan shades of black and white.

WORKS CITED

Becker, John E. *Hawthorne's Historical Allegory*. Port Washington, NY: Kennikat Press, 1971.

Hansen, Chadwick. *Witchcraft at Salem*. New York: Signet, 1969.

Hawthorne, Nathaniel. *Nathaniel Hawthorne Selected Tales and Sketches*. 3rd ed. New York: Holt, Rinehart and Winston, 1970.

Mather, Cotton. *On Witchcraft: Wonders of the Invisible World*. Authorized xerographic reprint. Ann Arbor, MI: University Microfilms, 1970.

Newman, Lea Bertani Vozar. *A Reader's Guide to the Short Stories of Nathaniel Hawthorne*. Boston: G. K. Hall, 1979.

Records of Salem Witchcraft Copied from the Original Documents. Burt Franklin Research & Source Works Series. New York: Lenox Hill, originally published 1864, reprinted 1972.

Turner, Arlin. *Nathaniel Hawthorne: A Biography*. New York: Oxford University Press, 1980.

3

Formalism

Poetry does not inhere in any particular element but depends upon the set of relationships, the structure, which we call the poem.

ROBERT PENN WARREN, "Pure and Impure Poetry"

Formalism probably has the distinction of having more names than any other recently developed school of criticism. The model, as defined by American and English critics, has been called the New Criticism (long after it was no longer new), as well as aesthetic or textual (because of its primary concerns) or ontological (because of its philosophical grounding). Then, too, there is **Russian formalism**, which shares some fundamental characteristics with its Western cousin, but it is the ideas of the writers known as the New Critics, referred to here as *formalist criticism,* that in the 1930s revolutionized the work of scholars, critics, and teachers in the United States. For decades people learned to read, analyze, and appreciate literature using this approach, making it one of the most influential methods of literary analysis that twentieth-century readers encountered.

Formalism's sustained popularity among readers comes primarily from the fact that it provides them with a way to understand and enjoy a work for its own inherent value as a piece of literary art. Emphasizing close reading of the work itself, formalism puts the focus on the text as literature. It does not treat the text as an expression of social, religious, or political ideas; neither does it reduce the text to being a promotional effort for some cause or belief. As a result, formalism makes those who apply its principles and follow its processes better, more discerning readers.

HISTORICAL BACKGROUND

Any new school of criticism is both an offspring of those that have preceded it and a reaction against them. The New Criticism, with its emphasis on unity and form, is the direct descendant of the aesthetic theories of the romantic poets (and the philosopher-critics before them). Samuel Taylor Coleridge, for example, believed that the spirit of poetry must "embody in order to reveal itself; but a living body is of necessity an organized one—and what is organization but the connection of parts to a whole, so that each part is at once end and means!" Form to him was not simply the visible, external shape of literature. It was something "organic," "innate." He explained that "it shapes as it develops itself from within, and the fulness [*sic*] of its development is one and the same with the perfection of its outward form. Such is the life, such the form."

The New Criticism was more directly born as a reaction against the attention that scholars and teachers in the early part of the twentieth century paid to the biographical and historical context of a work, thereby diminishing the attention given to the literature itself. Instead of dealing directly with a poem, for example, the previous generation's critics were likely to treat it as a sociological or historical record. It could be an excuse to indulge one's fascination with the lives of writers and their friends. When the critics and scholars did directly address the text, they tended to describe their own impressions of it. Clearly, something more scientific was called for, some better way of understanding and evaluating a poem or play.

Enter New Criticism, a theory of literature that would have a reader understand and value a work for its own inherent worth, not for its service to metaliterary matters. The movement began informally in the 1920s at Vanderbilt University in discussions among John Crowe Ransom, Robert Penn Warren, Allen Tate, Cleanth Brooks, and others who were interested in getting together to talk about literature. For three years, they published a literary magazine called *The Fugitive*. Not only influenced by one another but also bolstered by the work of theorists from abroad, such as T. S. Eliot, I. A. Richards, and William Empson, they began to develop their own ideas of how to read a text. Important to their thinking, for example, was Eliot's announcement of the high place of art as art rather than as expression of social, religious, or political ideas. They were influenced, too, by Eliot's explanation of how emotion is expressed in art. He called it the *objective correlative,* "a set of objects, a situation, a chain of events which shall be the formula of that *particular* emotion; such that when the external facts, which must terminate in sensory experience, are given, the emotion is immediately evoked." From Richards, who was concerned with the investigation of meaning, they adopted the practice of working toward the scrupulous explication of poems. Although the Fugitives would later become well known for their own poems and stories, they are also remembered for beginning to formulate principles of literary analysis that would shape the habits of serious readers for several decades to come.

The New Criticism went on to develop a sense of the importance of form (leading at some point to this area of criticism being called *formalism*), their practice emphasizing the close reading of texts and an appreciation of order. It asserted that understanding a work comes from looking at it as a self-sufficient object with formal elements, laws of its own that could be studied. To know *how* a work creates meaning became the quest. In time, formalist principles were set firmly in place with acceptance by such prestigious literary journals as the *Kenyon Review* and *Sewanee Review* and by college adoptions of Brooks and Warren's texts *An Approach to Literature* (with John Purser in 1936), *Understanding Poetry* (1939), *Understanding Fiction* (1943), and *Understanding Drama* (by Brooks and Robert Heilman in 1948). It was also supported by the publication of anthologies such as *The House of Fiction*, by Caroline Gordon and Allen Tate (1950), which features commentary on how to read the short fiction collected in the volume. The wide dissemination of formalist principles led, finally, to their dominance of American, and to some extent English, literary studies through the 1940s and 1950s and into the 1960s.

Russian Formalism

Critics involved with the formalist movement that took place in the United States and the Russian formalists are sometimes thought to be members of the same group, or at least closely related, because of the movements' similar names. In actuality, the two groups are only distantly connected. The latter flourished in Moscow and St. Petersburg in the 1920s, and although the principles they espoused have some similarity to those of the New Critics, they are two separate schools. In fact, because the work of the Russian formalists was based on the theories of Ferdinand de Saussure, the French linguist, they are probably more closely related to the structuralists, who were to garner attention in the 1950s and 1960s (see Chapter 8). Saussure's influence is seen, for example, in the Russian formalists' argument that literature is a systematic set of linguistic and structural elements that can be analyzed. They saw literature as a self-enclosed system that can be studied not for its content but for its form.

Even the Moscow formalists and the St. Petersburg formalists did not agree on everything, although they did hold some beliefs in common. For example, both rejected the nineteenth-century view that literature expresses an author's world-view, making biographical criticism the key to understanding a text. They also agreed that literature could (and should) be studied in a scientific manner, with the purpose of understanding it for its own sake, not as a medium for discussing other subjects. Consequently, form was more important to them than content. Their focus was on **poetics**—the strategies a writer used—rather than on history, biography, or subject matter.

The Russian formalists also asserted that everyday language is just that: everyday or ordinary. Literary language is different. It deviates from the expected, using all the devices an author has the power to manipulate to make what is familiar seem strange and unfamiliar. In fact, Victor Shklovsky coined the term ***defamiliarization*** to refer to the literary process that gives vitality to language that might otherwise be all too predictable. Defamiliarization is the artful aspect of a work that makes the reader alert and alive; it causes the reader to intensify the attention paid to the text, to look again at an image in an effort to take in the unexpected.

Another difference between reality and its representation in words is evident in the Russian formalists' distinction between story (*fibula*) and plot (*sjuzhet*). The former refers to the actual sequence of events in a narrative; the latter, to the artistic presentation, which can jumble the sequence, repeat episodes, or include surprises. The literary treatment defamiliarizes the world and heightens the reader's awareness of it.

In 1930 the Soviet government forced the Russian formalists to disband because they were unwilling to treat literature as an expression of Soviet ideology. Some of the leading proponents moved to Prague, where they continued their work. Eventually two of them, Roman Jakobson and René Wellek, emigrated to America, where they met with the New Critics. Whatever influence may have come of those discussions, it is now evident that both groups shared a belief in the acceptance of literature as a language separate and distinct from its everyday form, one that deserves close analysis of its characteristics and elements.

Mikhail Bakhtin

Mikhail Bakhtin (1895–1975), another Russian literary theorist of the twentieth century, does not fit easily into any one school of modern literary criticism. His thinking ranged through a widely diverse set of academic disciplines and interests that included philosophy, ethics, cultural criticism, literary history, and more, making it difficult to put him into a single category of study. He has sometimes been identified with the Russian formalists, but he clearly has differences with them. At other times he has been called a Marxist critic, since he was writing in the Soviet Union as early as the 1920s, but those doctrines never dominated his work. Although he is difficult to fit into any single classification, the impact of his thinking on many fields of study makes it impossible to overlook him. Because he was at work at generally the same time as the American formalists and the Russian formalists, despite his differences with them, his ideas will be discussed at this point.

The breadth of Bakhtin's interests has brought his views to the attention of scholars in many fields, making him influential in such varied disciplines as semiotics, religious criticism, and structuralism. He is held by many to be one of the outstanding thinkers of his era. Tzvetan Todorov called him perhaps the greatest twentieth-century theorist of literature.

Some of the difficulty of studying Bakhtin is due to his being during his lifetime a fairly obscure writer, even in his own homeland, until he was rediscovered by Russian scholars in the 1960s. Few of his works were published in authoritative editions during his lifetime, and disagreement still exists over which texts he actually wrote. Some of those that he coauthored are simply attributed to "the Bakhtin group." Others, including his work on the eighteenth-century German novel, which had been accepted for publication, disappeared during the German invasion of World War II, and a manuscript on the *Bildungsroman* he himself damaged by using its pages to roll cigarettes. He did not come to the notice of the West until the late 1960s when Julia Kristeva and Tzvetan Todorov brought him to the attention of the French literary world. Notice then quickly spread to the United Kingdom and the United States, and by the late 1980s he had become a leading scholar and thinker among those interested in language and culture.

The details of Bakhtin's life are equally uncertain. Information was routinely suppressed during his lifetime, and the political unrest in Russia at that time has made personal records difficult to come by. We know that he was born in Oryol, Russia, outside of Moscow, to an old family of the nobility, and that he spent his childhood in various cities. After earning a degree in classics and philology in 1918, he moved to Nevel (Pskov Oblast), a small city in western Russia, where he worked as a schoolteacher for two years. At that time the first "Bakhtin Circle," a group composed of intellectuals with varying interests, came together. Bound by their shared passion for discussing literary, religious, and political subjects, with German philosophy as one of the chief topics, they provided stimulus for the birth of some of the concepts that Bakhtin would develop throughout his career. The group included, among others, Valentin Voloshinov and P. N. Medvedev. In 1923 Bakhtin was diagnosed with osteomyelitis, a bone disease that eventually cost him his leg.

His troubles were not solely physical. Throughout his lifetime Bakhtin struggled with the politics of Russia. He did not have Communist Party credentials, a lack that sometimes denied him public notice, although it may also have saved him from the Stalinist purges. In 1929, shortly after publication of *Problems of Dostoevsky's Art*, his first major work, he was accused of participating in an antigovernment movement of the Russian Orthodox Church and of "corrupting the young," a charge that was never proven, and sentenced to ten years in exile in Siberia. Appealing on the basis of his health, he received a reduced sentence of six years of internal exile in Kazakhstan, where he worked as a bookkeeper and wrote several important essays, including "Discourse in the Novel."

In 1924 Bakhtin moved to Leningrad and later to Moscow, where he wrote a dissertation, "Rabelais and His World," to earn a postgraduate degree. The dissertation could not be defended until the end of World War II, and when it was, its unorthodox ideas sharply divided the scholarly community. In the end he was granted the doctorate, though he could not publish his dissertation. It went unread until it was rediscovered by graduate students at the Gorky Institute in the 1960s and finally published in 1965. He taught at Mordov Pedagogical Institute (now University of Saranak) from the late 1940s until 1961.

The published works for which he is best known are *Problems of Dostoyevsky's Poetics* (the only book to be published under his name before Stalin's death), *Rabelais and His World* (his dissertation), and *The Dialogic Imagination: Four Essays by M. M. Bakhtin*. "Discourse in the Novel," often referenced by those who think and write about Bakhtin's theories, is one of the essays in *The Dialogic Imagination*. In these works, all of them from a relatively early part of his life, he introduces the key concepts of his literary and cultural theory. They include dialogism, unfinalizability, heteroglossia, polyphony, and carnival.

Dialogism At the core of Bakhtin's literary theories is the concept of **dialogism**, the seeds of which are evident in some of his earliest known writings from the 1920s in which he criticizes Russian formalism for its abstract nature, which is evident in its lack of attention to the content of literary works. He then censures linguistics, and the work of Saussure in particular, for separating texts from their social context, for ignoring the relations that exist between speakers and texts. He argues that the structuralists (see Chapter 8) look only at the shape (the structure) of language and ignore how people use it. Such thinking eventually led him to assert that language (all forms of speech and writing) is always a dialogue, which consists of at least one speaker, one listener/respondent, and a relationship between the two. Language, for him, is the product of the interactions between (at least) two people. It is not monologic, an utterance issuing from a single speaker or writer.

The idea has applications on several levels. For the individual, it means that because it is language that defines a person, and one utterance is always responding to other utterances (even in those internal conversations in our heads), one is always in a process of becoming. And since the individual is always changing, nobody can be wholly understood or fully revealed. Bakhtin calls the condition in which people cannot be completely known **unfinalizability**.

On a more general level, dialogism sees works of literature to be in communication with each other and with other authors. One shapes the other, not just by influencing new works but by adding to the understanding of those that have preceded it as well as those that follow it. Works of literature do not merely answer or correct each other but inform and become informed by them. In an even more global manner, such thinking means that all language exists in response to what has already been said and in anticipation of what will be said. All thought is dynamic, growing and changing with each utterance.

Heteroglossia Many different languages exist in any single culture, and an individual uses a wide variety of them in any given day. Think about your day so far, considering how you have shifted languages, probably all of them English, but different types of English, as you changed listeners (or readers). How did the self you put forward in the different situations change with the languages you were using? How did the language both create and affect your relationship with the listener/reader? How did the context generate meaning?

Heteroglossia is the term Bakhtin uses to refer to the interplay of the numerous forms of social speech that people use as they go about their daily lives. It refers to the manner in which their diverse ways of speaking—their differing vocabularies, accents, expressions, and rhetorical strategies—mix with each other. It can be described as living language because it features multiplicity and variety; it carries suggestions of different professions, age groups, and backgrounds that intersect and shape each other, generating meaning through what he calls the "primacy of context over text."

Bakhtin maintains that two forces are in operation whenever language is used. Borrowing terms from physics, he calls them centripetal and centrifugal forces. The former pushes things toward a central point; centrifugal force pushes them away from the center and out in all directions. Heteroglossic language, according to Bakhtin, is centrifugal because of its dynamism and relativism. Its opposite, monologic language, is centripetal, because it forces everything into a single form or statement that comes from one authority. It standardizes language and rhetorical forms, ridding itself of differences in an effort to establish a single way of speaking and writing that is a pure, regimented discourse cleansed of differences that interrupt the accepted way of using language.

To apply his theories to literary genres, Bakhtin examines poetry and the novel in particular. Acknowledging that poetry has historically been the more highly valued form, he asserts that because the two genres have different purposes, they use language (create meaning) in different ways.

Poetry, he asserts, is an art form; it has an aesthetic function. It does not do anything. Operating as a self-sufficient whole, it is aware only of itself. It exists unconnected to its context and does not acknowledge its respondent. For example, in a poem a word refers only to itself or to an object that exists as an abstraction, not as a specific item. Consequently, Bakhtin concludes that poetry is essentially monologic. (He also views the epic and drama as monologic, but he pays particular attention to poetry.)

In contrast, prose (indeed, rhetoric in general—which seeks to use language to persuade or convince), has a social purpose; it does something. The novel in particular holds the attention of Bakhtin because it is dialogic (centrifugal), and with its diversity of voices, it is heteroglossic. It can be said to be characterized by **dialogized heteroglossia**. That is, it is composed of multiple experiences and worldviews in ongoing dialogue with each other, creating numerous interactions, some of them actual, some of them fictive, making it well positioned to oppose the standardization promoted by monologic genres. (Even the novelist is part of the interaction, as he or she is aware of a reader who is likely to have responses that affect what is written.) Bakhtin deems the commenting narrator's dialogic utterances to be the most important ones because through them a complex unity of diverse voices, interactions, and relationships form. He celebrates the novel for its "dialogically agitated and tension-filled environment of alien words, value judgments and accents" that form complex, ever shifting patterns. In it a multiplicity of languages clash, just as they do in any given culture.

Polyphony

Bakhtin uses the term **polyphonic** to describe the novel that depicts a world in which the dialogue goes on ad infinitum without reaching a conclusion or closure. The structure is not predetermined to demonstrate the author's worldview, nor are the characters drawn to exemplify it. It is typified by the novels of Dostoyevsky, in which the reader hears many voices uttering contradictory and inconsistent statements in the context of a real-life event. Truth in Dostoyevsky's works is perceived through multiple consciousnesses and expressed in many simultaneous voices, not conceived in a single mind and spoken by a single speaker. There is no central voice in his novels, only multiple unfinalizable characters that talk about ideas in their distinctive, individual ways. They exist with each other and through each other as they interact in social circumstances. In addition to the characters that participate in the experience, there are the author and the reader, too, who with the characters help to create the novel's "truths," not simply one certain truth. Characters influence characters. Readers watch as they shape each other and listen as their utterances conflict with each other, all the while filtering the characters' observations through their own experiences and understanding. Bakhtin contrasts Dostoyevsky's approach with that of the nonpolyphonic monologism of Tolstoy, who reveals his own understanding of truth by expressing it through his characters' words, actions, and choices.

Carnival Another key concept in Bakhtin's theory of the novel is that of **carnival**, an idea that made its first appearance in his dissertation, "Rabelais and His World," and was further developed in *Problems of Dostoyevsky's Poetics*. His notion of carnival builds on the ancient tradition of the Saturnalia, a Roman festival that mocked and reversed the official culture, if only for a short while. For a limited period of time the powerless became the powerful, the outsider became the insider, slave and master exchanged roles.

Bakhtin judges the novel to operate with a similar social impact. Building on his study of Rabelais's novel cycle *Gargantua and Pantagruel,* the protagonists of which he sees not only as a challenge to an official culture ruled by dogmatism and deadly seriousness but also as producers of energy and vitality, he extends that analysis to consider the novel as a genre that uses laughter and parody to challenge restrictive social forces, such as the tyranny and repression of his own day. It obliterates social hierarchies and blurs distinctions between young and old, rich and poor, public and private, in short reversing the traditional systems of authority and order. In doing so, it opens the way to joyful renewal.

The polyphonic nature of the novel, in which the reader hears conflicting statements from many voices interacting and helping to shape each other, is carnivalesque. The clash of ideas destroys any notion of regular conventions, standardization, or rules, and even suggests a certain freedom of being. Each character is individually defined, and at the same time the reader witnesses how each is influenced by the other. Each one is touched by the others, and in turn shapes the character of the others. Carnival is the context in which voices are singly heard but interact together.

READING AS A FORMALIST

To understand the following discussion, you should read the short story "Araby," by James Joyce, which begins on page 327.

The critic who wants to write about literature from a formalist perspective must first be a close and careful reader who examines all the elements of a text individually and questions how they come together to create a work of art. Such a reader, who respects the autonomy of a work, achieves an understanding of it by looking inside it, not outside it or beyond it. Instead of examining historical periods, author biographies, or literary styles, for example, he or she will approach a text with the assumption that it is a self-contained entity and that he or she is looking for the governing principles that allow the text to reveal itself. For example, the correspondences between the characters in James Joyce's short story "Araby" and the people he knew personally may be interesting, but for the formalist they are less pertinent to understanding how the story creates meaning than are other kinds of information that the story contains within itself.

Because formalism calls for a close reading of the text, the first time through a given work you cannot expect to notice all the subtleties and details that will ultimately figure in your analysis. It is on subsequent readings that the formalist perspective begins to take shape. The second time around, you may begin to notice repetition of words and images, patterns of sound, multiple meanings, and ambiguous dialogue. You will ultimately investigate every detail of a work for its contribution to and connection with the whole. Such observations made by the scrupulous reader are the key to discovering how all the formal elements of the text work together. Some of the main elements that call for attention are form, diction, and unity, as well as the various literary devices they subsume.

Form

Coleridge's concept of the organic, innate nature of form in a literary work (noted earlier) is reflected in the formalists' assumption that although the external, easily noted ordering of a poem or story (e.g., its rhyme scheme or sequence of events leading to a climax) may be significant in an analysis, form is actually the whole that is produced by various structural elements working together. Form grows out of the work's recurrences, repetitions, relationships, **motifs**—all the organizational devices that create the total effect. Together they are the statement of the work. Thus, form and content are inseparable.

Because what a poem or prose work means depends on how it is said, to understand it the formalist reader-writer pays attention to how all the parts affect each other and how they fit together. In early readings, then, you may find it helpful to make marginal notations where words and phrases recur. Even if the wording is not repeated exactly, there may be synonyms that echo important words. Images, too, can gain significance by appearing more than once. They may be random or may form a regular pattern; either way, they deserve to be noted, because they begin to create form and unity.

In a narrative, the **point of view** from which a story is told is a significant shaping force. Because the reader is given only the information that the narrator knows, as he or she understands it and chooses to share it, the storyteller controls the reader's perception of the fictive world and thereby determines how the reader grasps the integral and meaningful relationship of all its parts. Of course, the omniscient narrator, who speaks with a third-person voice, is assumed to see all, but if a major or minor character in the narrative recounts the narrative, the reader must question how that teller's part in the story affects his or her understanding and presentation of it. Is the narrator reliable? Biased? Does the narrator have a reason to leave out events or reshape them? What is the teller's ethical stance?

You can also use your reading log to address a number of issues regarding the formal qualities of a text. Some relevant questions, such as the following, can help you start to think about these qualities.

- Does this work follow a traditional form, such as the Petrarchan sonnet, or does it chart its own development?
- How are the events of the plot recounted—for example, in sequential fashion or as a flashback?
- How does the work's organization affect its meaning?
- Does the denouement in a plot surprise or satisfy you?
- Does the denouement provide closure to the narrative or leave it open?
- What is the effect of using a particular meter—say, anapestic tetrameter?
- What is the effect of telling a story from this point of view?
- What sounds are especially important in developing this piece? (In poems, be sure to look for more than end rhyme.)
- What recurrences of words, images, and sounds do you notice?
- Do the recurrences make a pattern, or do they appear randomly?
- What rhythms are in the words? (This question is applicable to prose as well as poetry.)
- Where do images foreshadow later events?
- How does the narrator's point of view shape the meaning?
- What visual patterns do you find in this text?
- What progressions of nature are used to suggest meaning—for example, sunrise/sunset, spring/winter?
- If you were to make a chart of the progress of this plot or poem, what would it look like?

Sometimes, particularly in works written in the past few decades, form is hard to determine. Conventions that serve as guideposts for the reader may be few. Theater of the absurd, for instance, delights in a lack of traditional elements that an audience would look to for help. However, no form is also form. Notice how the seeming absence of form suggests a chaotic world in which there is no meaning.

As a formalist, then, you will look for meaning in all the organizational elements at hand, even those that seem distorted or "absurd." But simply listing them is not enough. You must then determine how their interaction creates meaning. What is the effect of the whole? How do the parts of the poem that give it order come together to assume a unique shape that presents readers with a unique experience? How does **structure** become meaning?

Looking at "Araby," for example, the reader easily recognizes that the narrative unfolds chronologically, but he or she also perceives that more is taking place here than a simple sequence of events involving a romantic desire to go to a bazaar. On the surface of the story, little seems to happen, but beneath it, more subtle conflicts and changes are transpiring. With that recognition, it is possible to see "Araby" as an initiation story in which the protagonist begins with childish dreams, moves through a test of will and commitment, and arrives at a new, adult sense of the world. The boy's maturation could be described as a downward emotional spiral as he moves from a sense of the holiness of the world to frustration with its obstacles and then rage at its emptiness. The bottom of the spiral is marked by his recognition of the futility of his efforts to make it otherwise. Though the journey begins as he listens to the sounds of innocent child's play, it ends with a recognition of humankind's aloneness in a darkened world.

The form of "Araby" can also be described in other ways. You could, for example, compare it with other stories of quest, in which the protagonist searches for a holy relic, traveling from place to place (in this case making the train journey, which he must take alone) and enduring ordeals in the service of his mission. You could also describe it as circular, for it begins with physical death (a priest had died in the back room, where the air is still musty, and the garden is yellowed and "straggling") and ends with the death of innocence and belief, which those earlier images foreshadowed. You could even say that it is a mythic pattern, as it recounts a single episode from childhood to suggest the larger pattern of human experience in which innocence is succeeded by knowledge, dreams by reality, childhood by adulthood.

Diction

Words hold the keys to meaning. A formalist will look at words closely, questioning all of their **denotations** (explicit dictionary meanings) and **connotations** (implied but not directly indicated meanings). As Brooks posited, the reader must consider how a word or phrase creates meaning that no other word or phrase could. **Etymology** (the history of a word) becomes significant, and allusions to other works may import surprising meanings. Tracing **allusions** is a sticky point for formalists, because it means going outside the text to find meaning. Nevertheless, if the reader is to explore all facets of the text, it is important to discover everything that a given reference suggests.

Locution that has more than a single possibility for interpretation is valued for the richness it brings to the whole. Unlike the scientist, who strives for directness and singularity of meaning, the poet, who speaks of experience, uses **ambiguity** to reach for meaning through language that is suggestive, compressed, and multileveled. The poet may, for example, choose words that can bear the load of several, sometimes divergent meanings, as Gerard Manley Hopkins did in "The Windhover." In that poem, he used the word *buckle,* which can mean "crumple" but also suggests "join" or "bend" and perhaps other possibilities.

When an incident, object, or person is used both literally (as itself) and figuratively (as something else), it becomes a **symbol**. In other words, a symbol refers simultaneously to itself and to something beyond the self in order to expand the meaning of the text and provide additional possibilities for the discovery of meaning. The U.S. flag is a flag, for instance, but it may also make a viewer think of freedom and country. Symbols are often recognizable because they grow out of images or phrases that recur with higher-than-expected frequency or that receive an inordinate amount of attention by the narrator. Such is the case with the train trip the boy in "Araby" must take to reach the fair. As he travels alone through the dark night, the journey becomes more than a physical one; he is also moving psychologically from innocence to knowledge, from childhood to adulthood. Because it is meaningful in the context of the images, plot structure, and other elements of the story, the symbol contributes to the story's **unity**.

In your reading log, you will find it helpful to note the quality of language in a selection:

- Record any words you do not know.
- Find words that appear more than once. Do their meanings change with subsequent use? Or do they grow more powerful?
- Look for words that suggest meanings they do not explicitly state.
- Identify terms (titles of books, quotations, paraphrases) that point to other works that would add meaning to the one you are reading.
- Look up the history of words that appear at important points of a story or poem. Do other, older meanings suggest anything about their use here?
- Where did you find ambiguity? How does it suggest additional meanings?
- What are the important symbols, and how do they create unity?

When applied to "Araby," these approaches reveal that its language is particularly rich and subtle, with connotations radiating out of words that initially seem to be merely literal or factual. The opening paragraph alone—with its use of *blind* (twice), its reference to the school as a prison (at the end of the day setting the boys "free"), and its description of the uninhabited, detached house in a neighborhood of "brown imperturbable faces"—suggests a society in which something important has been lost, a world in which dreams will not survive. It stands in contrast to the language used to describe the boy's private, inner world, where he worships the sister of his friend Mangan, whom he thinks of as a holy figure surrounded by an aura of light. Describing his devotion, he stresses its sacred nature by using Christian language. He says, "I imagined that I bore my chalice safely through a throng of foes. Her name sprang to my lips at moments in strange prayers and praises which I myself did not understand." The ambiguity in "Araby," its use of words that suggest more than a single meaning, creates a sense of mystery that is part of both the boy's devotion to holy mysteries and the mystery of human life. For instance, the descriptions of Mangan's sister, who does little and says only a few words, imply that she is both human and holy. When the boy recounts his vision of her, he says, "The light from the lamp opposite our door caught the white curve of her neck, lit up the hair that rested there and, falling, lit up the hand upon the railing. It fell over one side of her dress and caught the white border of a petticoat, just visible as she stood at ease." In his words, she is both a sexual and a sacred being. He is attracted by her sensuality but also sees her as a holy icon surrounded by light.

Obviously the diction of "Araby" suggests more than a first reading might indicate. The formalist critic will push on the story's language to reveal meanings that are not readily noticed in an effort to find suggested meanings rather than explicit ones. The result is an enriched understanding of the experiences of the boy, his world, and his understanding of it.

Unity

If a work has unity, all of its aspects fit together in significant ways that create a whole. Each element, through its relationship to the others, contributes to the totality of the work, its meaning. Patterns that inform and give relevance to the rest often appear as verbal motifs, images, symbols, figurative language, meter, rhyme, or sound. The narrator's point of view can also be an important unifying element.

Unity is created, for example, when a single **image** or **figure of speech** is extended throughout a work or when several images or figures form a pattern. The appearance may be a relatively simple repeated reference to a color or sound or the more complicated use of figurative language, an intentional departure from normal word meaning, such as a metaphor. For example, when a word or phrase is used to refer to a person or object to which it is not logically applicable, as in Emily Dickinson's assertion that "hope is the thing with feathers," the metaphorical statement is an imaginative way of identifying one thing with another. Stretched and elaborated, images and figures grow rich and complex, as is easily noticed in the poems of the metaphysical poets, whose works the New Critics celebrated. To see how the protracted, embellished use of an image or figure can enhance and complicate meaning, read John Donne's "A Valediction: Forbidding Mourning" or shorter poems, such as "The Silken Tent," by Robert Frost, or Emily Dickinson's "I Like to See It Lap the Miles."

In the most powerful works, the elements do not come together easily or comfortably. In fact, the formalist critic looks for these elements to resist one another, creating what Tate called **tension**, or the push of conflicting elements against each other. Tension often appears in the form of **irony** (the use of a word or a statement that is the opposite of what is intended), **paradox** (a contradiction that is actually true), and ambiguity (a word, statement, or situation that has more than one possible meaning). For example, a piece of fiction's point of view becomes more complicated, and more interesting to a formalist, if the narrator is not aware of the whole story but must tell it from limited knowledge or understanding. The possibilities for paradox, irony, and ambiguity grow when the storyteller operates without fully comprehending the dimensions of the events and characters of the narrative.

In your reading journal, you may want to ask some questions about the unity of the selection you are studying:

- What images are extended or elaborated?
- Where do several images work together to create meaning?
- What is paradoxical in the work? How is it both contradictory and true? What is ironic in the work?
- Do all the elements cohere in ways that generate meaning?
- Are the verbal motifs, images, figures of speech, symbols, meter, rhyme, and sound consistent? If not, what did you have to reconcile?

"Araby" is rich in paradox, ambiguity, and irony, though it is the last one that most clearly creates tension in this story. For example, when the boy finally arrives at the bazaar, the hall is in darkness and silence, "like that which pervades a church after a service." He recognizes that despite his devotion, his fidelity, and his desire to serve his dream, he has come too late. What he has expected, indeed what the reader feels he has deserved, has not come to pass. His situation is an ironic one in which he finds the opposite of what he made his journey to reach. Araby, the place of romance and enchantment, is as mundane as his own neighborhood. His holy quest has led to darkness.

Paradox often occurs along with irony, and many elements in Joyce's story are paradoxical. The boys' school, for example, is called the Christian Brothers' School, but it is described as a prison. In fact, the references to Christian objects and symbols, which abound in the story, are mostly paradoxes. The boy's garden, for example, has a central (dying) apple tree, he prays in the back room (where the priest died), and at the end of the story, a voice calls out, in an inversion to God's command "Let there be light," that the light has gone out. There is paradox, too, in the boy's devotion; it is simultaneously sad (because it is doomed) and laughable (because it is childish). And Mangan's sister, both holy and profane, is perhaps not simply ambiguous but paradoxical.

As with irony and ambiguity, such paradoxes require the reader to reconcile them to resolve the tension they create so that the text becomes a unified whole. The opposition of formal elements, which must be overcome if the work is to achieve wholeness, gives it the complexity one finds in life itself. As Warren pointed out in his essay "Pure and Impure Poetry," the poet "wins by utilizing the resistance of his opponent—the ambiguity, irony, and paradox, which, since everything in the work has to be accounted for, the reader must resolve to discover meaning."

What Doesn't Appear in Formalist Criticism

Just as the formalist critic must approach a work with a heightened awareness of form, diction, and unity (including finding and examining the significance of ambiguity, paradox, and irony), some other analytical techniques are to be avoided strenuously. They include the heresy of **paraphrase**, the **intentional fallacy**, biographical examination, and the **affective fallacy**. Because these techniques lead the reader away from the poem, instead of into it, formalist critics do not consider them valid critical tools.

Paraphrase If a reader accepts the principles of formalism, any change to a text—whether it be in form, diction, or unifying devices—makes the work no longer itself. To restate a poem or summarize a story is to lose it. Its uniqueness disappears. Any alteration of wording or structure or point of view changes the meaning of the original and cannot, therefore, be valid.

Intention What an author intended to do is not important, argue the formalists. What the author actually did is the reader's concern. To indulge concern about what he or she had planned to do is to commit the intentional fallacy. In *The*

Verbal Icon, William Wimsatt and Monroe Beardsley question whether an author's intentions can ever be known, as those intentions often lie below the conscious level. Even if the author's intentions are overtly stated, they may not have been carried out. Authors, they observe, are not necessarily reliable witnesses of such matters. One can add that neither are they necessarily good critics of their own work. Sometimes they don't even recognize how good it actually is.

Biography Studying the details of an author's life, and by extension the social and historical conditions in which a text was produced, may be interesting, but it does little to reveal how a poem creates meaning. The work is not the writer, nor is the writer the work. To confuse the two is to be led away from what happens in the work.

Affect Just as readers digress by paying attention to the writer's biography, they also go astray by paying attention to their own reactions to the work. By asking about its effect on an audience, particularly the emotional effect, the critic shifts attention to results rather than means, from the literary text to the responses of someone outside it. Such an approach will lead to no single meaning. It can impose no standards. It results, say the formalists, in pure subjectivism.

Obviously, the formalist approach is not without its weaknesses and, needless to say, those who would point them out. Chief among the complaints is that the formalists have elevated the study of technique to the exclusion of the human dimension—that they have turned reading into the solving of clever puzzles and have lost the connections literature has with people and their lives.

Other objections come from those who find formalism too restrictive. David Daiches, for example, argued against such a narrow focus on a piece of literature as a work of art. Literature is, he asserted, many things at once: a social document, a record of a writer's thoughts and experiences, a commentary on life. To narrow the range of its possibilities is to diminish it.

Finally, critics have charged that formalism works less well with some works, perhaps even certain genres, than with others. It has proved to be especially helpful with lyric poetry but less effective in understanding the essay or long, philosophical poems. (Obviously, it is easier to deal with the formal elements of short texts than with those of long ones.) That formalism has not worked particularly well for analyzing contemporary poetry suggests that, for the time being, it is more likely to be found as part of other critical approaches than in essays that are purely formalist in their techniques. Certainly formalism is alive and well in classrooms, where students still learn to read closely and analytically and to support their interpretations with examples drawn from the text under consideration.

WRITING A FORMALIST ANALYSIS

Prewriting

When you approach the actual writing of your analysis, you may find that your reading log is mostly filled with definitions of words or lists of images. It is now time to see how those words and images are woven together, even those that do not naturally fit. You may want to revisit the text, looking for patterns (recurrences that appear with such regularity that they are eventually anticipated), visual motifs, and repeated words and phrases; for significant connotations, multiple denotations, allusions, and etymological ramifications to meaning; for unity, as expressed by the meaningful coherence of all elements of the work; and for the tension produced by paradox and irony.

Another approach to prewriting is to spend some time freewriting about what you have read. You can begin with a symbol or a strong image and see where it takes you. If the text has the unity a formalist looks for, any single observation is likely to lead you to an understanding of the other aspects of the text to which it is connected.

Drafting and Revising

The Introduction A common way to begin a formalist analysis is to present a summary statement about how the various elements of the work come together to make meaning. Such an opening announces the core of the analysis that the rest of your paper will explain in more detail. Of course, if you choose this approach, you will need to write at least a draft of your discussion before working on the introduction, because you have to know what you are going to say before you can summarize it. An introduction that follows this pattern will undoubtedly clarify your topic and intentions for your readers, but it may not be the most attractive or interesting way to address them. A more colorful alternative is to begin by directly referencing the text itself. For example, if you are working with a short story, you can recount a particularly meaningful incident from it, or if you are writing about a poem, you can quote a few lines, followed by an explanatory comment of why the excerpt is important to understanding the work as a whole.

The Body The main part of your paper will be devoted to showing how the various elements of the text work together to create meaning. You will want to touch on the form, diction, and unity, citing examples of how they operate together and reinforce one another to develop a theme—a meaning that has some universal human significance. Your job is to describe what you find in the work, then to assess its effect on the whole. Where you find conflicts, or aspects of the work that do not seem to lead to the same ends, you must work to resolve the tension they create.

If a repeated image is dominant in a story, or a repeated phrase particularly insistent, you may want to give it first place in your discussion. That is, you can choose to begin with the most significant element in the work, letting it subsume the other aspects that formalists consider important. On the other hand, you may decide to treat form, diction, and unity as equally significant, giving roughly the same amount of consideration to each.

You will also want to give a good bit of attention to any instances of paradox and irony, explaining how their presence in the work creates tension and how their resolution provides satisfaction. This is a good opportunity to draw examples from the text or to quote significant passages. As in all critical essays, references to the work that illustrate your discussion will both strengthen and clarify what you are saying.

Keep in mind that it is more effective to organize your discussion around the literary elements you have examined rather than follow the sequence of events in a narrative or the stanzaic progression of a poem. For the writer who tries to move sequentially through the text as the author has constructed it, making analytical comments along the way, the temptation to forsake analysis and simply summarize the work is hard to resist.

The Conclusion The end of your paper is an appropriate place to state (or reiterate) the connection between form and content. Up to this point, you have been describing how the text operates in particular ways and explaining the meaning that emerges from those ways. Now you have the opportunity to make some generalizations about the overall relationship of form and content. You can decide whether you have explored a text that has its own laws of being and operates successfully within them, or whether it is a work in which the formal elements, not easily reconciled, are eventually harmonized to make meaning.

SUGGESTED READING

Brooks, Cleanth. *The Well Wrought Urn: Studies in the Structure of Poetry*. Rev. ed. London: Dobson, 1968.

Brooks, Cleanth, and Robert B. Heilman, eds. *Understanding Drama: Twelve Plays*. New York: Holt, 1948.

Brooks, Cleanth, John T. Purser, and Robert Penn Warren, eds. *An Approach to Literature*. 5th ed. Englewood Cliffs, NJ: Prentice Hall, 1975.

Brooks, Cleanth, and Robert Penn Warren, eds. *Understanding Fiction*. 3rd ed. Englewood Cliffs, NJ: Prentice Hall, 1979.

———. *Understanding Poetry*. 4th ed. New York: Holt, Rinehart, and Winston, 1976.

Cowan, Louise. *The Fugitive Group: A Literary History*. Baton Rouge: Louisiana State University Press, 1959.

Daiches, David. *The New Criticism*. Portree, Isle of Skye, Scotland: Aquila, 1982.

———. " The New Criticism: Some Qualifications." *College English* 39 (February 1950): 64–72.

Eliot, T. S. *The Sacred Wood: Essays on Poetry and Criticism*. London: Methuen, 1964.

Empson, William. *Seven Types of Ambiguity*. 3rd ed. New York: Noonday Press, 1961.

Krieger, Murray. *The New Apologists for Poetry*. Westport, CT: Greenwood Press, 1977.

Ransom, John Crowe. *The New Criticism*. Westport, CT: Greenwood Press, 1979.

Richards, I. A. *Practical Criticism: A Study of Literary Judgment*. New Brunswick, NH: Transaction Publishers, 2004.

Tate, Allen. *Collected Essays.* Denver: Alan Swallow, 1959.

Wimsatt, W. K., Jr. *The Verbal Icon: Studies in the Meaning of Poetry*. Lexington: University Press of Kentucky, 1954.

For up-to-date information on the many Web sites addressing formalist critical approaches, visit www.cengagebrain.com.

Model Student Analysis

Robinson's "Richard Cory": A Formalistic Interpretation

FRANK PEREZ

For readers who are inclined to extract didactic moral lessons from poetry, the central theme of Edwin Arlington Robinson's short poem "Richard Cory" may appear to be that wealth, charm, and popularity, at least for the people in the poem, do not necessarily equate to personal happiness and fulfillment. However, a close reading of the poem suggests that the real theme of the poem is that appearances can sometimes be misleading. In the poem, the townspeople admire Richard Cory and "wish that we were in his place." But this adulation is misguided, for in the last line, we learn that Richard Cory commits suicide. That this climactic bit of information comes at the end of the poem is important because it contributes to the thematic and structural potency of the poem and resolves the ironic tension that the poem also creates.

The poem consists of four heroic (or elegiac) quatrains and is written in iambic pentameter. In the first stanza, the townspeople describe Richard Cory and state that they "looked at him" when he went downtown. The description continues in the second stanza but takes on an air of admiration: "But still he fluttered pulses when he said,/'Good-morning,' and he glittered when he walked." This admiration is directly stated in the third stanza: "In fine, we thought that he was everything/To make us wish that we were in his place." The positive descriptions and the emulation of Richard Cory suddenly stop in the fourth stanza as the poem shifts instead to a description of the daily misery of the townspeople. The last two lines of the poem deal with Richard Cory's suicide. The abrupt ending of the poem (indeed, the brevity of the poem itself) serves to effectively convey the sense of shock and "unfinished business" that normally accompanies news of a suicide or sudden death.

The chief irony of the poem is that the speaker(s)—in this case, the ambiguously plural "We people on the pavement"—are quite taken with a man who is miserable to the point of suicide. This situation is paradoxical and can be explained only in terms of the tension that the last line of the poem creates. This tension is twofold. First, there is the tension between the outward description of Richard Cory as given by the townspeople and the inner description of Richard Cory as indicated by the fact that he kills himself. Second, there is a conditional tension between Richard Cory and the state of the townspeople. Not only does the startling revelation of Richard Cory's suicide in the last line create this tension, but it also simultaneously forces an interpretation of the poem that resolves the tension.

The first of the aforementioned tensions is most clearly illustrated in the poem's diction, particularly in the title and in the words used to describe Richard Cory in the first ten lines. His name may suggest "rich man" or may even be an allusion to Richard the Lionhearted (Richard Coeur de Lion). The townspeople's description of Richard Cory is filled with words laced with regal connotations: "He was a gentleman from sole to crown," "imperially slim," "he was rich—yes, richer than a king." In addition, Richard Cory is described as charming: "He was a gentleman," "he fluttered pulses when he said,/'Good morning,' and he glittered when he walked," he was "admirably schooled in every grace." Such sycophantic adoration reaches a zenith in lines 11–12: "In fine, we thought that he was everything/To make us wish that we were in his place." Yet, despite his popularity, Richard Cory is in reality a suffering figure. But this dark side of Richard Cory is lost on the townspeople, who appear to be enraptured with the outward trappings of wealth and success. This dichotomy between the outward appearance of success and the reality of inner turmoil is not fully realized until we learn of Richard Cory's death in the last line of the poem.

The fact that the townspeople do not realize this dichotomous tension between Richard Cory's outward and inner states is evidenced in the second tension of the poem—the tension between Richard Cory and the state of the townspeople. In stark contrast to the description of Richard Cory's apparent life of ease, the townspeople are depicted as miserable, hardworking sorts: "So on we worked, and waited for the light,/And went without the meat, and cursed the bread." That sentence comes immediately after the line "To make us wish that we were in his place," thereby suggesting these people were driven by material urges to emulate Richard Cory.

There is no indication in the poem that the townspeople realize the error of their positive assumptions about Richard Cory. In addition, there is no internal evidence within the poem to indicate that the people cease their material striving after Richard Cory's death; the most any close reader can say on this matter is that he or she simply does not know what the townspeople's reaction is to Richard Cory's death. To infer anything else would be to read into the poem something that is not there—a critical no-no in the interpretive analysis of poetry. Also, the poem gives absolutely no evidence whatsoever for the cause of Richard Cory's suicide. Hence, it would be a mistake to interpret the poem as a moral lesson warning against the dangers of materialism. Rather, the safest interpretation is that appearances can sometimes be misleading.

4

Psychological Criticism

Novelists who go to psychiatrists are paying for what they should be paid for.
UNKNOWN SOURCE

Human beings are fascinating creatures. Readers can be said to take a psychological approach when they try to understand them. The questions readers ask about characters are the same ones we might ask about a friend or family member. "Why would he want to do something dumb like that?" one might say. Another might shake her head and comment, "I knew that wasn't going to work. I don't see why she had to try it." People never seem to run out of speculations about others' motives, relationships, and conversations or, for that matter, their own. They also speculate about dreams, puzzling as to their source. Bizarre in their form and ambiguous in their meaning, dreams are yet powerful enough to frighten, please, and intrigue us.

HISTORICAL BACKGROUND

Aristotle knew that human beings are endlessly interesting. As far back as the fourth century BC, Aristotle commented on the effects of tragedy on an audience, saying that by evoking pity and fear, tragedy creates a catharsis of those emotions. He was the earliest of many writers and critics down through the centuries to question why we are drawn to writing stories and poems and why we like reading them. Does literature make us better individuals? Matthew Arnold believed it could. Poetry, he said, could "inspirit and rejoice the reader." Where does the impulse to write come from? William Wordsworth said poetry springs from "emotion recollected in tranquillity." What is creativity? Samuel Taylor Coleridge thought there were two types of creativity: the primary imagination, which he described as "the living power and prime agent of all human perception," and the secondary one, which was capable of re-creating the world of sense through its power to fuse and shape experience. As Coleridge explained it, "[Creativity] dissolves, diffuses, dissipates, in order to recreate." Even Friedrich Nietzsche spoke of personalities as being Apollonian, by which he meant they were guided by the use of critical reasoning, or Dionysian, referring to personalities ruled by creative-intuitive power.

All such questions and theories are psychological. They are efforts to explain the growth, development, and structure of the human personality. Until the latter part of the nineteenth century, however, such speculation lacked the broad theoretical basis that would support those early attempts at understanding ourselves. It was then that Sigmund Freud (1856–1939) advanced his startling theories about the workings of the human psyche, its formation, its organization, and its maladies. His students and followers, such as Alfred Adler, Otto Rank, and Carl Jung, later built on Freud's ideas of probing the workings of the human psyche to understand why people act as they do. Of particular interest to literary critics is Jung, who provided the concepts of the **collective unconscious**, **myths**, and **archetypes**, which have helped readers see literature as an expression of the experience of the entire human species. Later, in the 1950s, Northrop Frye developed Jung's ideas in ways that were more directly applicable to literature. More recently, Jacques Lacan has received serious attention for his efforts to build on Freud's work, turning to linguistic theories to assert that language shapes our unconscious and our conscious minds, thereby giving us our identity.

Preceding the significant contributions of Jung, Lacan, and others, however, Freud began the quest for understanding by providing new ways of looking at ourselves. The power of his theories is evident in the number and variety of fields they have affected, fields as disparate as philosophy, medicine, sociology, and literary criticism. Although they do not provide an aesthetic theory of literature, which would explain how literature is beautiful or why it is meaningful in and of itself, their value lies in giving readers a way to deepen their understanding of themes that have always been present in Western literature—themes of family, authority, and guilt, for example. In addition, they provide a framework for making more perceptive character analyses. With Freudian theory it is possible to discover what is not said directly, perhaps even what the author did not realize he was saying, and to read between (or perhaps beneath) the lines.

The absence of an aesthetic theory makes psychoanalytic criticism both more and less useful to a reader. On the one hand, because it does not contradict other schools of criticism, it can be used as a complement to them. That is, instead of ruling out other perspectives on a text, it can exist alongside them, even enrich and extend them. The French feminist critics, a case in point, have made good use of Lacan's ideas in forming their own critical approaches. On the other hand, the lack of an aesthetic theory means that psychoanalytic criticism can never account for the beauty of a poem or the artistry that has created it. The reader must turn to other types of analysis to explore those other dimensions of literature.

PRACTICING PSYCHOLOGICAL CRITICISM

To understand the discussion that follows, you should read the short story "Young Goodman Brown," by Nathaniel Hawthorne, which begins on page 307.

Today the psychological literary critic can base his inferences on the works of numerous important theorists, but it is Freud's ideas that have provided the basis for this approach, and his ideas are still fundamental to it. To work as a psychological critic, whether you are directly applying Freudian theory or working with the ideas of his followers, it is necessary to understand some of his concepts about the human psyche.

Freudian Principles

As a neurologist practicing in Vienna in the late nineteenth century, Freud was troubled that he could not account for the complaints of many of his patients by citing any physical cause. Diagnosing his patients as hysterics, he entered upon analyses of them (and himself) that led him to infer that their distress was caused by factors of which perhaps even they were unaware. He became convinced that fantasies and desires too bizarre and unacceptable to admit had been suppressed, buried so deeply in the unconscious part of their being that, although the desires did not have to be confronted directly, they led to neuroses that caused his patients' illnesses. He concluded that the unconscious plays a major role in what we do, feel, and say, although we are not aware of its presence or operations.

Freud did not come by these ideas easily or quickly. As early as 1895, he published, with Joseph Breuer, *Studies in Hysteria,* an important work asserting that symptoms of hysteria are the result of unresolved but forgotten traumas from childhood. Five years later, he wrote *The Interpretation of Dreams,* in which he addressed the fundamental concepts of psychoanalysis, a treatment in which a patient talks to an analyst about dreams, childhood, and relationships with parents and authority figures. Using free association, slips of language, and dreams, Freud found ways for an analyst to help a patient uncover the painful or threatening events that have been repressed in the unconscious and thus made inaccessible to the conscious mind. In psychoanalytic criticism, the same topics and techniques form the basis for analyzing literary texts.

Just after the turn of the century, Freud himself began to apply his theories to the interpretation of religion, mythology, art, and literature. His first piece of psychoanalytic criticism was a review of a novel by the German writer William Jensen, "Delusions and Dreams in Jensen's *Gradiva*" (1907). In it he psychoanalyzed the novel's central character, noting the Oedipal effects behind the plot. (Freud was not alone in asserting the close relationship between dreams and art. In 1923 Wilhelm Stekel published a book on dreams, saying that no essential difference exists between them and poetry. Around that same time, F. C. Prescott, in *Poetry and Dreams,* argued for a definite correspondence between the two in both form and content.) The concern with literature soon turned to the writers themselves and to artists in general, as Freud questioned why art exists and why people create it. In that search, he wrote monographs on Dostoyevsky,

Shakespeare, Leonardo da Vinci, Goethe, and others. Freud's sense of the artist, finally, was that he is an unstable personality who writes out of his own neuroses, with the result that his work provides therapeutic insights into the nature of life not only for himself but also for those who read. As Freud commented in *Introductory Lectures on Psycho-Analysis,* "The artist has also an introverted disposition and has not far to go to become a neurotic."

In 1910 the depth that Freud's approach could add to literary analysis was made apparent in a (now classic) essay on *Hamlet* by Ernest Jones, in which Jones argued that Hamlet's delay in taking revenge on Claudius is a result of the protagonist's own "disordered mind." More specifically, Jones saw Hamlet as the victim of an Oedipal complex that manifests itself in manic-depressive feelings, misogynistic attitudes, and a disgust for things sexual. According to Jones, Hamlet delays his revenge because he unconsciously wants to kill the man who married his mother, but if he punishes Claudius for doing what he himself wished to do, that would, in a sense, mean that he was killing himself. Also derived from his Oedipal neurosis, his repressed desire for Gertrude, who is overtly affectionate toward him, causes him to treat Ophelia with cruelty far out of proportion to anything she deserves. When he orders her to a nunnery, the slang meaning of *brothel* makes it clear that he sees all women, even a guiltless one, as repugnant. Throughout the play, his disgust toward sexual matters is apparent in the anger evoked in him by the marriage of Claudius and Gertrude as well as in his repulsion of Ophelia.

Since Freud's era, and since Jones's landmark essay appeared, psychoanalytic criticism has continued to grow and develop, generating, for example, the related genre of psychobiography, which applies psychoanalytic approaches to a writer's own life. Today psychoanalytic criticism shows few signs of slowing down. Nevertheless, Freud's work continues to provide the foundation of this approach. Although not all of his explanations of how the mind operates are applicable to literary criticism, the six concepts that follow have had enormous impact on the way we understand what we read. They have even affected the way writers construct their works.

The Unconscious Probably the most significant aspect of Freudian theory is the primacy of the unconscious. Hidden from the conscious mind, which Freud compared to that small portion of an iceberg that is visible above the surface of the water, the unconscious is like the powerful unseen mass below it. Because the conscious mind is not aware of its submerged counterpart, it may mistake the real causes of behavior. An individual may be unable to tell the difference between what is happening and what she thinks is happening. In short, our actions are the result of forces we do not recognize and therefore cannot control.

In Hawthorne's short story "Young Goodman Brown," for example, Brown finds himself in just such a dilemma. Even well past the events of his night in the forest, he is not sure of what was real and what was a dream. His journey is psychological, as well as physical, for he moves from the security of consciousness to the unknown territory of the unconscious, a powerful force that directs him in ways he neither expects nor understands. He leaves the village of Salem, where social as well as spiritual order prevails, to go into the forest, where the daylight, and the clarity of vision and understanding it seems to confer, gives way to darkness and frightful confusion of perceptions. In the end, Brown can no longer tell reality from dreams, good from evil.

The Tripartite Psyche In an effort to describe the conscious and unconscious mind, Freud divided the human psyche into three parts: the **id**, the **superego**, and the **ego**. They are, for the most part, unconscious. The id, for example, is completely unconscious; only small parts of the ego and the superego are conscious. Each operates according to different, even contrasting, principles.

The id, which is the repository of the **libido**, the source of our psychic energy and our psychosexual desires, gives us our vitality. Because the id is always trying to satisfy its hunger for pleasure, it operates without any thought of consequences, anxiety, ethics, logic, precaution, or morality. Demanding swift satisfaction and fulfillment of biological desires, it is lawless, asocial, amoral. As Freud described it, the id strives "to bring about the satisfaction of the instinctual needs subject to the observance of the pleasure principle."

Obviously the id can be a socially destructive force. Unrestrained, it will aggressively seek to gratify its desires without any concern for law, customs, or values. It can even be self-destructive in its drive to have what it wants. In many ways, it resembles the devil figure that appears in some theological and literary texts, because it offers strong temptation to take what we want without heeding normal restraints, taboos, or consequences. Certainly the id appears in that form in "Young Goodman Brown." It is presented in the person of Brown's fellow traveler, who appears to Brown immediately after he thinks to himself, "What if the devil himself should be at my very elbow!" The narrator suggests the embodiment of Brown's id in the figure by describing him as "bearing a considerable resemblance" to the young man. Even before the older man's appearance, from the very outset of the journey, Brown recognizes that he is challenging acceptable behavior by leaving the highly regulated life of Salem; the pull of the id to disregard the usual restrictions and to participate in acts normally forbidden in the village intensifies as he walks deeper into the forest. As Hawthorne points out, Brown becomes "himself the chief horror of the scene."

To prevent the chaos that would result if the id were to go untamed, other parts of the psyche must balance its passions. The ego, which operates according to the reality principle, is one such regulating agency. Its function is to make the id's energies nondestructive by postponing them or diverting them into socially acceptable actions, sometimes by finding an appropriate time for gratifying them. Although it is for the most part unconscious, the ego is the closest of the three parts of the psyche to what we think of as consciousness, for it mediates between our inner selves and the outer world. Nevertheless, it is not directly approachable. We come closest to knowing it when it is relaxed by hypnosis, sleep, or unintentional slips of the tongue. Dreams, then, become an important means of knowing what is hidden about ourselves from ourselves.

The third part of the psyche, the superego, provides additional balance to the id. Similar to what is commonly known as one's conscience, it operates according to the morality principle, for it provides the sense of moral and ethical wrongdoing. Parents, who enforce their values through punishments and rewards, are the chief source of the superego, which furnishes a sense of guilt for behavior that breaks the rules given by parents to the young child. Later in life, the superegois expanded by institutions and other influences. Consequently, the superego works against the drive of the id and represses socially unacceptable desires back into the unconscious. Balance between the license of the id and the restrictions of the superego produces the healthy personality. But when unconscious guilt becomes overwhelming, the individual can be said to be suffering from a guilt complex. When the superego is too strong, it can lead to unhappiness and dissatisfaction with the self.

For Goodman Brown, the descent into the unconscious (the night in the forest) presents a conflict between the superego (the highly regulated life he has known in Salem) and the id (the wild, unrestrained passions of the people in the forest). Lacking a viable ego of his own, he turns to Faith, his wife, for help. Unfortunately, she wears pink ribbons, a mixture of white (purity) and red (passion), which indicates the ambiguity of goodness and Brown's clouded belief in the possibility of goodness throughout the remainder of his life.

The Significance of Sexuality Prior to Freud, children were thought to be asexual beings, innocent of the biological drives that would beset them later. Freud, however, recognized that it is during childhood that the id is formed, shaping the behavior of the adult to come. In fact, Freud believed that infancy and childhood are periods of intense sexual experience during which it is necessary to go through three phases of development that serve specific physical needs, then provide pleasure, if we are to become healthy, functioning adults. The first phase is called the oral phase, because it is characterized by sucking—first to be fed from our mother's breast, then to enjoy our thumbs or, later, even kissing. The second is the anal stage, a period that recognizes not only the need for elimination but also the presence of another erogenous zone, a part of the body that provides sexual pleasure. In the final phase, the phallic stage, the child discovers the pleasure of genital stimulation, connected, of course, to reproduction. If these three overlapping stages are successfully negotiated, the adult personality emerges sound and intact. If, however, these childhood needs are not met, the adult is likely to suffer arrested development. The mature person may become fixated on a behavior that serves to fulfill what was not satisfied at an early age. The early years, therefore, encompass critical stages of development because repressions formed at that time may surface as problems later.

Around the time the child reaches the genital stage, about the age of five, he or she is ready to develop a sense of maleness or femaleness. To explain the process by which the child makes that step, Freud turned to literature. Referring to the plot of Sophocles's *Oedipus Rex,* Freud pointed out that the experience of Oedipus is that of all male children. That is, just as Oedipus unknowingly kills his father and marries his mother, a young boy forms an erotic attachment to his mother and unconsciously grows to desire her. He consequently resents his father because of his relationship with the mother. Fearing castration by the father, the male child represses his sexual desires, identifies with his father, and anticipates his own sexual union. Such a step is a necessary one in his growth toward manhood. The boy who fails to make that step will suffer from an Oedipal complex, with ongoing fear of castration evident in his hostility to authority in general.

In the case of girls, the passage from childhood to womanhood requires successful negotiation of the Electra complex. In Freudian theory, the girl child, too, has a strong attraction for her mother and sees her father as a rival, but because she realizes that she has already been castrated, she develops an attraction for her father, who has the penis she desires. When she fails to garner his attentions, she identifies with her mother and awaits her own male partner, who will provide what her female physiognomy lacks.

In "Young Goodman Brown," Hawthorne clearly implies that Brown's troubling impulses are sexual and that they are not his alone. The sermon of the devil figure promises Brown and Faith that they will henceforth know the secret sins of the people of Salem: "how hoary-bearded elders of the church have whispered wanton words to the young maids of their households; . . . how fair damsels—blush not, sweet ones—have dug little graves in the garden, and bidden me, the sole guest to an infant's funeral." The catalog leaves no doubt that sexual passion is part of the human condition, and left unrestrained, it leads to grave offenses. Freud explains that as both boys and girls make the transition to normal adulthood, they become aware of their place in a moral system of behavior. They move from operating according to the pleasure principle, which dictates that they want immediate gratification of all desires, to an acceptance of the reality principle, in which the ego and superego recognize rules, restraint, and responsibility. Goodman Brown, unable to discern reality or define moral behavior, remains outside the adult world. We are told, "A stern, a sad, a darkly meditative, a distrustful, if not a desperate man did he become from the night of that fearful dream." On the Sabbath, he cannot bear to listen to the singing of the psalms nor hear the words of the minister's sermon. He lives separate and apart from his society.

The Importance of Dreams The vast unconscious that exists beneath the surface of our awareness seems closest to revelation when we sleep. Our dreams, according to Freud, are the language of the unconscious, full of unfulfilled desires that the conscious mind has buried there. Their content is rarely clear, however, for even in sleep the ego censors unacceptable wishes. Through the use of symbols that make repressed material more acceptable, if not readily understandable to us, the ego veils the meaning of our dreams from direct apprehension that would produce painful recognition. As in literature, the process may take place through **condensation**. For example, two desires of the psyche might be articulated by a single word or image in a dream, just as they are in a poem. Condensation can also take place through **displacement**—moving one's feeling for a particular person to an object related to him or her, much as metonymy uses the name of one object to replace another with which it is closely related or of which it is a part. When dreams become too direct and their meanings too apparent, we awaken or, unconsciously, change the symbology. As noted, Young Goodman Brown is never certain whether he has dreamed his experience or lived it. Indeed, the ambiguity and uncertainty about the other villagers and their part in the satanic communion haunt him for the rest of his life. He returns to the village and the light of day, but what is real and what is fantasy elude him. The meanings of the symbols remain unrevealed to him.

As a window into the unconscious, dreams become valuable tools for psychoanalysts in determining unresolved conflicts in the psyche, conflicts that a person may suspect only because of physical ailments, such as headaches, or psychological discomfort, such as claustrophobia. When dreams appear in literature, they offer rich insights into characters that the characters' outer actions, or even their spoken words, might never suggest. Because dreams are meaningful symbolic presentations that take the reader beyond the external narrative, they are valuable tools for critics using a psychoanalytic approach.

Symbols Freud's recognition of the often subtle and always complex workings of sexuality in human beings and in literature led to a new awareness of what symbols mean in literature as well as in life. If dreams are a symbolic expression of repressed desires, most of them sexual in nature, then the images through which they operate are themselves sexual ones. Their sexuality is initially indicated by shape. That is, physical objects that are concave in shape, such as lakes, tunnels, and cups, are assumed to be female, or **yonic**, symbols, and those that are convex, or whose length exceeds their diameter, such as trees, towers, and spires, are assumed to be male, or **phallic**.

Although Freud objected to a general interpretation of dream symbols, insisting that they are personal and individual in nature, such readings are not uncommon. Although this approach to understanding symbols has sometimes been pushed to ridiculous extremes, it undeniably has the capacity to enrich our reading and understanding in ways that we would not otherwise discover.

The symbols in "Young Goodman Brown" are replete with sexual suggestion that is rarely made explicit in the story. Many of those that play a part in Brown's initiation, such as the devil's staff, which is described as "a great black snake … a living serpent," are male images, suggesting the nature of Brown's temptation. The satanic communion is depicted as being lighted by blazing fires, with the implication of intense emotion, especially sexual passion. The burning pine trees surrounding the altar, again masculine references, underscore that the repressions of nature exercised in the village give way to obsessions in the forest. There are female symbols, too. For example, entering the forest suggests returning to the dark, womblike unknown. What if Young Goodman Brown had not actually undergone the experience and had only dreamed it? The event is still significant, because dreams can function as symbolic forms of wish fulfillment.

Brown's nighttime journey, the nature of which is powerfully deepened by the symbolic imagery, leaves its mark on him. He is thereafter a dark and brooding man, leading Richard Adams in his essay "Hawthorne's Provincial Tales" to argue that Brown fails to mature because he fails to learn to know, control, and use his sexual feelings. That is, he cannot love or hate; he can only fear moral maturity. He never manages to emerge from his uncertainty and consequent despair. He has been required to acknowledge evil in himself and others, including his wife, so that he can recognize goodness, but having failed the test, he is left in a state of moral uncertainty. The result is moral and social isolation.

Creativity The connection between creative expression and the stuff of dreams was not lost on Freud. His curiosity about the sources and nature of creativity is reflected in the monographs he wrote on creative artists from various times and cultures, including Leonardo da Vinci, Shakespeare, and Michelangelo. Freud recognized that the artist consciously expresses fantasy, illusion, and wishes through symbols, just as dreams from the unconscious do. To write a story or a poem, then, is to reveal the unconscious, to give a neurosis socially acceptable expression. Such a view makes the writer a conflicted individual working out his or her problems. Freud explained the idea this way in *Introductory Lectures on Psycho-Analysis:*

> The artist has also an introverted disposition and has not far to go to become a neurotic. He is one who is urged on by instinctual needs which are too clamorous. He longs to attain to honor, power, riches, fame, and the love of women; but he lacks the means of achieving these gratifications. So, like any other with an unsatisfied longing, he turns away from reality and transfers all his interest, and all his libido too, to the creation of his wishes in the life of fantasy, from which the way might readily lead to neurosis.

In the process of engaging in his or her own therapy, said Freud, the artist achieves insights and understanding that can be represented to others who are less likely to have found them.

Such views have led some critics to focus their attention not on a text but on the writer behind it. They see a work as an expression of the writer's unconscious mind, an artifact that can be used to psychoanalyze the writer, producing psychobiography. (A good example of this genre is Edmund Wilson's *The Wound and the Bow.*) Of course, to do such a study, one needs access to verifiable biographical information, as well as expertise in making a psychological analysis. Most literary critics, though they may be able to find the former, usually lack the latter. Indeed, one might ask whether such an undertaking is literary criticism at all.

Summing Up In the end, when you make a Freudian (psychoanalytical) reading of a text, you will probably limit yourself to a consideration of the work itself, looking at its conflicts, characters, dream sequences, and symbols. You will use the language Freud provided to discuss what before him did not have names, and you will have an awareness that outward behavior may not be consonant with inner drives. You will avoid oversimplification of your analysis, exaggerated interpretations of symbolism, and excessive use of psychological jargon. If you do all this, you will have the means to explore not only what is apparent on the surface but what is below it as well. As Lionel Trilling pointed out in *The*

Liberal Imagination, Freud has provided us with "the perception of the hidden element of human nature and of the opposition between the hidden and the visible."

Carl Jung and Mythological Criticism

Once a favored pupil of Freud, Carl Jung (1875–1961), a Swiss physician, psychiatrist, and philosopher, eventually broke from his mentor, then built on his teacher's ideas in ways that made Jung an important figure in the new field of psychoanalysis. His insights have had significant bearing on literature as well.

Like his teacher, Jung believed that our unconscious mind powerfully directs much of our behavior. However, where Freud conceived of each individual unconscious as separate and distinct from that of others, Jung asserted that some of our unconscious is shared with all other members of the human species. He described the human psyche as having three parts: a **personal conscious**, a state of awareness of the present moment that, once it is past, becomes part of the individual's unique **personal unconscious**. Beneath both of these is the **collective unconscious**, a storehouse of knowledge, experiences, and images of the human race. It is an ancestral memory—shared and primeval—often expressed outwardly in myth and ritual. Young Goodman Brown's presence at the forest gathering, for example, can be described as participation in a ritual binding the past to the present. As Jung explained it, "This psychic life is the mind of our ancient ancestors, the way in which they thought and felt, the way in which they conceived of life and the world, of gods and human beings." Its contents, because they have never been in consciousness, are not individually acquired. They are inherited.

Literary scholars began to understand the relevance of these ideas to literature as they found correspondences in plots and characters in works by writers in disparate circumstances who could not have been known to each other. Gilbert Murray, for example, was so struck by the similarities he found between Orestes and Hamlet that he concluded they were the result of memories we carry deep within us, "the memory of the race, stamped ... upon our physical organism." That is why such criticism is sometimes called a mythological, archetypal, totemic, or ritualistic approach, with each name pointing to the universality of literary patterns and images that recur throughout diverse cultures and periods. Because these images elicit perennially powerful responses from readers the world over, they suggest a shared commonality, even a world order. As a result, archetypal criticism often requires knowledge and use of nonliterary fields, such as anthropology and folklore, to provide information and insights about cultural histories and practice.

Although the collective unconscious is not directly approachable, it can be found in archetypes, which Jung defined as "universal images that have existed since the remotest times." More specifically, he described an archetype as "a figure ... that repeats itself in the course of history wherever creative fantasy is fully manifested." It is recognizable by the appearance of nearly identical images and patterns—found in rituals, characters, or entire narratives—that predispose individuals from wholly different cultures and backgrounds to respond in a particular way, regardless of when or where they live.

Although archetypes may have originated in the unchanging situations of human beings, such as the rotating seasons or the mysteries of death, they are not intentionally created or culturally acquired. Instead, they come to us instinctually as impulses and knowledge, hidden somewhere in our biological, psychological, and social natures. As critic John Sanford explained it, archetypes "form the basis for instinctive unlearned behavior patterns common to all mankind and assert themselves in certain typical ways." In literature we recognize them and respond to them again and again in new characters or situations that have the same essential forms we have met before and have always known. For example, when we meet Huckleberry Finn or the Ancient Mariner (as Maud Bodkin pointed out in *Archetypal Patterns in Poetry*), we are connecting with archetypes, re-creations of basic patterns or types that are already in our unconscious, making us respond just as someone halfway around the world from us might.

Archetypes appear in our dreams and religious rituals, as well as in our art and literature. They are media for the telling of our myths, which, according to Jung, are the "natural and indispensable intermediate stage between unconscious and conscious cognition." By becoming conscious of what is generally unconscious, we integrate our lives and formulate answers for things that are unknowable, such as why we exist, why we suffer, and how we are to live. By uniting the conscious and unconscious, archetypes make us whole and complete.

Living fully, Jung believed, means living harmoniously with the fundamental elements of human nature. In particular, we must deal with three powerful archetypes that compose the self. They are the **shadow**, the **anima**, and the **persona**. All three are represented in literature.

The shadow is our darker side, the part of ourselves we would prefer not to confront, those aspects that we dislike. It is seen in films as the villain, in medieval mystery plays as the devil, and in powerful literary figures like Satan in *Paradise Lost*. Young Goodman Brown clearly confronts (and rejects) his shadow in the figure of his nocturnal traveling companion. The anima, according to Jung, is the "soul-image," the life force that causes one to act. It is given a feminine designation in men (like Brown's Faith), and a masculine one (animus) in women, indicating that the psyche has both male and female characteristics, though we may be made aware of them only in our dreams or when we recognize them in someone else (a process Jung referred to as *projection*). The persona is the image that we show to others. It is the mask that we put on for the external world; it may not be at all what we think ourselves to be inside. The persona and anima can be thought of as two contrasting parts of the ego, our conscious personality. The former mediates between the ego and the outside world, the latter between the ego and the inner one.

To become a psychologically healthy, well-balanced adult—or, as Jung put it, for **individuation** to occur—we must discover and accept the different sides of ourselves, even those we dislike and resist. If we reject some part of the self, we are likely to project that element onto others—that is, we transfer it to something or someone else, thereby making us incapable of seeing ourselves as wrong or guilty. Instead, we see another person or institution to be at fault. In these terms, Young Goodman Brown's despondency can be seen as the result of his failure to achieve individuation. He projects his shadow on the forest companion and later on the entire community. He fails to nurture his anima, leaving Faith behind and, in the end, suspecting her of the faithlessness he has committed. And, finally, his persona, the face that he shows to the world, is a false one. He is not the "good man," the pious Puritan, he claims to be. The healthy individual develops a persona that exists comfortably and easily with the rest of his personality. Young Goodman Brown, unable to integrate all parts of his personality, dies an unhappy neurotic, or as Hawthorne puts it, "They carved no hopeful verse upon his tombstone, for his dying hour was gloom."

There are, of course, many different archetypes, with some more commonly met than others. Some of the characters, images, and situations that frequently elicit similar psychological responses from diverse groups of people can be found in the lists that follow. Whenever you meet them, it is possible that they carry with them more power to evoke a response than their literal meanings would suggest.

Characters

- **The hero**. Heroes, according to Lord Raglan in *The Hero: A Study in Tradition, Myth, and Drama,* are distinguished by several uncommon events, including a birth that has unusual circumstances (such as a virgin mother); an early escape from attempts to murder him; or a return to his homeland, where, after a victory over some antagonist, he marries a princess, assumes the throne, and only later falls victim to a fate that may include being banished from the kingdom only to die a mysterious death and have an ambiguous burial. The archetype is exemplified by such characters as Oedipus, Jason, and Jesus Christ. Sometimes the story may involve only a journey during which the hero must answer complex riddles, retrieve a sacred or powerful artifact, or do battle with superhuman creatures to save someone else, perhaps a whole people. The quests of some of the knights in Alfred, Lord Tennyson's *Idylls of the King,* such as those made by Gawain and Galahad, are examples.
- **The scapegoat**. Sometimes the hero himself becomes the sacrificial victim who is put to death by the community in order to remove the guilt of the people and restore their welfare and health. On occasion, an animal suffices as the scapegoat, but in literature, the scapegoat is more likely to be a human being. Again, Jesus Christ is an example, but a more recent retelling of the story is found in Shirley Jackson's "The Lottery."
- **The outcast**. The outcast is a character who is thrown out of the community as punishment for a crime against it. The fate of the outcast, as can be seen in *The Rime of the Ancient Mariner,* is to wander throughout eternity. Hawthorne's Young Goodman Brown also finds himself separated from his community following his refusal to join in the forest communion. He cannot listen to the hymns of the assembled congregation on the Sabbath, kneel

with his family at prayer, or trust in the virtue of Faith, his wife. He is lonely and alone.

- **The devil**. The figure of the devil personifies the principle of evil that intrudes in the life of a character to tempt and destroy him or her, often by promising wealth, fame, or knowledge in exchange for his or her soul. Mephistopheles in the legend of Faust is such a figure, as is the old man whom Young Goodman Brown meets in the forest. The latter, with his snakelike staff, purports to have been present at ancient evil deeds. Brown even refers to him as "the devil."
- **Female figures**. Women are depicted in several well-known archetypes. The good mother, such as Ma Joad in *The Grapes of Wrath,* is associated with fertility, abundance, and nurturance of those around her. The temptress, on the other hand, destroys the men who are attracted to her sensuality and beauty. Like Delilah, who robs Samson of his strength, she causes their downfall. The female who inspires the mind and soul of men is a spiritual (or platonic) ideal. She has no physical attractions but, like Dante's Beatrice, guides, directs, and fulfills her male counterpart. Finally, women are seen as the unfaithful wife. As she appears in Flaubert's *Madame Bovary,* the unfaithful wife, married to a dull, insensitive husband, turns to a more desirable man as a lover, with unhappy consequences.
- **The trickster**. A figure often appearing in African American and American Indian narratives, the trickster is mischievous, disorderly, and amoral. He disrupts the rigidity of rule-bound cultures, bringing them reminders of their less strict beginnings. For example, in the tales of Till Eulenspiegel, which date back to the sixteenth century, Till, a shrewd rural peasant, outwits the arrogant townspeople and satirizes their social practices.

Images

- **Colors**. Colors have a variety of archetypal dimensions. Red, because of its association with blood, easily suggests passion, sacrifice, or violence. Green, on the other hand, makes one think of fertility and the fullness of life, even hope. Blue is often associated with holiness or sanctity, as in the depiction of the Virgin Mary. Light and darkness call up opposed responses: hope, inspiration, enlightenment, and rebirth in contrast with ignorance, hopelessness, and death.
- **Numbers**. Like colors, numbers are invested with different meanings. The number three points to things spiritual, as in the Holy Trinity; four is associated with the four seasons (and, by extension, with the cycle of life) and the four elements (earth, air, fire, and water). When three and four are combined to make seven, the union produces a powerful product that is perfect and whole and complete.
- **Water**. Another common image, water is often used as a creation, birth, or rebirth symbol, as in Christian baptism. Flowing water can refer to the passage of time. In contrast, the desert or lack of water suggests a spiritually barren state, as it does in T. S. Eliot's *The Waste Land.*

- **Gardens**. Images of natural abundance, such as gardens, often indicate a paradise or a state of innocence. The best-known, of course, is the Garden of Eden.
- **Circles**. Circles can be presented simply or in complex relationships with other geometric figures. By their lack of beginnings and endings, circles commonly suggest a state of wholeness and union. A wedding ring, for example, brings to mind the unending union of two people.
- **The sun**. Like the seasons, the sun makes one think of the passage of time. At its rising, it calls to mind the beginning of a phase of life or of life itself; at its setting, it points to death and other endings. At full presence, it might suggest enlightenment or radiant knowledge.

Situations

- **The quest**. Pursued by the hero, mentioned earlier, the quest usually involves a difficult search for a magical or holy item that will return fertility and abundance to a desolate state. Certainly, the boy in James Joyce's "Araby" goes to the bazaar in search of a fitting offering for the sister of his friend Mangan, whom he has sanctified with his young love. It is both a holy quest and a romantic one. A related pattern is that of the need to perform a nearly impossible task so that all will be well. Arthur, for example, must pull the sword from the stone if he is to become king. Often found as part of both these situations is the journey, suggesting a psychological, as well as physical, movement from one place, or state of being, to another. The journey, like the travels of Ulysses, may involve a descent into hell.
- **Death and rebirth**. Already mentioned in connection with the cycle of the seasons, death and rebirth are the most common of all archetypes in literature. Rebirth may take the form of natural regeneration, that is, of submission to the cycles of nature, or of escape from this troubled life to an endless paradise, such as that enjoyed before the fall into the sufferings that are part of mortality. For example, in "Kubla Khan," Coleridge presents a landscape that is both savage and holy, a landscape of heaven and hell, ending with a vision of a transcendent experience in which the speaker/holy man has "drunk the milk of Paradise."
- **Initiation**. Stories of initiation deal with the progression from one stage of life to another, usually that of an adolescent moving from childhood to maturity, from innocence to understanding. The experience is rarely without problems, although it may involve comedy. In its classic form, the protagonist goes through the initiation alone, experiencing tests and ordeals that change him so that he can return to the family or larger group as an adult member.

Northrop Frye and Mythological Criticism

In 1957, Northrop Frye advanced the study of archetypes, at least as they apply to literature, with the publication of *Anatomy of Criticism,* in which he presented a highly structured model of how myths are at the basis of all texts. Although he did not accept Jung's theories in their entirety, he used many of them as the basis of his efforts to understand the functions of archetypes in literature. He spoke of a "theory of myths," by which he really referred to a theory of genres as a way of understanding narrative structures. All texts, he concluded, are part of "a central unifying myth," exemplified in four types of literature, or four **mythoi**, that are analogous to the seasons. Together they compose the entire body of literature, which he called the **monomyth**.

The mythos of summer, for example, is the romance. It is analogous to the birth and adventures of innocent youth. It is a happy myth that indulges what we want to happen—that is, the triumph of good over evil and problems resolved in satisfying ways. Autumn, in contrast, is tragic. In the autumn myth, the hero does not triumph but instead meets death or defeat. Classic tragic figures, like Antigone or Oedipus, are stripped of power and set apart from their world to suffer alone. In the winter myth, what is normal and what is hoped for are inverted. The depicted world is hopeless, fearful, frustrated, even dead. There is no hero to bring salvation, no happy endings to innocent adventures. Spring, however, brings comedy: rebirth and renewal, hope and success, freedom and happiness. The forces that would defeat the hero are thwarted, and the world regains its order. According to Frye, every work of literature has its place in this schema.

Currently the mythic or archetypal approach is less frequently used than it was in earlier decades. Some readers complain that it overlooks the qualities of individual works by its focus on how any given text fits a general pattern. When a novel is seen as but one of many instances of death and rebirth, for example, its uniqueness is ignored and its value diminished. However, the process of relating a single work to literature in general and to human experience as a whole gives the work of literature stature and importance in the eyes of other readers. It relates literature to other areas of intellectual activity in a reasoned, significant manner. Certainly the archetypal approach is worth knowing and sometimes using, for it yields insights about both literature and human nature that other approaches fail to provide. It considers a work in terms of its psychological, aesthetic, and cultural aspects, making such an analysis a powerful union of three perspectives.

Jacques Lacan: An Update on Freud

Since the 1960s, the Freudian approach, which had waned in popularity, has experienced a renaissance due to the ideas of a French psychoanalyst named Jacques Lacan. His work has been described as a reinterpretation of Freud in light of the ideas of structuralist and poststructuralist theories (see Chapter 8). Looking at Freudian theory with the influence of the ideas of the anthropologist Claude Lévi-Strauss and linguists Ferdinand de Saussure and Roman Jakobsen, Lacan's work is far-ranging and complex, innovative, and not easily understood. Some would even call it obscure.

In the mid-1950s, Lacan startled the world of psychoanalysis by calling for a new emphasis on the unconscious but with significant differences from the Freudian approach. His ideas and practices were at such odds with those of many other psychoanalysts that he was expelled from the International Psychoanalytical Association, leading him to form a new professional organization with colleagues and followers of like mind. From that point on, Lacan set himself on a course of developing new theories independent of the established profession. He explained these theories in publications called *Écrits,* which were actually lectures for graduate-level students.

Lacan's remarks upset his colleagues not because he was interested in understanding the behavior of the conscious personality by analyzing the unconscious, as the Freudians tried to do, but because he was interested in defining the unconscious as the core of one's being. Freud's concept of the unconscious as a force that determines our actions and beliefs shook the long-held ideal that we are beings who can control our own destinies; Lacan further weakened the Western humanist concept of a stable self by denying the possibility of bringing the contents of the unconscious into consciousness. Whereas Freud wanted to make hidden drives and desires conscious so they could be managed, Lacan claimed that the ego can never replace the unconscious or possess its contents for the simple reason that the ego, the "I" self, is only an illusion produced by the unconscious. It was a monumental challenge to our sense of who we are.

Lacan's concept of adult psychology also set him apart from Freud, who believed that the healthy psyche was characterized by unity. In contrast, Lacan recognized that it is always fraught with fragmentation, absence, and lack. This stance has, of course, made Lacan's ideas particularly attractive to the poststructuralists (see Chapter 8).

Another difference from the Freudians was Lacan's notion that the unconscious, "the nucleus of our being," is orderly and structured, not chaotic and jumbled and full of repressed desires and wishes, as Freud conceived of it. In fact, Lacan asserted that the unconscious is structured like a language. He expanded such ideas by turning to Saussure, though with a few significant modifications. Saussure (see Chapter 8) pointed out that the relationship between a word and a physical object is arbitrary, not inherent, and that it is maintained by convention. We know one signifier from another not because of meanings they naturally carry but because of the differences signifiers have from one another. Unlike Saussure, who saw a **signifier** and a **signified** as two parts of a **sign**, Lacan saw in the unconscious only signifiers that refer to other signifiers. Each has meaning only because it differs from some other signifier. It does not ultimately refer to anything outside itself, and the absence of any signified robs the entire system of stability. In these terms, the unconscious is a constantly moving chain of signifiers, with nothing to stop their shifting and sliding. The elements of the unconscious are all signifiers, but they have no reference beyond themselves, making them unstable. The signified that seems to be "the real thing" is actually beyond our grasp, because, according to Lacan, all we can have is a conceptualized reality. Language becomes independent of what is external to it, and we cannot go outside it. Nevertheless, we spend our lives trying to stabilize this system so that meaning and self become possible.

As evidence for his argument that the unconscious is structured like language, Lacan pointed out that analysts routinely study language as a means of understanding the unconscious. He states in particular that two elements identified by Freud as part of dreams, condensation and displacement, are similar to metaphor and metonymy. More specifically, condensation, like metaphor, carries several meanings in one image. Likewise, displacement, like metonymy, uses an element of a person or experience to refer to the whole. In addition, the importance that Freud attributed to other linguistic devices, such as slips, allusions, and puns, to provide insight into the unconscious is, according to Lacan, further evidence of the linguistic basis of the unconscious. Thus, the unconscious, the very essence of the self, is a linguistic effect that exists before the individual enters into it, leaving it open to analysis. If the linguistic system is extant before one enters into it, however, there can be no individual, unique self, a concept that is profoundly disturbing to many.

To the reader coming to Lacan's theories for the first time, they may seem to be more philosophical than literary. They have a bearing on literary analysis, however, in several important ways.

Character Analysis First of all, Lacan's rejection of the unique self changes our way of examining characters. Rejecting the traditional view of the human self as a whole, integrated being and accepting Lacan's view of it as a collection of signifiers that point to no signified, leaving one fragmented, means changing the way we think and talk about characters. If the psychologically complete personality is not possible, how is the reader to view the figures found in narratives?

Lacan's description of how the psyche evolves is helpful in developing new ways of reading to accommodate his views of the self. As he explained it, our movement toward adulthood occurs as several parts of our personality develop in search of a unified and psychologically complete self, which, though it can never be achieved, can be approached by stabilizing the sliding of signifiers. Consequently, we move through three stages, or orders as Lacan calls them—the real, the imaginary, and the symbolic, corresponding to the experience of need, demand, and desire. It should be noted that this evolution is not entirely sequential, as the orders sometimes overlap each other. Underlying the process, so the assumption goes, is language as the shaper of our unconscious, our conscious minds, and our sense of self.

It should be noted that disagreement exists among scholars about the nature and significance of Lacan's orders, due partly to the complexities of the concepts that underlie them and also because he revised his thinking from time to time. (He is also accused by some of being a bad writer.) Consequently, the explanations provided here may not entirely concur with explanations provided in other texts.

The new infant exists in a state of nature, a psychological place characterized by wholeness and fullness. It does not recognize itself as an individual that is complete and distinguishable from other people or objects. It knows only that it has needs (food, for example) and does not distinguish itself from the mother or any object that satisfies them. It exists in the **Real Order**, a psychological state characterized by unity and completeness.

Somewhere between six and eighteen months of age, the baby sees its own reflection and begins to perceive a state of separation between itself and the surrounding world, an experience known as the **mirror stage**, which is part of the **Imaginary Order**. In a preverbal state, the baby becomes aware of its body only in bits and pieces—whatever is visible at any given moment—but does not yet conceive of itself as whole, although it can recognize other people as such. The mirror stage introduces a sense of possible wholeness, because the image looks like other objects with discrete boundaries. However, to have boundaries means recognizing that the child is separate from the mother, not one with her. It is an awareness that is accompanied by a sense of loss. The sense of unity with others and with other objects has been lost and, along with it, the sense of security that it provided.

The infant thinks the reflection is real and uses what it sees to create the ego, the sense of "I." It is only an illusion, however, and she is, in actuality, not whole and complete. Thus the "self" is always manufactured by the mistaken acceptance of an external image for an internal identity. Lacan refers to it as the "**other**" because it is not the actual self, only an image outside of the self. He spelled it with a small "o" to distinguish it from the "**Other**," or those remaining elements that exist outside the self, objects and people that the infant comes to know before becoming aware of its own "other." It is known as an "ideal ego," because it is whole and nonfragmented and has no lack or absence. In other words, the individual makes up for the union that has been lost by misconceiving the self as whole and sufficient; but such an assumption is illusory and, hence, referred to as the Imaginary.

When the awareness of being separate comes, as it must if the individual is to move from nature to culture, the baby desires to return to that earlier period of oneness with the mother. Its needs at this point turn into demands, specifically demands for attention and love from another that will erase the separation that the baby knows, but such a reunion is not possible. One can never return.

When the infant realizes it is not connected to that which serves its needs, when it recognizes the Other and its own other, it begins to enter the **Symbolic Order**. (During that process it overlaps to some degree with the Imaginary.) The symbolic introduces language that takes the place of what is now lacking. It names what is missing and substitutes a sign for it, stopping the play and movement of signifiers so that they can have some stable meaning. Because a person must enter language to become a speaker and thereby name the self as "I," it masters the individual and shapes one's identity as a separate being. In the Symbolic Order everything is separate; thus, to negotiate it successfully, a person must master the concept of difference, difference that makes language possible (that is, we know a word such as *light* because it is not the word *fight*) and difference that makes genders recognizable.

The Symbolic also initiates socialization by setting up rules of behavior and putting limits on desire. Whereas the Imaginary Order is centered in the mother, the Symbolic Order is ruled by what Lacan calls the Law of the Father, because it is the father who enforces cultural norms and laws. According to Lacan, there are biological sexual differences, but gender is culturally created. This means that because the power of the word and being male are associated, the boy child must identify with the father as rule giver, and the girl must acknowledge that, as such, the father is her superior. Both male and female experience a symbolic castration, or a loss of wholeness that comes with the acceptance of society's rules.

Actually, Lacan refers to the ultimate center of power by several names. He calls it the **phallus**, referring not to a biological organ but to a privileged signifier, the symbol of power that gives meaning to other objects. Neither males nor females can possess the phallus totally, though males have a stronger claim to it. Instead, human beings go through life longing for a return to the state of wholeness when we were one with our mother, manifested in our desire for pleasure and things. But wholeness will always elude us.

He also calls it the Other, all that world beyond the self. To be the Other would be to bridge the separation that exists between the self and the center of language, the center of the Symbolic. Because such an act is not possible, the human being experiences an ongoing "lack," which Lacan calls "desire," an unsatisfiable yearning to merge with the Other and rule all.

Not surprisingly, Lacan has met with some criticism about his description of the Symbolic Order, with its emphasis on the superiority of the father that the girl must acknowledge. Positive outcomes of the challenge that his ideas present have been found in the adaptations and extensions of his theories by such feminist critics as Julia Kristeva Kristeva and Hélène Cixous. On the other hand, there are those who share Francois Roustag's opinion that Lacan's work is an "incoherent system of pseudo-scientific gibberish."

Obviously Lacan's ideas are interesting to the literary critic because they provide more ways of understanding and analyzing characters. A reader can look for symbolic representations of the Real Order, the Imaginary, and the Symbolic to demonstrate how the text depicts the human being as a fragmented, incomplete being. In "Young Goodman Brown," for example, evidence of the three orders points to lack and absence that make wholeness impossible. The protagonist longs for the wholeness provided by the Real, but it eludes him. He does not know and can never know the true "self," and he resists the acceptance of society's rules, the power of the group. Clearly suffering from a loss that he can never recover, he exemplifies the fragmented being who is unable to achieve the completeness he desires.

Antirealism In addition to changing the way characters are analyzed, Lacan's theories of language, in particular his assertion that language is detached from physical reality, also affect literary analysis. For example, his theories make it difficult to read a narrative as being realistic. The traditional assumption that a fictive world exists as a real one is no longer valid if language is not connected to referents outside of it. Instead, the reader must accept that a narrative is likely to be broken and interrupted. It may, like other signifiers, refer to other narratives. Lacan's early association with surrealist writers and painters is evident in the tendency of his followers to favor bizarre and nonlinear narratives.

Jouissance Lacan's ideas are also germane to the work of the critic, because he acknowledged that literature offers access to the Imaginary Order and a chance to reexperience the joy of being whole, as we once were with our mother. The word Lacan used, ***jouissance***, means "enjoyment," but it also carries a sexual reference ("orgasm") that the English word lacks. As Lacan used it, it is essentially phallic, although he admitted that there is a feminine *jouissance*.

WRITING PSYCHOLOGICAL CRITICISM

Prewriting

Once you are accustomed to taking a Freudian, mythological, or Lacanian approach, you will begin to notice meaningful symbols and will pay close attention to dream sequences as a matter of course. If you are not used to reading from these perspectives, however, you may want to be intentional about noting aspects of a work during prewriting that could be significant.

If you are interested in using Freudian theory, you can begin by making notes about a selected character, then writing a descriptive paragraph about him or her. The following questions can help to get you started:

- What do you see as the character's main traits?
- By what acts, dialogue, and attitudes are those traits revealed?
- What does the narrator reveal about the character?
- In the course of the narrative, does the character change? If so, how and why?
- Where do you find evidence of the id, superego, and ego at work?
- Does the character come to understand something not understood at the outset?
- How does the character view him- or herself?
- How is he or she viewed by other characters?
- Do the two views agree?
- What images are associated with the character?
- What principal symbols enrich your understanding of the characters?
- Which symbols are connected with forces that affect the characters?
- Does the character have any interior monologues or dreams? If so, what do you learn from them about the character that is not revealed by outward behavior or conversation?
- Are there conflicts between what is observable and what is going on inside the character? Are there any revealing symbols in them?
- Are there suggestions that the character's childhood experiences have led to problems in maturity, such as uncompleted sexual stages or unresolved dilemmas?
- Where do the characters act in ways that are inconsistent with the way they are described by the narrator or perceived by other characters?

- Who is telling the story, and why does the narrator feel constrained to tell it? How can you explain a character's irrational behavior? What causes do you find? What motivation?

An archetypal approach can start with these questions:

- What similarities do you find among the characters, situations, and settings of the text under consideration and those in other works that you have read?
- What commonly encountered archetypes do you recognize?
- Is the narrative like any classic myths you know?
- Where do you find evidence of the protagonist's persona? Anima/animus? Shadow?
- Does the protagonist at any point reject some part of his or her personality and project it onto someone or something else?
- Would you describe the protagonist as individuated, as having a realistic and accurate sense of self?

You can begin a Lacanian approach by considering the following questions:

- Where do you recognize the appearance of the Real, Imaginary, and/or Symbolic Orders?
- How do they demonstrate the fragmented nature of the self?
- Are there instances where the Imaginary interrupts the Symbolic Order?
- Is the character aware of the lack or absence of something significant in the self?
- Are there objects that symbolize what is missing or lacking?
- Do you find examples of the mirror stage of the developing psyche?
- Is the text an antirealist one that subverts traditional storytelling?

Drafting and Revising

The Introduction When you write an analysis of a work of literature from any of these three forms of psychological criticism—Freudian, mythological, or Lacanian—your reader will find it helpful if you announce at the outset what your primary focus will be. Because such studies can look at a single character, the relationships among characters, meaningful symbolism, narrative patterns, or even the life of the author, an indication of the direction your paper will take makes it easier for others to follow the development of your discussion.

Another approach is to comment on similarities and differences between the work with which you are dealing and other works by the same author. If you have determined that the elements of the poem or story you are analyzing are typical of a given writer—for example, that the conflicts faced by a particular character are similar to those that have been developed in some of the author's other works—noting those correspondences in the introduction can help convince the reader that what you say is valid. However, if the work under analysis is atypical of what one anticipates from a given writer, then revealing at the beginning that this work is a departure from the expected can garner attention as well.

If you have discovered parallels between the text you are writing about and others that you have read, you may want to mention the similarities you have discovered. If the situations or relationships among the characters have reminded you of those found in classic myths, fairy tales, Greek drama, or even more modern works, mentioning those correspondences will turn your discussion toward a mythic perspective.

The Body Because of the number and diversity of topics you have to choose from when doing psychoanalytic (and related) criticism, there is no formula for the organization of the body of the paper. There are only suggestions that may help you structure the way you report your ideas.

As always, you cannot expect your audience to accept your analysis simply as stated. You will have to prove your case by using tenets of psychological or critical theory to explain, for example, that a certain character cannot keep a job because he is resistant to authority because he has unresolved issues with his father, or that another is projecting an undesirable part of her personality when she blames a good friend for provoking a quarrel that she herself began. You do not have to refer to all the principles explained in this chapter, but you should incorporate all the points that help support your position.

If you have chosen to take a character as the principal topic of a Freudian analysis, you may have already discovered what you want to reveal about him or her when you prewrote. If not, it may be necessary to return to those notes to expand and deepen them so that you eventually arrive at an understanding of some struggle the character is living through, an epiphany he or she experiences, or the motivation behind some particular behavior. You will address that understanding in the body of your discussion. You may find the following strategies helpful:

- Reveal what is happening in the character's unconscious as suggested by images, symbols, or interior monologues.
- Identify the nature of the character's conflicts; look for indications of whether he or she has the attitudes of a healthy adult male or female. If not, then the neurosis needs to be identified and its source examined.
- Because any changes in the outlook or behavior of a character signal that some struggle has been resolved, for good or ill, assess their meaning.
- Examine whether a character operates according to the pleasure principle, the morality principle, or the reality principle.
- Explain a character's typical behavior by determining whether the personality is "balanced" or dominated by the id or the superego.
- Look carefully at any dreams that are recounted or alluded to. What repressed material are these dreams putting into symbolic form? What are they really about?

- Probe the meanings of symbols by thinking about them in terms of their maleness and femaleness.
- Find some particular behavior that a character is fixated on, then trace it to some need or issue from childhood that went unsatisfied or unresolved.
- Note any conflicts or events in the author's life that are reflected in the text.

Using a mythological approach, you can explore one or several of the following topics:

- Show how characters follow (or vary from) well-established patterns of behavior or re-create well-known figures from literary history—for example, from Greek mythology.
- Look at similarities and contrasts in the personal conscious and personal unconscious of a character to determine whether they reflect the same desires and impulses or are in conflict.
- Locate any instances in which the collective unconscious of a character is revealed, perhaps through a dream or vision.
- Identify archetypal images and situations, and explain how they work together to create meaning.
- Examine instances in which the persona, anima/animus, and shadow of a character are revealed, including instances of rejection and projection.

To use Lacan's ideas as the basis of your discussion, you can apply the following analytical strategies:

- Identify the Real, Imaginary, and Symbolic Orders in the narrative, and explain the position of a character in relation to each.
- Note instances where a character's fragmentation or lack is evident.
- Locate those occasions on which a character recognizes that he or she is a fragmented being yearning for wholeness, and explain the causes of those occasions.
- Explain how certain objects symbolize that which is lacking in a character's life.
- Note those occasions on which the unconscious controls and shapes a character.
- Pay attention to characters' needs, demands, and desires, noting how they indicate the characters movement towards adulthood.
- Examine familial interactions of a character's childhood and adolescence in an effort to understand adult behaviors.
- Point out antirealistic elements of a narrative, noting what those elements suggest about the inaccessibility of a whole, integrated self.
- Identify any mirror-stage experiences and explain how they demonstrate Lacan's ideas about the developing psyche.

The Conclusion The psychological analysis is one occasion in which a reader may welcome a summary conclusion. Because the discussion is likely to have covered some unusual ground and used some unusual terminology (in terms of literary criticism), a brief reiteration of the major points followed by a general conclusion may be in order. Take care not simply to say everything again but to assume a more global view, looking at the analysis as a whole. If you discussed multiple points, for example, you will probably need to rename them and tie them all together, showing how they extend and reinforce one another. If you focused on only one topic, such as character or imagery, then a simple reiteration of the themes that grew out of what you found should suffice.

SUGGESTED READING

Benvenuto, Bice, and Roger Kennedy. *The Works of Jacques Lacan: An Introduction.* New York: St. Martin's Press, 1986.

Bergler, Edmund. *The Writer and Psychoanalysis.* Madison, CT: International Universities Press, 1991.

Bodkin, Maud. *Archetypal Patterns in Poetry.* New York: AMS Press, 1978.

Campbell, Joseph. *The Hero with a Thousand Faces.* Princeton, NJ: Princeton University Press, 2004.

Felman, Shoshana. *Jacques Lacan and the Adventure of Insight: Psychoanalysis in Contemporary Culture.* Cambridge, MA: Harvard University Press, 1987.

Fiedler, Leslie. *Love and Death in the American Novel.* Normal, IL: Dalkey Archive Press, 1997.

Frazer, Sir James. *The Golden Bough.* New York: Oxford University Press, 1998.

Freud, Sigmund. *Introductory Lectures on Psycho-Analysis.* Trans. Joan Riviere. London: Heron Books, 1970.

———. *The Interpretation of Dreams.* Trans. A. A. Brill. Mineola, NY: Dover, 2006.

Frye, Northrop. *Anatomy of Criticism: Four Essays.* Toronto: University of Toronto Press, 2006.

Hoffman, Frederick J. *Freudianism and the Literary Mind.* Westport, CT: Greenwood Press, 1977.

Holland, Norman. *The Dynamics of Literary Response.* New York: Columbia University Press, 1989.

Jung, Carl. *The Integration of the Personality.* Trans. Stanley Dell. New York: Farrar and Rinehart, 1939.

———. " Psychology and Literature." In *Modern Man in Search of a Soul*, trans. W. S. Dell and Cary F. Baynes, pp. 175–199. New York: Harcourt, 1955.

———. *The Archetypes and the Collective Unconscious.* Trans. R. F. C. Hull. Princeton, NJ: Princeton University Press, 1980.

Lesser, Simon O. *Fiction and the Unconscious.* Boston: Beacon Press, 1957.

Murray, Gilbert. *The Classical Tradition in Poetry.* New York: Russell and Russell, 1968.

Phillips, William, ed. *Art and Psychoanalysis.* New York: World Publishing, 1963.

Trilling, Lionel. *Freud and the Crisis of Our Culture*. Boston: Beacon Press, 1955.

Wheelwright, Philip. *Metaphor and Reality*. Bloomington: Indiana University Press, 1962.

Winnicott, D. W. *Playing and Reality*. New York: Tavistock, 1980.

Wright, Elizabeth. *Psychoanalytic Criticism: Theory in Practice*. New York: Methuen, 1984.

CENGAGENOW

Web sites devoted to some of the topics covered in this chapter should be used with particular caution. Although some can be helpful, many sites that are connected to philosophical, psychological, and religious slants, both traditional and nontraditional, are not. Some take extreme positions of belief. In particular, the Web surfer looking for information on Carl Jung, archetypes, and myths must be aware that a search can lead to so many different topics that the initial quest can get lost. For these reasons, it is recommended, as before, that you begin by consulting www.cengagebrain.com for creditable online information.

Model Student Analyses

A Mythological Analysis

"'Thou Hast They Music Too': Loss as Art in John Keats's 'To Autumn'"

MEAGAN CASS

In mainstream contemporary American culture, we are often told to grapple with death, heartbreak, and loss as though they were contagious diseases. Phrases like "dealing with grief," "finding closure," "the four stages of grief," and "the grieving process" sanitize the experience of death and encourage us to classify, abandon, or silence our suffering as quickly as possible, moving on to enjoy more pleasurable experiences and emotions. Within this context, John Keats's "To Autumn" represents a rich, contrasting vision. The poem invites readers to ruminate on the fleeting nature of happiness and to appreciate the evocative beauty of loss. Through archetypal images of sensuality and pain, abundance and loss, Keats insists that not only do death and loss powerfully connect to the other seasons of human experience, they also contain (and engender) their own, worthy art.

Keats begins his portrait with the hinge between summer and fall, a time just before the harvest and long associated with the sensual, pleasurable aspects of life. The season's "mists" suggest a calm blurring of landscape, and its "mellow fruitfulness" connotes ease and fecundity (fruit here symbolizes both the literal abundance of the harvest and fertility). Summer, that "maturing sun," is imagined as Autumn's old lover, a masculine presence who "conspires" with *her* to "load and bless" the landscape. The images throughout the stanza further connote sexual pleasure and impregnation, lending to the opening stanza the feel of a sensual love poem. Autumn and summer "fill all fruit with ripeness to the core," "swell the gourd," and "plump the hazel shells/with a sweet kernel." This round fruit might also symbolize the archetypal nurturer woman, with "ripeness" connoting the transition from girlhood to womanhood. The closing image of plenty—"set budding more,/still more flowers for the bees"—alludes to copulation as well as to honey, the food of the holy land.

Keats further emphasizes this relished abundance through the sound of his language: *-ing* verbs (*conspiring, budding*) slow the rhythm of the lines, and the repetition of "more/and still more" accentuates the preharvest plenty. Words like "bless," "bend," "fill," "swell," "plump," and "sweet" let the reader taste and feel the weight of abundance. It's also interesting to note that these images of plenty are intertwined with images of domestic life. The fruit-heavy vines wind "round the thatch-eves," and the apples come from the "cottage-trees." This is not some uninhabited, uncharted wilderness, but rather a kind of home-grown Eden, symbolic of biblical paradise and innocence. Happiness and safety, Keats seems to say here, are within the bounds of ordinary human life.

Yet the garden is also vulnerable to death, to time passing. The penultimate line of the stanza, "until they think warm days will never cease," hints at the death and scarcity to come. While the bees have been tricked into believing their good fortune to be immutable, the speaker knows that there is much more to autumn, and to human experience, than this sensual brush with summer. The stanza's closing line, "For summer has o'er-brimmed their clammy cells," further warns of a loss of prosperity and joy, as "clammy" connotes sickness. Also, the term "clammy cells" suggests the cold interiors of coffins.

The second stanza represents a sharp shift in tone, as Keats's thus far loving portrait of autumn deepens (as the season progresses) to include symbols of isolation, death, and despair. Here the poem veers more clearly toward what Northrop Frye has identified as the "autumn myth" found in literary works dealing with tragedy, loss, and isolation. While this is the time of the harvest, when the hazel shells of the earlier stanza are broken for their sweet kernels, when the plenty is reaped and enjoyed, Keats emphasizes the "granary floor" and "the half-reaped furrow," drawing our attention to the barrenness the harvest leaves behind, and thus to approaching death. (We think of the brow *furrowed* with age, and later in the stanza, of that other kind of reaper).

In contrast to the first stanza's intuitive calm, this is a world of disorder. Separated from her "close bosom-friend," and from her (re)productive, pleasurable work, autumn haunts our "stores," or what we deem to be valuable and necessary in life. "Sitting careless," her hair lifted by a "winnowing wind," she is both diminished (as we are by time) and more menacing. While she is "Sound asleep," drugged on poppy seeds, she carries a hook and "spares the next swath and all its twined flowers"—the words echo the tightly knit world of the first stanza, and human connection itself (twine is a thing human beings make). The flowers themselves refer to summer, and the many buds of that time of plenty. The implication is that those of us who are safe from Autumn as reaper remain so accidentally and only temporarily. Moreover, there is no rationale behind who dies and who remains: death will eventually wake and find each of us with its "hook."

As the stanza closes, Autumn emerges more fully as the grim reaper archetype. Her hook symbolizes the grim reaper's scythe, and Keats also describes her as a "gleaner," a person who picks up what few bits of crops that have been left behind by the reapers, harvesting the last of the alive-things from the world, ensuring that nothing escapes death. She has no clear, benevolent purpose as she watches the brook, a symbol of time passing, of life running its course. If those "last oozings" of the cider press symbolize our fading vitality as we near death—the apples are being drained of all of their juices; the word "ooze" connotes blood and slow decay—then autumn's "patient look" implies sure knowledge of death's inevitability. Life will, at last, run out, and Autumn need only be patient. The rhythm of the stanza's last line adds to this sense of futility and inertia, as the comma after "oozings" emphasizes both that word and the phrase "hours by hours." Instead of ending in any conventional sense, the stanza unravels, leaving us in despair, leaving the speaker to ask, at the start of the next stanza, "Where are the songs of Spring?" For Northrop Frye, the spring mythoi connotes rebirth, renewal, and order—an order firmly disassembled in stanza two.

Yet the lament does not continue. Addressing Autumn again, this time like an admirer in a courtly love poem, he assures her, "thou hast thy music too." The remainder of this surprising stanza powerfully imagines that music without declawing death or making loss cheerful. First consider the image "barred clouds bloom the soft-dying day." There is beauty, in that the clouds "bloom" (connoting spring flowers), and the day's dying is "soft" (a reference to the first stanza's "mellow" softness). Yet "barred" reminds of the finality of death, a season from which we do not escape. Likewise, the image of the clouds touching "stubble plains with rosy hue" situates beauty firmly alongside the ugliness and decay of death. While "rosy" suggests the flowers of spring and summer, "stubble" brings to mind both the gleaner's meager harvest and the face of a man who has gone a few days without shaving, a man who has perhaps begun to neglect himself.

The next lines develop and extend this concept of a music of death and loss through the imagery of insect life cycles and bird migration (both of which are archetypal images of death, the departing and dying creatures leaving the landscape abandoned). Again, while songs are painful, they are still *artful.* The small gnats at the mercy of "the light wind," who like us have no control over when or how they will die, "mourn" in a "wailful choir." The word "choir" echoes "bless," in the first stanza, in evoking a religious ceremony. For Keats there is as much "high art," as much of the sacred in "wailful" suffering as there is in blessed happiness. Moreover, the least esteemed among us are capable of this powerful grief. (How different the line would read if Keats had chosen to anthropomorphize butterflies or some graceful migratory bird.)

We next get the songs of the humble hedge-crickets, whose "treble soft" implies that they are singing their winter song, a plaintive sound that echoes the lamb's "loud bleat" in the preceding line. Finally, the poem closes with much more casual, yet evocative music: the redbreast "whistling" and the migrating swallows "twitter." These images of mundane art—in the case of the latter, of shallow laughter—bring us back to the ordinary world of human sorrows, within the walls of the garden where we began. While the swallow's twitter is perhaps not significant enough to justify a "wailful choir," it is nonetheless meaningful in Keats's taxonomy of autumn music. There is a "full grown" dignity in death as well as in more trivial forms of suffering and loss contained within the pleasurable garden in which the poem began.

In one sense, then, "To Autumn" is a journey through time and through the human life cycle. Yet it is also a kind of glancing love poem, an honest, if ambivalent ode to death as muse. In attempting to paint a full, loving portrait of a woman who is both "mellow fruitfulness" and angel of death, Keats asks the reader to appreciate the full complexity and resonance of experience, to love the "last oozings" as well as the "ripeness," the "moss'd cottage-trees" as well as the "hilly bourn," to listen for the "wailful choir" as well as for the songs of spring. If we strive to hear everything from the percussive "full-grown lambs loud bleat" to the softer "twitter" of the "gathering swallows," we'll find, if not solace, a way to see death more clearly, to make something beautiful of our suffering, and thus to love and appreciate our own lives more completely.

A Psychological Analysis

"Power and Desire in Ernest Gaines's 'The Sky Is Gray'"

EMILY BROUSSARD

Ernest Gaines's short story "The Sky Is Gray," as a nonclimactic narrative about a boy and his mother's sojourn into the town of Bayonne, leaves much for the reader to sort out. We have next to no information about the pair, so little in fact that their names are barely used throughout. They go to the dentist, they eat at a café, and they meet a few kind strangers. It may seem that not much occurs, only a few trivial events in an ordinary day. There is no discernible climax to the story, no beatific revelation to speak of. In this text, action is replaced by multilayered tensions between the boy, his mother, and society. By using a psychoanalytic (Freudian) reading to explore these relationships in "The Sky Is Gray," the reader discovers that the boy is a troubled and guilty young man controlled by his superego and his castrating mother, that an Oedipal relationship exists between the two, and that the boy unconsciously desires to be free of her.

Because the story is told in the first person by the boy, all the information the reader receives comes straight from him. As such, it is heavily colored by his devotion to his mother and shows the overbearing presence of his superego. He keeps quiet about his sore tooth so as not to burden his mother financially, and he feels terribly guilty about the money she spends on him. When he is finally found out and they go to town, he never complains despite the bitter cold and his hunger, all because he doesn't want to upset his mother. In the café, his mother buys him three cakes, and he is "so hungry right now, the Lord knows I can eat a hundred times three, but I want my mother to have one" (p. 298). Where most children are unaware of their parents' personal and financial hardships, the boy is vigilant in his efforts to put his mother above even his most basic needs. He constantly reminds himself to obey his mother and not anger her, suppressing even his urge to hug her, because he's "not supposed to do that. She says that's weakness and that's crybaby stuff, and she don't want no crybaby around her" (p. 282).

In this story, everything begins and ends at the mother, and though there are several factors contributing to the boy's silence, they all spring from her. His mother has absolutely no patience for any childlike behavior, and she expects him to be "the man" (p. 282) in his father's absence. Because of this role, the boy's Oedipal feelings toward his mother emerge. He desires to "stand close beside her" (p. 291), and he dreams of buying her a red coat. That he wants to replace her drab black coat with one in the color of desire exposes his feelings to be more than filial. These Oedipal impulses drive him to please her at all costs. Another reason the boy does not question his mother is divulged in the boy's recounting of a memory in which his reticence to obey his mother's demand that he kill two small birds for food earned him repeated blows from her. Though he was only eight, she brutally punished him. He knows the consequences of disobeying his mother too well. Finally, because he has kept his sore tooth a secret to spare his mother worry, he cannot speak without pain. The cold air now causes his tooth to ache and he must keep his mouth firmly shut. In all these ways, the mother castrates the boy's power.

The mother in "The Sky Is Gray" can only be known through her actions on the day of the story and through the narration of her son. Since she rarely speaks herself, her motivations are somewhat difficult to decipher. Her actions paint her to be an extremely aggressive figure. She is often depicted by the boy as carrying a phallic symbol: a fork she uses to kill birds, an ax, and a knife she brandishes at a man in the café. It is as if he is trying to attribute the phallic power to his mother, in the absence of his own power and that of his father. The image of her forcing him to kill redbirds with the fork suggests that by giving him a tool she is trying to give phallic power to her young son. His mother's desire is for him to be powerful and strong, to fill the role his father left empty. The mother's use of these symbolic instruments in an attempt to create power is ironic, because, in reality, she is powerless. She is a destitute, black, single mother in rural Louisiana, and thus castrated as effectively as she castrates her son. In her relationship with her son, however, she is not relegated to the second-class status attributed to her by society, and she may exert all the power she is not able to use anywhere else over him.

Let us return to the red coat. Red may certainly be recognized as a signifier of desire, thus suggesting the boy's Oedipal feelings toward his mother. However, several other meanings may also be construed from the boy's choice of color. Red is the color of power and violence. The desire to buy his mother a red coat is another way the boy attempts to restore his mother's authority and dominance. Another way this coat may be interpreted refers to his mother's place in Southern, pre–Civil Rights era society. Black women were not encouraged to wear bright, flamboyant colors such as red or purple. They were expected to fade into the background, further negating their power and influence. The boy uses the red coat to free his mother from societal invisibility.

The reader never finds out if the boy got his tooth pulled, if they walked home or rode the bus, or if the boy finally rebelled against his tough, unforgiving mother. A scene in the dentist's office, however, gives a clue to the future the boy imagines for himself. A young man is reading in the waiting room, and he remarks, "That's the trouble with the black people in this country today.... We don't question is exactly our problem. We should question and question and question-question everything" (p. 289). This assertion begins a theological argument between the young man and a preacher that ends with him striking the young man twice across the face. The boy admires the bold young man and wishes "to be just like him" (p. 292) when he grows up. The young man could not be more different in behavior from the little boy. He does not cower in fear before the huffing preacher, as the boy does before his mother. Instead, he "looks at that preacher jus's hard's the preacher looks at him" (p. 289). After the preacher hits him twice, the second at the young man's goading, the young man says, "This hasn't changed a thing" (p. 291). While the boy lives in fear of beatings and scorn, the young man in the waiting room seems to welcome abuse, and refuses to let anyone sway him from the ideals that he holds dear. Freudian psychoanalysis relies heavily upon themes of the unconscious, and in this identification between the reserved boy and the audacious, freethinking young man, the reader can see the boy's unconscious desire to get out from under his mother's stifling influence. The young man, proudly affirming his virility in a society that represses and ignores him, represents the phallic power missing from the boy and his mother.

The young boy and the reader of "The Sky Is Gray" experience bewilderment and frustration together. Because the story is told by such a young narrator, the underlying issues at play in his family are not explained in any obvious, comprehensible way. A Freudian reading of this text facilitates understanding of these issues, and through it the reader can understand that the mother lashes out at her son because she feels helpless and alienated by the social order of the rural, Southern Louisiana of her day. The young boy is also rendered impotent by society, and he is further castrated by his mother's anger. Finally, though the wartime absence of the boy's father forces an unnatural, Oedipal bond between himself and his mother, the boy's admiration for the bold young man reveals his unconscious desire to shake his mother's hold. Freudian psychoanalysis lays bare the troubles at the heart of this family, and thus lights the way for the reader.

5

Marxist Criticism

The Marxist analysis has got nothing to do with what happened in Stalin's Russia: it's like blaming Jesus Christ for the Inquisition in Spain.
TONY BENN, *British Labor politician*

A comment that has made the rounds of many English departments over the past few years is that since the fall of the Berlin Wall and the subsequent opening of Russia to the West, Marxism has died a quiet death—except in English departments, where it is still alive and well. Even if it weren't for Cuba and some other places in the world, where Marxist theory is securely in place, this idea would be inaccurate; but it does point to the lasting viability of Marxist literary criticism, which continues to appeal to many readers and critics. It is interesting to note, however, that the principles of Marxism were not designed to serve as a theory about how to interpret texts. Instead, they were meant to be a set of social, economic, and political ideas that would, according to their followers, change the world. They are the basis of a system of thought that sees inequitable economic relationships as the source of class conflict. That conflict is the mechanism by which Western society developed from feudalism to capitalism, which, according to Marxism, will eventually give way to socialism, the system that will characterize world economic relationships. Since its inception, Marxist theory has provided a revolutionary way of understanding history.

HISTORICAL BACKGROUND

Marxism has a long and complicated history. Although it is often thought of as a twentieth-century phenomenon, partly because it was the basis of the Soviet

Union's social-governmental system, it actually reaches back to the thinking of Karl Heinrich Marx (1818–1883), a nineteenth-century German philosopher and economist. The first announcement of his nontraditional way of seeing things appeared in *The German Ideology* in 1845. In it Marx argued that the means of production controls a society's institutions and beliefs, contended that history is progressing toward the eventual triumph of communism, and introduced the concept of **dialectical materialism**, the theory that history develops as a struggle between contradictions that are eventually synthesized.

When Marx met the political economist Friedrich Engels (1820–1895) in Paris in 1844 and they discovered that they had arrived at similar views independent of one another, they decided to collaborate to explain the principles of communism (which they later called Marxism) and to organize an international movement. These ideas were expounded in the *Communist Manifesto* (1848), in which they identified class struggle as the driving force behind history and anticipated that it would lead to a revolution in which workers would overturn capitalists, take control of economic production, and abolish private property by turning it over to the government to be distributed fairly. With these events, class distinctions would disappear. In the three-volume work *Das Kapital* (1867), Marx argued that history is determined by economic conditions, and he urged an end to private ownership of public utilities, transportation, and the means of production. Despite the variations and additions that occurred in the century that followed, on the whole, Marx's writings still provide the theory of economics, sociology, history, and politics called Marxism.

Although Marxism was not designed as a method of literary analysis, its principles were applied to literature early on. Even in Russia, where literature was sometimes accepted as a means of productive critical dialogue and at other times viewed as a threat if it did not promote party **ideology**, literature was linked to the philosophical principles set down by Marx and Engels. Although the place of literature was uncertain and shifting—culminating finally in the Soviet Writers' Union, founded (and headed) by Joseph Stalin to make certain that literature promoted socialism, Soviet actions, and its heroes—it was apparent that Marxism provided a new way of reading and understanding literature.

The first major Marxist critic, however, appeared outside of Russia. Georg Lukács (1885–1971), a Hungarian critic, was responsible for what has become known as **reflectionism**. Named for the assumption that a text will reflect the society that has produced it, the theory is based on the kind of close reading advocated by formalists. But it is practiced by the **reflectionists** for the purpose of discovering how characters and their relationships typify and reveal class conflict, the socioeconomic system, or the politics of a time and place. Such examination, goes the assumption, will, in the end, lead to an understanding of that system and the author's worldview, or ***weltanschauung***. Also known as **vulgar Marxism**, reflection theory should not be equated with the traditional historical approach to literary analysis, which provides background and context for a work. Instead, vulgar Marxism seeks to determine the nature of a given society, to find "a truer, more concrete insight into reality," and to look for "the full process of life." In the end, the reflectionists attribute the fragmentation and alienation that they discover to the ills of capitalism.

Another important figure in the evolution of Marxism is the Algerian-born French philosopher Louis Althusser (1918–1990), whose views were not entirely consonant with those of Lukács. Whereas Lukács saw literature as a reflection of a society's consciousness, Althusser asserted that the process can go the other way. In short, literature and art can affect society, even lead it to revolution. Building on Antonio Gramsci's idea that the dominant class controls the views of the people by many means, one of which is the arts, Althusser agreed that the working class is manipulated to accept the ideology of the dominant class, a process he called **interpellation**. One way in which that manipulation takes place is by reinforcing capitalistic ideology through its arts. Althusser went on to point out, however, that the arts of the privileged are not all the arts that exist. The possibility remains that the working class will develop its own culture, which can lead to revolution and the establishment of a new **hegemony**, or power base. Althusser's ideas are referred to as **production theory**.

Marxism established itself as part of the American literary scene with the economic depression of the 1930s. Writers and critics alike began to use Marxist interpretations and evaluations of society in their work. As new journals dedicated to pursuing this new social and literary analysis sprang up, it became increasingly important to ask how a given text contributed to the solution of social problems by the application of Marxist principles. Eventually the movement grew strong enough to bring pressures to bear on writers to conform to the vision, resulting in a backlash of objection to such absolutism from such critics as Edmund Wilson in "Marxism and Literature" in 1938.

Currently two of the best-known Marxist critics are Fredric Jameson and Terry Eagleton. Jameson is known for using Freudian ideas in his practice of Marxist criticism. Whereas Freud discussed the notion of the repressed unconscious of the individual, Jameson talks about the political unconscious, the exploitation and oppression buried in a work. The critic, according to Jameson, seeks to uncover those buried forces and bring them to light. Eagleton, a British critic, is difficult to pin down, as he continues to develop his thinking. Of special interest to critics is his examination of the interrelations between ideology and literary form. The constant in his criticism is that he sets himself against the dominance of the privileged class. Both Jameson and Eagleton have responded to the influence of poststructuralism; in the case of the latter, this resulted in a radical shift in his thinking in the late 1970s. (For definitions and a discussion of poststructuralism, see Chapter 8.)

In some ways, Jameson and Eagleton are typical of the mixture of schools in literary criticism today. For instance, it is not uncommon to find psychoanalytic ideas in the writing of a feminist critic or postcolonial (see Chapter 10) notions influencing a Marxist. As groups that share an active concern for finding new ways of understanding what we read and the lives we live, their interaction is not surprising. The borrowing back and forth may make it difficult to define discrete schools of criticism, but in practice, it makes the possibilities for literary analysis all the richer.

READING FROM A MARXIST PERSPECTIVE

To understand the discussion that follows, you will need to read the short story "The Diamond Necklace," by Guy de Maupassant, which begins on page 332.

Many of the principles of Marxism, and the approach to literary criticism that it spawned, have already been mentioned in the brief historical survey you just read. Now it will be helpful to examine them in more detail and to see how they can be applied to literary texts.

Economic Power

According to Marx, the moving force behind human history is its economic systems, for people's lives are determined by their economic circumstances. A society, he says, is shaped by its "forces of production," the methods it uses to produce the material elements of life. The economic conditions underlying the society are called **material circumstances**, and the ideological atmosphere they generate is known as the **historical situation**. This means that to explain any social or political context, any event or product, it is first necessary to understand the material and historical circumstances in which they occur.

In Guy de Maupassant's short story "The Diamond Necklace," we are given a clear picture of a society that has unequally distributed its goods or even the means to achieve them. Madame Loisel has no commodity or skills to sell, only her youth and beauty to be used to attract a husband. Without access to those circles where she can find a man with wealth and charm, she is doomed to stay in a powerless situation with no way to approach the elegant lifestyle she desires. The material circumstances of her society have relegated her to a dreary existence from which she can find no exit. Her husband is so conditioned to accept the situation that he does not understand her hunger to be part of a more glamorous and elegant world. He is content with potpie for his supper because he has been socially constructed to want nothing more.

If a society is shaped by its "forces of production," the way in which society provides food, clothing, shelter, and other such necessities creates among groups of people social relations that become the culture's foundation. In short, the means of production structure the society. Capitalism, for example, has a two-part structure consisting of the **bourgeoisie**, who own property and thereby control the means of production, and the **proletariat**, the workers controlled by the bourgeoisie and whose labor produces their wealth. (Although in American society today, we have come to use the term *bourgeoisie* to mean "middle class," it originally designated the owners and the self-employed as opposed to wage earners.) Because those who control production have a power base, they have many ways to ensure that they will maintain their position. They can manipulate politics, government, education, the arts and entertainment, news media—all aspects of the culture—to that end.

The division of the bourgeoisie and proletariat in the society depicted in "The Diamond Necklace" is firmly established and maintained. Mme. Loisel's husband is a "petty clerk," and although she has a wealthy friend from her convent days, she has none of the accoutrements that would fit her to attend a reception to which her husband has (with some manipulation) managed to be invited. The haves are separated from the have-nots in this story by what they own and what they lack and by their ample or limited opportunity to acquire wealth and power. The division grows more apparent and unbridgeable as the couple works at increasingly demeaning jobs to acquire the money to pay off their loans. Because of the debts owed to the bourgeoisie, incurred because of the loss of the necklace owned by Mme. Loisel's well-to-do friend, they sink lower and lower in the social scale, losing what little hold they once had on social position or physical comfort. In the end, Mme. Loisel has become old and unkempt, unrecognizable to her friend. And in the most unjust irony of all, she learns after ten years that her efforts have been in vain. The bourgeoisie has tricked her once again by lending her a necklace not of diamonds but of cut glass.

Marx saw history as progressive and inevitable. Private ownership, he said, began with slavery, then evolved into feudalism, which was largely replaced by capitalism by the late eighteenth century. Evident in small ways as early as the sixteenth century, capitalism became a fully developed system with the growing power of the bourgeoisie in the mid-nineteenth century. At every stage, it had negative consequences, because it was a flawed system that involved maintaining the power of a few by the repression of many. The result was ongoing class struggle, such as the one depicted in the "The Diamond Necklace" between the bourgeoisie and the proletariat. The Marxist, then, works to reveal the internal contradictions of capitalism so that the proletariat will recognize their subjugation and rise up to seize what is rightfully theirs. As Marx stated in a famous passage from *The Communist Manifesto*, "Let the ruling classes tremble at a Communistic revolution. The proletarians have nothing to lose but their chains. They have a world to win. Working men of all countries, unite!" Although Mme. Loisel makes no move to create a revolution, she is keenly aware of the source of her sufferings. As she tells her affluent friend, "I have had some hard days since I saw you; and some miserable ones—and all because of you." The fall of the bourgeoisie and the victory of the proletariat Marx deemed to be "equally inevitable," and the new system born of such a revolution would be a classless society in which everyone has equal access to its goods and services, such as food, education, and medical care.

Some of the damage caused by the economics of capitalism, according to Marxists, is psychological. In its need to sell more goods, capitalism preys on the insecurities of consumers, who are urged to compete with others in the number and quality of their possessions: a newer car, a bigger diamond engagement ring, a second house. The result is **commodification**, an attitude of valuing things not for their utility **(use value)** but for their power to impress others **(sign value)** or for their resale possibilities **(exchange value)**. Both Mme. Loisel and her wealthy friend are victims of their society's emphasis on sign value. The former is so dazzled by the glitter of jewels and gowns and fashionable people that she can find little happiness in the humble attentions of her husband-clerk, and her friend's interest in the necklace apparently extends no further than the fact that it is impressive evidence of her wealth, for she substitutes glass for the real thing. When the acquisition of things that possess sign value and/or exchange value becomes extreme, an individual can be said to be practicing **conspicuous consumption.**

Because the economic system shapes the society, the methods of production are known as the **base**. The social, political, and ideological systems and the institutions that they generate—the values, art, legal processes—are known as the **superstructure**.

Because the dominant class controls the superstructure, it is, by extension, able to control the members of the working classes. Marxists are not in complete agreement as to whether the superstructure simply reflects the base or whether it can also affect the base. The group known as reflectionists (who subscribe to the vulgar Marxism mentioned earlier) see the superstructure as being formed by the base, making literature (and other such products) a mirror of society's consciousness. In a capitalist society, for example, the superstructure would exhibit the alienation and fragmentation that, according to the Marxists, the economic system produces. Controlled by the bourgeoisie, texts may, at least superficially, glamorize the status quo in order to maintain a stable division of power and means. Readers may not be aware of manipulation, especially when it appears in the form of entertainment, but it is no less effective for its subtle presentation.

Other Marxists, who assume that the superstructure is capable of shaping the base, recognize that literature (as well as art, entertainment, and such) can be a means for the working class to change the system. By promoting their own culture, they can create a new superstructure and eventually a different base. Even Marx and Engels admitted that some aspects of the superstructure, such as philosophy and art, are "relatively autonomous," making it possible to use them to alter ideologies.

The economic base in "The Diamond Necklace" is significant to all that is depicted in the story. Mme. Loisel's husband is a clerk whose employers have power over his professional life and over their social relationships with him. He and his employers lead very different kinds of lives. The bourgeoisie give elegant parties, while the clerk and his wife eat potpie. The "petty clerk" is not expected to fraternize with his betters except by the rare invitation (so eagerly sought after by him) that comes his way. And on such occasions, it is with difficulty that Mme. Loisel can achieve the appropriate appearance—dress, jewels, wrap. As they take on less attractive jobs to pay back what is owed, they are even less acceptable in the corridors of wealth and power. In the end, as noted, Mme. Loisel's friend does not even recognize her.

To examine the economic forces in a narrative, you can begin by asking questions such as these:

- Who are the powerful people in the society depicted in the text?
- Who are the powerless people?
- Are the two groups depicted with equal attention?
- Which group are you encouraged to admire?

- Which do you have sympathy for?
- Why do the powerful people have their power?
- Why is this power denied to others?
- From what is the power in the narrative derived? For example, is it inherited? Based on money? A result of violence?

Materialism versus Spirituality

Marx maintained that reality is material, not spiritual. Our culture, he said, is not based on some divine essence or the Platonic forms or on contemplation of timeless abstractions. It is not our philosophical or religious beliefs that make us who we are, for we are not spiritual beings but socially constructed ones. We are not products of divine design but creations of our own cultural and social circumstances.

To understand ourselves, we must look to the concrete, observable world we live in day by day. The material world will show us reality. It will show us, for example, that people live in social groups, making all of our actions interrelated. By examining the relationships among socioeconomic classes and by analyzing the superstructure, we can achieve insight into ourselves and our society. For example, the critic who looks at instances of class conflict or at the institutions, entertainment, news media, legal, and other systems of a society discovers how the distribution of economic power undergirds the society. Such analyses uncover the base (the economic system) and the social classes it has produced. Because the base and the superstructure are under the control of the dominant class, the people's worldview is likely to be false; the critic's obligation is to expose the oppression and consequent alienation that have been covered over. The Marxist is rarely content simply to expose the failings of capitalism and often goes on to argue for the fair redistribution of goods by the government.

It is the material world that has created Mme. Loisel, for example, and it is the material world that destroys her. Her desire for expensive objects and the circles in which they are found, generated by the capitalistic system she lives in rather than by any character flaw, leads her to make a foolish request of a friend. When she loses the "diamond" necklace, she too is lost. Her relationship with her friend, as well as any hope for a return to the glittering world of the reception, is shattered. She is destroyed not by spiritual failure but by an economic system that has created a superstructure that will not allow her to have a better life. She is trapped by material circumstances, and the final revelation about the false jewels will only deepen her sense of alienation and powerlessness, according to a Marxist perspective.

Such insights come from asking questions such as the following:

- What does the setting tell you about the distribution of power and wealth?
- Is there evidence of conspicuous consumption?
- Does the society that is depicted value things for their usefulness, for their potential for resale or trade, or for their power to convey social status?

- Do you find in the text itself evidence that the work is a product of the culture in which it originated?
- Where do you see characters making decisions based not on abstract principles, but on the economic system in which they live?

Class Conflict

One of the basic assumptions of Marxism is that the "forces of production," the way goods and services are produced, will, in a capitalist society, inevitably generate conflict between social classes created by the way economic resources are used and who profits from them. More specifically, the struggle will take place between the bourgeoisie, who control the means of production by owning the natural and human resources, and the proletariat, who supply the labor that allows the owners to make a profit. The conflict is sometimes realized as a clash of management and labor, sometimes simply as friction between socioeconomic classes. They are two parts of a whole that struggle against each other, not just physically but also ideologically. Marx referred to this confrontation as dialectical materialism. Actually the term includes more than class conflict, for it refers to the view that all change is the product of the struggle between opposites generated by contradictions inherent in all events, ideas, and movements. A thesis collides with its antitheses, finally reaching synthesis, which generates its own antithesis, and so on, thereby producing change.

The Marxist is aware that the working class does not always recognize the system in which it has been caught. The dominant class, using its power to make the prevailing system seem to be the logical, natural one, entraps the proletariat into holding the sense of identity and worth that the bourgeoisie wants them to hold, one that will allow the powerful to remain in control. Monsieur Loisel, for instance, is content with his lot. He aspires to be nothing more than he is and has difficulty understanding his wife's dreams. As for Mme. Loisel, she longs for things that "most other women in her situation would not have noticed." She believes herself born for luxuries—that is, born as a misplaced member of the middle class. They both experience the consequent debilitation and alienation described by Marx. Before the loss of the necklace, M. Loisel is given little credit for what he does. As a "petty clerk," he has little personal connection to his labor and is given no credit for what he produces. After the loss of the necklace, the situation is intensified, for the couple are finally shut out of all social contact with bourgeois society. In the end, Mme. Loisel moves to carry out what Marx calls upon the proletariat to do. She realizes that her life has been controlled by others. Freed of the debt she has owed her wealthy friend, she determines to free herself of the social enslavement to her friend by speaking openly and honestly at last. In doing so, she becomes painfully aware of the unsuspected depth of the control the latter has had over her. The necklace is false. She has been stripped of her dreams and forced to suffer for nothing. Finally, by speaking clearly, she engages in revolution by refusing to want any longer what the bourgeoisie values.

You can find evidence of class conflict and its repercussions by asking some of the following questions about the text you are analyzing:

- How many different social classes do the characters represent?
- Where do they struggle with each other?
- Do you find repression and manipulation of workers by owners?
- Is there evidence of alienation and fragmentation?
- Does the bourgeoisie in the text, either consciously or unconsciously, routinely repress and manipulate less powerful groups? If so, what are the tools they use? News media? Religion? Literature? Art?
- Do the working-class characters realize their lack of power?
- Does the work of literature advocate reform or revolution, either overtly or obliquely?

Art, Literature, and Ideologies

Ideology is a term that turns up frequently in Marxist discussions. It refers to a belief system produced, according to Marxists, by the relations between the different classes in a society, classes that have come about because of the society's modes of production. An ideology can be positive, leading to a better world for the people, or it can be negative, serving the interests of a repressive system. The latter rarely presents itself as an ideology, however. Instead, it appears to be a reasonable, natural worldview, because it is in the self-interest of those in power to convince people that it is so. Even a flawed system must appear to be a success. An ideology dictated by the dominant class functions to secure its power. When such cultural conditioning leads the people to accept a system that is unfavorable for them without protest or questioning—that is, to accept it as the logical way for things to be—they have developed a **false consciousness**. Marxism works to rid society of such deceptions by exposing the ideological failings that have been concealed. It takes responsibility for making people aware of how they have unconsciously accepted the subservient, powerless roles in their society that have been prescribed for them by others.

Marx himself was a well-educated, widely read German intellectual who could discourse on the poetry, fiction, and drama of more than a single culture. He enjoyed the theater and frequently made references to literature of all kinds. He was aware, however, that art and literature are an attractive and effective means of convincing the proletariat that their oppression is just and right. Literature is a particularly powerful tool for maintaining the social status quo because it operates under the guise of being entertainment, making it possible to influence an audience even when its members are unaware of being swayed. Because it does not seem to be didactic, it can lead people to accept an unfavorable socioeconomic system and to affirm their place in that system as the proper one. By doing so, it serves the economic interests of those who are in power. Marx points out that controlling what is produced is not difficult, because those who create art must flatter (or not offend) their clients who pay for it—the bourgeoisie.

Although Marxist views about literature coexist comfortably with the principles of some other schools of criticism, they stand in direct opposition to the concerns of the formalists. Marxist critics see a literary work not as an aesthetic object to be experienced for its own intrinsic worth but as a product of the socioeconomic aspects of a particular culture. In general, Marxists accept that critics must do more than explain how a work conforms to certain literary conventions or examine its aesthetic qualities. Marxist critics must be concerned with identifying the ideology of a work and pointing out its worth or its deficiencies. The good Marxist critic is careful to avoid the kind of approach that concerns itself with form and craft at the expense of examining social realities. Instead, the Marxist critic will search out the depiction of inequities in social classes, an imbalance of goods and power among people, or manipulation of the worker by the bourgeoisie and will then point out the injustice of that society. If a text presents a society in which class conflict has been resolved, all people share equally in power and wealth, and the proletariat has risen to its rightful place, then the critic can point to a text in which social justice has taken place, citing it as a model of social action.

In the former instance, the Marxist critic operates a warning system that alerts readers to social wrongs; in the latter, he is a mentor to the proletariat, pointing out how they can free themselves from the powerless position in which they have been placed. The intent of both approaches is highly political, aimed as they are at replacing existing systems with socialist ones. The function of literature is to make the populace aware of social ills and sympathetic to action that will wipe those ills away.

The ideology that a text inevitably carries can be found in either its content or its form. That is, a text has both subject matter and a manner of presentation that can either promote or criticize the historical circumstance in which it is set. To many Marxists, it is content that is the more significant of the two; the "what" is more revealing than the "how."

The "what" is important because it overtly expresses an ideology, a particular view of the social relations of its time and place. It may support the prevailing ideology of the culture, or it can actively seek to show the ideology's shortcomings and failings. It can strengthen a reader's values or reveal flaws through characters and events and editorial comment.

If the subject matter is presented sympathetically, then it depicts the social relationships—laws, customs, and values—that are approved by that society in a way that legitimizes them and, by extension, the underlying economic system that has produced them. If, on the other hand, it criticizes the prevailing ideology, it can be equally powerful and persuasive. By depicting the negative aspects of a socioeconomic system—injustice, oppression, and alienation—literature can awaken those who are unfavorably treated by that system. It can make them aware that they are not free, that they (members of the working class) are controlled by the oppressive bourgeoisie (a self-appointed elite). It can be a means of changing the superstructure and the base because it can arouse people to resist their treatment and overthrow unfair systems. At the very least, it can make social inequities and imbalances of power public knowledge.

What is the ideology expressed by the content of "The Diamond Necklace"? It is doubtful that de Maupassant wrote the story to foment revolution among his countrymen. Yet, in it the destructive power of the bourgeoisie's cool lack of concern for the proletariat is unmistakably depicted. The minor clerk and his wife are almost beneath notice to those who employ them, and the lower the couple falls in their ability to live well, or comfortably, or to survive at all, the less visible or recognizable they become. The denial of beautiful clothes and jewels to Mme. Loisel (while they are available to others no more deserving than she) and the suffering that such inequities cause her carry with them a clear social commentary. Such a society is uncaring and unjust. It exists on assumptions that allow the powerful to keep their comfortable positions only if the powerless remain oppressed and convinced that it is right that they are oppressed.

The manner of presentation (the "how") can also be instrumental in revealing the ideology of a text, especially when it brings the reader close to the people and events being depicted. For that reason, realistic presentations that clearly depict the time and place in which they are set are preferable to many a Marxist reader because they make it easier to identify with an ideology or to object to it. However, others find in modern and postmodern forms evidence of the fragmentation of contemporary society and the alienation of the individual in it. Although the narrative that is presented in an unrealistic manner—that is, through stream of consciousness or surrealism—may make a less overt identification with the socioeconomic ills of capitalism or with socialist principles, it can nevertheless criticize contradictions and inequities found in the world that capitalism has created. The effect of forms on the development of social commentary in a text can be understood by imagining how "The Diamond Necklace" would be changed if, instead of being a realistic depiction given by an omniscient narrator, the story were presented as an internal monologue taking place in the mind of Mme. Loisel or that of her husband or even that of her convent friend. In that presentation, the ideology would shift with each one's perception of what the social system is and should be, as well as what each has to lose or gain by changing it.

Believing that all products of a culture, including literature, are the results of socioeconomic and ideological conditions, the Marxist critic must have not only an understanding of the subject matter and the form of a work but also some grasp of the historical context in which it was written. The critic must also be aware of the worldview of the author, who wrote not as an individual but as one who reflects the views of a group of people. Such grounding helps the reader identify the ideology that inevitably exists in a text, so that he or she can then analyze how that ideology supports or subverts the power structure it addresses.

Asking some of the following questions will lead you to a deeper understanding of the work you are analyzing. Your answers should lead you to insights about the ideology expressed in the text and perhaps about your own.

- What ideology is revealed by your examination of economic power, materialism, and class conflict in a given work?

- Does the work support the values of capitalism or any other "ism" that institutionalizes the domination of one group of people over another—for example, racism, sexism, or imperialism? Or does it condemn such systems?
- Is the work consistent in its ideology? Or does it have inner conflicts?
- Do you find concepts from other schools of literary criticism—for example, cultural studies, feminism, postmodernism—overlapping with this one?
- Does this text make you aware of your own acceptance of any social, economic, or political practices that involve control or oppression of others?
- Does the work accept socialism as historically inevitable as well as desirable?
- Does it criticize repressive systems? Or does it approve of a system that exists by promoting one group of people at the expense of another—for example, a particular ethnic or minority group?
- Where do you see similar situations in your own world?

WRITING A MARXIST ANALYSIS

There is no prescribed form for writing a Marxist analysis. Doing so is simply a matter of applying Marxist principles in a clearly ordered manner. As a result, one such written critique may look quite different from another but be equally Marxist in its content.

Prewriting

If you have thoughtfully answered the questions listed in the previous section, you will have material to begin your prewriting. If you take those items that yielded the most information or generated your strongest opinions and use them as the basis of a free-write, your thinking will begin to develop along some identifiable lines. It may be that you need only see where the responses you made to some of the questions are evident in the text. Those passages should provide you with examples of your generalizations.

Some questions that will require you to go outside the text for answers, but that can be rewarding to pursue, are those that deal with the historical circumstances of the writer and the text. You may want to take time to do some library work to examine the following topics:

- What are the values of the author's time and place? Where are they reflected in the text?
- What biographical elements of the author's life can account for his or her ideology? For example, to what social class did the author's family belong? Where is that evident in the text?
- What are the socioeconomic conditions of the writer's culture? Where are they reflected in the text?

- Who read the work when it was first published? How was it initially received? Was it widely read? Banned? Favorably or unfavorably reviewed?
- What were the circumstances of its publication? Was it quickly accepted, widely distributed, highly promoted? Or was it published with difficulty? Was it given limited distribution?

Regardless of which topics you ultimately decide to develop, the four most important goals of your prewriting are (1) to clarify your understanding of the ideology of the work; (2) to identify the elements of the text that present the ideology; (3) to determine how those elements promote it—that is, convince the reader to accept it; and (4) to assess how sympathetic or opposed it is to Marxist principles. It is important to remember that a text does not have to be Marxist in its orientation to yield itself to an interesting reading from this perspective. Even one that is capitalist or sexist in its outlook can be fruitfully examined to determine how it attracts the reader into accepting its ideology.

It is also reassuring to recognize that Marxist critics do not always agree with each other's reading of a given text. If your interpretation differs from that of others, it is not necessarily wrong, because no single Marxist reading of a work results even when the same principles are applied. In the same manner, Marxism lends itself to combination with other schools of criticism, giving it even more possibilities for variation.

Drafting and Revising

The Introduction In a Marxist analysis, it can be effective to announce the ideology of the text and its relationship to Marxist views at the outset. Because the rest of your essay will be concerned with where and how the ideology is worked out, it is important that your reader share your understanding of the stance taken by the text. If you find this approach to be too dry, boring, and didactic, you might begin with a summary of an incident in the work that illustrates the social relationships of the characters or some other socioeconomic aspect of the society as preparation for your statement of the work's overall worldview.

The Body The central part of your essay will demonstrate the acceptance or rejection of Marxist principles in the text you are analyzing. It is in this part that the organizational principles will be of your own design. That is, you may choose to discuss each major character, assess the nature of the social institutions depicted, or point out the struggles between groups of people. The approach you take will in large part be dictated by the work itself. For example, an analysis of "The Diamond Necklace" could be built around the decline of the power and place of M. and Mme. Loisel as they are forced to repay the cost of the necklace, or it could illustrate the unjust treatment they receive from those in the powerful, controlling classes of society. It could even compare and contrast the differences between the lives of the Loisels and those of the rich and powerful. Of course, these are overlapping issues, and it is difficult to focus on one without noting the other. Once you have addressed any such topic, you will quickly find yourself with comments to make about others that are related to it.

Because there is no particular form to follow in writing a Marxist analysis, you may fall back on some of the techniques discussed in Chapter 2, "Familiar Approaches." It might be helpful to think about the usefulness of explication, comparison and contrast, and analysis. In any case, during revision you will want to be sure that each of your points is equally developed and that all are linked together in a logical sequence. Making an outline (*after* drafting) to check whether you have managed to provide adequate coverage and coherence is helpful because it can give you an overview of what you have done. If the parts are not balanced in length, depth, or content, you will need to make adjustments.

The Conclusion The conclusion of a Marxist analysis often takes either the form of an endorsement of classless societies in which everyone has equal access to power and goods or of criticism of repressive societies when that is not the case. The conclusion may once again make a case for social reform, pointing out where the literary work under consideration has either supported or rejected social change. In either case, to write the conclusion you will need to consider how the ideology in the text affirms or conflicts with your own.

That assessment may lead to a second possibility for your conclusion. That is, you may find it interesting to reflect on what the work has revealed to you about your own ideology. Perhaps you discovered that you have uncritically accepted the principles of socioeconomic-political movements that are controlling and oppressive. Perhaps your analysis has made you aware that principles you took as "given" or "natural" or "just the way things are" are actually socially constructed and can be changed in ways that make society more just and balanced. If so, explaining your realization can provide a powerful ending to your analysis.

SUGGESTED READING

Ahearn, Edward J. *Marx and Modern Fiction*. New Haven, CT: Yale University Press, 1989.

Arvon, Henri. *Marxist Aesthetics*. Trans. H. Lane. Ithaca, NY: Cornell University Press, 1973.

Baxandall, Lee, and Stefan Morawski, eds. *Marx and Engels on Literature and Art*. New York: Telos Press, 1973.

Eagleton, Terry. *Criticism and Ideology: A Study in Marxist Literary Theory*. London: Humanities Press, 1976.

———. *Marxism and Literary Criticism*. New York: Routledge, 2002.

Frow, John. *Marxism and Literary History*. Cambridge, MA: Harvard University Press, 1986.

Haslett, Mayra. *Marxist Literary and Cultural Theories*. New York: Palgrave, 2000.

Hicks, Granville. *The Great Tradition*. New York: Biblo and Tannen, 1967.

Jameson, Fredric. *Marxism and Form: Twentieth-Century Dialectical Theories of Literature.* Princeton, NJ: University Press, 1972.

———. *The Political Unconscious: Narrative as a Socially Symbolic Act.* Ithaca, NY: Cornell University Press, 1981.

Laing, Dave. *The Marxist Theory of Art: An Introductory Survey.* Boulder, CO: Westview Press, 1986.

Mulhern, Francis, ed. *Contemporary Marxist Literary Criticism.* New York: Longman, 1992.

Robinson, Lillian. *Sex, Class, and Culture.* Bloomington: Indiana University Press, 1986.

Slaughter, Cliff. *Marxism, Ideology, and Literature.* Atlantic Highlands, NJ: Humanities Press, 1980.

Williams, Raymond. *Marxism and Literature.* Oxford: Oxford University Press, 1977.

For up-to-date information on the many Web sites addressing Marxist critical approaches, visit www.cengagebrain.com.

Model Student Analysis

Silence, Violence, and Southern Agrarian Class Conflict in William Faulkner's "Barn Burning"

LIBERTY KOHN

William Faulkner's short story "Barn Burning" demonstrates the political and economic power disparities between the bourgeoisie, represented by the justice system and aristocratic landowners, and the proletariat, represented by the Snopes family. Taking place within living memory of the Civil War, the story is a critique of the southern sharecropping system and captures the immorality, greed, and lack of caring by the South's affluent classes. Yet the story also suggests that "barn-burning" nihilism is not the answer to class conflict. As young Sarty's flight suggests at story's end, for a true Marxist revolution, false consciousness, violence, and self-interest must be erased from people's actions.

The story opens as Abner Snopes is on trial for burning a barn. When his young son and main character, Colonel Sartoris Snopes, is called as a witness, Sarty's struggle begins. Although he identifies with his father and has inherited his father's ideas of the relationship between the bourgeoisie and proletariat, the story focuses on Sarty's burgeoning awareness that his father's barn burning is not a legitimate or helpful response to class inequality. Although Sarty ultimately warns Major de Spain of his father's attempted barn burning at story's end, signifying a break with his father's values, he supports and identifies with his father in the story's opening courtroom scene.

Abner Snopes typifies the powerlessness of the proletariat. In the opening trial scene, he does not speak until after the judgment is pronounced, underscoring his lack of voice in the political system as a whole. (He is equally silent after a lone statement in a second trial for barn burning.) He is ordered to leave the county. After their travel and relocation to Major de Spain's plantation, Abner states that he wishes to have a word with the man who will own him "body and soul for the next eight months." After leaving Major de Spain's house, Abner remarks that it was built with "nigger sweat" and that Major de Spain intends to add some "white sweat" as well. This comment demonstrates that race does not matter in Marxist class division. Those who own land and control the means of production hire workers to toil for small wages or life's necessities while the landowners themselves reap great benefit.

Although Abner's silence and control seem respectable, they demonstrate that he has been fully interpellated to accept the class system that offers him no opportunity. Instead of speaking representatively of himself in court, he chooses silence. He burns barns instead of calling for a redistribution of the means of production, landownership, and other material inequalities. Although Abner recognizes the injustices of sharecropping, he cannot imagine an alternative system. This acceptance of the way things are represents Abner's false consciousness. He can imagine only violence as a solution to class conflict. His violence becomes nihilism, destruction without reconstruction. However, as the family's nomadic life proves, nihilism provides only revenge, not economic opportunity.

Faulkner's language choice during the pivotal scene where Abner steps in horse droppings and walks across Major de Spain's rug demonstrates the inevitable social construction of individuals' beliefs. As Abner walks toward the house, Sarty notes that his father could have avoided the droppings with a "simple change in stride." Once inside, Abner's foot comes down on the floor "with clocklike finality." When Mrs. de Spain addresses him, Abner once again does not speak but simply turns and exits. Abner's unchanging stride suggests that he knows no other way to deal with class conflict. His reactions are socially constructed with a clocklike finality of their own. His silence when addressed by Mrs. de Spain parallels the silence of the courtroom scenes and underscores Abner's false consciousness: He believes he cannot gain power through speaking, only through destroying.

Marxist oppression continues across generations. The women in the family amply demonstrate the political and economic oppression and false consciousness of Marxist class division. Sarty's sisters are often described as cattle instead of humans. Attention is drawn to the cheapness of their clothes. The women are not allowed to exist as graceful upper-class women. Yet Faulkner suggests that the "inertia" surrounding them is their own. Like Abner, the sisters' problems are socially constructed and to some degree of their own making.

Sarty's mother and aunt also sustain the system of oppression. They save the little money that they have to buy Sarty a half-size ax, a gift that symbolizes the movement of the next generation into the working class and its false consciousness. Later, when Abner believes Sarty will flee to warn Major de Spain of the barn burning, Abner instructs his wife to hold her son, denying both his wife's and Sarty's ambitions to see Sarty escape the family's entrapment in the vicious cycle of southern agrarian sharecropping.

Throughout the story, Sarty himself wrestles with his father's ideas about class conflict and violence. In the opening scene, Sarty is hungry, underscoring the family's destitute status. Early on, we see him making mental efforts to make "his father's enemy" into his enemy as well. Upon exiting the trial, he scraps with the boy who yells "barn burner." However, as the family pulls away from the trial in their wagon, Sarty hopes that his father is satisfied and will not continue the cycle of destruction based on violence and nihilism without the production of economic opportunity.

Sarty's development is next seen when he and his father walk toward the de Spain house for the first time. Sarty intuits that his father can't harm such an aristocratic family. He realizes that his father's violence would be a "buzzing wasp" capable of only an annoying sting but no more. Sarty hopes that his father realizes this as well and will change from what "*he couldn't help but be.*" This line suggests that Sarty understands how his father has been socially constructed to understand class relationships and social mobility only through the current system based upon inequality and irresolvable conflict.

Sarty's disavowal of his father's nihilistic barn burning is the story's climax. As Abner rushes to burn the de Spain barn to the ground, Sarty protests by saying that before other burnings, a messenger was sent to warn the landowners. Abner only continues to prepare for the conflagration. Sarty understands that he could flee from the system of conflict, poverty, and interpellation in which his family is trapped. He says, "*I could run on and on and never look back, never need to see his face again. Only I can't.*" Ultimately, Sarty does break with his father. He warns the de Spain household of his father's actions, and he runs from his family, spending the night in the woods. The story ends with the sun about to rise, symbolically letting Sarty begin a new life. He understands that his father's nihilistic, ideological stranglehold kept the family from realizing a better life of economic and political opportunity.

"Barn Burning" presents an economic and political system that perpetuates class conflict, robs the working class of power and equality, and creates a false consciousness that destroys the proletariat's ability to imagine a different system based upon economic and political equality. Faulkner illustrates the interpellation throughout the entire Snopes family. While Abner Snopes is caught in material and social circumstances that allow him only nihilistic protest through barn burning, Sarty represents the true Marxist mind that realizes that an alternative system is needed, one where the bourgeoisie do not control the means of production and the proletariat are not in eternal insurgency. Although Sarty himself may be too young to think in such precise Marxist terms, the story "Barn Burning" itself suggests that successful economic and political systems must redistribute the means of production and allow society to recognize the equality and humanity of all people.

6

Feminist Criticism

> Throughout history people have knocked their heads against the riddle of the nature of femininity.... Nor will you have escaped worrying over this problem—those of you who are men; to those of you who are women this will not apply—you are yourselves the problem.
>
> SIGMUND FREUD, LECTURE 33, *New Introductory Lectures on Psychoanalysis and Other Works*

> If a woman has her Ph.D. in physics, has mastered quantum theory, plays flawless Chopin, was once a cheerleader, and is now married to a man who plays baseball, she will forever be "former cheerleader married to star athlete."
>
> MARYANNE ELLISON SIMMONS, *wife of Milwaukee Brewers' catcher Ted Simmons*

When a school of literary criticism is still evolving, trying to make a definitive explanation of it can be a perilous undertaking. Feminist criticism, a case in point, is difficult to define because it has not yet been codified into a single critical perspective. Instead, its several shapes and directions vary from one country to another, even from one critic to another. The premise that unites those who call themselves feminist critics is the assumption that Western culture is fundamentally **patriarchal**, creating an imbalance of power that marginalizes women and their work. In the case of queer theory critics, whose work is also covered in this chapter, parallel concerns include **heterosexual privilege** and the marginalization of homosexuals and their work. The social structure that enforces the same gender and sexual norms for all, according to feminists and queer theorists, is reflected in religion, philosophy, economics, education—all aspects of the culture, including literature. They work to expose such ideology and, in the end, to change it so that the worth of everyone can be fully realized and appreciated.

HISTORICAL BACKGROUND

Although the feminist movement stretches back into the nineteenth century, the modern attempt to look at literature through a feminist lens began to develop only in the early 1960s. Emerging alongside feminist criticism was a movement toward queer theory criticism, which reached a critical point by the 1980s, as the following overview explains.

Feminism

Feminism was a long time coming. For centuries, Western culture had operated on the assumption that women were inferior creatures. Leading thinkers, from Aristotle to Charles Darwin, reiterated that women were lesser beings, and one does not have to look hard to find comments from writers, theologians, and other public figures that disparage and degrade women. The Greek ecclesiast John Chrysostom (ca. AD 347–407) called women "a foe to friendship, an inescapable punishment, a necessary evil," and *Ecclesiasticus*, a book of the biblical apocrypha, states, "All wickedness is but little to the wickedness of a woman." The Roman theologian Tertullian (ca. AD 160–230) lectured to women that "the judgment of God upon your sex endures even today; and with it inevitably endures your position of criminal at the bar of justice. You are the gateway to the devil." Even the Book of Genesis blames Eve for the loss of paradise. Revered writers of later ages have been equally ungenerous in their descriptions of the nature of women. Alexander Pope (1688–1744) asserted, "Most women have no character at all," and John Keats (1795–1821) explained, "The opinion I have of the generality of women—who appear to me as children to whom I would rather give a sugar plum than my time—forms a barrier against matrimony which I rejoice in."

It is not surprising, given widespread acknowledgment of the inferiority of the female, that women too accepted their lesser status. Even the French writer Madame de Staël (1766–1817) is said to have commented, "I am glad that I am not a man, as I should be obliged to marry a woman." When women did recognize their talents, they sometimes worked to conceal them. Jane Austen (1775–1817), for example, advised, "A woman, especially, if she have the misfortune of knowing anything, should conceal it as well as she can." Or as Mae West (1893–1980) put it, "Brains are an asset, if you hide them." Women are the staple of jokes, too. As an example, James Thurber (1894–1961), an oft-quoted misogynist, once commented, "Woman's place is in the wrong."

In the late eighteenth century, however, Mary Wollstonecraft took issue with the assumptions that allow people to make jokes and cause women to hide their creativity. In 1792 she published *A Vindication of the Rights of Woman*, a book in which she depicted women as an oppressed class regardless of social hierarchy. Her views were radical in a place and time that did not recognize women's political or legal rights, offered them few opportunities for employment, and, if they married, gave their property to their husbands. Having experienced as a child the imbalance of power between her own mother and father and having observed as an adult the indignities suffered by women of all classes, she recognized that they are born into powerless roles. As a result, Wollstonecraft asserted, women are forced to use manipulative methods to get what they want. She argued for women to be "duly prepared by education to be the companions of men" and called for the members of her sex to take charge of their lives by recognizing that their abilities were equal to those of men, to define their identities for themselves, and to carve out their own roles in society. She wrote,

> I earnestly wish to point out in what true dignity and human happiness consists—I wish to persuade women to endeavour to acquire strength, both of mind and body, and to convince them that the soft phrases, susceptibility of heart, delicacy of sentiment, and refinement of taste, are almost synonymous with epithets of weakness, and that those beings who are only the objects of pity and that kind of love, which has been termed its sister, will soon become objects of contempt.... I wish to shew that elegance is inferior to virtue, that the first object of laudable ambition is to obtain a character as a human being, regardless of the distinction of sex.

Her stand was not welcomed by all. Horace Walpole, for example, called her a "hyena in petticoats," but Wollstonecraft's words were out, and they were impossible to ignore ever again.

In 1929 another eloquent analysis of the position of women was published by Virginia Woolf, best known as a writer of lyrical and somewhat experimental novels. Called *A Room of One's Own*, the book questioned why women appear so seldom in history. Woolf pointed out that poems and stories are full of their depictions, but in real life they hardly seem to have existed. They are absent. In the chapter entitled "Shakespeare's Sister," she pondered what would have happened to a gifted female writer in the Renaissance. Without an adequate education or a room of her own, "whatever she had written," Woolf concluded, "would have been twisted and deformed, issuing from a strained and morbid imagination." Woolf went on to argue that

> if we [women] have the habit of freedom and the courage to write exactly what we think; if we escape a little from the common sitting room and see human beings not always in their relation to each other but in relation to reality; and the sky too, ... when she [Shakespeare's sister] is born again she shall find it possible to live and write her poetry.

Individuals like Wollstonecraft and Woolf stand out as eloquent spokespersons for women. Along with them are many others whose names are less well known but whose efforts have been important to the development of women's history, both social and literary. Some of that history has been traced by Elaine Showalter, who divided it into three phases: the feminine phase (1840–80), the feminist phase (1880–1920), and the female phase (1920–present). In the first, female writers imitated the literary tradition established by men, taking additional care to avoid offensive language or subject matter. Novelists such as Charlotte Brontë and Mary Ann Evans wrote in the forms and styles of recognized writers, all of whom were male. Sometimes female writers even used men's names (Currer Bell for Brontë and George Eliot for Evans, for example) to hide their female authorship.

In the second phase, according to Showalter, women protested their lack of rights and worked to secure them. In the political realm, Susan B. Anthony, Elizabeth Cady Stanton, and others pushed to secure equality under the law, and some of the more radical feminists envisioned separate female utopias. In the literary world, they decried the unjust depictions of women by male writers.

The third phase, at its beginnings, concentrated on exploring the female experience in art and literature. For female writers, this meant turning to their own lives for subjects. It also meant that the delicacy of expression that had typified women's writing began to crumble as a new frankness regarding sexuality emerged. For feminist critics, it meant looking at the depiction of women in male texts in an effort to reveal the **misogyny** (negative attitudes toward women) lurking there. More recently they have turned their attention to an examination of works by female writers. These latest efforts Showalter refers to as **gynocriticism**, a movement that examines the distinctive characteristics of the female experience, in contrast to earlier methods that explained the female by using male models.

During the third period that Showalter identified, a host of important spokespersons have raised public awareness of issues surrounding women's rights. Simone de Beauvoir in *The Second Sex* (1949) argued that French culture, and Western societies in general, are patriarchal. In those societies, the males define what it means to be human. Lacking her own history, the female is always secondary or nonexistent. Beauvoir believed that women are not born inferior but rather are made to be so. She called for women to break out of being the "other" and to realize their possibilities. Betty Friedan shocked some and cheered others with her attack on the image of the happy, mid-twentieth-century, American, suburban housewife and mother in *The Feminine Mystique* (1963). By the next decade, feminists were taking their models from other social protests, such as the civil rights movement. Kate Millett, in *Sexual Politics* (1970), objected to the repressive stereotyping of women by probing the differences between biological (sexual) and cultural (gender) identities. Millet also pointed out that power in both public and domestic life is held by males, and literature is a record of the collective consciousness of patriarchy. That is, much literature is the record of a man speaking to other men, not directly to women. At about the same time, Germaine Greer documented images of women in popular culture and literature in *The Female Eunuch* (1970) in an attempt to free women from their mental dependence on the images presented by these sources.

Showalter acknowledges that today there is no single strand of feminism or feminist criticism, no single feminist approach to the study of literature, but there do seem to be some similarities among feminists in particular countries. American feminism, which has its stronghold in academia, has worked to add texts by female writers to the canon. Sandra Gilbert and Susan Gubar, authors of *The Madwoman in the Attic* (1979), have been influential in American feminist criticism, calling for a recognition that male writers have too long stereotyped women as either "the angel in the house" (the woman who lives to care for her husband) or "the madwoman in the attic" (the woman who chooses not to be the angel). They call for writing by women, even a woman's sentence with linguistic qualities of its own, that will more accurately capture the complexity of women's lives and nature.

Showalter points out that French feminists are primarily psychoanalytic. For their theoretical basis, they have turned to their fellow countryman Jacques Lacan. They are, consequently, concerned with language, particularly with how women in the **Symbolic Order** (a phase of development) are socialized into accepting the language and Law of the Father and are thereby made inferior (see Chapter 4). Hélène Cixous goes so far as to assert that there is a particular kind of writing by women, which she calls ***l'écriture féminine***, that is characterized by non-linear texts and cyclical writing that is the antithesis of phallocentric writing. She urges women to write themselves out of the linear system of writing and thinking devised by men for men.

The British feminists, according to Showalter, generally take a Marxist position. Protesting the exploitation of women in life and literature, which they view as connected by virtue of being parts of the material world, British feminist critics work to change the economic and social status of women. They analyze relationships between gender and class, showing how power structures, which are male dominated, influence society and oppress women. Like Marxists in general, they see literature as a tool by which society itself can be reformed.

All three groups are gynocentric, trying to find ways to define the female experience, expose patriarchy, and save women from being the other. Those involved with literature—critics and writers—try to expand the canon to include female writers and to correct inaccurate depictions of women in the works of male writers. Interest in such topics has led to increased notice of works written by females who had been ignored or forgotten but whose texts deserve examination. *The Awakening*, by Kate Chopin, is a case in point. Rediscovered in the 1960s, it became a popular and critical success more than sixty years after its initial publication.

The growing strength of the feminist movement has also led to the establishment of women's studies programs, further fueling the interest in gender studies, which question the qualities of femininity and masculinity, and in feminist literary criticism. Such programs ask questions about the nature of the female imagination and female literary history. What, after all, is a female aesthetic? Do women use language in ways that are different from those of men? Do women have a different pattern of reasoning? Do they see the world in a different way?

Several significant studies have tried to answer such questions. They do not all agree, but in general, they have challenged assumptions about how males and females use language, view reality, solve problems, and make judgments. They all suggest that women and men have different conceptions of self and different modes of interaction with others. Some of the findings call for recognition of the differences, because ignoring them inevitably leads to a suppression of women's ways of understanding and acting.

Nancy Chodorow, for example, argued in *The Reproduction of Mothering* that girls and boys develop a different concept of self because of different relationships with the mother, the primary parent in the home. Girls maintain an ongoing gender role identification with the mother from the beginning, but boys, in addition to dealing with an **Oedipal attachment**, give up their primary identification with her. The result is that men tend to deny relationships, whereas women remain relational.

In another study, Carol Gilligan focused on differences in how males and females talk about moral problems. Her interest in the subject grew out of her objections to the theories of psychologist Lawrence Kohlberg regarding the development of moral reasoning, which he believed to be the basis for ethical behavior. Expanding the theories of Jean Piaget by examining the stages of development beyond the ages first studied, Kohlberg concluded that the process of moral development can be observed in six stages, which are broken into three levels, each responding better to moral dilemmas than the last. His research also showed that girls, on average, reach a lower level of moral development than do boys. Gilligan took issue with Kohlberg's findings in her book *In a Different Voice* by objecting to his research methods. As she pointed out, the participants in Kohlberg's basic study were all male, thereby forming a false standard of measurement. She also noted that the scoring method Kohlberg used tended to favor a principled way of reasoning that is more common to boys, over moral argumentation concentrating on human relationships, which is more natural to girls.

Gilligan's conclusions were that men are more likely to see morality as a matter of rights and rules to be dealt with by formal reasoning. Women, on the other hand, are more likely to deal with moral issues contextually. That is, instead of applying "blind justice" provided by abstract laws and universal principles, they recognize that moral choice must be determined from the particular experiences of the participants. Conflicting responsibilities are to be resolved in a narrative, consensual manner. Such ideas eventually led to Gilligan being known as the founder of "difference feminism," because unlike some feminists, she acknowledged that significant differences exist between men and women—specifically, that men think in terms of rules and justice, whereas women are more likely to think in terms of caring and relationships. More recently, Gilligan worked with Nora Lyons to examine the implications of self-definition, finding that many more women than men define themselves in terms of their relationships and connections to others.

Another feminist writer, Robin Lakoff, has argued that women's language is inferior to that of men. She has pointed out its patterns of weakness, uncertainty, and triviality. She went on to assert that women should adopt the stronger male utterance if they wish to achieve equality.

A fourth study of significance comes from Mary Field Belenky, Blythe McVicker Clinchy, Nancy Rule Goldberger, and Jill Mattuck Tarule. Entitled

Women's Ways of Knowing, it is concerned with women's intellectual development. Recognizing that male experience has served as the model in defining the processes of intellectual maturation, the authors argue that the ways of knowing that women value "have been neglected and denigrated by the dominant intellectual ethos of our time." That is, "thinking" has traditionally been defined as the mental processes attributed primarily to men—processes such as abstract reasoning, the scientific method, and impersonal judgments. Belenky et al. aver that this kind of thinking does not come naturally to many women, who instead are more comfortable with personal and interpersonal ways of knowing. They are more likely to value "connection over separation, understanding and acceptance over assessment, and collaboration over debate." Based on interviews with 135 women from a variety of backgrounds and ages, the study found that women develop intellectually as they find their voice, as they move from silence (in which they take their identification from external authorities) to subjective knowledge (when they turn away from others but still lack a public voice) and then to constructed knowledge (when they integrate their own intuitive knowledge with what they have learned from others).

Despite (or perhaps because of) such studies, members of the feminist movement today, as well as the critics, male and female, who make its principles and methods the basis of their critical approach to literature, are not yet in complete agreement about what those principles and methods are. In fact, there are currently many different forms of feminism and many different kinds of feminist critics, partly because of their tendency to borrow from other social and literary movements—a practice that has both enriched and complicated their work. As a result, they now find themselves the inheritors of several decades of evolution that has led to significant differences, and even some disagreements, among them.

Minority feminists—women of color and lesbians, for example—do not always align themselves with what they see as a primarily white, middle-class movement that has historically marginalized them. Their exclusion is ironic, given that their victimization has been greater than that of their white counterparts. Not only has history taken less notice of them than it has of white women, but literature too has generally overlooked them, at least until recently. Compounding their grievances is the fact that they have more than a single battle to fight. The African American feminist critic, for example, finds herself pressured by two forces of oppression: racism and sexism. The two are bound together in her experience, but she does not find that circumstance represented by mainstream feminism, which is focused only on sexism. The same situation is true for the poor, the aged, and other women who find themselves without access to power, leaving them outside the movement as it has developed with leadership vested in educated—and relatively affluent—white women. The response of minority feminist critics is therefore likely to be more political than that of white critics. And when one makes reference to feminism as a worldwide movement, the situation becomes even more complex, because the roles and power of women in different countries vary widely. A feminist living and working in Los Angeles is likely to have a very different life from that of a mother of five in Chad or Sudan, so how can there be "sisterhood"?

The political edge found among minority feminist critics, the Marxist feminists, and others has not been welcomed by everyone. Some complain that extreme positions regarding social policy ultimately cause a reader to ignore the literary text. They object that a radical stance diverts the critic from the main task at hand, which is to pay attention to the aesthetics of literature, not to impose a political agenda on it. Such comments are formalist in nature, for they urge the reader to see the work as an autonomous entity with its own rules of being. It is an approach that lies at a great distance from the methods of those who would use literature as a tool of social protest and reform.

The definition of feminist criticism was also destabilized by the introduction of deconstruction, which, since the middle 1970s, has been a disruptive and transformative way of thinking about what it means to be male or female (see Chapter 8). When the definition plays with the reversal of those binaries, it also overturns all the other binary oppositions that are related to them: rational/emotional, active/passive, objective/subjective. The result is that it complicates what we mean when we refer to sexual identity. It forces us to ask, What do we mean when we describe someone as masculine or feminine? Another field of criticism that takes this question seriously is queer theory.

Queer Theory

By the 1980s, the fissures in the feminist movement were growing deep. Accusations from minority groups claimed that it had become just as exclusive as the patriarchal system it had initially opposed. As noted, African American women charged the leading feminists with defining the movement by the experiences of white, middle-class women. They objected that the world of black women had been marginalized, thereby recreating the social inequalities that feminism had objected to. In 1982, *Ain't I a Woman: Black Women and Feminism*, by bell hooks, gave voice to some of those who felt left out. Lesbian critics raised similar objections, protesting that feminism continued to privilege heterosexual orientation to the exclusion of gay women.

The objections and protests led, perhaps inevitably, to the development of gay and lesbian studies, a movement that seeks to make sexual orientation central to critical analysis and understanding. The interests of such researchers and critics include literary criticism but are not purely, or perhaps even chiefly, literary: practitioners of gay and lesbian studies clearly have political and social goals, chief among them being to work against **homophobia** and **heterosexual privilege**. To achieve those goals, its adherents focus on sexual differences. The term *queer theory* reflects an evolving alliance between gay men and lesbians, as opposed to the usual male studies and female studies that characterized the earlier gay and lesbian movements. At first glance the choice of such a term would seem to be counterproductive, as *queer* had, for many years, been a pejorative reference to a homosexual. A second look, however, indicates an effort to reverse the meaning of the term and thereby change the attitudes of society, a strategy well-known to Marxists (see Chapter 5). It is also a more inclusive term than might first be assumed, as it takes as its subject matter all sexual topics that are considered abnormal or odd—in other words, "queer"—by the mainstream in an effort to challenge traditional views of sexual identities.

Queer theory has sometimes been put in the category of third-wave feminism because of its interest in essentialist versus social constructionist theories that the earlier movement had explored. That is, the thinking of the early queer theorists often centered on questions about how sexuality is contrived: Is it socially created or a natural given? Can it be changed, or is it inescapable? In the late 1960s, Kate Millett had drawn distinctions between sex, a biological determination, and gender, a socially constructed one. Whereas sex is fixed and stable, she argued, gender is not, because it is determined by society and thereby subject to its changing conventions and structures. Those involved in the lesbian movement had argued that accepting the premise that a woman is born with a true essence that cannot be varied meant denying their own experience. In turn, the queer theorists, like many feminists and lesbians before them, opposed the assertions of **essentialism**, or the idea that a person's true identity is composed of fixed and unchanging properties, those that make one human. They instead supported the idea that human identity is formed by the culture into which one is born. Recognizing that gender, what it means to be a man or a woman, is a constantly changing concept, they became **social constructivists**.

Along with the work of Millet, Judith Butler's book *Gender Trouble* has been highly significant in this discussion. In it she argues that some early feminists were wrong in asserting that women are a group with inherent characteristics and interests that they hold in common. Instead of accepting that gender shifts and changes with times and contexts across a wide range of behaviors and attitudes, that stance limited the choice of gender to two possibilities: male and female. The result has been to continue the traditional binary of masculine/feminine, thereby making it more difficult for individuals to choose their authentic identities. Instead of being innate, Butler says, identity is **performative**, by which she means that what a person does at particular times determines gender and identity. Identity is constantly moving among possibilities. Acknowledging that notions about gender are difficult to change because they are generally accepted, without question, to be naturally the way they are and should be, Butler calls for social action that will revise the norms and the masculine/feminine binary so that many genders, and therefore identities, are available and accepted. She speaks for queer theorists in general who want to destabilize assumptions about sexual identity, which, they maintain, is far more complicated than the simple binary of male/female. By so doing, they hope to weaken simplistic assumptions and reduce prejudices.

Another queer theorist who argues for fluidity of identity is Eve Kosofsky Sedgwick, who has done much to bring the subject to the attention of the public. In her *Tendencies*, she attempts "to find new ways to think about lesbian, gay, and other sexually dissident loves and identities in a complex social ecology where the presence of different genders, different identities and identifications, will be taken as a given." Identity, to Sedgwick, is a complex mixture of choices, life experiences, and professional roles. Her intent is clearly to make a more humane world in which differences among people are not only tolerated but also accepted.

Queer theorists use the strategies of deconstruction to demonstrate the fluidity of gender identity. By reversing sexual binary oppositions, such as heterosexual/homosexual, they show that these are not fixed essences. Queer theory claims that such terms are not absolute because they cannot be understood without one another, and they are not stable because they can be reversed to a binary that privileges homosexual over heterosexual, showing by their reversal different possibilities of identity and power, and thereby opposing the notion of an essential, unchangeable relationship. Sedgwick highlights the importance of questioning notions of homosexuality and heterosexuality in her *Epistemology of the Closet*: "Virtually any aspect of modern Western culture, must be, not merely incomplete, but damaged in its central substance to the degree that it does not incorporate a critical analysis of modern homo/heterosexual definition."

In sum, interested in questions regarding sexual identity, queer theorists view individuals not simply as male or female but as a collection of many possible sexualities that may include various degrees of heterosexuality, homosexuality, or bisexuality. In other words, sexuality is neither stable nor static. In their view it is dynamic and changing, affected by the experience of race and class and subject to shifting desire. It is a force of its own that is not just biologically conferred. Thus, heterosexuality cannot be viewed as the norm against which other sexual identities are measured.

It should be noted that queer theory is interested in a wide range of sexual practices and identities, many of which were considered abnormal not too many years ago. Its practitioners turn their attention to a wide variety of topics running from gay marriage to cross dressing to bisexuality and more. The "odd" (queer) is considered to be an opportunity to examine social organization and practices with the purpose of redefining how we see and understand ourselves. With the explosion of information and discussion on the Internet, conversation about once-taboo subjects has moved into new prominence. No longer controlled by institutions such as publishing houses, government agencies, and schools, public discourse has expanded to include sexual topics seldom found in open discussion only a few decades ago. Given the changing norms of popular culture that continue to break traditional strictures, sexuality, in all its manifestations, can be expected to receive extensive attention for some time to come.

What are the applications that queer theory has to offer literary criticism? They are the same as those that are applied to real-life people and experiences. The queer theory critic will look at gender, sexual practices, identity, defining choices, sexual stereotyping, assumed norms, types of masculinity and femininity, and other such issues. He or she examines lesbian and gay episodes in canonical works (especially those instances that have previously been ignored or explained away) and exposes homophobic literary practices. Genres that have been instrumental in establishing conventional ideas of what is masculine and what is feminine are of particular interest to this critic. And, needless to say, he or she also works to identify works by gay and lesbian writers as well as increase the reading public's appreciation of them. Although much of queer theory is more focused on social reformation than on literary analysis, it has a place in contemporary criticism.

One final note is that realistic fiction, which assumes fixed identities of characters and which usually maintains consistent points of view (an essentialist stance), is less interesting to the queer theory critic than narratives that feature the surprising and the unusual. Traditional moral outlooks, a linear sequence of unfolding events, and recognizable and socially sanctioned characters provoke less curiosity than does fiction that interrupts or disturbs the realistic outlook.

Whether examining an unconventional piece of literature or a more traditional one, you can ask the following questions to approach the text as a queer theory critic:

- Does the work challenge traditional ways of viewing sexuality and identity?
- Does it depict human sexuality as more complex than the essentialist terms *male* and *female* suggest?
- What ranges of male and female identity do you find?
- Does the work assume an essentialist view of gender—that is, does it accept that there is a fixed, unchanging self?
- Does the work or narrator assume that the self is a constructed one?
- If the self is assumed to be constructed, what performative acts construct a character's identity?
- What sexual topics do you find in the work that are odd or peculiar—that is, queer?
- Where is gender destabilized? What destabilizes it?
- Does the work show how sexual identities are indeterminate, overlapping, changing? If so, where?
- Does the work complicate what it means to be homosexual or heterosexual?

READING AS A FEMINIST

To understand the discussion that follows, you should read the letters of Abigail Adams, written on March 31 and April 5, 1776, and the one from her husband, John, written on April 14, 1776, which begin on page 254.

Although feminist criticism has many strands, most critics hold some general approaches in common. More specifically, they look at literary history to rediscover forgotten texts by women, to reevaluate other texts, and to examine the cultural contexts in which works were produced. They analyze the male/female power structure that makes women the other (the inferior), and they reject it. They work to abolish limiting stereotypes of women. They seek to expose patriarchal premises and the prejudices they create. Often, they challenge traditional, static ways of seeing gender and identity. In short, by changing the literature that people read and the ways that they read it, feminist critics hope to change the world so that everyone is valued as a creative, rational being. That makes feminist critics, as a group, highly ideological, even visionary.

Despite the sprawling nature of feminist studies, it is possible to group some of the different perspectives into several overlapping approaches. Three major groups of feminist critics are those who study difference, those who study power relationships, and those who study the female experience. Queer theory critics also intersect with these groups and will be discussed where relevant.

Studies of Difference

Feminist critics who are interested in determining the differences in male and female writing work from the assumption that gender determines everything, including value systems and language. Not all feminist critics agree, for they recognize that historically the concept of female difference has resulted in an assumption of female inferiority, leading them to argue that difference should no longer be an issue. Nevertheless, studies like those of Belenky and Gilligan have led critics to look for distinctive elements in texts by men and women. They compare and contrast what men and women write and how they write it. They examine not only the subjects but also voice, syntax, and diction. Although such matters remain largely unresolved, the concern with male and female writing characteristics has resulted in increased attention to gay and lesbian texts and, as noted earlier, has been influential in the establishment of gay and lesbian studies programs.

One way this approach has influenced current criticism is evident in an expanded concept of which genres are to be accepted as literature. If works by female writers are to be deemed worthy of study, then the forms they have traditionally turned to, such as journals and letters, have to be included in the canon. The correspondence between Abigail Adams and her husband, John, who was away from home because of the Revolutionary War, is an example of the sorts of texts that interest feminist critics. For one thing, the letters allow the voice of Abigail, a woman who had much to say, to be heard. She was not likely to write a political treatise or poems exhorting the troops to battle, but she did write to her husband, and through those letters, her concerns are still articulated. Her letters are also typical of the kind of writing women have always done. Do they constitute literature? A feminist critic would argue that they do.

The correspondence between Abigail and John Adams is interesting because of the contrast of content as well as the style of the two writers. Abigail begins both of the letters included here with a plea for more communication from John. She complains that he writes infrequently and that his letters are too brief. In answer, he does not apologize but explains that the "critical state of things" necessitates the brevity of his writing. He is involved in matters of importance that make it impossible for him to write at greater length. Of course, he also alludes, without excuse or apparent irony, to a "multiplicity of avocations" that presumably take up his time. Abigail also opens by inquiring about John's work—asking about the state of the revolution and even devoting a short paragraph to patriotic sentiment that is sure to please him—before she turns to news of their home, the town, and finally her own state of mind. She ends with an overt feminist statement, calling men tyrants and asking her husband to recognize the rights of women to have voice and representation in the new government. John, on the other hand, after explaining that he has been too busy to write much, turns quickly to recounting the progress of the revolt and its effect on the colonies. It is an impersonal account, with no reference to his direct involvement with it. When he does address more personal issues, in answer to her description of the state of their home Boston, he assumes a patriarchal tone and discourses on issues of morality. Finally, in a response to her requests for his attention to the rights of women, he turns lighthearted, referring to her "*gaieté de coeur*" and describing her as "saucy." He treats her comments playfully, declaring that because men are already masters in name only, they cannot even think to repeal the system in which they seem to hold control lest they become completely subjected to "the despotism of the petticoat." He gives her appeals no serious thought.

The style of the two letters also has contrasts. Abigail's is full of personal references, marked by the use of the pronoun *I*, whereas John's makes little reference to himself. John speaks primarily in the third person, narrating at much greater distance than does his wife. Abigail also describes her sentiments, explicitly stating her feelings. She says, for instance, "I wish you would ever write me a letter half as long as I write you," "I am fearful of the small-pox," and "I feel very differently at the approach of spring from what I did a month ago." John, in contrast, makes little reference to his own feelings. He says that he pities the children of the solicitor general, but instead of indulging the sentiment, he uses it to make stern comments about morality. Later he speaks of being charmed by Abigail's gaiety, the sign of innocent femininity, and at the end expresses amusement, even laughter, at her silliness that asks for equality. The final mood is implicit in the ironic treatment he gives her concerns. The two not only choose to discuss different topics but also approach them from quite different perspectives: the personal and the impersonal, the subjective and the objective, the explicit and the implicit.

If you are interested in studying differences in the writing of men and women, you will find it helpful to consider the following questions:

- Has the writer chosen to write in a genre typical of male or female writers of the period?
- Do you consider the content of the piece typical or atypical of a male or female writer?
- Does the voice sound characteristic of a male or female writer? That is, is it personal or impersonal, subjective or objective, implicit or explicit?

Studies of Power

The sociological aspects of feminism broached so delicately by Virginia Woolf become overt and explicit with today's outspoken feminists who complain of the imbalance of power between the sexes. They assume that the economic system is at the root of the inequitable relationship and thus attack both the economic and the social exploitation of women. They charge that women are oppressed by a group that consciously works to hold them down through its ideology. Michèle Barrett, who writes from a Marxist point of view, argues that the way households and families are organized is related to the division of labor in a society, the systems of education, and the roles men and women play in the culture. Building on Woolf's belief that the conditions under which men and women produce literature affect how they write and what they write about, Barrett argues that gender stereotyping is tied to material conditions.

Feminist critics who are interested in examining and protesting power relationships of men and women in literature have expanded their focus to include a number of subgroups that have also been marginalized in society. Thus, they frequently look at writers from cultures as varied and different as those of blacks (African Americans and other people of color), Hispanics, Asian Americans, American Indians, Jews, and lesbians. Some blacks, the most outspoken of the minorities, describe critics as racists and misogynists, object to the amount of attention paid to black male writers (instead of black female writers), and even charge white feminist critics with being interested only in white, upper-middle-class women. Their efforts have not all been directed to protest, however. They have also produced some valuable scholarship by compiling bibliographies of ignored black writers and their works, studying black female folk artists, and publishing slave narratives. They have traced the growing power and authority of black females, whose history in this country began in slavery. And they have celebrated the family and community nurtured by those women. Like the Marxists, these critics have highly political purposes.

The common thread uniting these disparate groups is the belief that the social organization has denied equal treatment to all its segments and that literature is a means of revealing and resisting that social order. To them, art and life are fused entities, making it the duty of the critic to work against stereotyping in literature, media, and public awareness; to raise the consciousness of those who are oppressed; and to bring about radical change in the power balance between the oppressors and the oppressed.

Whereas feminist critics in general have sometimes been criticized for having too little to say about the quality of literary texts, those concerned with issues of power and economics have been especially chided for their lack of attention to questions of aesthetic value. More interested in the sociological aspects of texts than in making a close reading of them, these readers have an especially political intent. Many of the English feminist critics who work from a Marxist perspective would belong to this group.

Critics who take this approach would be interested in the letters of Abigail and John Adams because they show contrasting views of labor and economics. Abigail's letters express concern for the state of their personal property. She comments that their house, left empty by a doctor who has now moved on, is like a new asset, because it was worthless to them while it was occupied. She has asked a friend to take stock of what is left, as part of the process of evaluating their holdings. The house has been left dirty, obviously an objectionable state, but one that is less distressing than its destruction would have been. She also mentions the fate of others whose homes have been used by the enemy, noting that in some cases the inhabitants have left rent for their use or for damage done to furniture. She even mentions the state of the president's unfinished "mansion-house," in Washington. Abigail's is a practical inventory of households—her own, those of her neighbors, and those of their leaders.

John, too, makes observations about the economy, but they are less personal than those of his wife. Attracted to an analysis of the broader situation, he is more philosophical than she. Speaking of the defense of Virginia, he comments, "The gentry are very rich, and the common people very poor. This inequality of property gives an aristocratical turn to all their proceedings." He recognizes the value of a less hierarchical society, one in which the classes are less distinctly defined. When he mentions their personal holdings, he maintains his impersonal tone, referring to "a certain house in Queen Street" rather than naming it as their own. He assumes the same attitude he held toward the "aristocratical turn" of the Virginians and applies it to his own family, warning, "Whenever vanity and gayety, a love of pomp and dress, furniture, equipage, buildings, great company, expensive diversions, and elegant entertainments get the better of the principles and judgments of men or women, there is no knowing where they will stop, nor into what evils, natural, moral, or political, they will lead us." His call for less attention to material acquisition and his desire for a less hierarchical society foreshadow the ideas to be later espoused by the Marxists.

The division of labor between man and woman, husband and wife, is also clear in these letters. It is John's duty to be away, directing the affairs of the colonies, but Abigail is expected to remain at home with the family. Such a situation is not surprising to see in the eighteenth century. More interesting is the nature of the work they are expected to do. Whereas John's may involve physical courage but probably has more to do with using his authority to plan operations and direct groups of people, Abigail's responsibility for maintaining the family is considerably more lowly. In answer to his inquiry as to whether she has yet made saltpeter, she replies that she will try to do so after she makes soap and remarks that making clothes for the family takes much of her time. In addition, she is concerned about planting and sowing, about finding and providing food for all.

Finally, despite the candor with which Abigail presents her case to John regarding her desire for the equality of women, the terms she uses and the spirit in which he receives them indicate the reality of their relationship. She charges men with being "naturally tyrannical," acknowledges that they hold "the harsh title of master," and implores him to "put it out of the power of the vicious and the lawless to use us with cruelty and indignity with impunity." Despite his comments elsewhere about the desirability of equality among people, he fails to take her seriously. As he says, "As to your extraordinary code of laws, I cannot but laugh."

Obviously Abigail and John Adams do not belong to any of the minority groups named here. They were white, Anglo-Saxon founders of the United States, members of what in retrospect is definitely deemed to have been the "inner circle." They lived much of the time on a farm in Braintree, just south of Boston, which was a center of culture, had access to education, and through John wielded power and made policy. What would the minority feminist critics make of their correspondence?

Although there would seem to be less here for the minority critics to address than there is for the other groups of feminists, the final paragraph in John's letter is significant where their interests are concerned. In it he mentions, in a lighthearted manner, a number of minority groups: apprentices, students, Indians, "negroes," and "another tribe," women. Later he refers to "Tories, land-jobbers, trimmers, bigots, Canadians, Indians, negroes, Hanoverians, Hessians, Russians, Irish Roman Catholics, Scotch renegadoes," too. Clearly his intent is to treat the matter with humor, but by linking Abigail's "foolish" request with the unruly conduct of what he considers to be groups under the control and domination of their betters, he reveals his own prejudices. He betrays his own sense of superiority, his acceptance of the right to oppress and repress, despite his protestations against aristocracy. It could be charged, and certainly would be by minority feminists, that such attitudes are at the root of the racial and ethnic divisions that have marked the entire course of American history.

Studies of power as depicted in literature often begin with the following questions:

- Where do you find an imbalance of power among the characters?
- Who are the powerful ones, and who are the powerless? Are the latter women and/or minority figures?
- What divisions of labor exist between men and women in the work?
- Does the work resist a social order that denies equal treatment to all? Or does it accept it?

Studies of the Female Experience

The interest of some feminists in probing the unique nature of the female personality and experience has led the critics and writers among them to try to identify a specifically female tradition of literature. Such explorations have been particularly interesting to French feminists, who have found in Lacan's extensions of Freudian theory a basis for resisting the idea of a stable "masculine" authority or truth. Rejecting the idea of a male norm, against which women are seen as secondary and derivative, they call for a recognition of women's abilities that goes beyond the traditional binary oppositions, such as male/female and the parallel oppositions of active/passive and intellectual/emotional. Searching for the essence of feminine style in literature, they examine female images in the works of female writers and the elements thought to be typical of *l'écriture féminine*, such as blanks, unfinished sentences, silences, and exclamations. Early female images and goddesses become important as symbols of the power of women to resist and overcome male oppression. Images of motherhood are significant too, for childbearing and rearing involve power and creation. Of course, this approach runs the risk of creating female chauvinists who argue for a special, superior gender. It also risks creating a ghetto in which women's writing stands separate from the male tradition and is thereby weakened.

One such critic who has been influenced by Lacan is Hélène Cixous, who in "The Laugh of the Medusa" (1976) explores the nature of the female unconscious and issues a call for women to put their bodies into their writing. Connecting female writing with Lacan's Real Order, a prelinguistic phase of development characterized by oneness between the child and the mother, she sees women's writing as coming from a primeval space that is free of the elements of Lacan's Symbolic Order, such as the Law of the Father (see Chapter 4). In it, the Voice of the Mother becomes the source of feminine power and writing. Cixous's visionary perspective, which calls upon women to invent their own language, possibly heads toward the terminal marginalization of women's writing, despite the passion with which it is put forth.

Feminists have often reacted negatively (even angrily) to some of Freud's ideas about women—for example, that women suffer from an inevitable penis envy that makes them see themselves as *hommes manqués*. Since Lacan, however, some of these feminists have been able to accept the "phallus" as a symbolic concept, using it as it once was used in ancient fertility cults. From him they take the position that males and females alike lack the wholeness of sexuality of full presence, leaving both with a yearning that can never be filled.

Abigail Adams would not have been able to think of herself in such terms, but throughout her letters it is clear that she looks at life around her and at her own responsibilities in a way that John does not. She is the nurturing caretaker of the family, fulfilling the expected, stereotypical female role. She offers, for example, to copy and send the instructions for the "proportions of the various sorts of powder fit for cannon, small-arms, and pistols" if it would be useful to John.

However, Abigail is more than just a helpmate or facilitator. She is a thinking individual, one who reverses the rational/irrational binary. John engages in a serious conversation with her about "Dunmore," and it is clear that he values her intellectual grasp of the situation. Her accounts of the work she does to maintain the household—making clothes, soap, and perhaps saltpeter—are evidence of the reversal of the active/passive binary often invoked in regard to male/female. She is a hardworking, involved, industrious woman, without whose efforts and energies the family, and by extension the society, could not survive.

Rhetorically, as noted in the discussion of studies of power, Abigail is careful to write what is likely to be pleasing to John. She inquires about his work, reiterates the rightness of the cause for which he is fighting, speaks at length about personal matters, and reveals her own feelings. Her voice is not that of her husband, even when she agrees with his sentiments. It is a distinctly female voice full of concern for others that comes from a particularly personal perspective.

To study the nature of the female personality and experience in literature, you can begin by asking the following questions:

- Where do characters speak with mannerisms that seem to be characteristically female, such as unfinished sentences, silences, exclamations?

- Does the text include images of motherhood or references to goddesses that suggest creativity and power?
- Do you find the female characters conforming to expected norms? Are they nurturing, giving, passive, emotional?
- Are there reversals of the expected norms? Do some female characters take on what are considered to be masculine characteristics?
- According to this work, what does it mean to be female?

Queer theorists might be quick to acknowledge that Abigail and John would themselves espouse an essentialist point of view, but it is also easy to see that the two are clearly products of their day and time, socially constructed beings. They carry out the roles of man and wife, male and female as society expects them to. Even so, Abigail challenges the traditional concept of the essentialist female both by what she says and what she does. The overt appeal appears in her request that John be favorable to "the ladies" in the new code of laws. A more subtle challenge lies in the acts she performs. In his absence, she is running the household, raising the children, providing food and clothing, and, one assumes, handling the family finances. Her performative identity removes her from the role of helpless dependent female and reveals her to be a strong, skillful manager of a complex social unit. She has extended the range of what it means to be female, thereby complicating its meaning as well.

WRITING FEMINIST CRITICISM

For those readers who are interested in examining issues concerning women and literature but who do not have a defined agenda to follow or promote, making a feminist reading of a male author's text (which includes most of the canon) involves realizing from the outset that it is **androcentric** and then resisting that point of view. It means not necessarily reading from a traditionally male perspective. In a similar way, queer theory critics recognize and resist a heterosexual point of view. How does that resistance take place? For a female feminist reader, it involves consciously refusing to reverse her role (that is, take on a male one) in order to identify with a male protagonist or to share a male point of view of a narrative. Instead of assuming that the masculine point of view, system of values, or manner of thinking is the universal norm, she will recognize that there is an alternative perspective: a woman's. Without such realization, the female reader finds herself in a double bind. She is expected to identify with the male perspective while being reminded that to be male is not feminine. For a male feminist reader, it means adopting a new and possibly surprising perspective—that of trying to experience the narrative through the lens of the opposite gender. Of course, making a feminist reading of a feminist text means using a different approach. Instead of resisting, the reader will try to connect, try to find commonality and community.

A feminist reader will also look for new female writers, as well as help revive interest in forgotten or ignored ones. A study by Nina Baym showed that as late as 1977, the American canon of major writers did not include a single female novelist, even though female novelists have been a significant force in the field since the mid-nineteenth century. An androcentric canon generates androcentric interpretation, which leads to canonization of androcentric texts and the exclusion of gynocentric ones. The feminist reader will try to reverse that process by asserting the quality of texts produced by particular female writers, finding and promoting undervalued writers from the past, questioning the values that underlie literary acceptance, and defining a female tradition of letters. She will also make alternative readings of traditional works.

Prewriting

If you have the opportunity to choose the text you will examine for your feminist critique, you may want to select something by a female writer, especially if the work has not already received a good bit of notice from feminist critics. An alternative, especially if you are reading from the perspective of queer theory, is to choose a text in which identity is not assumed to be fixed. Regardless of the selection you are working on, you will initially find it helpful to focus on the characters in the text, as they are an easily accessible indication of the author's attitudes and ideology. Some of the questions you can ask include the following:

- What stereotypes of women do you find? Are they oversimplified, demeaning, untrue? For example, are all blondes understood to be dumb?
- Examine the roles women play in a work. Are they minor, supportive, powerless, obsequious? Or are they independent and influential?
- Is the narrator a character in the narrative? If so, how does the male or female point of view affect the reader's perceptions?
- How do the male characters talk about the female characters?
- How do the male characters treat the female characters?
- How do the female characters act toward the male characters?
- Who are the socially and politically powerful characters?
- What attitudes toward women are suggested by the answers to these questions?
- Do the answers to these questions indicate that the work lends itself more naturally to a study of differences between the male and female characters, a study of power imbalances between the sexes (or perhaps other groups), or a study of unique female experience?
- Can any characters be viewed not simply as male or female but as a collection of many possible sexualities? That is, do they exhibit various degrees of heterosexuality, homosexuality, or bisexuality?
- Is sexuality assumed to be stable and static or dynamic and changing?
- Is the sexuality of the characters affected by the experience of race and class?
- Is heterosexuality viewed as the norm against which other sexual identities are measured?

Drafting and Revising

Once you have determined which of the three approaches you want to follow, or how they work together to form the text, you can begin drafting your analysis.

The Introduction One interesting way to open your discussion is to point out why a feminist or queer theory critique is particularly appropriate for the text you are analyzing. For example, many established works have acquired traditional readings that can be challenged from a new point of view. You can easily explain that you intend to show why the accepted understanding is not the only possibility. In the case of the letters exchanged by John and Abigail Adams, for example, a feminist explanation would point out that it is his writings that are ordinarily examined by historians, not hers. Because she presents a different perspective on some of the same incidents and experiences he observed, her writings also deserve attention. Other rationales for a feminist or queer theory analysis may lie in the characters, the situation, the cultural context in which a text was produced, or the author. Whatever your reason for making a reading based on feminist theory or queer theory, explaining why it is a fitting one will help your reader follow the analysis more easily.

An alternative beginning is to connect the characters or events of the situation with a similar situation that has actually occurred. Because many critics see literature as a way to understand and reform society, making such a connection can be powerful.

The Body Because feminist studies serve so many different interests, your discussion can take a variety of approaches. To simplify your decision making, you can try working within one of the three categories discussed earlier: studies of difference, studies of power, or studies of the female experience. You may want to apply the principles of queer theory by asking some of the questions listed earlier. Of course, these are overlapping areas of attention, but you will probably want to center your analysis in one of them.

If the issue of gender differences attracts your attention, you will almost certainly want to select a work by a female writer for your study, because you will be looking for what makes a female text different from one written by a male. You can ask questions such as the following:

- Is the genre one that is traditionally associated with male or female writers?
- Is the subject one that is of particular interest to women, perhaps one that is of importance to women's lives?
- What one-word label would accurately capture the voice of the narrator? Why is it appropriate?
- Is the work sympathetic to female characters?
- Are the female characters and the situations in which they are placed presented with complexity and in detail?
- How does the language differ from what you would expect from a writer of the opposite gender?

- How does the way the female characters talk influence the reader's perception of them?
- What are the predominant images? Why are they (or why are they not) associated with women's lives?
- Does the implied audience of the work include or exclude women? In the case of a male writer, is the work addressed to a mixed audience, or does it sound more like one man telling a story to another man?
- How do the answers to these questions support a case for this work's having been written in a particularly masculine or feminine style?

If you are interested in the relationships of the characters or in how things get done in the world of the text, you will probably investigate the balance (or imbalance) of power depicted in it. The following questions can help you arrive at some conclusions. Some of these questions are similar to those you asked during your prewriting.

- Who is primarily responsible for making decisions in the world depicted: men or women?
- Do the female characters play an overt part in decision making? Or do they work behind the scenes?
- Who holds positions of authority and influence?
- Who controls the finances?
- Do the female characters play traditional female roles? Or do they assume some unusual ones?
- Are there any instances in which women are unfairly treated or ill treated?
- What kind of accomplishments do the female characters achieve?
- Are the female characters honored for their accomplishments?
- Do the male characters consult the female characters before taking action, or do they merely inform them of it?
- Does the story approve or disapprove, condemn or glorify, the power structure as revealed by your answers to these questions?
- How is the female reader co-opted into accepting or rejecting the images of women presented in the work?

You may be interested in examining how the unique female experience is captured in the work you are to analyze. If so, you will want to consider questions like the following:

- Does the text reject the idea of a male norm of thinking and behavior that is stable and unchanging? If so, where?
- Is the writer's style characterized by blanks, gaps, silences, or circularity?
- Are images of the female body important in the text?
- Do you find references to female diseases or bodily functions?

- Do motherhood, or those attitudes and behaviors characteristic of motherhood, figure significantly in the text?
- Can you find instances in which the traditional binaries of male/female, intellectual/emotional, objective/subjective, and active/passive are reversed?
- What new circumstances do the reversals suggest?
- Can you find instances in which wholeness rather than otherness is associated with the female characters?
- What generalizations about the uniqueness of the female experience can you make based on the answers to these questions?

The Conclusion The end of your paper is an appropriate place to state the generalizations and conclusions drawn from your questions. It should pull all of your references to the text into a single statement about what is particularly female (or male) about the way the work was written, about the power relationships depicted in it, or about its presentation of the nature of the female experience.

SUGGESTED READING

Abelove, Henry, Michèle Aina Barale, and David Halperin, eds. *Lesbian and Gay Studies Reader.* New York: Routledge, 1993.

Barrett, Michèle. *Women's Oppression Today: Problems in Marxist Feminist Analysis.* London: NLB, 1980.

Beauvoir, Simone de. *The Second Sex.* Trans. H. M. Parshley. New York: Knopf, 1993.

Braidotta, Rosi. *Nomadic Subjects.* New York: Columbia University Press, 1994.

Butler, Judith. *Gender Trouble: Feminism and the Subversion of Identity.* New York: Routledge, 1999.

Chodorow, Nancy. *The Reproduction of Mothering: Psychoanalysis and the Sociology of Gender.* Berkeley: University of California Press, 1999.

Cixous, Hélène. " The Laugh of the Medusa." *Signs* 1(1976): 875–93.

Fetterly, Judith. *The Resisting Reader: A Feminist Approach to American Fiction.* Bloomington: Indiana University Press, 1978.

Friedan, Betty. *The Feminine Mystique.* New York: Norton, 2001.

Gates, Henry Louis, Jr., ed. *Reading Black, Reading Feminist: A Critical Anthology.* New York: Meridian, 1990.

Gilbert, Sandra M., and Susan Gubar. *The Madwoman in the Attic: The Woman Writer and the Nineteenth-Century Literary Imagination.* 2nd ed. New Haven, CT: Yale University Press, 2000.

Green, Gayle, and Coppélia Kahn, eds. *Making a Difference: Feminist Literary Criticism.* New York: Routledge, 1991.

Greer, Germaine. *The Female Eunuch.* New York: Farrar, Straus and Giroux, 2001.

Gubar, Susan. *Critical Condition: Feminism at the Turn of the Century*. New York: Columbia University Press, 2000.

Heilbrun, Carolyn. *Hamlet's Mother and Other Women*. New York: Columbia University Press, 1990.

Jackson, Stevi, and Sue Scott, eds. *Feminism and Sexuality*. New York: Columbia University Press, 1996.

Meese, Elizabeth. *Crossing the Double-Cross: The Practice of Feminist Criticism*. Chapel Hill: University of North Carolina Press, 1986.

Millett, Kate. *Sexual Politics*. Urbana: University of Illinois Press, 2000.

Sedgwick, Eve. *Epistemology of the Closet*. Berkeley: University of California Press, 1990.

Showalter, Elaine, ed. *The New Feminist Criticism: Essays on Women, Literature, and Theory*. New York: Pantheon, 1985.

Warner, Michael, ed. *Fear of a Queer Planet: Queer Politics and Social Theory*. Minneapolis: University of Minnesota Press, 1993.

Wollstonecraft, Mary. *A Vindication of the Rights of Woman*. New York: Penguin Books, 2006.

Woolf, Virginia. *A Room of One's Own*. Orlando, FL: Harcourt, 2005.

For up-to-date information on the many Web sites addressing feminist and queer theory critical approaches, visit www.cengagebrain.com.

Model Student Analysis

The Road from Mother: A Daughter's Struggle

CINDY CHILDRESS

One of the dominant themes in Jill Ker Conway's autobiography, *The Road From Coorain* (1989), is the writer's attempt to detach herself from her mother. This theme is important because the form it takes in the text deviates from the traditional style of autobiography, contributing to a distinctly female mode of self-writing in which the daughter's autobiography contains her mother's biography. I read the struggle for authority between these genres within the text, opening it to interpretation of the mother/daughter struggle for identity. This struggle is particularly interesting, given feminist psychoanalyst Nancy Chodorow's theory that daughters do not fully individuate from their mothers. The autobiographer, however, represents both the interrelation with her mother and a painful wrenching away from her, and she works to reconcile her feminist leanings with abandoning her mother, which is necessary for survival yet fraught with contradiction.

Ker Conway says in an interview with C-SPAN's Brian Lamb that she wrote *The Road from Coorain* in a self-conscious attempt to fulfill the goal of second-wave feminists, which was to tell women's stories, providing new narratives and prototypes for women's ways of being, and to tell the truth about women's lives. This agenda was undertaken in the 1960s and 1970s by female confessional poets, but women's autobiographies had remained comparatively stifled by the genre's masculine conventions. As Patricia Spacks and others have noted, for centuries when women wrote about themselves, they wrote either religious conversion narratives or self-effacing narratives that enlarged their failures while diminishing their successes and the work it took to make them happen (Spacks 112–132). All this changed with women's autobiographies in the 1980s and early 1990s, as Audre Lorde, Kim Chernin, and their contemporaries revolutionized the genre of self-writing by creating a space for feminine forms within it—a space inhabited by *The Road from Coorain.*

Carolyn Heilbrun suggests in *Writing Women's Lives* (1989) that one way in which women's self-writing is different from men's is that women acknowledge the others in their lives, so that female autobiographers' identities are linked to those of others (24). In reading Ker Conway's autobiography, however, I was struck by the degree to which the story of her life is enmeshed in that of her mother, so that in narrating her life, the writer also tells a cautionary counter tale about her mother. Heilbrun's work does not focus exclusively on the role of the mother in self-writing, but criticism that builds upon Heilbrun's work seizes upon her idea and expands it to explore the dynamic between the writer/ daughter and her mother.

Jo Malin offers the most thorough examination of the mother/daughter relationship as it appears in women's autobiography. She suggests,

> Every woman autobiographer is a daughter who writes and establishes her identity through her autobiographical narrative. Many twentieth-century autobiographical texts by women contain an intertext, an embedded narrative, which is a biography of the writer/daughter's mother. (1)

The existence of the two genres—autobiography and biography—in the one hybrid text shows a resistance to the dominant literary tradition of male autobiography, which is monologic—that is to say, it has one authoritative voice (9). The writer then "not only 'thinks' her mother's story … but her [the writer's] voice and her mother's voice are dialogic" in the text (11). The dialogue is established as the mother becomes the "biographical protagonist," and as such, her voice engages the "autobiographical protagonist" voice; as the text alternates between voices, their stories vie for meaning.

The daughter's representation of her mother's embedded biographical narrative may or may not be accurate or fair. Tess Cosslett notices that there are problems with the autobiographer writing her mother's story, because "the mother being dead, or so far estranged, or of a different culture" can't respond (141). Cosslett notes that writers are "often ready to attribute thoughts and feelings for their mothers, to speak for them," which leads to a situation of speaking for a silent other, which has patriarchal ramifications (141). The ways in which Ker Conway's autobiography is in conversation with her mother's embedded biography are telling; for instance, the mother's first name and maiden name are never revealed, suggesting that even as Ker Conway seeks to free her mother of the patriarchal codes that robbed her of identity, she may fare little better in Ker Conway's autobiography. On the other hand, just as Virginia Woolf critiques nineteenth-century biographies for being biased toward progress and patriarchy in *A Room of One's Own* (1921), so might Ker Conway's writing her mother's story contain biases relevant to her proclaimed feminist agenda. And the narrative begins as though this might be the case.

She describes her mother as a "New Woman" in that she was a nurse and lived independently until her late twenties, when she married the author's father. The two settle on a sheep farm called Coorain in a remote part of the Australian bush. Deprived of social activities and a job, her mother focuses her energy on domestic tasks and reading. The descriptions of her mothering reveal a desire to liberate her daughter from gender stereotypes (when her brother hits Ker Conway and she hits him back, her mother approves), but in doing so enforces masculine traits, including reining in emotion to the point of being forbidden to cry when her father dies. I share the writer's value that her mother should have allowed healthy mourning to occur, and yet through the counter narrative of her mother's biography, I understand that because of her own oppressive childhood experiences, the mother thinks her daughter needs to minimize traditionally feminine traits to survive the harsh, male public sphere.

Chodorow postulates that in Western society, the female child has a "continued identification with her mother," whereas the male child is encouraged early to identify himself against, not with, his mother. This becomes relevant to women's self-writing, because we see the adult daughter struggling against, while also perpetuating, her identification with her mother. Ker Conway describes a scene that occurred before her father's death in which the three of them are at the dinner table when the farm is failing; she feels that both parents depend upon her good behavior and success to redeem their lives. This feeling intensifies after his death, as her mother increasingly depends upon Ker Conway to care for her emotional needs, reversing the mother-daughter roles. As she explains, her mother "found sleeping alone a nightmare, and ... said she needed my company in her bed. After that it was I who had trouble resting, for she clung to me like a drowning person" (75). This image is apt to describe their relationship throughout the book.

One way that the mother clings is through her daughter's financial dependence. Although Ker Conway gives a realistic depiction of the hard work her mother did in order to provide opportunities and material goods, such as working two jobs so Ker Conway might attend a private school, those gifts are depicted as having strings attached. When the family's finances improve, they visit Europe. Upon returning home, her mother constantly nags the writer and her brother; the writer then realizes "that my mother's gifts came at a considerable price ... There would come a time afterward when they would have to be earned" (135). The power dynamic of money yokes mother to daughter, suggesting that maternal love is not unconditional but may be withheld to elicit certain attitudes and behaviors in the daughter. The mother manipulates her daughter's emotions by making her feel unworthy of her mother's generosity and love in order to make Ker Conway stay at home all the time, forsake her friends, and indulge her mother's increasingly violent fits of anger.

Another misfortune of the continued identification between mother and daughter is that mothers often relive their lives through their daughters. As she would have liked to do herself, Ker Conway's mother was determined that her daughter attend college. The writer records the experience thus: "Each day she asked me hungrily what I was learning, hoping to live out her thwarted longing for education through me." Her disappointment with the answers reminded her daughter "that at my age she had already been working and supporting herself for many years. If I ever mentioned needing more pocket money for train fares, she raised her eyebrows ... and changed the subject" (158). The author begins to achieve autonomy from her mother by getting a job and being able to buy her own clothes, at which point she wears things her mother disapproves of and yet earns her respect for making a living.

Cosslett warns against the "mythologizing" tendency of daughters toward their mothers, which usually results in a failure to investigate the elder's material circumstance (149). Ker Conway, however, takes pains to explore her mother's past by paying attention to her working-class home life and limited education.

A decade before second-wave feminists such as Adrienne Rich and Betty Friedan critiqued their suburban housewife lives, Ker Conway critiqued her mother's similar situation; as Ker Conway grew up, she witnessed her mother being prescribed sedatives as a solution for depression and boredom— a chemical dependence that morphed into alcoholism. While observing the older woman's deterioration, the writer says she "would place beside her [mother] in my mind's eye the young competent woman" she had once been (195). The author continues describing her impression of her mother's situation thus:

> I was living with a tragic deterioration brought about because there was no creative expression for this woman's talents. Lacking a power for good, she sought power through manipulating her children.... She, once a rebel, had acquiesced in settling down to live the life of an affluent woman. Society encouraged a woman to think her life finished after her husband's death and encouraged a woman's emotional dependence on her children. (195)

Rather than mythologizing, Ker Conway seems to demythologize, situating her mother in the historical circumstance of overly medicated and disgruntled 1950s housewives. The writer positions herself to escape from that household and her mother's fate therein when her acceptance to Harvard allows her to leave her mother and motherland for the United States. However, she describes leaving her mother not as a success, as one might frame leaving a tyrant, but rather as acceptance of defeat—a lacking of fortitude and even violating "the code of my forefathers" by not standing by her deteriorated mother (232).

Although she physically distances herself from her mother, Ker Conway remains mired in her identification with the older woman, resolving that "the only way I could pay her respect now would be through some sublimated expression of my guilt, generalized toward caring for all frustrated and angry older women" (237). By transferring the debt she feels she owes her mother onto other women, Ker Conway identifies her status as daughter within a larger network of women, which also opens opportunities to identify with healthier models of womanhood. The tragedy of her mother's biographical narrative gives birth then to her daughter's heroic autobiographical one, a double tale of women's selfhood that is only possible within the female mode of self-writing.

WORKS CITED

Cosslett, Tess. "Matrilineal Narratives Revisited." In *Feminism and Autobiography: Texts, Theories, Methods*. Eds. Tess Cosslett, Celia Lury, and Penny Summerfield. New York: Routledge, 2000.

Heilbrun, Carolyn. *Writing a Woman's Life*. New York: Ballantine Books, 1988.

Ker Conway, Jill. *The Road from Coorain*. New York: Knopf, 1989.

Lamb, Brian. Interview with Jill Ker Conway. Book Notes. C-SPAN. 24 May 1998. May 2007 <http://www.booknotes.org/Transcript /?ProgramID=1414>.

Malin, J. *The Voice of the Mother: Embedded Maternal Narratives in Twentieth-Century Women's Autobiography*. Carbondale: Southern Illinois University Press, 2000.

7

Reader-Response Criticism

'Tis the good reader that makes the good book.
RALPH WALDO EMERSON, AMERICAN ESSAYIST, POET, PHILOSOPHER

The name *reader-response* tells the story. This approach to literary criticism turns the spotlight on the reader, without whose attention and reactions the text would be inert and meaningless. In one sense, the work would not exist at all. It would be like the proverbial tree that makes no sound when it falls because there is nobody there to hear it.

HISTORICAL BACKGROUND

Readers have always responded to what they read, of course. But with the advent of reader-response analysis, the worst fears of the formalists came true: The audience was expected to shake off its deference to the authority of the text (or to the published critic's or classroom teacher's explanation of the text) and become an active participant in the creation of meaning. The focus moved away from thinking of a work as a self-contained aesthetic object to considering the experience that transpires when the reader and the work come together. No longer could any reading be taken as unbiased and objective. The reader had moved to center stage.

The ancient Greek orators and rhetoricians, with their concern for how to move and persuade an audience, could be called the literary ancestors of today's reader-response theorists. Both Plato and Aristotle were aware of the power of words to stir or convince people, though they did not hold the same opinions about the impact of doing so. Whereas the former had serious misgivings about using literature to arouse people's emotions, the latter recognized in it the capacity to quiet and strengthen an audience, as, for example, a tragedy can effect a catharsis that cleanses people of debilitating feelings and attitudes. Aristotle also explored the many ways in which an argument can be made convincing to listeners. He thereby influenced Longinus, Cicero, Quintilian, and other rhetoricians to this day in making choices about organization and style, so that what they have to say will appeal to a particular group of people.

The more recent lineage of reader-response critics can be traced to the work of I. A. Richards in the 1920s and Louise Rosenblatt in the 1930s. Richards, recognizing the wide variety of interpretations a group of readers is likely to have for a single work, asked his students at Cambridge University to write responses to short poems so that he could analyze their approaches. At that point, however, Richards backed away from becoming a fully developed reader-response theorist, because he categorized his students' reactions according to their "accuracy." That is, he ranked the reactions according to their closeness to or distance from what he deemed to be the correct interpretation.

Rosenblatt, who was largely ignored by readers pursuing formalist principles of criticism when her first works were published, offered a "transactional" theory of reading. As she explained it, a given text is not always read in the same way. Instead, readings vary with the purpose, needs, experiences, and concerns of the reader, who adopts a "stance" toward a text, an attitude that determines what signals to respond to, so that certain results can be achieved. The two opposing stances are the "efferent" one, in which the reader concentrates on information to be extracted from the writing, and the "aesthetic," which involves senses, feelings, and intuitions about "what is being lived through during the reading event." According to Rosenblatt, a piece of literature comes into being when it receives an aesthetic reading, which is produced by a merging of reader and text. As Rosenblatt explained in *The Reader, the Text, the Poem* (1978), "At the aesthetic end of the spectrum, . . . the reader's primary purpose is fulfilled *during* the reading event, as he fixes his attention on the actual experience he is living through. This permits the whole range of responses generated by the text to enter into the center of awareness, and out of these materials he selects and weaves what he sees as the literary work of art."

The early work of Richards and Rosenblatt received renewed attention with the appearance of Walker Gibson and Wayne Booth, who, around the mid-twentieth century, raised questions about the roles readers play. Gibson, pointing out that a text asks a reader to become what he called a "mock reader," reintroduced the reader who becomes a participant in the creative act by playing the role the writer has designed for him or her. The issue of where and how meaning is created thereby reemerged as a significant concern among literary theorists. Booth recognized that a writer controls a reader through rhetorical strategies, but he did not go so far as to give readers the principal responsibility for making meaning. The question, simply put, had become, Does the interpretation of a text depend primarily on the reader, the text itself (which can manipulate the reader), or a combination of the two? Further questions then ensued: What is a text? Is the reader the book holder, the reader conceptualized by the writer, or an ideal reader?

Reader-response critics do not answer such questions with a single voice. In fact, their approaches cover such a wide variety of concerns that sometimes the term *reader-response* seems to refer to a chaotic jumble of theories that may or may not have anything to do with each other. They do, however, agree on a few basic principles, the most important of which is the effect that a work has on a reader and the strategies that produce that effect. Interpretation of meaning is assumed to be an act of reading, thereby making the ultimate authority not the writer or the text but the reader. A literary work thus becomes an evolving creation, as it is possible for there to be many interpretations of the same text by different readers or several interpretations by a single reader at different times. As Wolfgang Iser explained in *The Act of Reading* (1978), "The significance of the work, then, does not lie in the meaning sealed within the text, but in the fact that that meaning brings out what had previously been sealed within us."

The result? When readers accept the assumption that there is no one true interpretation, they discover rich, complex, diverse possibilities. When they recognize that there is no right or wrong answer but instead a variety of readings that grow out of individual experiences and feelings, literature becomes alive for them. When their own lives intersect with the text, that text takes on vitality. According to Rosenblatt, "The reader brings to the work personality traits, memories of past events, present needs and preoccupations, a particular mood of the moment, and a particular physical condition." A reader's experience is determined by "these and many other elements in a never-to-be-duplicated combination." The effect is not limited to the understanding of a text, however. It extends to the understanding of the self as well. Because reader-response criticism calls for introspection and reflection on one's own values and beliefs, it can lead the reader to deeper personal knowledge and greater cultural awareness.

Not surprisingly, some critics object to the intense subjectivity of such an approach. If a poem can have as many meanings as it has readers, they ask, can there be any shared experience of it? Can there be an intellectual discussion of it? Others complain that digressions into self-analysis diminish textual analysis. It makes the reader's life, rather than the literary work, the primary focus of attention. Though such arguments may have some merit, there is little doubt that, in the end, a reader-response analysis powerfully engages readers to move analytically both inward and outward, finding meaning in the text, the self, and the world.

It should be noted that in the 1960s, another, somewhat different, form of reader-response criticism emerged that asked the critic to examine the public's response to authors and works during a particular era. Known as **reception theory**, it recognizes that readers in different historical periods are not likely to interpret or judge a given work in precisely the same way, and that as literary fashions and interests change, the characteristics that find favor in one century may be disparaged in the next. The receptionists peruse newspaper articles, study magazine reviews, and read personal letters to find evidence of how the public once viewed written material. They try to determine the expectations that readers were likely to have had at a given time, based on the receptionists' understanding of genres, works, and language. They look for what Hans Robert Jauss called the **horizon of expectations** of the reading public—that is, what readers valued and looked for in a work.

The focus of the receptionists is easily understood by considering works that at some point in time were rejected by the reading public but were held in high esteem at other times. For example, Kate Chopin's *The Awakening*, today a popular and frequently taught novel, was given a hostile reception by the critics of her day. Her depiction of Edna Pontellier, a woman who remained unapologetic for her sensuality, was called "trite and sordid," and the author and the novel were deemed to be unacceptable in polite society. The America of a century ago was not ready to admit such a frank portrayal of female desire and indulgence; its horizon of expectation did not include stories of such behavior. Sometimes this process is reversed, and a work that is well received early on receives negative criticism later. Mark Twain's *Huckleberry Finn,* for instance, has had the curious history of being alternately revered and castigated as readers in different eras proclaimed it to be sensitive or insensitive to various social issues.

The receptionists, whose work leads to interesting inferences about readers, authors, and their works, cannot make a final evaluation of the worth of a poem or story, because they demonstrate how its appeal may change from one time to another. Instead, they engage the past in a dialogue with the present, helping readers view the work from contrasting historical and cultural perspectives.

MAKING A READER'S RESPONSE

To understand the discussion that follows, you should read the short story "The Masque of the Red Death," by Edgar Allan Poe, which begins on page 338.

Getting Started

For some people, a reader-response approach is startlingly different from the approach they are accustomed to taking. Instead of memorizing historical information, recognizing literary forms and techniques, or learning a prescribed interpretation, you will be asked to look inside and around yourself for ways to make the work meaningful.

Interacting with the Text

Although the focus is always on the reader, there are several ways of thinking about the relationship he or she has with the text. Rosenblatt describes two of them, then advocates letting the two work together in an approach that she calls **transactional analysis**. As she explains it, in "the actual reading event," the reader interprets the text (the reader acts on the text), or the text produces a response in the reader (the text acts on the reader). However, each of these phrasings, because it implies a single line of action by one separate element on another separate element, distorts the actual reading process. In the end, the relationship between reader and text is not linear. It is a situation, an event at a particular time and place in which each element conditions the other.

In preparation for making a transactional analysis— one that shows how reader and text come together to create meaning—it will be helpful to consider how the two "linear" processes work; that is, to consider separately, for a moment, how the text controls the reader and how the reader makes the text.

The Text Acts on the Reader When you examine how a text controls the reader's responses, you acknowledge that the text is a powerful manipulator. As Henry James once commented, "In every novel the work is divided between the writer and the reader; but the writer makes the reader very much as he makes his characters."

To examine a text by looking for how it produces certain effects on a reader means to look at it in much the same way that the group of critics known as the **structuralists** do (see Chapter 8). Both reader-response critics and the structuralists assume that because readers come to a work with a certain literary competence, or what Jonathan Culler called a set of shared reading conventions, they recognize signals that they are accustomed to finding there. They then use those signals to make the expected interpretation. Both groups know how they are expected to respond, and they react accordingly. They use the familiar cues to make new interpretations. Thus, looking at the text to see how it causes readers to react in certain ways involves asking how the codes, signs, signals, and rules work together to produce meaning. It entails examining the relationships among the parts in an effort to define the system—known as the **grammar**—that governs them. The able reader recognizes the grammar because of her own life experiences and her reading background.

If the meaning of a text is recognizable because "informed" readers know the accepted conventions that underlie it, then a work cannot be subject to an infinite number of interpretations. This means that it is less important for readers to record their personal responses than it is to make generalizations about how interpretation is governed by the system under which the text was written. Although critics who have a structuralist bent recognize that different readers will produce different interpretations, they focus on the regularities they find in readers' strategies. Such generalizations also extend beyond the text in question, for the text is not autonomous; it exists in the context of other texts, with which it shares common elements and, hence, meanings.

It is important to realize that sometimes an author can use recognizable conventions to "fool" the reader. As Stanley Fish pointed out in *Surprised by Sin* (1998), a text can use predictable responses, such as the expectations typically evoked by a particular genre, to cause readers to make interpretations that later prove to be wrong. Consequently, readers must be sophisticated enough to make adjustments to their interpretations as needed.

If you are primarily interested in how the text controls your response, you will want to examine how it shows you what you should be thinking and feeling as it unfolds. This may involve considering the author's intention and how it was carried out. Certainly it will entail looking closely at each element of the work for what it implies about the reader's behavior.

In "The Masque of the Red Death," for example, the reader gradually moves from enjoyment of (and vicarious participation in) the lighthearted revelries of the courtiers to "unutterable horror" at the final "dominion" of the Red Death. The isolation of the setting, the images of silence and darkness, and the diction ("gaudy," "fantastic," "blood-tinted panes," "ghastly," "grotesque," "delirious fancies," "bizarre") imply a world in which madness is the norm and the supernatural rules. Indeed, every component of the story—plot structure, patterns of expectation and satisfaction or expectation and disappointment, characterization, revelations and reversals, contrasting elements, image, symbol, figurative language, tone—contributes to the mounting uneasiness and final terror experienced by the reader. Consider, for example, the description of the rooms, one small element of the tale. The progress through each of the seven (a magical number) chambers disquiets the reader. The rooms are "irregularly disposed," we are told, with a "sharp turn at every twenty or thirty yards." Their colors, repeated in the stained glass windows to produce a claustrophobic effect, move in a disturbing sequence—from blue to purple, then green, orange, white, violet, and finally black—that is accentuated by windowpanes of "scarlet—a deep blood color." It is a sequence that begins with suggested innocence (blue) and ends in mystery and death (black and blood color). Or consider the effect of the contrasting sounds in the story. We are told, for example, that "the wild music of the orchestra" and light laughter of the dancers are interrupted when the hour is "stricken" (a word that carries the suggestion of illness) by the ebony clock, which has a sound that is "clear and loud and deep and exceedingly musical, but of so peculiar a note and emphasis that . . . the giddiest grew pale." The sound of the clock is made even more ominous by its contrast with the jovial noises of the partygoers and its effect on them. All the information given is disposed to create in the reader a sense of the fantastic that is threatening and dangerous.

To examine how a text controls a reader's response, you will find it helpful to ask questions such as these:

- What did the author intend for you to feel while reading this work, and how did he or she make you feel it?
- What are you dependent on in this work to help you make sense of what you read—descriptive passages, the narrator's voice, contrasting viewpoints of characters?
- Do the events fall into a pattern you have met before?
- Are there opposites in the text that surprise you? Inform you? Keep you from anticipating what is coming?
- How do your previous experiences with this genre set up your expectations for how this text will operate?
- What images and events in the story are you already conditioned to approve or disapprove?
- How does the point of view affect (or control) your understanding?
- What information has been withheld from you? How does that affect your inferences?
- What similarities do you recognize between this work and other works—for example, in terms of themes, setting, characters?

- How does the text call upon what you know of the world to produce your response to the work?
- Did the work cause you to make interpretations that you had to revise later?
- What events or experiences were you led to anticipate? What mysteries were you asked to solve? What judgments were you expected to make?

The Reader Acts on the Text When the focus is turned directly on the reader as the chief source of interpretation, all of your thoughts, experiences, fantasies, and beliefs play a part in creating meaning. You will bring to a text a multitude of qualities that are yours alone: expectations, prejudices, stock responses, values, personal experiences, gender, age, past readings, even the circumstances of the present reading. These forces, according to Norman Holland, make a given work serve "highly personal, even idiosyncratic ends."

According to Holland, who uses psychology to explain the process of reading, each of us receives a "primary identity" from our mother. It is our understanding of the kind of person we are. Because an "identity theme," like a musical theme, can have variations even as it remains central to our being, when we read, we play our identity theme by re-creating the text in our own image. We "use the literary work to symbolize and finally replicate ourselves." As we do so, we find the means to cope with fears and desires buried in our own psyches. Consequently, responses vary just as personalities do. No two people will work through a text in the same way or arrive at the same point of understanding. That is not to say that a text lacks its own themes and structure. Nevertheless, any interpretation of them is, in the end, subjective.

David Bleich bases his case for the reader's importance on the denials of modern scientists, such as Thomas Kuhn, that an objective world of facts exists. Because what is observed is inevitably changed by the circumstances of the observation, there can be no knowledge except subjective knowledge. Bleich, applying such theories to literature, argues that a text does not exist outside its readers, who are the observers. Whatever is offered as an "objective" analysis actually has roots in a personal response, for instead of discovering meaning in a text, readers develop meaning for it. The process begins with the individual but is subsequently shaped communally through question, challenge, and amendment in a group setting. What becomes known as fact (the meaning that is developed) depends, he says, on the community's needs.

Stanley Fish, calling his approach *affective stylistics,* argues that readers create a text as they read it—word by word and sentence by sentence. He is interested in how readers' responses develop as the words and sentences succeed each other one by one—that is, how the style affects the reader. Fish describes interpretation as the product of **interpretive communities**, or groups of informed, linguistically competent readers who read and make meaning based on assumptions and strategies that they hold in common. He denies the existence of an individual, subjective response, because, as he points out, we have all internalized interpretive strategies based on assumptions about literature that have come to us from our institutions and cultural groups. We may belong to more than one such community. As Fish explains the process, a reader does not make an individual response that is altered by negotiation with others' responses; instead, she makes a response that, from its inception, is the product of a wider community of readers who share certain assumptions about how a text is read. In these terms, readers do not interpret a text. They create it.

In the case of "The Masque of the Red Death," your response can be affected by a number of forces that lie completely outside the text. If you have already read a number of stories by Poe, you will probably begin this one expecting something out of the ordinary, probably something mysterious and scary. Anticipation based on experience will predispose you to accept a confrontation with the fantastic. Once you begin to read, you will notice that much is not told. Despite the seemingly detailed descriptions of the castle apartments, for instance, the reader is left to supply the exact images mentioned only as a "multitude of gaudy and fantastic appearances" created by the tripod "bearing a brazier of fire" and the visual outlines of the "glare and glitter and piquancy and phantasm" of the great fete. The way they take shape for you will depend on other fiction you have read, movies you have seen, or possibly places you have been. Your impression may be altered even by where you read this story—perhaps at home alone late at night or in the school library's browsing room on a sunny spring morning.

When so much importance is placed on individual responses or those of interpretive communities, it almost seems as if a text can mean anything a reader says it means. It is critical to remember, then, that "wrong" readings can exist even when the reader is using the reader-response model. Mistaking one word for another or misunderstanding the definition of a word, for example, can lead a reader to make inferences that are clearly off the mark. Although a variety of interpretations of a single work are possible using this approach, some simply will not fit. To make sure your interpretation is on point, ask yourself how much of it includes various features of the text and how much of it deals with aspects that do not reflect the text.

The following questions can help you discover your role in creating the texts you read:

- What did you expect to feel while reading this work?
- What was unsettling in what you read?
- How did you adapt to what made you uncomfortable so that it more clearly fit what you desired?
- With what or whom did you most closely identify in the work? What identification gave you the most pleasure? The most displeasure?
- Did the work fit your picture of the way life is?
- What adjustments did you have to make so that the work did not challenge the world as you know it?
- What does the work fail to tell you about characters and/or events? What imaginary or personal material did you use to supply what was missing?
- What memories does this work recall for you?

- Can you be sure you have not simply misread a passage—for example, by making a vocabulary mistake?
- If you reread this work using a different critical strategy, how would it become a different work?

The Transactional Model In practice, most reader-response critics do not think singly about how a text affects the reader or how a reader creates the text. Instead, they tend to apply both perspectives interactively. They work from the assumption that it is in the meeting of the two shapers of meaning that literature is created. As Rosenblatt argued, "'The poem' cannot be equated solely with either the text or the experience of a reader"; instead, it is the relationship that exists between them. The former serves as a pattern that controls what the reader can make of it. The latter is called upon to fill in gaps to hypothesize, imagine, and, in general, be a coproducer of the text. The poem (or the story) is created by the transaction that occurs between the two creators. As a result, new readings of a given text are always possible, and yet a text cannot mean whatever a given reader chooses to think it means. Any reading must be true to the work and to the reader.

Another way of explaining the interaction of reader and text was offered by Wolfgang Iser, a German **phenomenologist** who argued that it is impossible to separate anything from the mind that knows it. That makes the reader and text cocreators of meaning. A literary work, Iser said, is an intended act of the writer's consciousness, an artistic effort that is then reexperienced in the consciousness of a reader, who engages in an aesthetic endeavor. The text supplies the materials and determines the boundaries for the creative act of reading. It creates for itself an **implied reader** and uses certain structures to predispose the actual reader, who brings his own unique set of experiences to the act of reading the text, to respond as the implied one. (Both are competent to decode the text.) The text engages "the reader's imagination in the task of working things out for himself." As readers give life to the material presented by the text, as they deal with its "indeterminacy," which is created by the missing material and information, they influence the effect of what has been written. If the work is successful, it supplies neither too much nor too little but simply guides readers through to self-discovery.

If Poe's story pulled you through the series of lurid chambers to the final acknowledgment of the presence of the Red Death, leaving you hardly breathing, eyes fixed intently on each line, then the story worked for you. You recognized that you were to be an imaginative reader who was able to disregard the limitations of a realistic setting, and you thereby responded to the swift pace and mounting intensity of the narrative. Perhaps you identified with the guests and shared their response to the entrance of the masked figure, which, the narrator explains, is marked by terror, horror, and disgust. On the other hand, if you were unwilling to succumb to such a surreal plot, finding it simply too unbelievable even to generate sweaty palms, it was not a success. Either way, your job is to explain what the effect on the reader was and to analyze how the text and the reader were responsible for that effect.

Taken one step further, the transaction may occur between the mind of the author and the mind of the reader. The **Geneva critics**, for example, try to enter the writer's mental universe, experiencing his or her unique consciousness. Individual works of literature grow unimportant in this process, as the purpose is not to understand a single work but to reconstitute in criticism the writer's world. The goal is to share the author's inner reality by considering his or her entire output. As J. Hillis Miller explained it, "All works of a single writer form a unity, a unity in which a thousand paths radiate from the same center." The Geneva critic looks for the center from which the paths spring, searching for the essential wholeness of the writer and his or her work. For beginning critics, finding such a center would be an ambitious undertaking, requiring, as it does, close familiarity with a writer's entire canon, along with an understanding of all the hallmarks of his or her style.

To use the transactional model, you can begin by asking yourself some of the following questions:

- What kind of reader is implied by this text? For example, does it address you as if you are intelligent and well informed, or as if you are inexperienced and innocent?
- What aspects of the text invite you to respond as the implied reader?
- How do you, as an actual reader, differ from the one that is implied?
- What gaps and vague outlines did you find yourself filling in?
- How did your perceptions and responses change as the work unfolded? What caused them to change?
- What contradictions did you perceive in the text—for example, characters who represent differing viewpoints? How did you resolve them?
- What do you know of the author's intent?
- List the most vivid images you remember from the text. How have you reconstructed them from your own experiences?
- What experiences of your own have you used to visualize and understand those presented in the text?

WRITING A READER-RESPONSE ANALYSIS

Prewriting

To find a starting point for exploring where your personal experience and the text converge, you will find it helpful to make a few personal observations before, during, and after reading the text. These observations will help you discover interpretive points for discussion. It is easy to begin; simply ask questions such as these before you even pick up the book:

- How do I feel about reading this piece? Am I eager to begin? Curious about what I will find? Reluctant?

- What do I already know about this work or this author?
- What do I already know about the time, place, or characters depicted?
- What does the title suggest to me?

Noting your responses in a journal or log during a first reading can help you make generalizations later. You may still be at the questioning stage when you do this, or your ideas may have reached an advanced degree of development. Regardless of how far along you are in your thinking, here are some suggestions to consider during the initial reading:

- Does the work include quotations that I would like to copy and save? What questions would I like to ask the author?
- What objections can I raise to what I am reading?
- Where do I experience confusion, disagreement, approval, or any other attitude or feeling?
- What experiences does the text bring to mind that I can describe or narrate?

You can also make short responses after the first reading. These responses may be appropriate for a journal entry, or you may write them as separate texts.

- As soon as you finish reading the work, describe how you feel about it.
- Write a brief summary of the plot.
- Freewrite about a single line from a poem or about a sentence from a piece of prose.
- Identify a line or an image that immediately caught your attention or that you remember clearly. Why do you find it to be powerful?
- Think of someone or some experience that a character or situation in this work brings to mind.
- List the things you like about the work. Why do you like them?
- List those aspects of it that bother you. Why do they bother you?
- Identify any passages you do not understand.
- Choose what you would tell someone about this work if you could make only one comment.
- Consider how you might have acted had you been one of the characters.
- What else would you like to know about the characters or events?
- What values, beliefs, or assumptions of your own does this work affirm? Which of your values, beliefs, or assumptions does it challenge?
- Compose a letter (not to be sent) to the author or to one of the characters.
- Speculate on who should play the various roles in a filmed version of the work.

Drafting and Revising

The Introduction Because you are making a reader-response analysis, it is appropriate to involve your audience in the introduction to your essay. In other words, try to provoke a strong response from your own reader. One way of doing so is to begin by recounting an incident from the work that elicits a particularly powerful reaction or quote a passage that holds strong emotion for most readers. For example, Edgar Allan Poe's description of the mysterious stranger who suddenly appears at the ball in "The Masque of the Red Death"—"The figure was tall and gaunt, and shrouded from head to foot in the habiliments of the grave"—is not likely to provoke an inattentive yawn from anyone who reads it. It can send shivers down the spine of even the most passive reader. An essay that begins by quoting such a line will catch a reader's attention; it can also effectively lead into a more detailed examination of how the reader and text are responsible for making the literary work.

The Body The core of your paper will explain how the text controls the reader's understanding and sympathies, identify the personal material you have put into the text, and describe how the two interact to create the text. In other words, it will show how you acquired information about the text and what responses that information created.

Part of your discussion, then, will center on the guidelines embodied in the text. It will note stereotypes, points of view, connotations, patterns, metaphors, foreshadowing, and images that guide your responses. It will question the accuracy of the information that is given and the reliability of the various characters who provide that information. It will remark on those instances in which only partial information is provided and where the reader knows more than the characters know. Even points at which the reader is misled will be significant.

You may want to describe your general impression of the work or how your initial impression of it changed to become your final judgment. You may even want to point out what you have found that was recognizable from your own experiences, both personal and literary. Note any incidents and characters that produced either validation of or challenge to your sense of the world (noticeable because of your own comfort or discomfort on meeting them). It may be helpful to profile the character with whom you most closely identified or the incident that gave you the most pleasure or pain. If you found yourself remembering a personal experience that made the text more credible or moving, you will want to include it here. If you supplied material by imagining events that did not actually take place, you should mention any fantasies or speculations that helped explain a character's motivation or enhance a bit of action. If you made adjustments in how you initially saw the text so that it was more in keeping with your usual way of seeing things, you will have a direct means of discovering your part in making this text. Even the expectations you had before reading it may be significant in explaining how you created the work.

Finally, you should explain what resulted when the text and the reader came together. You may want to note how the text invites responses by predisposing the reader to read in certain ways, and you might examine how the images provided by the text are modified by the reader's personal experience. Although the text proffers certain norms or values, it is the reader who decides whether or to what degree they should be accepted or rejected. The critic's job is to raise meaningful questions and to look for meaningful answers. In the process, a new reading of the text may emerge, and the reader may be changed as well.

The Conclusion The body of your analysis will have presented numerous observations backed up by even more citations from the text. The conclusion, then, is the place to pull all the disparate pieces of information together into generalizations about the text. It need not be lengthy, but it should state the major effects the work has had on a reader and the causes that produced those effects. Finally, the conclusion should include an evaluation of how effectively the text elicited the desired responses, how deeply the reader became involved in constructing the text, and how the work was enriched by the mutual participation of text and reader. In other words, how well did the process work?

SUGGESTED READING

Bleich, David. *Subjective Criticism.* Baltimore: Johns Hopkins University Press, 1978.

Booth, Wayne. *Rhetoric of Fiction.* 2nd ed. Chicago: University of Chicago Press, 1983.

Culler, Jonathan. *Structuralist Poetics: Structuralism, Linguistics, and the Study of Literature.* New York: Routledge, 2002.

Fish, Stanley. *Is There a Text in This Class?: The Authority of Interpretive Communities.* Cambridge: Harvard University Press, 1980.

———. *Surprised by Sin: The Reader in "Paradise Lost."* 2nd ed. Cambridge: Harvard University Press, 1998.

Freund, Elizabeth. *The Return of the Reader: Reader-Response Criticism.* New York: Methuen, 1987.

Gibson, Walker. " Authors, Speakers, Readers, and Mock Readers." *College English* 5 (1950): 265–69.

Holland, Norman. *Five Readers Reading.* New Haven, CT: Yale University Press, 1975.

———. " Hamlet—My Greatest Creation." *Journal of the American Academy of Psychoanalysis* 3(1975): 419–27.

Iser, Wolfgang. *The Act of Reading: A Theory of Aesthetic Response.* Baltimore: Johns Hopkins University Press, 1978.

Jauss, Hans Robert. *Toward an Aesthetic of Reception.* Trans. T. Bahti. Minneapolis: University of Minnesota Press, 1982.

Mailloux, Steven. *Interpretive Conventions: The Reader in the Study of American Fiction.* Ithaca, NY: Cornell University Press, 1982.

Rosenblatt, Louise. " Writing and Reading: The Transactional Theory." *Reader* 20 (fall 1988): 7–31.

———. *The Reader, the Text, the Poem: The Transactional Theory of the Literary Work.* Carbondale: Southern Illinois University Press, 1994.

———. *Literature as Exploration.* 5th ed. New York: Modern Language Association of America, 1995.

Scholes, Robert. *Structuralism in Literature: An Introduction.* New Haven, CT: Yale University Press, 1974.

Tompkins, Jane. *Reader-Response Criticism: From Formalism to Post-Structuralism.* Baltimore: Johns Hopkins University Press, 1981.

For up-to-date information on the many Web sites addressing reader-response critical approaches, visit www.cengagebrain.com.

Model Student Analysis

Discovering the Way the World Works:

A Reader-Response Analysis of James Joyce's "Araby"

MICHAEL JAUCHEN

At the end of James Joyce's short story "Araby," the young narrator reaches a sudden, disheartening conclusion concerning the meaning of his recent experiences in Dublin and what those experiences reveal about his own personal shortcomings: "Gazing up into the darkness I saw myself as a creature driven and derided by vanity; and my eyes burned with anguish and anger." This final realization is the product of two separate but interrelated aspects of the narrator's life. First, it is a realization concerning a conventionally accepted truth about reality. Evidence from our own lives tells us overwhelmingly that the actual workings of the world rarely live up to the idealistic imaginings of youth; empirical experience makes us aware that the world does not play out like a fairy tale. Second, the narrator's realization at the end of the story is the product of his own private experience of that empirical reality. He reaches his conclusion only after the empirical evidence of the world has been filtered through his own perceptions and desires. This deeply personal quality is one reason the story's ending retains such power. The narrator's epiphany illustrates that the ultimate meaning of experience is found at the crossroads between empirical facts and the way our individual perceptions organize those facts into nuggets of meaning.

On one level, the narrator's experience in "Araby" resembles the experience contemporary readers undergo when they attempt to make meaning out of a text. Just as the young boy must attempt to make sense of Dublin's mysterious materials, we as readers are constantly on a journey of discovery, encountering new (and sometimes strange) textual worlds that encourage us to construct meaning out of them. And just as the meaning of the young narrator's experiences in "Araby" is a combination of the empirical facts of the outside world and the young boy's personal perceptions of that world, a reader's discovery of meaning is always a transaction between the reader and the text. The text provides us with empirical evidence—authorial devices such as diction, allusion, and imagery—that produces a particular range of rhetorical effects and guides our understanding of the story. During the act of reading, however, all this material is constantly filtered and processed through the perceptions of each individual reader and tinted by his or her idiosyncratic inklings, desires, and personal experiences. The ultimate "meaning" of a world or a text, then, is a combination of the two. It is a hybrid of the empirical and the personal, an ever-evolving transaction between the reader and the text.

This makes "Araby" a prime text to look at through the critical lens of reader-response theory. Many reader-response critics, such as David Bleich and Stanley Fish, emphasize the reader's role in the overall creation of a text's meaning. These critics argue that the subjective position of each reader alters the objective facts of any text and that instead of ignoring these personal intrusions, a complete reading of any text should actively incorporate them into the act of criticism. Unlike more conventional modes of reading, such as New Criticism (Formalism), a reader-response-driven criticism of "Araby" allows us to see that the ultimate "meaning" of Joyce's story is not something that can be pinned down conclusively, but is instead a moving, evolving activity of participatory reading.

Before considering how Joyce's story creates meaning through its transaction with the individual reader, a look at a few of the text's empirical aspects will help provide a foundational framework concerning some of the authorial tools Joyce uses to guide the reader through the work. In terms of plot, "Araby" is a very short story, and its action is fairly straightforward. The narrator has a typical Irish upbringing. He attends Catholic school, spends his nights playing with the other neighborhood boys, and develops his first crush on a girl down the street, the older sister of his friend Mangan. When Mangan's sister tells the narrator she will not be able to attend Araby, a traveling bazaar that is making a stop in Dublin, the young boy promises he will go to the fair and buy her a gift. After making this promise, the boy spends his time daydreaming about his new love interest. With his active imagination, he builds her up into a perfect, idealized figure of beauty and chivalric love. When the night of the bazaar finally arrives, the boy's journey is fraught with numerous mundane obstacles—his uncle is late from work and the train to Araby is delayed—and the boy gets to Araby just as it is closing. Amid the deserted rides and stalls, he approaches a booth and overhears a young salesgirl having a silly conversation with two boys. When the girl coldly asks the narrator if he would like to buy anything, the boy says no and walks away dejected. As the rest of the lights go out in the bazaar, the narrator realizes his entire mission and his idealized image of Mangan's sister have been products of his own foolish vanity.

Although this plot summary of "Araby" makes the story seem like a straightforward narrative, an investigation of the "implied reader," one approach common to reader-response criticism, demonstrates that the author has written the story with a knowledgeable and sophisticated individual in mind. There are a number of allusions throughout the story, for example, that subtly critique the Catholic religion. Many of these references, however, would not be obvious to a reader who is unacquainted with the conventional imagery and practices of the Catholic faith. At one point in the story, the narrator mentions some of the books—*The Abbot, The Devout Communicant, and The Memoirs of Vidocq*—that were left behind by the former owner of the house, a Catholic priest. While *The Devout Communicant* seems like typical reading fare for a priest, the inclusion of *The Abbot* (a historical romance about Mary, Queen of Scots) and *The Memoirs of Vidocq* (a sexually explicit and blasphemous autobiography) suggests a more sinister reality lying behind the priest's facade of piety and asceticism. A similar type of subtle allusion appears in the religious imagery Joyce uses to describe Mangan's sister, who is portrayed as a modern-day representation of the Virgin Mary. She is constantly haloed by a ring of light, and the narrator confesses that her name comes to mind during his "moments in strange prayers and praises." The narrator's idealized image of Mangan's sister is especially apparent in the twilit scene when he promises to buy her a gift at Araby:

> She held one of the spikes, bowing her head towards me. The light from the lamp opposite our door caught the white curve of her neck, lit up the hair that rested there and, falling, lit up the hand upon the railing. It fell over one side of her dress and caught the white border of a petticoat, just visible as she stood at ease.

The allusions here (the spikes through her hands, her bowed head, and the recurrence of the color white) suggest that in the imaginative world of the narrator, Mangan's sister represents much more than just a neighborhood girl. The young narrator has transformed her into an object of idolatry, which, as he comes to realize later, is not her true nature. For the reader who is aware of all these subtle religious references, Joyce's story becomes a conscious, methodical critique of the deceptive and idealized facades inherent to Catholicism, and the boy's experience can be read as a cautionary tale about the dangers of any type of extreme religious idolatry.

Even if the "implied reader" does not understand all these religious allusions, however, Joyce fills "Araby" with more easily recognizable patterns of imagery and language that guide the reader to an understanding of the story's central tension between idealized image and actual reality. All these authorial techniques further reinforce the story's overall theme of shattered, youthful illusions. The diction in much of "Araby," for instance, creates a strong contrast between the world of childhood and the world of adult responsibility. Joyce portrays the boy's childhood activities as positive, almost magical, things. The houses of his neighborhood come alive through personification, and the boy thinks of them as living creatures that "gazed at one another with brown imperturbable faces." In the chill of wintertime, the narrator plays outside with his friends until their "bodies glowed." At one point, he compares his own body to "a harp" and the sound of Mangan's sister's voice to the "fingers running upon the wires." The accumulation of these images in the reader's mind demonstrates that in "Araby" childhood is equated with possibility, openness, and imaginative freedom.

Starkly contrasting with this idealized world of childhood, the diction Joyce uses to describe the activities of the adult world persistently connotes responsibility, obligation, commerce, and dirtiness. On a trip to the market with his aunt, the narrator describes the "flaring streets," the "drunken men and bargaining women," "the curses of laborers," and the "shrill litanies" of the salesmen peddling their wares. The narrator's trip to Araby is also delayed due to innumerable obstacles from the world of adulthood. He has "to endure the gossip" of Mrs. Mercer, who stops in for an unexpected visit; dinner is postponed because the narrator's uncle has to work late; the train experiences an "intolerable delay" on the way to the bazaar; and the ticket taker at the gate is a "weary looking man." The accumulation of these images leads the reader to believe that, in the boy's mind, the activities of the adult world pale in comparison to the magic and possibility of childhood. Compared with the wonderful, idealized world of the narrator's youthful imagination, the "serious work of life," the obligations of adulthood, are nothing more than "child's play, ugly monotonous child's play."

There are also numerous images of blindness in the story, which further suggest the story's central theme of shattered illusions to the reader. The narrator's house is on a cul-de-sac, or "blind" street. Many times, he looks underneath a window blind in order to watch what Mangan's sister is doing down the street. Once, when he is lost in a reverie about the girl, he confesses, "I was thankful that I could see so little." And it is no coincidence that the story ends in complete darkness or that the boy's final feeling of "anguish and anger," his new insight into the true nature of his character, is centered in his eyes. All of these references to blindness in "Araby" point the reader to the narrator's metaphorical lack of sight in his idealization of Mangan's sister. These elements within the text work together to cause the reader to focus strongly on the story's theme of blind, youthful ideals and the way that blindness often leads to disenchantment with the world of adulthood.

In terms of my own reading of "Araby," however, I have to admit that there are also many points in the story where I am reminded of other stories of childhood and maturation I have read. These intertextual elements further shape my own experience of Joyce's text while still supporting my reading of the story's central theme. The narrator's maturation process in "Araby," for instance, follows a pattern similar to that of Stephen Daedalus in two of James Joyce's other novels, *A Portrait of the Artist as a Young Man* and *Ulysses*. In *A Portrait of the Artist*, Stephen ultimately rejects the Irish Catholicism of his boyhood, and, after a key scene at the beach involving another idealized female figure, he decides to leave Ireland for good and pursue an artistic career in Paris. When *Ulysses* begins, Stephen's dreams have experienced a severe setback, and he is working at a job for which he feels overqualified. Unlike "Araby," which ends the narrative at the beginning of the young boy's disillusionment, these later works offer Joyce's picture of the possible long-term consequences of foolish childhood dreaming. The future life of the young boy in "Araby" could very well play out much as Stephen's life did, with shattered dreams of greatness and a hatred for the machinations and responsibilities of adulthood. When the narrator of "Araby" notes how his constant daydreaming tested the patience of his schoolmaster, turning his face "from amiability to sternness," it was hard for me not to think of the adult Stephen Daedalus, who, once his dreams of artistry are gone, becomes a schoolmaster himself and scolds his students for being academically unprepared.

When the narrator of "Araby" goes up to the attic of his house to escape from the adult world of time (he mentions how the clock's "ticking began to irritate me"), I thought of J. D. Salinger's novel *The Catcher in the Rye*, which tells the coming-of-age story of Holden Caulfield, a sixteen-year-old who runs away from school and spends a few days wandering around New York City by himself. Like the narrator of "Araby," who pictures himself as a modern-day Lancelot searching for his love "through a throng of foes," Holden Caulfield has idealized dreams of escape. In one scene in particular, he asks his girlfriend if she will run away with him into the woods. Both Holden and Joyce's narrator want to escape the adult world of time and responsibility and live in the eternal world available to them through their imagination. The narrator of "Araby" notes how "the high cold empty gloomy rooms liberated me," and when he is up there alone, he loses all track of time. In a very important scene in Salinger's novel, Holden tells his little sister that his greatest dream in life is to stand in a field of rye and save the children who are playing there from running off of a cliff, metaphorically tumbling into the world of adulthood. All of these other works have helped shape my personal understanding of "Araby" to a great degree. Although I understand that the narrator's realization at the end of "Araby" is a deeply personal one, these intertextual influences allowed me to think of his experience in a more generalized light, suggesting that his epiphany is simply a unique manifestation of a larger theme common to many stories about childhood. The desire to escape the world of adulthood is a characteristic of the protagonist in almost any coming-of-age novel, whether it is Huck from *Huckleberry Finn*, Quentin Compson from *The Sound and the Fury*, or Billy Colman from Wilson Rawls's *Where the Red Fern Grows*. It is also characteristic that in many of these works, the protagonists have to come to terms with disconcerting new knowledge concerning the world around them. Huck learns about the dangerous and racist undercurrents in America on his trip down the river with Jim, Quentin's disillusionment over his sister's loss of innocence drives him to suicide, and Rawls's protagonist loses both of his beloved dogs in a horrible fight. All of these works suggest that the transition from childhood into adulthood is rarely easy and that, more often than not, it is a process fraught with pain and heartache. In this regard, the young boy's realization about the ultimately empty content of his wild daydreaming in "Araby" makes Joyce's story a prototypical example of the coming-of-age tale.

Even if it is a story that has been told innumerable times, however, I deeply empathize with the young narrator of "Araby." One of my main interests is creative writing, and I spend a good deal of time within the world of my own imagination. On top of that, I am a voracious reader. In book after book, I come across compelling worlds created by authors who write about love, death, desire, and romance. I have often had to come to terms with the fact that the world of fictional stories (a world in which anything can happen) does not match up with the world I actually inhabit. And even though this sense of disappointment has diminished with my own maturation into adulthood, I still find myself inclined toward daydreaming and idealization. Consequently, I see much of myself in Joyce's narrator. I often want the world to be better and more exciting than it is, and this often only sets me up for disappointment.

Ultimately, "Araby" is a short story that should be familiar to almost any reader who has experienced the shattering of a youthful illusion about the world. For the more sophisticated reader, Joyce also includes elements in the story that turn the narrative into a deeper critique of religious idolatry. For the general reader, however, the story's motif of blindness and the way Joyce draws a strong contrast between the magical world of childhood and the mundane world of adult responsibility demonstrate that the text is dealing with themes that are common to many stories of childhood. This does not make "Araby" an exercise in redundancy. Joyce's concision of action and his compression of imagery make "Araby" a text that tells its familiar story in a new and compelling way.

8

Deconstruction

Deconstruction's admirers see it as a way that begins to let us question the presuppositions of the language we think in. Its detractors condemn its subtle and convoluted readings as narcissistic self-reflexivity.

SHIRLEY F. STATON

The term *deconstruction* sends many readers running for cover, partly because it is one of the most radical approaches to reading that has appeared on the scene, but also because its terminology presents difficulties of its own. Why, then, does anyone want to understand it or use it to read a poem or story? Perhaps the best answer is that deconstruction provides a way of playing with language and meaning that teases and delights. It is not a fully developed critical method or school or even a philosophy. Instead, it is, says its founder Jacques Derrida (1930–2004), a strategy, some "rules for reading, interpretation, and writing."

HISTORICAL BACKGROUND

Deconstruction is the best known (and most significant) of a kind of literary criticism known as **poststructuralism**; in fact, many people use the terms interchangeably. To understand the revolution that poststructuralism has created in literary criticism, it is necessary to look at some of its predecessors, both **structuralism**—the movement that it both incorporates and undermines—and those that structuralism itself challenged.

The revolutionary nature of deconstruction can be summarized by saying that, in general, it challenges the way Western civilization has conceived of the world since Plato. More specifically, it overturns the principles that have provided basic beliefs about truth and meaning since the seventeenth-century French philosopher, scientist, and mathematician René Descartes (1596–1650) applied the rational, inductive methods of science to philosophy. Refusing to accept the truth of anything without grounds for believing it to be true, Descartes began with the one thing he could know—that consciousness of his thinking proved his own existence. *"Cogito, ergo sum,"* he declared. "I think, therefore I am." From that one certainty, all other knowledge could proceed. The Cartesian approach, which elevated the importance of reason over passion, superstition, and imagination as a means of finding truth in the natural world, has had an impact well beyond the seventeenth century. It has helped shape the thinking of humanists, artists, and philosophers into the twenty-first century, providing them with the conviction that they could make a better world. If meaning and truth could be found by thinking and acting rationally, humankind could solve social problems, cure illnesses, and create new technologies. In short, through the use of reason, progress was possible, perhaps inevitable.

The confidence inspired by such a worldview came into question toward the end of the nineteenth century when a radical re-visioning of "reality" took place in a wide variety of disciplines. The long-held view of the world as a knowable, objective entity that could be discovered through direct experience of the senses encountered serious challenges in fields as diverse as physics, linguistics, anthropology, and psychology. In philosophy, for example, thinkers such as Friedrich Nietzsche (1844–1900) began to question the existence of objective truth. Nietzsche even announced the death of God, by which he meant that human beings were no longer able to sustain belief. Without God, however, he worried that there would be no cosmic order or universal moral law that bound all human beings. Such a state of being carried with it the threat that humankind could fall into nihilism and perhaps lawlessness. Consequently, Nietzsche called for a reevaluation of basic beliefs that would make it possible for human beings to develop their creative powers in this world, not the next. In place of the limitations imposed by religion's commands and laws, and instead of the despair caused by lack of faith, he believed humankind could exercise newly found freedoms that would liberate the human spirit. He foresaw a "superman" (the ***Übermensch***) who would be strong and independent, freed from all values except those he deemed to be valid.

Using different terminology, spokespersons from other areas of study echoed Nietzsche's denial of an ultimate reality that is static, unified, and absolute, to be replaced by an understanding of the world as relativistic, dynamic, and open. In 1905, for example, Albert Einstein (1879–1955) published a paper that would change scientists' understanding of time, space, and reality. His ideas about the velocity of light challenged the assumption that there is such a thing as time that all clocks measure. In other words, the concept of absolute time was replaced with that of time as being relative to motion. Such thinking represented a fundamental shift in the way we see ourselves and our world. It would later lead to questions about the nature of human behavior, belief, and morality. "Is *everything* relative?" the twentieth century would ask.

The study of language was not immune to such probing. For two hundred years, language had been viewed as a transparent medium through which reality could be set down accurately and shaped into an aesthetic form. Finding meaning, which was assumed to be present, required finding the words that corresponded to the objects and experiences observed. Literature was taken to be mimetic, reflecting and presenting truths about life and the human condition. Because texts depicted life in a powerful way, they were thought to have a life of their own that could be discovered and analyzed. Enter the critic, whose job was to reveal the value and meaning of texts. For example, the formalists (the New Critics, as distinguished from the Russian formalists), who carried the nineteenth-century empirical worldview into the twentieth century, saw a poem as a self-sufficient object possessing unity and form and operating within its own rules to resolve ambiguities, ironies, and paradoxes (see Chapter 3). Formalists sought to determine not what the poem means but *how* it means. There was no doubt that with the application of intellectual analysis, an understanding of form would lead to meaning. Although an occasional doubter complained about the cold, unemotional nature of the formalists' close readings, there was no uncertainty about the presence of ultimate meaning.

The power of the formalists and their nineteenth-century heritage began to break down in literary criticism with the appearance of the **phenomenological critics**, who rejected the formalists' inability (or unwillingness) to question how readers know a literary work, as exemplified by their refusal to investigate the author's intentions. The phenomenologists, who believe that meaning resides not in physical objects but in human consciousness as the object is registered in it, emphasize the reader in making literature (see Chapter 7). Instead of a single best reading of a text, they accept the possibility of many readings, because a text cannot exist separate from the individual mind that perceives it. It cannot be explained as something unto itself; instead, it can be explained as an effect on a reader, and that effect will be different for each reader because of the unique experiences each brings to the reading. In addition, readers are called upon to supply missing material, to fill in textual gaps. They do so by using their own experiences with literature and life, thereby creating even more differences in interpretations. In other words, as in other fields, it is no longer a given in literature that truth is static, absolute, and unified. Now it is deemed to be relative, dynamic, and open.

STRUCTURALISM

From the early part of the twentieth century came another set of ideas that was to have a significant impact on how people understand the world. Called ***structuralism***, it is, in its broadest sense, a science that seeks to understand how systems work. It accepts the belief that things cannot be understood individually. Instead, they have to be seen as part of a larger structure to which they belong. Structuralists are not so much interested in the operations (or aesthetics or meaning) of a single entity as they are in trying to describe the underlying (and not necessarily visible) principles by which it exists. Assuming that individual characteristics that can be noted on the surface are rooted in some general organization, structuralists collect observable information about an item or practice in order to discover the laws that govern it. For example, a structuralist studying urban American architecture of the twentieth century will be interested in the characteristics of a single building only insofar as they provide data that help define the bigger category of architectural objects to which that building belongs. A structural anthropologist may examine the customs and rituals of a single group of people in some remote part of the world not simply to understand them in particular but also to discover underlying similarities between that society and the society of others.

Because behaviors that on the surface appear to be vastly different from each other may have commonalities beneath the surface that link the human beings who practice them, observations of concrete local phenomena allow the researcher to support assumptions about human society that cross cultural boundaries. He or she does not view objects or behaviors in isolation, but as part of a larger system. In short, structuralists are looking not for structures in a physical sense but for patterns that underlie human behavior, experience, and creation.

A critical question has to do with the source of the structures themselves. Traditionally, it has been assumed that the structures resided in the physical world. Human beings found meaning in what they perceived outside themselves. However, the structuralists argue from a different direction. According to them, structure comes from the human mind as it works to make sense of its world. Any given experience, they say, is so full of information that it would be overwhelming if there were no way of ordering it. The mind's defense is to sort and classify, make rules of process—that is, to create a structure. It is such conceptual systems that make it possible for individuals to distinguish one type of object from another or to differentiate among members of the same category. This fairly radical idea placed meaning in the mind of human beings rather than in external, objective reality. It is a short step from there to the idea that language, not sense experience or modes of consciousness, shapes who we are, what we think, and what we understand reality to be.

Ferdinand de Saussure

When the structuralist approach was applied to language, it caused a significant departure from the traditional methods of study practiced by nineteenth-century philologists, who had examined language **diachronically**—that is, by tracing how words evolved in meaning or sound over time. The philologists compared the changes they found with those that had occurred in other languages and then looked for causes. Their work assumed that language was mimetic—not a system with its own governing rules but one that reflected the world. A word, to them, was a symbol that was equal to the object or concept it represented. In contrast, Swiss linguist Ferdinand de Saussure (1857–1913), who is generally regarded as the father of modern linguistics, began to use a **synchronic** approach, a method that was deemed to be a more scientific study of language. It involves looking at a language at one particular time (as opposed to over a period of time) in search of the principles that govern its functions, principles of which its users might not even be consciously aware. As explained in *Course in General Linguistics* (1972), a posthumously published work based on student notes of lectures Sausurre presented between 1913 and 1915, he looked for the foundational system of language by observing its surface uses. At the outset, his work seemed to have the potential to discover basic principles of language and culture that could explain human behavior.

Saussure's studies led him to reject the idea that language is simply a tool to be used to represent a preexistent reality. That is, he did not accept the idea that it is mimetic or transparent. Instead, he argued that language is a system that has its own internal rules of operations. He called those general rules ***langue***, and he referred to the applications that members of a particular speech community make of those rules in their iterations as ***parole***. In other words, *langue,* sometimes referred to as a grammar, is the system within which individual verbalizations have meaning, and *parole* refers to the individual verbalizations. The rules of *langue,* which the individual speaker absorbs as a member of a culture, are manifested in *parole.* In his efforts to identify and explain how all this works, Saussure swept away the nineteenth-century correspondence model between words and things and gave us language that is connected only conventionally and arbitrarily to the world outside it.

One of the concepts important to Saussure's explanation of the language system is that of **signs**, which he describes as being composed of two parts: a written or sound construction, known as the **signifier**, and its meaning, called the **signified**. The spoken or written form of *hat,* for example, is a signifier. The concept that flashes into your mind when you hear or read it is the signified. With the introduction of these terms, and the theory underlying them, Saussure transformed the sense of what a word is. He made it no longer possible to speak of a word as a symbol that represents a thing outside of it, as it had conventionally been known. Because a signifier does not refer to some object in the world but to a concept in the mind, it is language, and not the world external to us, that mediates our reality. We see only what language allows us to see both outside and inside ourselves. It does not simply record our world or provide labels for what is in it. Instead, according to Saussure, language constitutes our world; it structures our experience. Consider, for example, how speakers of different languages tend to have differing views of the world. Structuralists would say that their views differ because language has made them see everything through different structures. At the same time languages hold certain underlying traits in common. For Saussure it is the larger system of relationships that warrants study.

The connection between the signifier and the signified has several important characteristics. First of all, it is not a natural relationship but an arbitrary one. The signifier *hat* has no inherent link with the physical object you wear on your head. It could just as easily have been called a rose or a bed. Then how do a signifier and a signified become tied together? The relationship comes about through convention, an agreement on the part of speakers that the two are associated. Finally, we know one sign from another not because of meanings they inherently carry but because of the differences among them. The signifier *bat* is distinguishable from *hat,* for example, because they have different initial letters. Words cannot be defined in isolation, because they exist as a chain formed by relationships with other words. Language, then, is arbitrary, conventional, and based on difference.

Structuralism has taken varied forms in different countries, partly because Sausurre's works were not translated into English until the 1950s and did not achieve widespread notice in the United States until the 1960s and 1970s. Consequently, the most influential theorists have been the French followers of Saussure. His ideas and theirs have been adopted and adapted by many disciplines in addition to linguistics. After all, wherever there is social behavior, there is likely to be a signifying system, though not necessarily one involving words. Any organized, structured set of signs carries cultural meanings, making it possible to "read" a culture by examining those signs. Saussure, in fact, proposed the development of a science called **semiology** that would investigate meaning through signs observable in cultural phenomena. Because language is the primary signifying system, it would be the chief focus of study, and research into other systems would follow the model used in studying it. It was thought that identifying the laws that govern signs would make it possible to explain the social behavior and cultural practices of human beings.

At the same time, in the United States, Charles Sanders Pierce was developing **semiotics**, which applied structuralist principles not just to language but to the study of sign systems in general and the way meaning is derived from them. The point is the same as in semiology: to treat all forms of social behavior as signifying systems that are defined by the structure of their interrelationships. The process provides anthropologists, sociologists, psychologists, and others with a way to go beneath external facts to examine the nature of the human experience. Semiotics has proved to be valuable in studying phenomena as disparate as Barbie dolls and the mythologies of little-known cultures. Unlike semiology, which failed to grow into the fully developed science that Saussure had hoped for, semiotics continues to mature as a field of research.

When structuralist principles are applied to literature, several new and interesting issues arise. Instead of trying to discover the meaning of a text, for example, the structuralist reader will look for the system to which the work belongs. Consequently, he goes in search of signs that operate by rules. The individual work is not the focus of interest. It only provides data that will lead to the larger organizing principles that are the object of the search. How literature conveys meaning, not what that meaning is, takes center stage. How a literary device functions is more important than how it depicts reality.

The process is scientific and objective, not transactional or emotional. The upshot is that the author is of little interest to the structuralist reader because a text is not deemed to be an author's own vision but rather a part of a system to which it belongs, a system by which it is governed. In his or her concern for finding structure and systems, the structuralist critic pays decreased attention to moral issues and creates instead a kind of diagram of how the text operates.

As a result, literary critics who subscribe to the tenets of structuralism work most often with prose narratives. Usually they seek to connect a text with a larger structure, such as a genre or some universal narrative form. They often establish connections with other texts that have similar patterns or motifs. On a broader scale, they sometimes find parallels between a literary work and the structure of language itself. They are also drawn to work derived from Saussure's ideas concerning semiology or Pierce's semiotics, causing them to look at the whole of Western culture as a system of signs, drawing inferences from artifacts that to others might seem trivial and insignificant. Such analyses sometimes lead critics to ask abstract questions more common to philosophy and sociology than to literature. Since doing so takes the critic away from the text, structuralist criticism is left open to charges that it is not primarily a literary strategy.

Scholars other than Saussure have also made significant contributions to structuralist thinking. Four whose ideas should be mentioned are Claude Lévi-Strauss, Roland Barthes, Vladimir Propp, and Jonathan Culler.

Claude Lévi-Strauss

Claude Lévi-Strauss was a French anthropologist who in the 1950s began to use structuralist principles to study cultures. Some of his work involved applying Saussure's ideas to narratives, specifically to myths he collected from around the world. Struck by the fact that he often found strong similarities in stories that came from widely separated cultures and ages, some of them even seeming to be different versions of the same narrative, he wanted to find the general structure that allowed them to have meanings reflective of human concerns that are not culturally bound. As Lévi-Strauss saw it, the fantastic, unpredictable characters and events of myths suggest that each is unique, but the commonalities among them clearly indicate that they are not. To resolve that paradox, he determined that each myth is a single instance of a universal law of human thought. To prove his assertion, he studied individual myths (the *parole*) in search of the structural elements they share—i.e., the larger system to which they belong (the *langue*).

Lévi-Strauss referred to the smallest structural elements of myths as **mythemes**, because they are analogous to phonemes in linguistics, the smallest sounds in a language, according to Saussure. Both are minimal building blocks, essential elements of myths and language, respectively. Mythemes, according to Lévi-Strauss, are always linked in complicated relationships with each other, one of which is opposition, or contradiction. Others work to resolve the opposition. As he pointed out, "Mythical thought always progresses from the awareness of oppositions toward their resolution." Studying their interactions can reveal the larger narrative structure.

Claude Lévi-Strauss's interest in oppositions was shared by his contemporary, Roman Jakobson. Both extended Saussure's ideas about the importance of difference by examining how opposites make meaning. The former, for example, came to see narratives as organizations of paired opposites, referred to as **dyadic pairs**, often referred to as **binary oppositions**. They are contrasting concepts such as male/female, right /left, day/night, each of which makes it possible for us to understand the other more fully. We are able to understand black because we understand white, noise because we know silence. The concept would become especially important for the deconstructionists, important with a twist, however.

In sum, by looking at individual items for the shared structural elements that would point to the general laws of their being, Lévi-Struass applied structuralist theory to mythology and to culture in general. He moved systematically from the particular to the general in an effort to locate individual works in their structural context. This methodology and the assumption that structures underlie all things eventually led the anthropologist to claim that it is not only myths that follow universal laws. All human thought, he declared, obeys universal laws.

Roland Barthes

Roland Barthes (1915–1980) was another cultural anthropologist who lived and worked in France at the same time as Claude Lévi-Strauss. Instead of traveling the world to look at diverse (some would say exotic) cultures, Barthes directed his attention to the culture of his native country, more specifically to elements of it that had never before been the object of intellectual scrutiny. He applied structuralist principles to social practices and public figures of modern-day France in an effort to find their meaning (their *langue*). In *Mythologies*, published in 1957, he questioned the meaning and significance of everything from eating fish and chips to the film image of Greta Garbo. In each case he examined the subject in its structural context so that he could understand its function in society.

By the 1970s structuralism had begun to achieve intellectual notice, and Barthes turned his attention to literature. It is for his lengthy analysis of Balzac's short story "Sarrasine," entitled *S/Z*, that he is best known. In good structuralist fashion, he divided the story into 561 "**lexies**," or units of meaning, then classified them into five codes that he deemed to constitute the basic structure of all stories. (His theory is analogous to the assumption that all sentences are governed by an identifiable set of grammatical structures.) The five codes are: the proairetic code, which includes indications of actions; the hermeneutic code, which poses questions that provide suspense; the cultural code, which includes references to common knowledge; the semic code, which reveals character and theme; and the symbolic code, which also deals with theme, but it does so through contrasting elements such as love and hate, life and death, male and female.

Building on the structuralist theory that human beings organize reality by recognizing contrasts and oppositions, Barthes infers that narratives are built on binary oppositions. To determine the meaning of a story requires that a reader note the binary oppositions in the text, observe their interactions and relationships, and thereby decode meaning. It is important to note that such a process ignores the author, the genre, and literary schools or periods. To read a narrative (*parole*) as one iteration of its larger context (*langue*) makes such traditional elements of analysis irrelevant and unnecessary.

Vladimir Propp

Vladimir Propp, a Russian Formalist critic, is associated primarily with **narratology**, yet another form of structuralism, this one principally concerned with the narrative structure of a text. Propp is best known for his investigation of Russian fairy tales, published in 1928 as *Morphology of the Folk Tale*, but not available in English until 1958. Because its concerns were not those favored by the Soviet regime, it disappeared until the structuralists rediscovered it in the 1950s. It was influential in Claude Lévi-Strauss's study of myths.

Following the structuralist process, Propp examined a sizeable number of folk-tales to discover the system that governs them, the *langue*. He concluded that all folk tales are constructed around 31 **narrative functions**—i.e., possible actions that always appear in the sequence he listed. A narrative can utilize any selected number of functions, but they must occur in the given order. For example, a narrative could use #11, "the hero leaves home"; #12, "the hero is tested, interrogated, attacked, etc., which prepares the way for his receiving either a magical agent or helper"; #16, "the hero and the villain join in direct combat"; #18, "the villain is defeated"; and #31, the hero is married and ascends the throne. No single tale will use all 31 functions, but their order is fixed simply because events must unfold according to a natural sequence. For example, the villain cannot be defeated (#18) before the hero and the villain join in direct combat (#16).

Characters receive less attention from Propp than do the functions. Since he treats them as seven **spheres of actions**, they are not so much individual characters as they are types of characters. They include the villain, the provider, the helper, the princess, the dispatcher, the hero, and the false hero.

Using selected functions and the seven spheres of action, a writer can generate a Russian folk tale. Knowing what they are can assist a reader in understanding how a tale operates. What is missing is any concern for literary style, authorial individuality, point-of-view, or social-historical relevance.

Jonathan Culler

Structuralism arrived in the United States in the 1970s, with Jonathan Culler (1944–) leading the charge. Influenced by Sausurre and Claude Lévi-Strauss, he published *Structuralist Poetics* (1975), in which he argued for the movement to devote less attention to examination of individual texts and more to *langue*. To do so, he called for a study of how people read and interpret literature. His theory is that it is a reader who makes structures and meanings in a text. He reasons that past experiences allow an individual to construct assumptions and expectations that make it possible for them to make sense of what they read. They develop literary competence that makes them active participants in generating the text.

Deconstruction, a product of the late 1960s, extended structuralist ideas about the nature of the sign, the importance of difference and binary oppositions, and the role of language in mediating experience, sometimes in ways that contradicted structuralist theories. When readers began to recognize gaps in the structures they were examining, they began both to build on and to break with structuralism, making deconstruction one of several poststructuralist theories that find their commonality in the idea that although some structuralist principles can be used to form a new understanding of reality, the earlier theorists did not take their ideas to their logical conclusions. That assumption led to several significant differences between the two groups.

For one thing, the poststructuralists objected that the structuralist interpretations of texts are too static and unchanging, producing readings that posit fixed meanings. Derrida attributed the problem to the structuralists' acceptance of a transcendental signified. As he pointed out, a concept of constant, universal meaning would be essential as an orienting point in such a closed-off system. The poststructuralists argued instead that texts are fluid, dynamic entities that are given new life with repeated readings and through interactions with other texts, thereby providing an ongoing plurality of meanings. Another objection was that although the structuralists seemed to have provided a broadly applicable new method of arriving at meaning through an analysis of underlying codes and rules, what a text means and how it means simply cannot be determined, because it is not possible to systematically find the grammar of a text. Meaning, they argued, is essentially undecidable, thereby denying the structuralists' belief in the possibility of establishing objective knowledge through systematic observation and logical deduction. For example, the poststructuralists point out that in a single text one can find many meanings, all of them possible and all of them replaceable by others. Instead of looking for structure, then, deconstruction looks for those places where texts contradict, and thereby deconstruct, themselves. Instead of showing how the conventions of a text work, deconstruction shows how they falter. The result is that a literary work can no longer have one unifying meaning that an authority (critic or author) can enunciate. Instead, meaning is accepted to be the outgrowth of various signifying systems within the text that may even produce contradictory meanings. One additional difference between the two groups is that the structuralists assume a scientific stance, which is reflected in the detached tone of their writing and their tendency to discuss abstract topics. The poststructuralists, on the other hand, tend to be more passionate and emotional.

In the 1970s, deconstruction became a major force in literary criticism, in large part because of the strong influence of its originator and namer, the philosopher Jacques Derrida (1930–2004). Derrida's main precursors were Friedrich Nietzsche and Martin Heidegger, (1889–1976) both known for their probing of such key concepts as knowledge, truth, and identity. In the United States, deconstruction became closely associated with Yale University, because some of deconstruction's better-known advocates were on the faculty. In fact, in many people's minds, deconstruction remains closely associated with (and is sometimes referred to as) the Yale school of criticism.

The impact of deconstruction has not been welcomed by all readers, some of whom object that it robs literature of its significance, trivializes texts as simple wordplay, and presents itself in unintelligible jargon. Humanists see deconstruction as a wedge between literature and life, even as a practice that shuts out ordinary readers unwilling to engage in the complex theorizing that deconstruction requires. In response, its defenders point out that it gives us a way to read more critically and honestly than previous systems have allowed us to do. It also provides a means of discovering premises and ideologies that lurk unacknowledged in the language we use.

PRACTICING DECONSTRUCTION

Working from the assumption that language is inherently ambiguous and not the clear, efficient tool for communication we would like to think it is, deconstruction recognizes that any human utterance has a multitude of possibilities for meaning. The simplest statement may be heard in a variety of ways, giving language a tendency to undermine itself by refuting what it appears to be saying. It contradicts itself as it moves from one meaning to another. How does this happen?

In deconstructive terms, Saussure's sign—the combination of a signifier and a signified that refers to a mental concept—is not a stable, unchanging entity. Using Saussure's theory that language is a system based on differences, Derrida went a step further, stating that any given signifier may point to several different signifieds. For example, a statement as uncomplicated as "The cherries are in the bowl" says more than the six words denote. The signifier "cherries" will evoke in our consciousness, and that of our listener/reader, a host of associations—other fruit, a still life, desserts, trees in bloom, allergies—obviously more than cherries in a bowl. Each of the signifieds (other fruit, a still life, and so on), in turn, becomes a signifier, because it leads to other associations, or other signifieds. In short, a signifier has no single signified, or mental concept, as the structuralists assume but instead leads to a chain of other signifiers.

The seemingly simple explanation of sign = signifier + signified can be complicated in other ways as well. A person can speak ironically, for instance, saying one thing but meaning another. Imagine that you say to someone who has just run a stop sign and hit your car while driving over the speed limit, "How could you have run into me? You say you were driving so carefully." Although you would seem to be sympathetic to the other driver, you are actually accusing him of being irresponsible behind the wheel. Tone of voice can also be meaningful. It can, by exaggeration, indicate irony. It may also indicate a specially intended meaning behind a statement. By changing the vocal emphasis to different words, you change the meaning. For example, try reading the second sentence aloud, stressing the first use of the word *you*: "*You* say you were driving so carefully." What does the statement imply? It suggests that the person who caused the accident is being defensive but is alone in claiming innocence. Now emphasize the second *you* and see how the meaning shifts. "You say *you* were driving so carefully" implies that the other driver has accused you of some improper driving practice. And so precise meaning slips away, suggesting many meanings, rather than a single, fixed, clearly identifiable one as the structuralist principles defined.

Saussure argued that language refers not to objective reality but to mental concepts. In deconstructive terms, it does not even refer to mental concepts but only to itself. It consists of the ongoing play of signifiers that never come to rest. Our thinking, then, is always in flux, always subject to changing signifiers that move from one to another. We may wish for stability, but we are caught in language, which refuses to stay fixed. Such play does produce illusory effects of meanings, but the seeming significations are the results of a **trace**, which consists of what remains from the play of signifiers. Because we recognize a word by its differences from other words, it continues to have traces of those that it is not. A word, which is present, signals what is absent. Derrida called this ongoing play ***differance***, a deliberately ambiguous coined term combining the French words for "to defer" and "to differ," suggesting that meaning is always postponed, leaving in its place only the differences between signifiers. (Interestingly, in spoken French, *differance* cannot be distinguished from *difference*, making its meaning even more uncertain.) *Differance* asserts that knowledge comes from dissimilarity and absence, making it dynamic and contextual. When these ideas are applied to a text, the concept of *differance* makes it impossible to think about that work in isolation. The meaning of any given text will be derived from its interrelatedness with other texts in an ongoing process that gives it a series of possible meanings and readings.

Many people are made uncomfortable by the absence of a stable meaning. When they realize the extended consequences of such a proposition, they are likely to be even more disquieted, for if meaning is derived from what is not there—absence—and it is, in the end, undecidable, then there is no such thing as objective truth. As Derrida explained it, there is no **transcendental signified**, no ultimate reality or end to all the references from one sign to another, no unifying element to all things. Human beings resist an existence that lacks the certainty of unchanging meaning, a fixed center, because, as Derrida pointed out, humankind, at least in the Western world, is **logocentric**; that is, human beings want to believe that there is a centering principle in which all belief and actions are grounded and that certain metaphysical ideas are to be favored over others. They want to believe that there is a presence behind language and text. Throughout history such a center has been given many names: truth, God, Platonic form, essence. The salient characteristic, regardless of the name, is that each is stable and ongoing. Each provides an absolute from which all knowledge proceeds.

Actually, this type of thinking goes back to Aristotle, who declared that something cannot have a property and not have it, leading to the dualistic thinking characteristic of Western civilization. Such reasoning is most apparent in the tendency of Western metaphysics to see the world in terms of pairs of opposed centers of meaning, or binary oppositions. As on other occasions, Derrida borrowed the idea from the structuralists, then elaborated on it by noting that in every such pair one member is privileged, or favored, over the other. For example, in the binary oppositions of male/female, good/evil, or truth/lies, the first in each pair is traditionally held by society to be superior. The privileged member defines itself by what it is not, its less-valued partner. Not only do such oppositions exist among abstractions, but they also underlie all human acts. The ideology of a situation or a text can be determined by locating the binary oppositions in it and noting which are the privileged members.

Poststructuralists test binary oppositions to determine whether they are indeed opposed, to challenge traditional assumptions and beliefs about what should be (and is) privileged, to question where they overlap and on what occasions they share their existence. The poststructuralists, including those who read from a deconstructive perspective, point out that oppositions are sometimes not so contrasting as they are thought to be. Perhaps something can be present and absent at the same time. Perhaps, they suggest, looking at the world as a series of opposed centers of meaning—such as right/wrong, good/evil, love/hate—oversimplifies its nature. Such thinking does not take into account the complexity of the way things are, leading to distortions of the truth.

Deconstruction requires that we suspend notice of contradictions in our effort to maintain the conventionally accepted arrangement of absolutes. It resists such simplification by reversing the oppositions, thereby displacing meaning, overturning hierarchies, and offering another set of possibilities of meaning that arise from the new relations of difference. Whenever a group seeks to reverse traditional hierarchies or destabilize privileged binaries, deconstruction becomes a valuable tool. In literary criticism, consequently, deconstructive strategies are often imported into other critical approaches, such as feminist readings or those based on queer theory, as a way to change social attitudes and perceptions.

One binary opposition of particular importance to Derrida was that of speech/writing. He objected to the practice of making speech the privileged member, a convention he called **phonocentrism**, because it implies that the presence of a speaker makes communication more direct and accurate. Written words, which are merely copies of speech, are traditionally deemed to be inferior, because they are less directly connected to the source. Speech is evidence of the presence of the speaker, but writing, which serves when the speaker is not there, points to absence. The binary emerging from this situation is presence/absence, with the former—declared through speaking—the privileged term. This is an essentially logocentric position, because it puts the human being in the center, announcing his or her presence through language. It asserts presence (being) through speaking.

If there is no transcendental signified, no objective truth, then such binaries are not fixed and static. They are fluid and open to change. They can, said Derrida, be reversed. Any center can be decentered, thereby providing a new set of values and beliefs. At the very least, such a reversal makes it possible to see any given situation from a new perspective. A bigger assertion is that by reversing the oppositions—displacing accepted meaning and reinscribing new values—one is able to get outside logocentric thought. Not only did Derrida reverse the speech/writing binary to see the terms in a new way, but he actually argued that writing must come before speech. That is, he reasoned that speech is a form of writing; the two share certain features, as they are both signifying systems. When we interpret oral signs, we must do so by recognizing a pure form of the signifier, one that can be repeated (and recognized) again and again, despite differences of pronunciation. But being capable of repetition is a characteristic of writing, whereas speech vanishes into the air. Because the repeatable signifier gives speech a characteristic of writing, Derrida said it is a special kind of writing.

Complicating the situation is the idea that binary oppositions may overlap each other. They are not necessarily discrete entities. There are too many contradictions and associations involved with language to be able to separate them entirely. At the same time that they reinforce presence, they also remind us of what is missing, thereby complementing each other. Derrida referred to the unstable relationship of binary oppositions as **supplementation**, suggesting that each of the two terms in such an opposition adds something to the other and takes the place of the other. In his hands, for example, writing not only adds something to speech but also substitutes for it, though the substitution is never exact; it is never precisely what it completes. Supplementation exists in all aspects of human life and behavior.

The various ideas traditionally subscribed to by Western civilization are based on the assumption that conscious, integrated selves are at the center of human activity. Derrida called that belief the **metaphysics of presence**. These ideas include our logocentrism (ties to words), our phonocentrism (ties to words produced as sounds), and our acceptance of a transcendental signified (ultimate source of all knowledge). In short, they are beliefs about language and being that have been influential since Plato. But Derrida challenged these beliefs as flawed and erroneous, because meaning is, in the end, undecidable. He defined the metaphysics of presence as "a set of themes whose character was the sign of a whole set of long-standing constraints," adding that "these constraints were practiced at the price of contradictions, of denials, of dogmatic degrees." Furthermore, Derrida "proposed to analyze the non-closed and fissured system of these constraints under the name of logocentrism in the form that it takes in Western philosophy." By deconstructing these constraints, he tried to open new ways of thinking and knowing. In terms of texts, he gave readers a new way to read.

MAKING A DECONSTRUCTIVE ANALYSIS

To understand the discussion that follows, you will need to read "Stopping by Woods on a Snowy Evening," a poem by Robert Frost, found on page 281.

Whereas a traditional critical reading attempts to establish a meaning for a text, a deconstructive reading involves asking questions in an effort to show that what the text claims to be saying is different from what the text is really saying (which, of course, is acknowledged to be provisional). It tries to undermine the work's implied claim of having coherence, unity, and meaning and to show that it does not represent the truth of its subject. In fact, no final statement about its meaning can be made, for each reading is provisional, just one in a series of interpretations that decenter each other in ongoing play. In the absence of a transcendental signified, a text cannot be said to be tied to some center that existed before and outside it, and meaning can have no place to conclude, nothing in which to be subsumed.

A number of people have tried to summarize the process of deconstructing a text. Derrida himself explained it by saying that "the reading must always aim at a certain relationship, unperceived by the writer, between what he commands and what he does not command of the patterns of the language that he uses." As Sharon Crowley describes the process in *Teacher's Introduction to Deconstruction,* it tries to "tease larger systemic motifs out of gaps, aberrations, or inconsistencies in a given text." It tries to find blind spots that a writer has absorbed from cultural systems. She adds that "deconstruction amounts to reading texts in order to rewrite them," just as Derrida tried "to reread Western history to give voice to that which has been systematically silenced." (Paul de Man has perhaps had the most to say about "blind spots." In *Blindness and Insight,* he goes so far as to assert that critics achieve insight through their "peculiar blindness." He finds that they say something besides what they mean.)

Barbara Johnson's frequently quoted definition of deconstruction says that it occurs by "the careful teasing out of warring forces of signification within the text itself." Jonathan Culler says that "to deconstruct a discourse is to show how it undermines the philosophy it asserts, or the hierarchical oppositions on which it relies." A more detailed comment comes from J. Hillis Miller:

> Deconstruction as a mode of interpretation works by a careful and circumspect entering of each textual labyrinth. . . . The deconstructive critic seeks to find, by this process of retracing, the element in the system studied which is alogical, the thread in the text in question which will unravel it all, or the loose stone which will pull down the whole building. The deconstruction, rather, annihilates the ground on which the building stands by showing that the text has already annihilated the ground, knowingly or unknowingly. Deconstruction is not a dismantling of the structure of a text but a demonstration that it has already dismantled itself.

Such definitions are helpful, but how does the deconstructive critic go about "unraveling" the text or finding a writer's blind spots or a text's "gaps, aberrations, or inconsistencies"? The process is actually somewhat similar to the one used in formalism. That is, the reader engages in a very close reading of the text, noting the presence and operation of all its elements. However, the ends of the two approaches are radically different. Whereas formalism seeks to demonstrate that a work has essential unity despite the paradoxes and irony that create its inner tension, that it expresses a realizable truth, deconstruction seeks to show that a text has no organic unity or basis for presenting meanings, only a series of conflicting significations.

One way to begin is to follow Derrida's own process, which he called "double reading." That is, you first go through a text in a traditional manner, pointing out where it seems to have determinate meanings. The first step in deconstructing Frost's "Stopping by Woods on a Snowy Evening," for example, might be to make a commentary on the narrator's desire for peace, the highly controlled form, or the cumulative effect of the images of night, winter, and sleep. On second reading, however, you would question what is accepted in the poem as natural or self-evident, looking to find places where the attitudes or assumptions identified on first reading are contradicted or undermined. When incompatible meanings are brought to light, the text deconstructs itself. These incompatible meanings undermine the grounds on which the text is based, and meaning becomes indeterminate. The text is not unitary and unified in the manner that logocentrism promises. Recognizing that a text has multiple interpretations, the reader expects to interpret it over and over again. No single reading is irrevocable; it can always be displaced by a subsequent one. Thus interpretation becomes a creative act as important as the text undergoing interpretation. The pleasure lies in the discovery of new ways of seeing the work. Of course, because the reader must express those discoveries in logocentric language, the interpretation will deconstruct itself as well.

How do you find alternative meanings, especially if you are accustomed to assuming that there is an inherent meaning to be found, that it will be recognizable to other readers, and that the picture it gives of the world will be consonant with the way the world really is? How do you find contradictory or incompatible meanings if you are used to finding *the* meaning of a text or passage?

You can begin by locating the binary oppositions in the text, identifying the member that is privileged and the one that is not. All key terms and characters are defined by their oppositions, and the deconstructive reader will show how the pairs are mutually dependent but also unstable. In "Stopping by Woods," for example, a number of hierarchical oppositions are quickly noted: silence/sound, nature/civilization, isolation/community, dark/light, stillness/activity, unconscious/conscious, and, by implication, death/life and dreams/reality. Looking at them carefully will give you a way of entering the poem deconstrucuively. For example, try to answer the following questions about the hierarchical oppositions, and then compare your answers with the commentary that follows each.

- What values and ideas do the hierarchies reflect? Your answer will define some of the preconceptions that influence the way the text is conventionally read.

  If you accept the first of each paired term to be the privileged one, you will read the poem as a statement about the value of experiencing peace, oneness with nature, acceptance of self. There is beauty in the moment and a sense of connection with primeval forces.

- What do you find when you reverse the binary oppositions? What fresh perspectives on the poem emerge? Because the hierarchy is arbitrary and illusory, it can be turned upside down to provide a new view of the values and beliefs that underlie it. The new, unconventional relationships may radically change your perception of the terms or of the text.

  The interesting aspect of the oppositions in this poem is that the "privileged" terms throughout most of it are reversed at the end when the traveler chooses to continue his journey. For the first three stanzas, silence is favored over sound, nature over civilization, isolation over community, and so on. When, however, the persona rejects the loveliness of the dark, deep woods and chooses to honor promises that lie outside them, he acknowledges that he lives in a world that expects him to renounce self-indulgent dreams and carry out his obligations. He is part of a society that honors community, activity, consciousness, and reality.

  Although in this case the poet himself has provided a reversal, the reader still must ask what has been changed by it. What else is affected? What would be different, for example, if the traveler opted for nature, darkness, and dreams? What if the forces that attracted him so powerfully throughout most of the experience remained the privileged ones? What would be different if isolation were deemed to be more attractive than community? What if it were preferable to be alone, outside the company of friends and family? Then the woods would belong to nobody, or at least the narrator would not acknowledge their claim, and there would be no self-consciousness about being observed.

Conformity to social norms and pressures (signaled by the horse) would cease to exist. The world would be marked by an absence of stress and the presence of peace. The narrator would be liberated from drudgery, labor, the burdens of responsibility, which are implied by the penultimate line. Structure and regimentation would disappear, and in their place would be spontaneity and natural reactions. And perhaps most important, one would feel a sense of unity with nature. To be alone is for the moment appealing, and this overturned hierarchy offers a new and provisional center of meaning.

- Do you find any contradictions in the privileged members? Or are they incompatible?

  The privileged terms silence, isolation, stillness, *and* unconscious *initially seem to fit easily into a single scene, but on closer analysis, some inconsistencies emerge. There are contradictions in the poem that go unacknowledged. For example, the traveler enjoys the pleasures of isolation but ultimately opts for community. He savors the beauty of nature but chooses civilization. When he continues his journey, isolation and nature are decentered by community and civilization. In the end, contradictory hierarchies (isolation/community and community/isolation, nature/civilization and civilization/nature) are privileged by the protagonist even though they are incompatible. The opposed conditions cannot exist together, though that is never overtly acknowledged in the poem. Their incongruity underscores the fragmented, conflicted nature of the traveler himself. It also asserts the lack of fixed, unchanging meaning in poems or in life itself.*

- What else do the terms make you think of? What other hierarchies do they lead to? Such associations will suggest alternative readings, new terms that can decenter the ones currently controlling the interpretation.

  Earlier it was noted that stillness, silence, isolation, and the rest seem, by extension, to suggest the unconscious and death. By establishing unconscious/conscious and death/life as major oppositions, the old reading about promises and duties is decentered and replaced with an interpretation having to do with renunciation of vitality and presence, a quite different set of concerns. In this way, the chain of signifiers rolls over and over, moving from one provisional meaning to another.

- How do the binary terms supplement each other? How does each help the reader understand its opposing term? How do they reinforce both presence and absence?

  At the end of Frost's poem, when the narrator exchanges the peace of aloneness (isolation) for reengagement with the world, nature and civilization, and countryside and village, are not opposites; rather they are experiences in the being of the narrator that decenter and supplement each other. He is attracted by the solace of the winter scene in the woods, but he chooses the world of obligations and work. He is not, of course, a unified being but a fragmented one who speaks from the unconscious and returns at the end to the conscious world. He exists in dream and reality.

Another deconstructive approach is to take what has heretofore seemed marginal and make it central. Elements customarily considered to be of minor interest can become the focus of interest, with binary oppositions and possible reversals of their own. The comment that ordinarily receives little attention is brought to the center to see what new understandings surface, or a minor character may be scrutinized as critical to what happens in the plot. For example, in "Stopping by Woods," a close look at the horse is revealing. Seemingly of slight importance to what happens in the poem or what it may mean, the horse turns out to be surprisingly significant. Described in this poem as "little" ("My little horse must think it queer / To stop without a farmhouse near"), he turns out to play a large role. He "gives his harness bells a shake," thereby reminding the narrator of responsibility, duty, and social judgments. He interrupts the silence with sound, supplanting the peacefulness of the moment with a call to activity and conformity, replacing absence with presence. The horse becomes, in a sense, the voice of the conscious and civilized world, which in itself is a commentary on that world. Nevertheless, the traveler exchanges his dreams for reality. The horse's bells, sounds that are not even language, displace isolation as a center of meaning and thereby change the direction of the poem. The animal's impact would easily go unnoticed, except that the deconstructionist moves him to center stage.

Any "hidden" contradictions and discrepancies between what the text seems to say and what it actually says are important. Such incongruities are often found in what is not said, in gaps of information, silences, tensions, questions, or sometimes figures of speech. The author's intent is of no help in this process, because what the author thinks was said may not be the case at all. In fact, by identifying those places where a slip of language occurs—that is, where something is said that was not meant to be said—you have found a point at which a text begins to deconstruct itself. By discovering a pattern of such inconsistencies and trying to account for it, a different interpretation becomes possible. The reader of this poem wonders, for instance, about the distance between the terms used to describe the woods. They are said to be "lovely, dark, and deep." The first descriptive word connotes aesthetic pleasure, the next two a sense of threat or mystery. The solace that the narrator imputes to the woods is threatened. It is, finally, not there, or at least it is there only momentarily. The woods have no permanent, stable, consistent self.

Looking at a binary opposition, such as presence/absence, for example, reversed by Derrida so that absence is favored, often helps a reader deconstruct a text. In "Stopping by Woods," it is significant that the narrator's words come unspoken from the inner self. They appear to exist only in thought. Phonocentric views would give them a privileged position because they are closest to the man. They represent him, stand in for him, displace him. The inner words ultimately appear in writing, however, displacing speech (which in this case is unvoiced), which displaced unspoken thought, which initially displaced the man. The presence of being is far removed. The words of the persona supplement (act as additions to and substitutions for) him. Further, the bells of the horse metaphorically make the horse a spokesperson for the community, thereby displacing the horse's center. Sound has replaced speech. Animal has replaced people. Absence is thereby privileged over presence.

In sum, the narrator of "Stopping by Woods" is seen to be a logocentric being who looks for a center where there is none. Finding only momentary meaning, he moves on to seek a center in work and community. He yearns for peace but displaces it with obligations, because although unity is desirable, it is absent, only fleetingly available in the moment in the woods.

Finally, the deconstructive reader will place all structures in question, because an ultimate meaning is always deferred, and ambiguity remains. The purpose is to decenter each new center, to cast doubt on previous theories, never coming to rest on any one meaning but generating an infinite number of possible interpretations. The meaning of the protagonist's experience in "Stopping by Woods," for example, cannot be determined in the long run. The repetition of the last line resists interpretation or provides multiple readings, because its metaphoric ramifications remain ambiguous, unclear, full of possibilities, none of them final.

On subsequent readings, new levels of meaning will emerge with the inversion of other binary oppositions. Some will appear only after others have been explored. You may find yourself moving back and forth between different interpretations or successively displacing one with another. In either case, the unending play of *différance* prevents you from arriving at any decidable meaning, or any set of multiple meanings, for anything you say or write. Instead, there is an unending process, with every new reading holding the possibility of a new interpretation. Acceptance of shifting meanings challenges the previously held views of the reader, offering freedom from the constraints of traditional assumptions and ideologies so that new ways of seeing are made possible.

WRITING A DECONSTRUCTIVE ANALYSIS

It should be noted at the outset that important voices have expressed concern about the appropriateness of viewing deconstruction as a critical approach. Not surprisingly, some critics resist what they see as the negativism found in deconstruction's philosophical attack on the existence of meaning in literature (and life). Others object less to its destructive effects than to what they see as its tendency to trivialize literature and the act of reading, thereby threatening the privileged place those people hold in academia. They accuse deconstruction of diminishing our capacity to appreciate and interpret literature. And almost everyone complains of its obscure and confusing terminology. David Hirsch's *The Deconstruction of Literature,* John Ellis's *Against Deconstruction,* and David Lehman's *Signs of the Times: Deconstruction and the Fall of Paul de Man,* for example, all question the validity of this approach.

Another kind of objection comes from Jane Tompkins, who argues against the practice of applying poststructuralist principles to texts, because it means using methods that are basically positivist and empirical and thereby contradictory to deconstruction.

> The point I want to make here is that you can't apply post-structuralism to literary texts. Why not? Because to talk about applying post-structuralism to literary texts assumes the following things: (1) that we have freestanding subjects, (2) that we have freestanding objects of investigation, (3) that there are freestanding methods, and (4) that what

> results when we apply reader to method and method to text is a freestanding interpretation. This series of assumptions revokes everything that Derrida is getting at in *"Différance,"* and that is implicit in Saussure's theory of language.... As we read literary texts, then, "we" are not applying a "method"; we are acting as an extension of the interpretive code, of those systems of difference that constitute us and the objects of our perception simultaneously.

Nevertheless, deconstructive readings can enrich one's experience with a text by providing an ongoing journey through it, with each journey revealing a new way of thinking about the text. Although such studies proceed in different ways, here are some suggestions to help you read from this perspective and to write about your observations.

Prewriting

A reading log can be particularly helpful with the deconstructive approach. As you go through a text for the first time, you can make notes as a formalist would, taking an interest in how meaning grows out of the work's various stylistic elements. You will identify tensions (in the form of paradox and irony) and be aware of how they are resolved. You will take note of how images, figurative language, and symbols come together to make a unified whole (see Chapter 3). During the second reading, you can set aside your willingness to accept that there is an identifiable, stable meaning produced by the diction, imagery, symbols, and the rest and begin to probe unresolved, unexplained, or unmentioned matters. In your reading log, you should record the undeveloped concerns that would, if they were explored, interrupt the assumed unity and meaning of the text.

The prewriting stage is also a good time to play with the binary oppositions that you find, first identifying those that initially seem most significant, then inferring the ideology that they present. You can recognize them by noting where the text makes a clear distinction between two items of the same genus: black/white (colors), men/women (gender), and so on. You can determine which is privileged by asking what the text accepts as normal, natural, worthy of being or doing. The next step, as noted in "Making a Deconstructive Analysis," is to reverse the terms, thereby creating an inversion of the recognizable world, a new world that is parallel to the world you are used to. This, in turn, allows you to look at the work in an unaccustomed manner. You can also look for contradictions in the binary terms by noting how each defines itself against its opposite or determine how they supplement each other by showing how a term that seems complete in itself is actually derived from something else. Even the most unified act or being is dependent on others for its existence, making all things incomplete or fragmented. It is likely that some of the steps in this process will help you find, in the terms of J. Hillis Miller, "the thread in the text in question which will unravel it all, or the loose stone which will pull down the whole building." And that is an important point, because deconstruction works not simply to reverse binaries but also to deconstruct entire hierarchies by illustrating their inherent instability.

Another prewriting activity involves examining the language of the text. You can begin by looking for paradoxes and contradictions, then move on to examining the figurative language. By making a list of metaphors, for example, you have information that may reveal slippages of the language. Because figures of speech do not mean what they literally say, there is room for them to misstate what the author intended for them to say. You may find it helpful to put the phrases on paper and then play with their possibilities in writing.

A more global view of the text involves looking for shifts in point of view, time, voice, vocabulary, or tone, because such shifts may signal that the narrative or the narrator (speaker) of the work is not unified or stable. What seems to be coherent is actually fraught with contradictions and conflicts. When these cannot be resolved, the text is said to have reached the point at which it deconstructs itself, a point known as **aporia**.

Much of the prewriting suggested here involves listing and note making. Although these strategies will aid analysis, they will be helpful in the drafting stage only insofar as they provide ideas and information. Consequently, the more material you can generate at this point, the better off you will be when you begin to write your first draft.

Drafting and Revising

The Introduction Given that deconstructive readings seek to displace previous ones, and sometimes to decenter standard, generally accepted interpretations, one way to open the discussion is to reiterate the conventional reading of a text. In other words, the introduction may simply be a restatement of the usual perception of what a work means or of how it operates. By explaining how a story is usually read or how a character is normally perceived, you have a basis for deconstructing those views. Once you have established what is usually deemed to be so, you are set to state why it is not the only possible reading. Your argument for multiple readings will be the central focus of the body of the discussion that follows, but it is helpful to introduce that idea early on.

The Body Your purpose in the body of your deconstructive analysis will be to demonstrate the limited perspective of the conventional reading. You may want to show how the ideology that the text tries to support is not supportable, an approach that is popular with Marxist and feminist deconstructive critics. In this case, as you study a particular text, you will also be deconstructing the larger contexts in which it exists. You will be suggesting, or overtly stating, that the order supported by it is also open to question, perhaps itself fraught with inconsistencies and illusory stability.

On the other hand, you may be more interested in presenting a series of possible readings, one decentering the other in an ongoing process. This approach will take the discussion a step further by showing how meaning is not simply an either-or situation but an unending series of possibilities, leaving meaning ultimately beyond deciding. In either case, you will want to demonstrate how and where the text falls apart because of its own inconsistencies, misstatements, or contradictions.

The thinking you did during the prewriting stage will be valuable here, but remember that all assertions need to be supported with quotations and examples drawn from the text. The following questions can help you generate the basis of your discussion. If you developed your prewriting stage thoroughly, you will have already covered some of these questions.

- What is the primary binary opposition in the text?
- What associated binary oppositions do you find?
- Which terms in the oppositions are privileged?
- What elements in the work support the privileged terms?
- What statement of values or beliefs emerges from the privileged terms?
- What elements in the text contradict the hierarchies as presented?
- Where is the statement of values or beliefs contradicted by characters, events, or statements in the text?
- Are the privileged terms inconsistent? Do they present conflicting meanings?
- What associations do you have with the terms that complicate their opposition? That is, what associations keep you from accepting that the terms are all good or all bad?
- What new possibilities of understanding emerge when you reverse the binary oppositions?
- How does the reversal of oppositions tear down the intended statement of meaning?
- What contradictions of language, image, or event do you notice?
- Are there any significant omissions of information?
- Can you identify any irreconcilable views offered as coherent systems?
- What is left unnoticed or unexplained?
- How would a focus on different binary oppositions lead to a different interpretation?
- Where are the figures of speech so ambiguous that they suggest several (perhaps contradictory) meanings?
- What usually overlooked minor figures or events can be examined as major ones?
- How does the focus of meaning shift when you make marginal figures central?
- What new vision of the situation presented by the text emerges for you?
- What new complications do you see that the conventional reading would have "smoothed over"?
- Why can you not make a definitive statement about the meaning of the text?

The Conclusion If you have begun by rehearsing the conventional reading of the text under analysis, an effective way to end your essay is by comparing that understanding with your deconstructive analysis, pointing out why the earlier one is not definitive. If you prefer, you may reiterate the several different ways in which the text can be read, thereby making the point that meaning is always provisional, always ready to give way to other meaning.

SUGGESTED READING

Abrams, M. H. " The Deconstructive Angel." *Critical Inquiry* 3(1977): 425–38.

Crowley, Sharon. *A Teacher's Introduction to Deconstruction*. Urbana, IL: National Council of Teachers of English, 1989.

Culler, Jonathan. *On Deconstruction: Theory and Criticism after Structuralism*. Ithaca, NY: Cornell University Press, 1982.

Derrida, Jacques. *A Derrida Reader*. Ed. Peggy Kamuf. New York: Columbia University Press, 1991.

———. *Of Grammatology*. Trans. Gayatri Chakravorty Spivak. Baltimore: Johns Hopkins University Press, 1998.

Johnson, Barbara. The Critical Difference: Essays in the Contemporary Rhetoric of Reading. Baltimore: Johns Hopkins UP, 1980.

Miller, J. Hillis. " Tradition and Difference." *Diacritics* 2(1972): 6–13.

Norris, Christopher. *Deconstruction: Theory and Practice*. London: Methuen, 1982.

Scholes, Robert. " Deconstruction and Criticism." *Critical Inquiry* 14(1988): 278–95.

Tompkins, Jane. " A Short Course in Post-Structuralism." In *Conversations*, ed. Charles Moran and Elizabeth Penfield, pp. 19-37. Urbana, IL: National Council of Teachers of English, 1990.

For up-to-date information on the many Web sites addressing deconstruction, visit www.cengagebrain.com.

Model Student Analysis

The Blame Game

KATHERINE MEISTER

Is there a single, unified meaning in Guy de Maupassant's "The Diamond Necklace," or does the tale offer a plurality of different meanings? At first glance, this is a difficult question to answer; however, an exploration of oppositions and contradictions within the text offers an avenue to begin investigation. One opposition that is particularly useful in exploring the question of meaning within the text is found in the opposition between the individual and society. As one reads through the text, it is difficult to determine whom or what the text is critical of. Is it critical of Mme. Loisel or of society? Is her discontentment an individual flaw, or is it a flaw created by the society in which she lives? These questions make it clear that the text does not offer one single meaning but several different meanings. As one examines the text, evidence to support both positions emerges, and because it contradicts itself, the text cannot offer a unified message. Ultimately, there are two different positions within this text. A first reading of the text favors a position that is critical of Mme. Loisel and of her discontentment; however, a second reading uncovers contradictions in the text that decenter this first reading, producing a reading that is sympathetic to Mme. Loisel. It views her discontentment as a flaw imposed upon her by societal pressure.

On a first reading of the text, it seems clear that "The Diamond Necklace" is only critical of Mme. Loisel; it views her discontentment as an individual flaw. Evidence of a negative opinion of Mme. Loisel appears early in the text. Her apartment is described as being "shabby" and "worn" and, "All these things, which another woman of her station would not have noticed, tortured and angered her." Other women in her place are content, but she as an individual is not, and consequently her discontentment is criticized. In addition, the strong language adds to this criticism of Mme. Loisel. Not only does she want things that other women do not, not having these things "tortured and angered her." This language shows the obsessive desire that possesses Mme. Loisel. Instead of being content with her middle-class life, as are the other women of her circle, she is "tortured" by the fact that she does not have "footmen in short trousers" and "old silks."

Later in the text, further evidence reaffirms that Mme. Loisel's discontentment is an individual flaw. When given the invitation to the ball, she says to her husband, "I have no dress and consequently cannot go to this affair. Give your card to some colleague whose wife is better fitted out than I." Her response is interesting, because a colleague's wife will have no more money and no more luxuries than Mme. Loisel. If a colleague's wife is fitted to go to the ball, why does Mme. Loisel feel that she is not? This statement reveals that Mme. Loisel possesses low self-esteem, and it is this individual flaw that drives her to chase after more than her middle-class life can provide. If she believed she was just as "fitted" as other women, she would not be discontented with her own life and would be happy to attend this "select" event in her theater dress.

At first, these and other similar passages throughout the tale point to a criticism that is focused solely on Mme. Loisel. However, a closer examination of the text reveals contradictions in it that produce a reading that is sympathetic to Mme. Loisel and that exposes social pressure as the source of Mme. Loisel's unhappiness. The first sentence of the tale produces sympathy for Mme. Loisel that is clearly contradicted by subsequent comments just noted: "She was one of those pretty, charming young ladies, born, as if through an error of destiny, into a family of clerks." First, this statement is not critical of Mme. Loisel but sympathetic toward her. It is not her fault that she has been born into this family; it was an "error of destiny." Furthermore, the use of *error* implies that she should have been born into a wealthier family; therefore, she is not wrong to want the fate that should have been hers. If destiny had not erred, she would have had the life that she desires, and at this point, the text is sympathetic to this fact.

In addition, throughout the tale, there are several slips in language that can be used to argue that it is not an individual flaw that has caused Mme. Loisel's discontentment, but that her discontentment is a flaw imposed upon her by society. One such passage occurs early in the text: "She had such a desire to please, to be sought after, to be clever, and courted." These are traits that are dependent upon how others see her, and because these traits are not fulfilled by her own attitudes, the statement constitutes a slip in the original language of personal flaw. She wants to please society, and in order to do so, she has been made to believe that she must be sought after, clever, and courted. These desires are formed through outside societal pressure that has made her believe that these things are important; however, these characteristics also demand a certain amount of wealth—wealth that Mme. Loisel does not possess. In the end, she cannot be blamed for her discontentment in life, because it is caused by the things society demands of her that she cannot give.

As Mme. Loisel prepares to attend the ball, further evidence is given to show that society is indeed the source of her discontentment. Her ball gown is almost ready, but instead of being excited, she is "disturbed" and "anxious," because she does not have a jewel to "adorn" herself. She is discontented because "there is nothing more humiliating than to have a shabby air in the midst of rich women." Just as society can make her feel sought after and clever, it can also make her feel humiliated. Society demands that she have a jewel to adorn her dress, and if she does not have one, she opens herself to ridicule and humiliation. She measures herself and her ball attire by the standards created by the society she wishes to impress, and in that comparison, she discovers that she does not live up to them. Again, Mme. Loisel cannot be blamed for her discontentment, because it is a discontentment that has been created by the social standards she cannot maintain.

Finally, it is interesting that Mme. Loisel is such a success at the ball. This success shows that the pressure placed upon her was a real pressure and not a pressure she created and placed upon herself. While at the ball, "All the men noticed her, asked her name, and wanted to be presented. All the members of the Cabinet wished to waltz with her. The Minister of Education paid her some attention." The demands of society have been reinforced at this ball. If she had worn her theater dress and fresh flowers, she would not have met societal standards, and it is doubtful that she would have been such a success at the ball. If she had not received as much attention by the public, it could have been argued that she had placed an imaginary pressure upon herself; however, her reception proves that the pressure she feels is real.

The opposition between the individual and society in "The Diamond Necklace" creates a tale that cannot offer a single unified meaning. The text may initially claim to be critical of Mme. Loisel; however, there is ample evidence to prove that it is actually sympathetic toward her. She cannot be blamed for her discontentment in life because it is a discontentment that has been created by a societal pressure to desire luxuries that her middle-class life cannot provide. Ultimately, this reading is revealed through the contradictions in the tale. In reading past the initial claims of the text and closely examining oppositions and contradictions within the text, the reader finds that it deconstructs itself and a new, different reading may be found that sheds a new perspective upon Mme. Loisel and her discontentment in life.

9

Cultural Studies: New Historicism

> The essential matter of history is not what happened but what people thought or said about it.
>
> FREDERIC W. MAITLAND, ENGLISH WRITER ON LAW

As we noted with feminist and other critical approaches, the more recent the appearance of a particular perspective, the more difficult it is to define. The field of cultural studies is a prime example of this problem. Emerging in the 1960s, this field has yet to settle into an accepted and agreed-upon set of principles and practices. In it you will recognize many theories that you have already met, including ideas drawn from Marxism, feminism, popular culture, racial and ethnic studies, and more. It is not a single, standardized approach to literature (or anything else) but a field that binds its adherents through some common interests and purposes, although they are addressed in widely divergent ways.

At present, three types of cultural studies that are getting particular notice are new historicism, postcolonialism, and American multiculturalism. Although each has its own distinct focus, all are concerned with social and cultural forces that create a community or that threaten it. Those who look at texts from these points of view are eager to make more voices recognized by a broader circle of readers. In the long run, their approaches to reading can change the way readers conceive of a culture. Because cultural studies is still finding its way, this discussion will identify only a few commonalities that are shared by its different subgroups.

AN OVERVIEW OF CULTURAL STUDIES

Part of the difficulty in defining ***cultural studies***, or even ***culture*** for that matter, is that the terms are so inclusive. If *culture* refers to the sum of the beliefs, institutions, arts, and behaviors of a particular people or time, then cultural studies can be said to address an almost unthinkably broad body of knowledge: language, customs, legal systems, literature, and more. Sometimes such a study is even interested in the culture of those who have responded to it. As it usually proceeds, however, a cultural study will address a particular topic, such as "Hispanic Women Writers of Texas," using the cultural context to arrive at generalizations about that topic. The intent is to connect historical, social, and economic knowledge surrounding the topic, a topic that may not seem to be very literary at all. Because any context is virtually unending, the critic never knows enough. As a result, interpretations made from a cultural studies perspective tend to be open-ended and continue to evolve as they are affected by new information. Nevertheless, a few generalizations can be made.

For the most part, groups engaged in cultural studies share the assumption that within any society there is a dominant group that determines what is acceptable and what is unacceptable for the larger body. It defines the culture's tastes and values—in short, its ideology. Cultural critics are interested in those groups of people who do not belong to the dominant parties and who challenge the hegemony of the powerful. In the world of literature, they are the people Antonio Gramsci called **subaltern** writers. However, wherever there is dominance, there is also, to some degree, defiance that makes it impossible for the powerful to prevent change indefinitely. Recognizing that **subjects** (people) are socially constructed, cultural critics work to change **power** structures where they are unequal, making the subjugated and marginalized more visible and influential makers of the culture. As James Berlin put it, "The subject is the point of intersection of various discourses—discourses about class, race, gender, ethnicity, age, religion, and the like—and it is influenced by those discourses." Consequently, it is necessary to "examine signifying practices in the formation of subjectivities within concrete material, social, and political conditions." Such a focus makes the field a highly politicized one, dedicated, as it is, to examining cultural forces in both literature and life with the intent of changing the way power is conceived.

The challenge presented to the power structure by groups such as African Americans, gay people, and women has led to challenges in other arenas as well. In literature, it has created a rejection of the concept of the "masterpiece." All the artifacts of a time or a people are of interest to the cultural critic, each to be treated with equal importance. There are no hierarchies of importance, no divisions between "fine art" and "popular art," between "high culture" and "low culture." Art itself is but one of many manifestations of a culture, one expression of it. Such an assumption makes cultural studies inevitably interdisciplinary. No single approach can provide the kind of analysis that broad social concerns demand. Literary criticism, in these terms, is a limited creature that needs the help of anthropology, sociology, psychology, linguistics, and more.

When literature is no longer given special reverence but is instead regarded as one of many areas of interest, its connections with the everyday world of work are inevitably involved; at this point, the influence of Marxism becomes particularly evident. Marxism is reflected, for example, in the interest that cultural studies researchers have in how a work was produced. They question how a book achieved publication, who bought it, and how it was marketed.

In sum, cultural studies takes a broad view of human communities. Its practitioners challenge the status quo by trying to displace the powerful (whether "the powerful" be a literary canon or discriminatory institutions) and promote the voices (and thus the power) of those seldom heard. They do so by using knowledge and methods adopted from nonliterary fields to serve their belief that they can effect cultural change. For them, literature is a particularly productive means by which a culture can call attention to itself and assert its significance and worth.

With the increased self-awareness that has burgeoned since the 1960s among groups of people bound by common ties of race, ethnicity, history, and gender, a thorough discussion of cultural studies would become a book of its own. Even a consideration of how it affects literary criticism in general is beyond the scope of this presentation. Consequently, only three types of cultural studies will be looked at in this book: new historicism is discussed in this chapter, while postcolonialism and American multiculturalism are taken up in the following one. Although they are not the only types of cultural studies that could have been selected, these three have received significant attention of late. The ways in which their adherents read and analyze texts can be applied to the literatures of other cultural groups.

ASSUMPTIONS, PRINCIPLES, AND GOALS OF NEW HISTORICISM

New historicism, which readers began to apply to texts in the late 1970s and early 1980s, attracted enough attention to challenge the prominent position then held by the deconstructionists. However, given that it is a radically new way of examining the human past, new historicism is difficult to pin down, partly because it is still changing and developing and partly because it draws on widely diverse fields that seem to have little in common except their interest in the study of cultures. Sometimes new historicism seems to be grounded in sociology, sometimes in psychology or economics; in any case, the scope of investigation by new historicists is never limited to any single field of study, because they see all parts of a given culture as shaping and being shaped by one another in such complex ways that any one approach is incapable of providing a complete picture of what has happened or, more important, what it means. Because new historicism is significantly different from traditional historical study, perhaps the best way to present its basic assumptions and principles is to begin by comparing it with its more familiar predecessor.

Traditional Historicism

At the simplest level, historians have traditionally been concerned with finding out what really happened at a given time and place. They worked to establish the factual accuracy of the stories that make up the record of the human past so that they could establish, with as much certainty as possible, that the account they rendered was a valid delineation of what had happened. To do so meant maintaining an objective stance, a position of distance from the scene of action that would allow them to see and state the truth about people and events. If they were successful in doing so, they would, by extension, manage to capture the sense of an entire age. They could find the essence of a period, the worldview that would unlock the meaning of that period's literature, art, politics, social behavior, and the rest. In looking at the broad sweep of history, they viewed the narratives as being linked to one another in a causal sequence that, it was assumed, would carry the world forward in a positive, progressive manner.

New Historicism

The new historicists, most of them literary scholars, have challenged and resisted the assumptions and goals of traditional historicism. They deny, for example, that anyone can ever know exactly what happened at a given time and place. All that can be perceived is what has been handed down in artifacts and stories, making history a narration, not a pure, unadulterated set of precise observations. Thus, all history is subjectively known and set down, colored by the cultural context of the recorder—usually a person of power—thus leaving untold the stories of those who were powerless. Traditionally, history has been recorded by the winners. The losers, or those who lack political or social power, have their stories to tell as well. Although they may not have published those stories in official documents or textbooks, they have circulated them as separate **discourses**, or ways of seeing and talking about the world. The new historicist would want to hear all the stories and recognize all the voices.

Imagine, for example, trying to understand what took place at the battle of Gettysburg and why it happened. No single explanation can account for the complexities and contradictions buried in the battle. A simple report of causes and effects behind the series of events would not explain what really happened. No reading of the battle in light of the spirit of the age would include all those who were involved: officers and volunteers, rural and urban troops, wives and children, blacks and whites. And, at the end of the battle, who could say that something positive had taken place? The new historicists do not claim to have the "truth" about a text or historical event; rather, they assert that the truth, if such a thing could even exist, would be narratologically and culturally contingent. History and literature, it seems, are more complicated than earlier readers had assumed.

Complicating the matter further is that not only are history's stories subjectively recorded, but they are also subjectively read and interpreted. A historian works from texts that have already been written (or told), recasting them in light of his or her own particular concerns. Regardless of his commitment to produce objective readings, the historian can never manage to do so, because he cannot transcend his own values, experiences, and knowledge. Inevitably caught up in his own social and cultural contexts, the historian cannot escape the viewpoints provided by the ideas and institutions of his own day. Like the literary analyst, the historian who reads a "text" is involved in interpretation, reinforcing the subjectivity of any account of history.

Because it is impossible to maintain pure objectivity in the examination of history, historians are obligated to acknowledge the biases that are likely to color their interpretations. The more unaware they are of their tendencies to "read" history in particular ways, the more biased their accounts are likely to be. They are, therefore, ethically bound to admit their political and philosophical tendencies. The act of announcing one's own leanings is known as **self-positioning**. As a result of the less-than-objective recordings and readings of the past, history becomes a text rather than a series of empirically verifiable events. Consequently, its study calls for a more interesting (and more valid) question than "What really happened?" In its place, the new historicist is drawn to ask: "What do the interpretations tell us about the interpreters?" or "How does what happened point to social conflicts?" or "How do the historical facts fit into ideologies of the day?" As Hayden White pointed out, what yesterday's historian would have seen as an event that actually occurred in the past, today's historian sees as a "text" to be interpreted, just as a poem or novel is interpreted by a critic.

The new historicists also challenge the existence of what is referred to as the "spirit of an age." Recognizing that any culture is made up of many disparate and conflicting strands, they deny that there is ever a single, unified worldview operating at a given period. To claim to have found the one perspective that would explain the beliefs, behaviors, and products of a time and place is an oversimplification. In place of a controlling narrative, the new historicists recognize many narratives produced by institutions and social strata that may hold contrasting bodies of belief and practice or differing modes of behavior. As they would put it, at any given period, many discourses, or ways of seeing and thinking about the world, operate simultaneously. These discourses clash and overlap and repeat, shaping and being shaped by one another. The political discourse of the court of Henry VIII in sixteenth-century England was not the discourse of the peasants who populated the country's rural villages. To claim understanding of that rich period by considering only what the court was talking about and how it saw current events (and the court itself had many different discourses operating), or by examining only how the church viewed them, would provide a severely limited sense of what was happening and what it meant. According to new historicists, there never was, and there never is, a single history or a single worldview. Instead, many discourses come together in a complex cultural interaction. In fact, some new historicists charge that the very notion of a standardized culture is a false one that has been imposed by powerful institutions and classes as a way of maintaining their own interests.

Because new historicists are aware that no single discourse can explain the complexities of any event or artifact, they search out sources that were overlooked in the past by critics who sought an overall explanation of a period's practices and products. Their investigations have led to an interest in the narratives of marginalized people as well as to some criticism for the importance they give to nonmainstream materials. Their quest is important, however, because it is through the stories people tell about themselves that those people come to know who they are. To hear only the narratives of the dominant group would mean ignoring others that have helped shape people and would provide only a partial understanding of what and how ideologies operated and interacted to form personal and group identities.

Consider, for example, the sketchy picture Americans had of antebellum life before the slave narratives began to appear in the 1960s. Obviously, without those stories, a large part of what was known about the pre–Civil War United States was missing. The new historicists would question what the absence (silencing) of the slaves' discourse indicated about antebellum culture, as well as about the culture of the century that followed it. They might ask, for example, why the works of Frederick Douglass, well known in his own day, were out of print (and circulation) for decades following the Civil War. They would also be interested in how the suppression fit the ideologies of the power structure.

The presence and use of power (and the lack thereof) is implicit in the search for previously silenced voices. Power is generated by shared discourses and wielded by those groups and institutions that are participants. These groups establish norms and define what is deemed acceptable. Discourses that differ from the norm and digress from what is acceptable are likely to be suppressed, or at least go unrecognized, for they threaten the values generally espoused by a culture and the dominance of the powerful. Stephen Greenblatt points out that we define ourselves in relation to what we are not, making it necessary to demonize and objectify what we are not as "others." Designated as disruptive, foreign, and perhaps mad, the "others" are evidence of the rightness of our own power. Nevertheless, the "others" are there, despite being ignored, scorned, or disapproved—that is, silenced; without an awareness of them, one cannot understand the power structure itself.

Even the most powerful discourse is not permanent. Power moves through all social levels by way of marriage, commerce, and intellectual exchange. Although power reinforces its base in some cases, it inevitably stimulates opposition in others. As a result, culture is dynamic, with unstable, changing concepts of what is good and bad, acceptable and unacceptable. It is by hearing the repressed discourses as well as the dominant ones that the historian is able to discover complex relationships among ideologies that eventually provide an interpretation of what the stories of the past mean. At the very least, unearthing lost discourses and giving them value works against making an oversimplification of history by accepting a master narrative and provides a more complete understanding of any text.

Finally, the new historicists deny that history has goals. In their reading of it, events do not necessarily march forward connected by cause and effect, nor do they necessarily constitute progress. After all, the concept of progress is likely to vary from one society to another, with the characteristics attributed to it usually being those that belong to the society defining it. There is also the problem that cultures wax and wane. Powerful, affluent peoples do not stay at their peak forever. Even the Roman Empire eventually fell to the invaders known as barbarians.

New Literary Historicism

Not surprisingly, such radical departures from the traditional ways of looking at history change the way we read literature. In fact, it should be noted that most of the new historicists are literary scholars. Under their aegis, the concept that a text imitates life—that it reflects its historical context—has either disappeared or seen serious changes. Gone are those approaches that used history, even history of the text, as background to literature and that saw the work as a replication of a period's people and behavior (see Chapter 2). History is not expected to validate a text by providing facts that will prove the text's truth. Indeed, history cannot do so. Because it has been subjectively rendered, the facts are not, and have never been, known with certainty.

The new historicist critic works in two directions. He or she seeks to understand a text by examining its cultural context—the anxieties, issues, struggles, politics (and more) of the era in which it was created. She also seeks to understand the culture by looking at its literature. Even a work that is not overtly political or ideological affects the culture that reads it and is in turn affected by that culture; the two are intimately bound up with each other, making it impossible to read a text in isolation. In particular, the new historicist critic is interested in understanding a culture's power structure. She may even try to explain one incident in a text in terms of the concerns of the period in which it was written. When dealing with a contemporary work, however, the critic may not be content with simply understanding the power structure. Instead, she may see a text as an instrument of political awareness and a statement of ideology. Critics who work from this perspective often want to change the culture, and the stories they bring to light are deemed to be tools for modifying it. Like the Marxists who preceded them, these critics assume that literature addresses cultural concerns and can affect society's attitudes and values.

With such revised assumptions, the questions for readers are not "Were the characters based on real people?" or "Do the events recounted in the text recreate experiences from the author's life?" or "Does the text capture the spirit of the times accurately?" Rather, the question is "How does the text reveal and comment on the disparate discourses of the culture it depicts?" With that new question, history moves from behind a literary work, and an era's various discourses, one of them being literature, become coparticipants in a complex interaction that is the subject of study. Just as the historian contextualizes historical texts in the many discourses of a culture, so the critic interprets literary texts by viewing them as part of the same interchange. A work of literature is no longer read as an autonomous entity.

The several discourses will not all be representative of "high art" or even what has been known as art at all. In fact, according to the new historicists, all texts are social documents and, as such, they both reflect and affect the world that produces them. Reading any single one renders an incomplete picture; understanding multiple documents requires piecing them together to produce an interpretation. Using such an approach means removing literature from its pedestal and accepting it as one discourse among many—some of them, such as scientific tracts, legal papers, and popular songs, seemingly distant from the sublimity traditionally attributed to literary works. Like other cultural artifacts, literature creates and is created. It demonstrates discourses as they conflict, overlap, and complement one another, and it conflicts with, overlaps, and complements other discourses. Literary interpretation involves acknowledging all the social concerns that surround a text—the customs, institutions, and social practices it depicts, as well as those that are part of the author's life.

The job of the good reader, then, is to negotiate the various forces claiming his attention and to find meaning in their interactions. The job is complicated, however, by the fact that culture affects critics as well as texts. Just as a literary work exists in the midst of other discourses, so a critic cannot escape those of his own time. He is influenced by cultural norms and values, both public and private, so that instead of finding (and perhaps explaining) the "true" meaning of a work, he inevitably arrives at a unique interpretation—his own.

In sum, reading literature from a new historicist perspective involves accepting a new understanding of what a text is. Instead of assuming that it is a static, reflective artifact of a definable culture, this approach treats literature as a participant in a dynamic, changeable culture. The potential for change becomes important, because it means that literature has a role to play in the reformation of the society. With its help, power bases can be restructured and the marginalized recognized. Working from this position, the critic accepts the interrelatedness of all human activities, making it necessary to examine how all discourses—those contemporary with a text and those of readers who came later—affect the interpretation of literature. Once it has been acknowledged that what is deemed acceptable is not the same in all eras, it becomes necessary for the reader to admit the prejudices that his own culture has generated.

The new historicists have not escaped criticism, even from postmodernists. Some have objected to their political edge and to their willingness to discard aesthetic hierarchies in their use of what are usually deemed nonliterary documents to add to the picture they are trying to formulate. New historicists answer such charges by saying that the value of their type of reading is that it provides a more complete understanding of a text than could be discovered under the older system.

A brief word needs to be said about the related British movement known as **cultural materialism**. Like new historicism, this movement calls for a renewed awareness of the interrelatedness of human society and a deeper understanding of our own habits and beliefs. However, it is more overtly political in its beliefs and goals than is new historicism. Originally organized in the mid-1960s as an outgrowth of Marxist criticism, cultural materialism argues that the dominant class dictates what forms of art are to be considered superior at the expense of the working-class culture, which, misunderstood and undervalued, is deemed to be inferior (see Chapter 5). The cultural materialists work to erase any distinction between "high" and "low" forms of art, arguing that any text can be analyzed to reveal how it shapes a people's experience. All texts are carriers of ideologies that have the power to reinforce or transform those they touch. The dominant class defines what is acceptable with the goal of strengthening its own position of superiority and power, but the art of the excluded also has the power to reinforce those for whom it speaks and even to affect the entire culture, including the persons and institutions of power. It may be helpful to note that whereas new historicism tends to look at the operations of power from the top down and to concentrate on the pervasive nature of dominant power structures, thereby emphasizing how the powerful produce (and appropriate) subversion in their own interest, cultural materialism looks at how power works from the bottom up and is more interested in the positive potential of subversion for producing real alternatives to dominant institutions of power and modes of knowing. Because literature is a means of effecting change, the job of the critic reading as a cultural materialist is to reveal the social purposes that may lie unrealized in a text, so that repressive ideologies of the powerful can be revealed and resisted.

HISTORICAL BACKGROUND

From the outset, the new literary historicism has challenged several movements that preceded it. In particular, it has disputed the principles of traditional historicism and New Criticism (formalism), both of which had dominated critical practice for several decades. Just as historians customarily viewed the past as a series of movements and events that reflected a period's particular way of seeing the world or as isolated achievements of individuals, literary historians tended to see literature as an expression of the spirit of a particular time and place or as a series of masterpieces produced by a limited number of creative talents (see Chapter 2). By positioning texts against a background of social and political information of the times in which they were produced or in the context of biography, literary historians provided readers with a way of understanding another way of life, another culture. As the formalists pointed out, sometimes such a perspective was more historical than literary.

The New Critics went so far as to ignore the historical context of literary works, arguing that those works belong to no particular era but instead are universal and timeless (see Chapter 3). The formalists believed that it was not necessary to know the author's biography or the cultural environment in which a work was produced, because the work held its own aesthetic rules of being within itself. In a sense, the text existed like Keats's Grecian urn—outside of or above time. To consider a poem only in terms of itself—without reference to why it came to be, who was influenced by it, what its purpose was, or how it changed the world—meant not asking questions that many readers believed to be fundamental to understanding it. Those who objected began to challenge such a stance, raising issues about how a reader can understand literature without knowing where it came from and how it was received. At about the time that the New Critics were under attack from various postmodern theorists, the new historicists joined the skirmish by raising questions that further challenged their own premises as well as those of traditional historical literary study.

The general social unrest of the 1960s laid the groundwork for change, even in academia, where the literature classroom grew increasingly politicized. A new generation of professors who were no longer mostly white males began to raise questions about the relationship of literature and culture, power, and authority. Representative of a wide cross section of society—females, minorities, working classes—these professors had a stake in finding and liberating voices that had not traditionally been heard in literature, because those voices were often their own.

An early shot on the literary front of the culture wars was fired by literary scholar Stephen Greenblatt, who is regarded by many as the founder of new historicism. At the least, he provided the name by which the movement is known in the United States when he used the term in 1982 in an introduction to a special issue of the journal *Genre*. Well schooled in the principles of New Criticism, Greenblatt resisted the narrowness of its view and began to publish articles and essays in which he probed the nature of literature and its relationship to the larger culture. His thinking attracted the interest of others, such as Louis Montrose, Jonathan Dollimore, and Catherine Gallagher, who were to become early new historicists. Together they questioned the objectivity of historians, the meaning of texts, the nature of literature, and the role of the critic. Several influences led them to do so.

The nineteenth-century philosopher Friedrich Nietzsche had opened the discussion much earlier by asserting that people shape facts to suit their desires. He wrote, "Ultimately, man finds in things nothing but what he himself has imported into them." Nietzsche rejected the possibility of absolute truths or objective knowledge; in their place, he found that what is accepted as truth is that which corresponds to what has already been described as truth by those in power, including political authorities, rulers, intellectuals, or simply the prevailing ideologies of the day. The new literary historicists have been more directly influenced by the French thinker Michel Foucault (1926–1984), who challenged many of the accepted concepts about history, culture, and society; by the ideas of Marxist scholars, who recognized the interconnected nature of society; and by the methodology of cultural anthropologists.

According to Foucault, history is neither linear nor teleological. That is, it cannot be explained as a series of causes and effects, and it is not necessarily going purposefully forward toward some known end. It is not a continuum in which truths about human nature and society remain constant. Instead, in Foucault's concept of history, what is accepted to be true changes. Each period establishes its own set of values or actions that people are expected to discuss, protect, and defend. Each develops its own standards of permissible behavior, its criteria for judging what is good or bad, and its system of rules for controlling what is to be said and for disseminating what is accepted as knowledge. Control may take the form of exclusion or prohibition, because what is considered normal or rational silences what is not, whether that be objects, rituals, or specific subjects. Foucault was particularly interested in discourse, the language of a particular time and place that controls and preserves social relations; discourse can be thought of as ideology in action. He examined discursive practices in an effort to find the **episteme**, or the rules and constraints outside which individuals cannot think or speak without running the risk of being excluded or silenced. The episteme designates which statements can be uttered, who or what institutions have the authority to name things and make judgments about them, how they are allowed to speak, the forms their expression can take, and what can be talked about. Persons and institutions representing "the norm," of which even they may be unconscious, have the power to determine that which is judged to be knowledge and truth, to dictate which subjects are valued and which are not.

Because human society is always more complicated than a single view can indicate, Foucault searched for those who had not been allowed to speak and topics that had not been valued. To do so, he borrowed techniques and terminology from archaeology. He dug down past "final" readings of history to find what had been suppressed, ignored, or silenced, which may be just as important to understanding a culture as what has been accepted as knowledge. He examined subjects such as madness, prisons, and sexuality, which he felt had been discourse taboos for centuries. As he put it, these topics were subject to "rules of exclusion." For example, madness, which Foucault saw as a changing, historically conditioned notion, became a threat to society once reason was considered to be supreme, and therefore it had to be banned from society.

In these terms, literature becomes one of many interactive discourses, and studying it requires putting together those discourses—the accepted with the excluded—even when they are contradictory. Thus literature is part of the record of human experience that was formed by the cultural conditions at a particular time and place. By reading literature in this way, one not only arrives at a more accurate picture of the past but also discovers knowledge that was lost in traditional historical and literary accounts, because it belonged to those who were shut out from participating in the discussion, even when it was about subjects that were of significance to those participants.

Lately the work of Mikhail Bakhtin (see Chapter 3) has provided new historicists with another way of thinking about the silenced and excluded. His concept of **carnival** features a culture behind the mainstream one, a marginalized culture that subverts sanctioned hierarchies by turning the privileged symbols upside down or by putting them into common experience. By doing so, it mocks authority and resists mandatory social behavior. And throughout the process, carnival remains officially sanctioned. Interestingly, resistance is always a part of subjection. Dominance creates opposition that makes social change inevitable. The principle is evident in literature too, where the meanings of texts are never permanently subscribed to but are modified by successive challenges from readers and critics. Continuously evolving interpretation makes it impossible to view a text as an organically unified entity.

Another key influence on new historicism has been Marxism, particularly its view of power, which recognizes that the dominant class tries to control the thinking of the people through many means, one of which is literature (see Chapter 5). Following both the Marxists and Foucault, the new historicists acknowledge that a culture's accepted practices keep the powerless in their place and serve the interests of the ruling classes by maintaining social divisions. However, texts can also be a means of overturning the status quo; according to new literary historicists—and more especially their British cousins, the cultural materialists—critics have a role to play in revealing the political subtexts that lie beneath the conventional ones. Marxism is also evident in the new historicists' assumption that a text can be understood only in its cultural context, that all actions in a society are connected to all other actions, and together they form the culture. From that position, the literary new historicists reason that because a work is connected to the world that produced it, any understanding that does not include an awareness of the concerns of both the culture in general and the author in particular is incomplete. That is, knowledge of the material and historical circumstances of the production of a text is fundamental to comprehending that text.

An additional influence on the practices of the new historicists comes from cultural anthropology. In particular, the methodology Clifford Geertz called **thick description** has proved to be helpful. (Greenblatt, in particular, acknowledges the influence of Geertz's thinking on his own work.) Actually, Geertz gives credit for the term *thick description* to Gilbert Ryle, who explained that a wink means nothing to the person who sees it unless it has a context, and with different contexts, that wink has different meanings. Extending the argument to all human behavior, Geertz distinguished between *thin description*, which would focus only on an isolated act (such as a wink), and *thick description*, which includes the context of the act. Thick description involves observing, collecting, and interpreting cultural details to find the codes by which people govern their choices and actions. Even small actions that seem to have no particular significance in themselves can, along with other actions, suggest how a given people see their world. In Geertz's methodology, everything is important. Nothing is to be overlooked, because it is through the interconnections of details that meaning is revealed. The observer, however, can never be fully objective, for we are all biased by our own cultural forces. As Foucault pointed out, because historians are also subject to their epistemes, they must confront their own biases.

The growing interest in the literatures of people who had previously been ignored by the mainstream tradition is a step toward adapting Geertz's techniques to the study of literature. By collecting the many strands of concurrent storytelling available in any given era, critics and scholars can construct a richer, more complete account of that literary period. Recognition of the interactions of various traditions helps explain both the traditionally anthologized texts and those known only to members of the group that produced them, and it helps to keep the latter alive.

In sum, influenced by Foucault, Marxism, and cultural anthropology, the new literary historicists no longer see history as factual background but as one of many concurrent narrative discourses that can be (and will be) read and reread in light of the worldview of succeeding cultures. Analysis of a literary text involves listening to all the discourses while recognizing the listener's inherently biased perspective. The process might be thought of as an ongoing conversation among authors and readers of various eras in which no participant has a complete or objective understanding of the whole.

READING AS A NEW HISTORICIST

To understand the discussion that follows, you will need to read "The Sky Is Gray," by Ernest J. Gaines, which begins on page 281.

A new historicist's analysis can pursue several different (but not unconnected) lines of inquiry. It can ask questions about the author's life and times, the life and times in which a work is set, the various discourses represented in the work, the author's intentions, the work's initial reception, and the various ways in which the work has been received since its initial appearance. The overlap of concerns in these queries will produce an interwoven analysis—a thick description—in which one topic complements and overlaps the others.

The World of the Author and the Text

A look at the life of Ernest Gaines, for example, reveals a number of significant social forces that resulted in his 1963 writing of "The Sky Is Gray," a story about a young black boy growing up in the segregated South of the 1940s. In the turbulent era in which Gaines wrote the story, individuals wrestled with changing concepts of racial relationships, civil rights, and poverty—all of which are important aspects of "The Sky Is Gray." The era the story recalls, however, was very different from the one that Gaines himself knows from personal experience, family stories, African American culture, and Southern tradition. Although Gaines had been living in California for fifteen years when he wrote the story, had graduated from San Francisco State College, and held a creative writing fellowship at Stanford University, those earlier times remained viable in his memory several decades later.

In some ways, the issues of race, rights, and poverty in 1963 were more powerful than they had been in Gaines's childhood. At the time he was writing the story, it had been six years since troops had been sent to Little Rock, Arkansas, to ensure desegregation of the high school. Thurgood Marshall, who almost a decade earlier had won the *Brown v. Board of Education* case that led to the desegregation of public schools, was soon to become the first black justice appointed to the U.S. Supreme Court. Lyndon B. Johnson's War on Poverty would begin the next year, and Johnson's Great Society, which would be enacted by legislation introduced in 1965, would provide programs such as Medicare and Medicaid. Likewise, the Civil Rights Act of 1968, stressing open housing, was on the horizon. Newspapers, magazines, and television news routinely reported changes in the social system that had been in place since the Civil War. In short, the limited access to opportunity and the inequitable division of power taken for granted in "The Sky Is Gray" were being questioned during the time of its writing. Indeed, the denial of African-Americans' rights to schools and universities (education), the voting booth (political power), and lunch counters (social intercourse) was under siege.

In the story, however, James and his family lack all such rights. They are powerless. They do not even live close to centers of power where they might catch the notice of those who could change the dynamics of their situation. In fact, at the time of the story, legal and social measures are firmly secured to keep blacks "in their place." Through the practice of segregation, maintained by those who have power, James and his family will remain powerless because of poverty, ignorance, and separation from the mainstream. For example, James and his mother sit in the bus behind the sign that says "Colored." When the dentist goes to lunch they leave his waiting room, and to find food and shelter from the cold, they must go "back of town," passing by whites-only cafés but not looking in. By law and by social practice, the two of them have no choice but to endure. In such a context, the story becomes a quietly compelling political document, testifying to social wrongs that cry out for attention and change. Gaines was able to re-create that earlier time because he carried in his memory a strong sense of the place, its land, its people, and its culture. Like most of his work, the story is set in rural Louisiana, among the poor, black, bilingual populace of his native Pointe Coupee Parish. James lives in such a family. On his trip to see the dentist, for example, there is so little money that he must choose between buying something to eat and riding home on the bus, and racial discrimination dominates every choice he and his mother make in Bayonne, the small, bleak town that seems urban by comparison with the plot of land where they share their small house with Ty, Auntie, Val, Louis, and Walker.

Having listened as a child to the stories of the old people, Gaines understands his culture's assumptions about family, attitudes, behavior, and values. From his early childhood experiences at River Lake Plantation, he has developed a sense of what it means to love the land but not own it, to live in the quarters in the shadow of the plantation house, to attend school and church in the same building and then in another town. In describing his identity, Gaines said,

> I see myself as a writer, and I happen to have been born here [Louisiana]. I was born black. I was born on a plantation. I've lived in that interracial, or ethnic, mixture of the Cajun, and the big house owned by the Creoles—not Cajuns, but Creoles—and the blacks. I was associated very early with the Baptist church; I was christened as a Baptist. But I went to Catholic school, a little school in New Roads, my last three years in Louisiana. I had to go through their kind of discipline. I had to go to mass. I didn't go to confession or anything like that. I didn't take the Holy Sacrament. I had to go through all these kinds of things. My aunt who raised me and who was crippled spoke Creole. Some of the old ladies on the plantation and some of the old men spoke Creole. (Gaudet and Wooton 1990, 80)

Gaines's young adulthood presented him with a broader context, one that included other races and ethnic groups and different relations between social classes. It introduced him to books and cities and a new world of experiences that would allow him to understand more clearly the nature of his own culture and the circumstances that had forged it. His respect for the strength of the people of the quarter, combined with his knowledge of that bigger world where the social dictates and rules of decorum were different, allowed Gaines to depict the limitations imposed on his characters without dishonoring their dignity. As a result, "The Sky Is Gray" illuminates the experience of people who up until its appearance had been mostly ignored, certainly underrepresented, and sometimes misrepresented in literature. In so doing, the story develops several important themes that recur throughout Gaines's fiction.

The most evident theme, perhaps, is the search for manhood, a manhood characterized by dignity that cannot be impugned by circumstances. The story ends with the words of James's mother who, in telling him to turn his collar down as it should be, explains, "You not a bum ... You a man." Long before that comment, however, her own behavior serves as a model of endurance and sacrifice. She goes hungry so that James can eat. "We don't take no handout," she tells Helena, the white lady who insists that his mother come into the kitchen and eat. His mother turns to leave the house rather than accept more salt meat than she has paid for. From such fierce determination and from such courage, James learns what is expected of him as a man. It is more than simple survival, which Mama also teaches him through the unpleasant duty of killing the redbird. It is survival with dignity in a harsh world that will systematically deny him his manhood.

Another of Gaines's themes deals with the old people who are connected to the land at the very time that change is approaching. There are tensions between the young, who are no longer willing to accept the burden the land imposes on them or the societal limitations they have inherited, and the old, who have endured both. The scene in the dentist's office is a case in point. The radical young man, who insists that everything, including the color of the grass and God himself, should be questioned, offends the preacher and others who see his ranting as an attack on the institutions and beliefs that have allowed them to live with honor. The young man impugns their traditions and makes rifts in their solidarity by introducing a new way of looking at their lives, a new social code. Change will not be easy within the black community, even change that brings with it desirable rights and opportunities. It may even mean losing treasured aspects of its culture. For example, with increased literacy, what will happen to the rich oral tradition that formed Ernest Gaines himself? Will there continue to be a Monsieur Bayonne to pray over a tooth that aches? Will there be resources, some of them superstitious, to fall back on when everything else fails? What is lost when solutions are standardized, when one size fits all?

Finally, there is the question of identity. Who is James to think he is? How does the black man define himself? In another Gaines story, "A Long Day in November," the character Munford says, "By looking at us he [the white man] knows what he is not." In a culture that has traditionally required that a person belong to one race or another, is the black man to do the same? In "The Sky Is Gray," James seems to recognize that although he honors his cultural background, being a man transcends racial designation. It requires acting responsibly and with integrity, traits not given to one race or another. Gaines explained the situation when speaking of himself:

> I know who I am. I know that I was born in Pointe Coupee Parish. I know that I grew up on a plantation. I know about the old people

> around me who sacrificed everything for me to educate me. I know that I have written books. I know that my books have been translated into many languages. I know all these things about myself. I know that I care for my family. I know that I care for my friends. I know that I don't give a damn for my enemies. I know that I don't judge all whites as my enemies; I don't judge them as my friends, either. I know I have white friends. I don't say that all blacks are my friends, because I don't have too many black friends here ... I say I must go on and do my work, I must earn my living, I must do my teaching yet communicate with my friends, be with my friends, and all this sort of thing. (Gaudet and Wooton 1990, 54)

An analysis that seeks to examine the world of the author and the text often begins with questions such as these:

- What assumptions did people hold about their lives and their culture during the author's lifetime?
- What traditional practices were being challenged?
- Who wielded power at the time the work was produced? Who wielded power during the period the work depicts?
- What shaping experiences in the author's life were unique to him or her?
- How did political and social events impact the writer's attitudes and choices?

Discourses in the Text

Many voices are heard in "The Sky Is Gray," some of them new to readers of the 1960s. Before this story's appearance, few narratives based on the experiences of African Americans had joined the mainstream. Gaines himself noted that black writers had no influence on him as he learned his craft, simply because he could not check out books from the library when he was a child in Louisiana; likewise, later in Vallejo, California, where he moved when he was fifteen, few books by black writers were available. Even in college in the early 1950s, he was asked to read only passages from *Native Son*, and *Invisible Man* was newly published. In short, books by black writers were not available to show Gaines the way during his development as a writer. Consequently, his depiction of black families and experiences represented for the reading public a glimpse into what was virtually a new world for them, one characterized by pressures, practices, and traditions they had not met in literature before.

In addition to introducing the discourse of rural, poor, Southern, black America, Gaines provided a depiction of another little-known culture, one composed of people of Creole and Cajun lineage. Kate Chopin, who had drawn characters and settings from the communities of French and Spanish descendants in Louisiana, had been largely forgotten by the time Gaines began writing. Though her stories, and certainly *The Awakening*, would later find popularity with readers, in the early 1960s "The Sky Is Gray" depicted a world little known to most people who lived outside it. The discourses in the story had been little heard or noticed. Most audible in Gaines's stories are the African American discourses. On the level of authenticity of expression, they resonate with rhythms and idioms that differ from those of urban white America. Gaines acknowledged that he absorbed these discourses as a child, listening to the stories people told sitting on the ditch bank or gathered around the fireplace at night. He said, "I came from a place where people sat around and chewed sugarcane and roasted sweet potatoes and peanuts in the ashes and sat on ditch banks and told tales and sat on porches and went into the swamps and went into the fields—that's what I came from" (Gaudet and Wooton 1990, 37). That was not urban. Those situations were not the ones James Baldwin was writing about. They were voices not heard before in American literature.

As Gaudet and Wooton pointed out in *Porch Talk*, Gaines's ability to catch the sound of these people talking was enhanced by his technical training and literary background: "Though he bases his narrative on the folk storytelling tradition, he is quite obviously not a folk storyteller. He is an artist who recognizes the value of the language and customs of his culture, and who consciously manipulates that material through techniques and in forms that occupy the mainstream of western literary tradition" (5). Consequently, Gaines is able to give readers not just black discourse but varieties of black discourse, not a one-dimensional perspective but conflicting and overlapping ones that deepen the authenticity of the portrayal. Even "The Sky Is Gray" has characters who represent differing discourses within the black community. Most obvious among them are the preacher and the revolutionary young man (who is probably more typical of the 1960s than the 1940s) in the dentist's office, who finally come to blows over their differences. Not only do they represent contrasting views, but they also reflect the diversity that results from education. Whereas some of the characters are probably illiterate, others study and question. More subtly, there is difference in the innocence of Ty's childhood view of events, the piety of Monsieur Bayonne, and the tight-lipped stoicism of James's mother. They face the world with different expectations and different defenses, though all of them are closely bound together in rural black culture, which is not monolithic. The culture is not a single body of stereotypical characteristics.

Discourses other than those reflecting the black, Creole, and Cajun cultures are also evident in "The Sky Is Gray." Gaines recognizes a number of significant influences on his writing that came from beyond the black community. The radio shows of the 1950s, "where you can only hear things and they tell you what's going on"; jazz saxophonist Lester Young, who instead of playing on the note, "plays around the note, or under the note, or above the note"; white writers (Mark Twain, F. Scott Fitzgerald, Ernest Hemingway, Ivan Turgenev); and the jumbled California culture (made up of blacks, Latinos, Filipinos, Japanese, Chinese, and whites) all played a part in the world Gaines writes about and from. His fiction presents no single discourse but rather a welter of complementary and conflicting and overlapping ones, just as one finds in society.

The following questions are helpful in identifying the various voices represented in a work. After answering them, you can ask how the information you have found is evident in the way the characters address the world.

- What ethnic and racial groups do the characters represent?
- How many different age groups are depicted?
- What levels of education have the characters achieved?
- How do the beliefs and expectations of the characters differ?
- What geographical areas do the characters come from?

Intentions and Reception

"The Sky Is Gray" could never be described as overtly supporting or undermining particular ideologies. It was not conceived as an explicitly political document. Nevertheless, in its poignant depiction of James (a boy old beyond his years), Mama (determined that James grow up to live with dignity), and Helena and Alnest (whose concern for suffering includes a sensitivity to the feelings of the sufferers), it challenges the power structure of the segregated society it depicts. The story recognizes the complexity of human interaction, both intraracial and interracial, while holding up the exchange between the older white couple and James and Mama as a model of what is possible, even in a society built on wildly unequal divisions of power. In this way, "The Sky Is Gray" can be said to undermine the discourses of the time and place in which it is set as well as clearly reflecting those in which it was produced. And although the legal strictures and mores of its setting have radically changed in the decades since its initial publication, the story still manages to touch the emotions and the sense of ethics of contemporary readers, reminding them of what was and what must never be again.

Although Gaines does not talk about his work in political terms and generally asserts that he does not write for any particular audience, he has, on occasion, admitted that he would like to think that he writes for the black youth and the white youth of the South. Never interested in publishing just for money, just to sell books, he has stated that his purpose is to produce good writing, and if that touches young people who will make a better world than their predecessors experienced, he will be pleased. Despite disclaimers about making money, however, economics has influenced publication of Gaines's fiction. His first novel, *Catherine Carmier*, went little noticed, making the stories he subsequently submitted unattractive to publishers. To get them into print, he had to produce a second novel before the stories were brought out. "The Sky Is Gray," which appeared in the collection *Bloodline*, had been earlier published in *Negro Digest*. When it appeared in *Negro Digest*, there seemed to be little recognition—except on the part of Dorothea Oppenheimer, who became Gaines's agent and close friend—of the story's artistry, authenticity, and power. Today it is difficult to realize that perceptive editors did not recognize the relationship the story would go on to have with audiences over time. Now frequently anthologized and taught in schools and colleges, it stands as a historical document of what once was, continues to offer political challenge to unbalanced power structures, and poses, through the interactions of James, Mama, Helena, and Alnest, a model of interracial accord. It does not suggest that all the problems of the poor, the rural, or the races have been solved. It cannot be read from the perspective that progress is inevitable. But it clearly shows that there have been changes in the social system of the American South.

Sometimes an author's intent is clearly evident in the work itself, but on other occasions, the critic must resort to finding interviews or book reviews to determine the purposes behind it. Such is almost always the case when one is interested in knowing how a work has been received since publication. These searches involve questions such as the following:

- What are the author's stated political views?
- Has the writer ever spoken publicly for or against some cause?
- Can one character be assumed to be speaking for the author?
- Was the work an immediate success, or was it largely overlooked upon publication?
- Did the work cause controversy when it was published?
- Has the work sustained its readership since it first appeared?

WRITING A NEW HISTORICIST LITERARY ANALYSIS

Throughout your analysis, and as you begin to shape it into a written report, you will hold certain assumptions about the text. You will assume that it has been marked by the time and place in which it was produced and that it reflects the time and place in which it is set. You will also presume that the text serves some purpose, even if the author and perhaps the reader are not consciously aware of what that intention is. In addition, you will accept that the reading you are making will be different from those of other readers, leading to multiple interpretations that are affected by changing cultural movements and evolving understandings of the time and place of production.

Prewriting

In the case of a new historicist analysis, prewriting may not be an accurate name for what you are likely to do. Because your attention will be on all the cultural forces surrounding (and infusing) the text with meaning, you will need to be well informed on a number of issues that lie outside it. Consequently, instead of pre*writing*, you may be pre*reading*. To acquire a comprehensive understanding of the cultural environment—to engage in thick description—you will probably need to do some library work, looking for information in the following areas:

- *The author.* Reading a biography can provide insight into the writer's concerns about personal experiences as well as about society in general. Such interests will affect the presentation of the people and times depicted in the text, whether or not the setting is the same as the one in which the author is working.

- *The cultural moment.* Not only will newspapers and magazines of the era report the issues of the day, but less explicitly they will also indicate the people's tastes. That is, they will provide information about the rules governing what was deemed to be acceptable and desirable at that time. The issues and the tastes of the day are forces, albeit nonliterary ones, that impinge on what the text means. The tastes of the period, which you may find to be the more revealing, can sometimes be found in the public figures of the day, who symbolize the codes of behavior approved by others. Sometimes the tastes lurk in seemingly insignificant details, such as dress, family customs, advertising, or home decoration. All such matters play a part in how a work is received by the reading public. If a work conflicts with what readers believe (or want to believe), it may meet with resistance. If it reinforces beliefs or satisfies curiosity about a topic, it is more likely to meet with favor. Such research becomes especially meaningful when the social codes and forces at work in a culture appear to conflict with each other.
- *The text.* Listening for all the voices—present and past as well as one's own—enriches and deepens possibilities for meaning. Although one narrative may be dominant, no text includes only a single one. The world that the text presents is an interaction of different, dynamic discourses that shape and are shaped by one another.

Drafting and Revising

The Introduction One way of opening your new historicist analysis is to present a general sketch of the era in which the text is set. An overall look at the narrative's time and place can ground the discussion that follows. The guiding word here is *general.* The body of the essay will present specific information about politics, behaviors, figures, and institutions, so the introduction should do little more than present a panoramic view of the environment. You may want to think of the opening as an aerial photograph that shows the layout of the countryside. In the course of the discussion, you will provide close-up shots of that overview.

If you prefer to be more probing than such an introduction permits, an alternative opening is to move directly into your discussion about what the work contributes to your understanding of human experience in the particular time and place in which it is set. This approach involves making some generalizations about the text's interpretation of the culture it represents, which your ensuing discussion will go on to support. For example, you may want to comment on whether (and how) the text supports or challenges the dominant discourses of its own era and those of later ones, or you may choose to explain how the text reveals the complexity of the period.

The Body One way to organize the body of your discussion comes directly from the prereading process described earlier. That is, you can address the three topics suggested by the prereading's categories of investigation: the world of the author, personal and public; the historical-cultural environment of the text, both the one it depicts and the one in which it was produced; and the internal world of the text itself, the discourses that generate the narrative. In the case of all three, you should be attentive to the power structure that is in place, questioning inequalities and pointing out social forces that build community and those that destroy it.

Information about the author's life can shed light on the forces and issues that helped create the text. People and events that were significant to the writer and whether they were positive or negative experiences can point directly to intent and purpose. Philosophical and political grounding can explain explicit and implicit social commentary. A writer's letters, interviews, and journals can provide comments that illuminate intended audiences and effects. To isolate such helpful information, you can ask some of the following questions.

- What were the formative experiences in the writer's life?
- Who were the significant people in the writer's life?
- What texts affected the writer's thinking?
- What religious-spiritual issues were important to the writer?
- What was the writer's general political stance?
- What social class did the writer's family occupy?
- As an adult what social class did the writer aspire to belong to?
- How much social power did the writer's family have?
- From how many different social classes and types of work did the writer draw friends?
- What social issues were important to the writer?
- What public roles did the writer assume?
- What one-word label would describe the voice of the narrator in this text?

Looking beyond the author to the culture in which he or she lived means examining events and texts that may seem to lie at some distance from the one under scrutiny. You will want to include social actions, relationships, and documents—all situations that involve exchanges of power. You will look for significance not only in major incidents but also in minor details. Helpful information can be found by asking several kinds of questions. The first has to do with historical events of the period:

- What were the major cultural and historical events of the period? What connections do they have with the text?
- What resistance was there to these events, and what was its source?
- What were the major controversies of the period? Are they explicitly or obliquely mentioned in the text?
- What or who represented the power bases in the controversy? Which group was dominant? Which ones were not?

- What professions and disciplines held power? The church? The law? Science? Academiia?
- Who were the major figures of the period?
- What characteristics did those figures embody that were deemed to be admirable? Which were deemed to be objectionable?
- What was the source of their power and influence?
- Who or what opposed (or at least resented) their power and influence?
- Where do you see power operating secretly—that is, not openly or explicitly?
- How did those who held power prevent opposition to or subversion of it?

Another avenue of inquiry regarding the work and the world outside of it deals with written texts of the period. It asks questions such as these:

- How is the style of this text similar to or different from other literary texts of the era?
- How do the purposes of this text repeat, conflict with, or repeat other texts of the day?
- How does this text fit (or not fit) into the nonliterary texts of the same period?
- How has this text influenced and been influenced by other texts?

A third group of questions dealing with the work of literature and the world beyond it examines the interactions of the two, including the connections between the text and the world it depicts, the one in which it was published, and those of subsequent periods. You can ask questions such as these:

- What would have attracted readers to this work at the time it was published? In later periods?
- What was the work's public and critical reception at the time of publication?
- What has changed about the way it has been read since publication?
- What models of behavior does this work support?
- What do the answers to the preceding four questions tell you about the various cultures represented?
- How have values changed since the work was published?
- How have values changed since the period in which the work is set?
- Has the text changed its culture or any other culture? If so, how?

In addition to examining the life and thought of the author and the cultural ambience of the work's times, you will also need to look intently at the text itself as a response to both of the other two areas of interest. To determine what commentary the text offers regarding the larger world outside itself, you can ask the following questions:

- What various discourses do you meet in the text?
- Which ones are powerful?

- Which represent the experience of people who have traditionally been overlooked, marginalized, or misrepresented?
- What conflicts do you discern in the text between the discourse of the powerful and that of the powerless?
- How do conflicting discourses in the text influence and shape each other by agreeing, complementing, or contradicting each other?
- How does this text support a particular discourse? What ideology does that support suggest?
- What are the social rules observed in the text?
- Is the text critical of those rules, or does it treat them as models of behavior?
- How does the text support or challenge the values, beliefs, and/or practices of the culture it depicts?
- What does the ideological stance imply about the culture it depicts, that of the author's times, and that of subsequent periods?
- How does this text suggest that history does not necessarily proceed in an orderly, positive direction?

The Conclusion If you have followed the suggestions offered here for drafting your essay, you may not have yet mentioned your own stance regarding the text. If that is the case, the conclusion provides an opportunity for you to make a disclaimer as to the certainty of your analysis. Because all readers are inevitably influenced by the times in which they live, nobody approaches a text from a completely unbiased perspective. In an effort to give as true an account of a text as is possible, the responsible new historicist critic will state his or her attitudes and the cultural principles that have led to the analysis. Such a self-positioning will not alter the slant of the critical comments, but it will give the reader a better chance of understanding their source and significance.

SUGGESTED READING

Ashcroft, Bill, Gareth Griffiths, and Helen Tiffin, eds. *Post-Colonial Studies Reader.* New York: Routledge, 2006.

Bhabha, Homi. *The Location of Culture.* New York: Routledge, 2004.

Brannigan, John. *New Historicism and Cultural Materialism.* New York: St. Martin's Press, 1998.

Colebrook, Claire. *New Literary Histories: New Historicism and Contemporary Criticism.* Manchester, UK: Manchester University Press, 1997.

Cox, Jeffrey N., and Larry J. Reynolds, eds. *New Historical Literary Study: Essays on Reproducing Texts, Representing History.* Princeton, NJ: Princeton University Press, 1993.

During, Simon. " New Historicism." *Text and Performance Quarterly* 11 (July 1991): 171–89.

Foucault, Michel. *The Foucault Reader*, ed. Paul Rabinow. New York: Pantheon, 1984.

Gallagher, Catherine, and Stephen Greenblatt. *Practicing New Historicism*. Chicago: University of Chicago Press, 2000.

Gaudet, Marcia, and Carl Wooton. *Porch Talk with Ernest Gaines: Conversations on the Writer's Craft*. Baton Rouge: Louisiana State University Press, 1990.

Greenblatt, Stephen. "The Power of Forms and the Forms of Power." *Genre* 15 (1982): 1–4.

Michaels, Walter Benn. *The Gold Standard and the Logic of Naturalism: American Literature at the Turn of the Century*. Berkeley: University of California Press, 1987.

Thomas, Brook. " The Historical Necessity for—and Difficulties with—New Historical Analysis in Introductory Literature Courses." *College English*. 49 (September 1987): 509–22.

Veeser, H. Aram, ed. *The New Historicism*. New York: Routledge, 1989. (Note esp. Catherine Gallagher, "Marxism and the New Historicism," and Stephen Greenblatt, "Toward a Poetics of Culture.")

For up-to-date information on the many Websites addressing new historicist critical approaches, visit www.cengagebrain.com.

Model Student Analysis

The Economics of Paranoia in Nadine Gordimer's "Once Upon a Time"

KYLE FELKER

In the short story "Once Upon a Time," Nadine Gordimer resists the dominant discourses of South African apartheid by examining the ways in which its social and economic machinery corroded and deformed the lives of the white upper class as much as it did the black and immigrant underclasses. She critiques the dominant political belief that black and white people under apartheid were free to develop separately but equally in their own homelands, and examines the ways in which the economic system underlying apartheid created isolation, paranoia, and violence not only for native Africans and immigrants but for the white ruling class that ostensibly benefitted the most from the system.

Like most of Gordimer's writings, "Once Upon a Time" can only be understood against the historical backdrop of South African apartheid. This collection of policies and laws was a massive social and political experiment that stretched roughly from 1948 to 1990 in the four southernmost provinces of Africa, which have come to be known collectively as South Africa. The southernmost region of Africa was colonized by Dutch immigrants fleeing European religious persecution in the sixteenth and seventeenth centuries. Along with Hugenots and British, they eventually formed the Afrikaner cultural group. This small (compared to the number of native Africans, Indians, and other nonwhite residents) white minority would form the nucleus of the ruling upper class during apartheid. Since the colonial period, there had been hostility to "uitlanders," or nonwhite foreigners, and restrictions on where native Africans could live and work. But the National Party victory in the general election in 1948, achieved mostly by manipulating the racial fears of the white population, paved the way for a much more systematic, methodical, and aggressive system of racial segregation that would become apartheid ("Apartheid" 117).

The ideology behind apartheid was deceptively simple: the various racial groups occupying South Africa were not compatible and should be kept as separate as possible. To this end, the government established "homelands" for the native African tribes, essentially reservations that were loosely based on traditional tribal geography. Apartheid policies then sharply limited the rights of nonwhites to travel beyond their tribal homelands. No area of life was unaffected. In the area of labor and education, apartheid policies and legal systems limited the educational opportunities afforded to nonwhites by setting up separate and inferior systems of schooling, legally limiting the types of professions nonwhites could work in to menial labor, and limiting their ability to form unions and protest unfair wages and working conditions. Apartheid made it illegal to marry or have sexual intercourse with someone not of your own race. Nonwhites were not allowed to live in urban areas and could not move about freely outside their native homeland. Theoretically, economic, social, and cultural development within the homelands was free and unfettered, but in reality, the Homelands were impoverished, had no infrastructure, and no means of development, which forced their inhabitants into perpetual dependency on the urbanized economic systems of the white ruling elite.

By 1991, when "Once Upon a Time" was published in *Jump and Other Stories*, the South African government had already announced that it would work toward a more democratic government. But that change would not come quickly, and the scars left on South Africa are numerous and enduring.

Gordimer's story is unusual in that it resists the dominant discourse of apartheid, but it does not do so by examining the plight of native Africans and immigrants under apartheid directly. Instead, the story focuses on the adverse effects of apartheid on the dominant economic and social class of apartheid, the white ruling class. Fiction such as this produced by a white writer during apartheid indicates that there existed dissenting discourses even within the dominant class. In short, white support of apartheid was not monolithic. Many liberal whites, especially British immigrants, were against apartheid policies. Discourse of dissenting whites of necessity centered around the difficulty of establishing a clear moral ground that would allow them to critique the practices and assumptions of their own social class. This was not an easy task. While Gordimer was never imprisoned or deported, as were many who attempted to condemn apartheid policies, she nevertheless came under sharp criticism, and many of her works were banned by the National Party (Rudikoff). Gordimer's fiction therefore represents one strand of a complex skein of discourses in which support of and dissent from apartheid was not clearly divided by class and racial lines.

"Once Upon a Time" can be divided into two major narrative sections. In the first section, the narrator utilizes images of fragility and violence, "windowpanes thin as rime" (p. 303) that "could shatter like a wineglass" (p. 303), and a bodiless creaking that the speaker eventually identifies as "A buckling, and epicenter of stress" (p. 303) to construct an atmosphere of tension and dread. The speaker's home, we learn, is perched precariously on "undermined ground" (p. 303) over a dark and unseen labyrinth of landslides and rockfalls peopled by native African migrant miners, "interred there in the most profound of tombs" (p. 303). The metaphor that Gordimer constructs in this first section is a representation of apartheid in miniature. The speaker's home is positioned much as the white ruling class was, perched economically and socially over an unseen but nevertheless very present black and immigrant underclass. Under apartheid, native Africans were required to live on reservation-like homelands where their economic impoverishment was unseen by the majority of the white upper class. In Gordimer's account, the entire fragile system threatens at any moment to dissolve into chaos, imprisoning the white upper class in a maze of paranoia and fear, and the native underclass is a dank and dripping tomb of poverty and despair.

To distract herself from this terrifying reality, the speaker decides to tell herself "a bedtime story" (p. 303). Current popular culture often treats fairy tales and fantasy as an escape from reality, but Gordimer skillfully intertwines the conventions of the literary fairy tale with those of realism in depicting the brutality, fear, and violence of real-life apartheid. The fairy-tale portion of Gordimer's story begins the way most traditional fairy tales end: with a couple living happily ever after. We are not told that the couple is part of the white ruling class, but there are numerous clues: they live in a suburb (nonwhites were not allowed to live in urban areas or own such property under apartheid), they have material wealth (nonwhites were typically kept in abject poverty in their homeland areas), and their intruder sign bears a masked man who "proved that the property owner was no racist" (p. 304). But like the narrator of the story, this couple is living under apartheid, where happily-ever-after is not so happy. True, the couple and their beloved son are wealthy and affluent, they have a caravan trailer and swimming pool and servants and insurance, but they live in increasing fear of the "people of another color" (p. 304) who are "quartered" outside the city, in much the same way that native peoples under apartheid were quartered on homeland territories while the white ruling class lived in suburbs and urbanized areas. Increasingly, the happy couple's idyllic happy-ever-after life is threatened by crime and the presence of the nonwhite underclass that the apartheid economic system itself creates, until more and more, the suburb begins to resemble a gulag of "prison architecture" (p. 306), with blaring alarms and security fences. In the final sentences of the story, the couple's child is mutilated on their own security fence, the outward manifestation of their paranoia.

An important dimension of "Once Upon a Time" is the way Gordimer incorporates the economic aspects of apartheid into her fiction. Under apartheid, the white ruling class and the native African and immigrant classes were locked into a very specific form of economic interdependence, in which native Africans and immigrants served as cheap, underpaid menial labor, and members of the white upper class occupied the specialized and highly educated professions such as medicine and law. Economic dependence is a key reason why development of the native homelands as sovereign states was impossible and failed in the late seventies and early eighties ("Apartheid" 89). While the white ruling class prospered economically from this interdependence, Gordimer points out that this very prosperity put them at risk. She describes how "intruders sawed the iron bars and broke into homes, taking away hi-fi equipment, television sets, cameras and radios, jewelry and clothing, and sometimes were hungry enough to devour everything in the refrigerator or paused audaciously to drink the whiskey in the cabinets or patio bars" (pp. 304–305). These incidents of theft are a very large part of the reason why the fairy-tale residents of the story's affluent suburb begin installing the formidable defenses that lead to tragedy at the story's end.

Gordimer's story dramatizes how the creation of an economic system that kept natives poor and concentrated wealth in the hands of a small ruling class created crime, paranoia, and fear. This corrosive fear, in turn, keeps the two classes apart, even to the extent that the white couple is afraid to bring bread and tea to the poor migrant workers who loiter near the suburb. Ultimately, it leads directly to the installation of security safeguards that turn the idyllic suburb of Happily-ever-after into "prison architecture" (p. 306), a hell of blaring alarms, razor-sharp wire, and pathetically festive painted pink spikes.

Gordimer also alludes to the violence and social unrest apartheid created. In the fairy-tale world, there are "riots, but these were outside the city" (p. 304). Despite the physical distance, the violence of the riots deeply affects the suburb, leading to the first installation of security devices. Gordimer may be alluding here to the Sharpeville riots of 1960, in which police opened fire on protestors, killing sixty-nine people. Or she may perhaps be referencing the Soweto uprisings of 1976, which were caused by legislation requiring that black students be taught in the Afrikaans language ("Apartheid" 118). Hundreds of people were killed when police again opened fire into crowds of protesting students. While the fairy-tale inhabitants of the story are far from these scenes of death and violence, they nevertheless have a brutalizing effect. It is the unseen but nevertheless present threat of chaos and violence that leads to the first fateful gestures of fear and the isolating effects of it, as realized metaphorically by the increasingly forbidding and cacophonous security measures.

Ultimately, "Once Upon a Time" is a fable about loneliness, isolation, fear, and the way in which the economic and social policies of apartheid annihilated human connection. The narrator lurks in her fragile house, worrying about burglar bars and knifings and unseen landslides that may bury the migrant workers and shatter her home like a wineglass. Even her fantasies are infected with the harsh realities of apartheid life. There is no escape for her, and less for the fairy tale denizens of her bedtime story. There is a crucial moment in the story where the fairy-tale wife sends out the housemaid with bread and tea for the beggars who loaf and sleep in the suburb. "You only encourage them with your bread and tea," her husband tells her, "They are looking for their chance..." The way in which this threat trails off into a nebulous but terrifying unknown is, in some ways, the heart of this story. The economic prosperity and safety the white couple enjoy is counterbalanced by the constant fears that both will be taken from them. Their fears, in the form of their aggressive security systems and alarms, grow increasingly powerful until they turn inward. Gordimer's story points out that under apartheid the line between the brutalized and the brutalizer is a thin one. The members of the dominant social class have material goods, but they are constantly prey to phantoms, jumping at every shadow, until they mutilate their own children out of sheer terror.

WORKS CITED

"Apartheid." *New Encyclopedia of Africa*. Ed. John Middleton and Joseph C. Miller. 2nd ed. Vol. 1. Detroit: Charles Scribner's Sons, 2008. 88-91. *Gale Virtual Reference Library*. Web. 17 April 2010.

"Apartheid." *Encyclopedia of Race and Racism*. Ed. John Hartwell Moore. Vol. 1. Detroit: Macmillan Reference USA, 2008. 117–20. *Gale Virtual Reference Library*. Web. 12 April 2010.

Rudikoff, Sonya. "Nadine Gordimer." African Writers. Ed. C. Brian Cox. Vol. 1. New York: Charles Scribner's Sons, 1997. *Literature Resource Center*. Web. 12 April 2010.

10

More Cultural Studies: Postcolonialism and Multiculturalism

It is from those who have suffered the sentence of history—subjugation, domination, diaspora, displacement—that we learn our most enduring lessons for living and thinking.

HOMI BHABHA, "THE POSTCOLONIAL AND THE POSTMODERN"

We have already seen how new historicism uses knowledge and information from many fields, some of which have not traditionally been associated with literary studies. Critics working from a postcolonial or American multicultural perspective share that interest in going beyond the study of literature as literature, and they too have been influenced by anthropology, sociology, Marxism, feminism, popular culture studies, and other nonliterary disciplines that examine distinct groups of people in an attempt to explain how a culture is created, maintained, and weakened. In addition to sharing the interests of other disciplines, they also adopt and adapt their methodologies, finding in the approaches of psychoanalysis or deconstruction the means of examining texts as part of a larger body of study—that of the culture itself.

POSTCOLONIALISM

To understand **postcolonialism** and its connection to literature requires looking first at its predecessor, **colonialism**, and then its successor, **neocolonialism**.

It hardly needs to be pointed out by now that because postcolonialism is a relatively new field of study, there is not total agreement about its principles and purposes. In this case, even its spelling (*post-colonialism* versus *postcolonialism*) is disputed. What follows, therefore, are generalizations that may not apply to everyone involved with postcolonial theory and the criticism of **postcolonial literature**.

Historical Background

Interest in postcolonialism dates back to the 1950s when Alfred Sauvy coined the term *Third World* to refer to developing nations, such as those in Africa or South America. They differ from what has come to be known as the First World countries—those in most of Europe and North America—which are characterized by industrialization, democracy, relative affluence, and similar cultural assumptions and beliefs. The white populations of countries once belonging to the British Empire (Australia, Canada, New Zealand) occupy a status of their own as they fulfill the definition of a First World country, but have more recently been linked with the colonizing power than some others, such as the United States. At the bottom of this hierarchy are the native populations who, although in some cases they compose the majority, are ruled by their white conquerors. Postcolonialism is interested in all but the First World; however, because many members of the First World have historically been the oppressors, they too are involved in the discussion.

Colonialism is, simply, the subjection of one population to another. It is most clearly seen in physical conquest, but in its more subtle forms, it involves political, economic, and cultural domination. The British rule in India, for example, involved not only the use of force to subdue the latter but also the imposition of British institutions and tastes. When people are colonized, their traditions and practices are supplanted by imitations of those of the colonizer. Parts of the indigenous culture as elemental as food, clothing, and recreation tend to disappear, because they are either hidden or replaced, thereby removing that culture from history. The term *colonialism* is sometimes used to challenge the meaning attributed to it by the colonizers, who use the term to refer to the positive, civilizing effects of their efforts. In this challenging usage, *colonialism* takes on Marxist overtones to reflect the perceptions of local peoples who have experienced (or who have known the legacy of) the burdens imposed by the colonizers: foreign social, business, and legal practices; exploitation of natural resources; and military occupation.

Although the term *postcolonial* was not in use until the late 1980s, theories surrounding its concerns have been published since the 1960s. Over the years, the study of postcolonialism has primarily attracted the interest of literary scholars and critics. However, because it is concerned with what happens to a culture from the beginning of colonization to the present, it is also making inroads in fields as diverse as political science, sociology, and psychology. Postcolonialism theories offer topics of interest to members of these fields because the formal termination of colonial rule does not wipe out its legacy, and the culture that is left is a mixture of the colonized one and that of the colonizer, often marked by contrasts and antagonisms, resentment and blended practice. The two are no longer recognizable as having separate cultures. Consequently, issues abound regarding the development of national identity, identification of cultural histories and knowledge, the precolonial nature of the colonized, and the colonized's resistance to the power base that has subjugated them.

Edward Said's *Orientalism*, published in 1978, was an important influence on what would become known as postcolonialism. In his analysis, Said called attention to the pejorative stereotypes that the British, other Europeans, and Americans create of the peoples unlike themselves, thereby making it easier to justify military or economic conquest. Their view of the "**other**" world—"orientalism"—is inevitably colored by their own cultural, political, and religious backgrounds, leading them to depict those unlike themselves as inferior and objectionable—for example, as lazy, deceitful, and irrational. The self, by contrast, is defined as good, upright, and moral. The Eastern nations are given all the negative characteristics that the West does not want to see in itself. For example, the first reports of the Oklahoma City bombing in 1995 attributed the deed to Middle Eastern terrorists, because it was impossible to think that an American would have done such a thing. In *Orientalism*, Said called upon the literary establishment to raise questions about colonization, imperialism, and constructions of the "other." Over the ensuing decades, postcolonial theorists have probed those issues by examining such subjects as language, feminism, oppression, cultural identity, race, and education. The intent is to study what happens when one culture is dominated by another.

Helen Gilbert and Joanne Tompkins point out the error of understanding postcolonialism simply as a "temporal concept," a period of time following the end of foreign governance. Instead, they say, it is a complex mixture of contesting discourses, social hierarchies, and power structures. In fact, it seems that the *post* part of *postcolonialism* may be an overstatement of the way things really are, for today a new kind of colonialism is taking place. Weaker powers are no longer as likely to be taken by military conquest, but they are no less economically and culturally dominated. Major international corporations, drawn by the availability of cheap labor and cooperative local governments, practice what is known as neocolonialism, which has much the same effect as traditional imperialism. Under neocolonialism's aegis, the customs and traditional "ways" of the subjugated peoples are weakened, changed, and sometimes destroyed.

Knowing exactly which works fall into the category of postcolonial literature was a simpler matter before the 1980s, when it was called Commonwealth literature. At that time, it was generally assumed that the term referred to the literature of cultures colonized by the British Empire, such as Australia, New Zealand, Canada, and parts of Africa, all of which were dominated by white Europeans who imposed their own cultural traditions at the expense of the native population's traditions. The problem with the label *Commonwealth literature* is its grounding in British culture. This term seems to indicate that the literatures of native cultures still belong to "the mother country." Such a position also ignores the literature of white settlers in colonized lands. Some readers still argue that white writers in Canada, New Zealand, or Australia should not be included, because they practice British traditions, share the same language, and belong to the same race. They have not been oppressed. They have not had to hide their traditions. Others argue, however, that although the settlers were the colonizers, they (or their descendants) do not and did not belong to Britain in the same way that native-born citizens do. Their home is in the colonized country. Consequently, the literature of white settlers is not dissimilar in its sense of double consciousness (double vision) as defined by W. E. B. DuBois (see "American Multiculturalism" later in this chapter). That is, their literature views the world through the contrasting perspectives of both the colonizer and the colonized. It reflects the sense of belonging to neither, of being culturally displaced, a quality Homi Bhabha refers to as **unhomeliness**. The broadest view of postcolonial literature is that it is the literature written in English by people in formerly colonized countries, some of it authored by the colonizers and their descendants, but more of it by those they colonized.

The term *postcolonial* has since replaced the label *Commonwealth literature*, although the uncertainty regarding what literatures it includes continues. At the least, it seems to broaden the field of interest by opening it to countries colonized by Western powers other than Great Britain, such as Spain, France, Russia, Portugal, and more. Currently the literature of any country that concerns itself with the legacy of colonial rule qualifies, including, to name only a few, that of African countries, India, Sri Lanka, and most recently the Middle East. Some readers assume that postcolonial literature refers to texts produced after the colonized countries became independent, but others take it to mean the texts produced from the time of colonization to the present.

The subject matter of postcolonial literature is marked by its concern for ambiguity or loss of identity. Written by culturally displaced people, it investigates the clash of cultures in which one deems itself to be superior and imposes its own practices on the less powerful one. Its writers examine their histories, question how they should respond to the changes they see around them, and wonder what their society will become. They recognize in themselves the old culture and the new, elements of the native one and the imposed one. The result is writing that is critical of the conquerors and promotional about its own ideologies.

Postcolonial literary criticism, which began to attract widespread notice in the early 1990s, looks at the works of postcolonial writers but is not limited to them. Because its practitioners are interested in how the colonized came to accept the values of the more powerful culture and to resist them too, it looks at canonical texts as well as postcolonial ones. Attitudes toward the "other" are evident in works that may not, on the surface, seem to deal with colonialism at all. Helen Tiffin argues in "Post-colonial Literatures and Counter-discourse" that because a precolonial past cannot be regained and contemporary identity cannot be free of that past, the real job of postcolonial criticism is "to investigate the means by which Europe imposed and maintained ... colonial domination of so much of the rest of the world." She suggests that the way to do so is to use "canonical counter-discourse," a process in which one examines "a character or characters, or the basic assumptions of a British canonical text, and unveils [colonialist] assumptions, subverting the text for post-colonial purposes." By extension, the whole colonialist discourse in which that text participates is revealed.

In looking at *Jane Eyre*, for example, Andrew Bennett and Nicholas Royle discover a strong racial theme in the novel. By bringing Bertha Mason, Rochester's Creole wife (from the West Indies), to the center of the narrative, they make the allusions and images that refer to slavery and the slave trade, heretofore mostly ignored, important keys to prevailing social attitudes. Whereas traditional criticism has in large part overlooked Bertha, who lives as a madwoman locked in the attic, and has left the assumptions about her unexamined, Bennett and Royle uncover the ideology implicit in the unquestioned acceptance of her invisibility, imprisonment, and displacement from her homeland. Before their analysis, she was seen as a threat because of her madness. They make it possible to view her, instead, as a sufferer who has been driven mad. The roles of villain and victim are reversed, providing through this new perspective on a much-read novel additional insight into colonialist and anticolonialist thinking.

Basic Assumptions

The lack of total agreement about what postcolonialism is or whom it involves makes it difficult to set down its basic principles and purposes. Further complicating the situation is that different cultures have responded to colonization in different ways, making it impossible to subscribe to any single way of approaching postcolonial studies. With those reservations in mind, the following assumptions and generalizations are by and large accepted as important to postcolonial theory.

- Colonizers not only physically conquer territories but also practice **cultural colonization** by replacing the practices and beliefs of the native culture with their own values, governance, laws, and belief. The consequence is loss or modification of much of the precolonial culture.
- When their own culture is forbidden or devalued, natives come to see themselves as inferior to the conquerors. They abandon (or hide) their own cultural practices to adopt (imitate) those of the assumedly "superior" one.
- Colonial subjects practice **mimicry**—imitation of dress, language, behavior, even gestures—instead of resistance. In *Black Skin, White Masks*, published in 1952, Frantz Fanon, a psychiatrist, reasoned that the inferiority complex created in black people who have accepted the culture of another country as their own will cause them to imitate the codes of their colonizers. As the colonized become better educated and able to live as their white counterparts, they become increasingly imitative. Homi Bhabha points out that the mimicry is never exact, however. It "is at once resemblance and menace." The colonizer both wants and fears that the colonized will be like him because the imitation honors and, at the same time, undermines the "authoritative discourse" of colonialism.
- European colonizers believed that their ideals and experiences were universal. As a concept, **universalism** is evident in the characters and themes in European (and, later, American) literature.

- The European colonizers assumed the superiority of their own culture and the inferiority of the conquered ones. They thought of themselves as civilized, even advanced, and of the colonists as backward, even savage. Using their own culture as the standard for what any culture should be, a practice known as **Eurocentrism**, the powerful justified the imposition of their own culture on those they deemed to be of lesser status, the **subalterns**.
- The practice of **othering**, viewing those who are different from oneself as inferior beings, divides people and justifies hierarchies. Sometimes the dominant culture sees the "other" as evil, in which case it is known as the **demonic other**.
- On other occasions, the "other" is deemed to have a natural beauty, to be the **exotic other**.
- Colonizers also become the colonized. In this two-way process, the Europeans too were affected by their contact with other cultures.
- The effects of past colonialism are still evident today, and a new form of colonialism is currently effected by international corporations operating in developing nations.
- The interaction of cultures creates blended ones, mixtures of the native and colonial, a process called **hybridity** or **syncretism**. Characterized by tensions and change, this process is dynamic, interactive, and creative. As Bhabha explained in an interview with Gary Olson and Lynn Worsham, "For me, hybridization is a discursive, enunciatory, cultural, subjective process having to do with the struggle around authority, authorization, deauthorization, and the revision of authority. It's a social process. It's not about persons of diverse cultural tastes and fashions."

Reading as a Postcolonialist

To understand the discussion that follows, you should read the excerpt from Jill Ker Conway's autobiography, The Road from Coorain, *which begins on page 257.*

A postcolonial analysis begins with the assumption that examining the relationship between a text and its context will illuminate not only the given work but also the culture that produced and consumed it. In the end, you may not agree with everything you find in either of them, but you will emerge with a deeper understanding of how and why a text is meaningful. In turn, the process gives greater validity to your judgments about a body of literature and the community associated with it. The postcolonial reader will generally be alert and sensitive to the presence of the following elements that recur in the literature.

Presentation of Colonialism The central question of postcolonial criticism addresses the stance of the text toward the mixed colonial culture that it depicts or that produced it. What attitudes does the text reflect regarding the colonizers and the colonized? A wide range of viewpoints is possible, for the historical development of a culture, the relationships between its cultural groups, and the daily stresses of mixing people of different backgrounds make for a complex situation. The understanding of such matters will likely be expressed in fairly subtle ways, and there may be no single unconflicted attitude, because questions of how the conquered and the conqueror can live comfortably with each other, even after years of trying, are not easily answered.

Colonialism is certainly one of the principal themes of Jill Ker Conway's autobiographical remembrance of growing up in Australia. In *The Road from Coorain*, she not only identifies the colonialist mentalities she met (and was led to share) but also traces the means by which they were inculcated and maintained. She tells the story of her awakening to the fact that she has unconsciously absorbed colonial attitudes from her family and other families living similar kinds of lives in the outback. Her recognition of the elitism and estrangement from native life on that continent takes her by surprise as she moves from Coorain, the remote sheep farm in the bush, to Sydney after the death of her father, later to graduate school in America, and finally to her appointment as the first female president of Smith College. The awareness of the duality of her cultural roots is accompanied by the corresponding surprise of finding that being female set her apart in a similar way. Just as she was subtly informed at home and school and in society that Australia was inferior to Great Britain, so she was also confronted with implicit, and sometimes explicit, assumptions that she was less capable than the males in her world. Ironically, it was because she was female that she was allowed to pursue higher education, for, unlike her brothers, she was not expected to return to Coorain to run the sheep farm.

You can begin to examine the attitudes toward colonialism that exist in a work by asking the following questions:

- Is the work critical of colonialism, approving of it, or ambivalent about its value?
- Does the narrator speak as an observer or a participant in the story's cultural setting?
- What traditions and practices serve to maintain the cultural hierarchy in the work?

Treatment of Characters It is in the portrayals of colonizers and the colonized that the larger picture becomes evident. The reader can begin by asking whether the depictions are positive or negative. Whose deeds are celebrated and whose reproved? The assumptions about characters, both spoken and unspoken, will indicate whether the work supports or resists the ideology and practices of colonialism.

Conway's depictions of the characters she knew as a girl are not simple. Some of the colorful personalities she met came to the sheep farm to work; others were landowning farmers like her parents. She remembers them with fondness, but she also recognizes that from the beginning, the class distinctions were clear and became more firmly drawn after her move to Sydney. It was the families with close English connections who stood high in the hierarchy; it was those with the most English behavior who were most admired. At Abbotsleigh, for example, the school in which Conway was enrolled after her brief exposure to public education, the headmistress, Miss Everett, represented the "European cultural ideal," and the girls were expected to emulate her straight back, British accent, and athletic carriage. Looking back, Conway recognizes that something was lost by what she refers to as her "colonization." She speculates that had she remained in a public school, she might "have been obliged to come to terms with the Australian class system." She adds, "It would have been invaluable knowledge, and my vision of Australia would have been the better for it. It was to take me another fifteen years to see the world from my own Australian perspective, rather than from the British definition taught to my kind of colonial." Though her criticism is not bitter and her depictions of Miss Everett and others at Abbotsleigh are affectionately drawn, her awareness of the limitations imposed by the colonial mentality is clear.

Insight into the attitudes of the characters can come from asking the following questions:

- What descriptive terms characterize the depiction of the characters who are the colonizers?
- What descriptive terms characterize the depiction of the colonized characters?
- What is the relationship between the colonized and the colonizers in the narrative?

Validity of the Narrative It is important to establish whether the events are exaggerated. Is political and cultural domination presented explicitly or allegorically? Is the whole story being told? Are some elements contrary to what actually happened? Are the rationalizations believable? Knowing something about the author, including his or her background, opinions, and purposes, can sometimes be helpful in this regard.

Because *The Road from Coorain* is autobiographical, and the writer has validity in the eyes of the reader, the narrative is straightforward and rings true. The writer does not indulge in exaggeration or even satire, except for an occasional comic look at human foibles. If you are interested in testing the validity of a narrative, the questions posed in the previous paragraph can be applied to any piece of postcolonial literature.

Expressions of Nativism (Nationalism) Out of a desire to resurrect the precolonial culture, some postcolonial writers consciously use elements of native culture and expunge elements of the imposed one. It is one way to rediscover native identity and declare its worth. Several problems lie in this approach, however. When writers publish works written in their own language, for instance, they usually meet a limited reading audience because too few people are likely to be proficient at comprehending it. Some people also argue that the attempt is inherently flawed, because all cultures change; even without the intervention of an outside oppressor, what once was, even if one could find it out, would no longer be. Finally, postcolonial cultures are hybrid ones, and any attempt to go back to a "pure" culture is unrealistic.

Conway, writing as a native-born Australian but not as a member of the indigenous population, makes no attempt to disavow her British heritage. Instead, she writes from the postcolonial perspective of a hybrid culture that combines both the native one and the dominating one. Sometimes the contrasts she experienced make for illogical or amusing situations. For example, the requirement at Abbotsleigh that the girls wear uniforms designed for an English climate leaves them in summer in "starched green linen dresses with cream collars, the same [green flannel] blazer, beige socks, a cream panama hat, and the same brown gloves." She continues, "Woe betide the student caught shedding the blazer or the gloves in public, even when the thermometer was over 100 degrees.... No one paused to think that gloves and blazers had a function in damp English springs which they lacked entirely in our blazing summers." Such irrational practices left the girls, as Conway says, "only partially at home in our environment." She is referring to the sense of unhomeliness, of being caught between two cultures and not entirely at home in either of them. Another way of describing her situation is to say that she is experiencing double consciousness, for she has an awareness of being part of both the colonized and the colonizing cultures and thus of being the recipient of all the conflicts and contrasts that exist between them.

The following are some questions that can help the reader examine the elements of nativism in a story:

- Does the story refer only to native elements of the culture, or does it depict a hybrid culture?
- Which characters experience unhomeliness?
- Where do you find instances of double consciousness?

Recurring Subjects and Themes Some postcolonial texts look to the past, rehearsing the pains of othering and the humiliations of mimicry. They retell the stories of the initial colonization and trace changes in the native culture. Others record the sense of double consciousness and unhomeliness experienced by those who belong to both past and present and to neither. Still other texts look to the future, reaching for a definition of the new hybrid identity (both personal and communal) and an ideology that will serve its needs. In all cases, postcolonial texts reveal the complexity of cultural identity in a colonized world.

As already noted, *The Road from Coorain* is the story of Conway's double consciousness and unhomeliness as it evolves into a personal identity. It also points to the practice of mimicry as one of the chief ways by which the colonizer's presence was maintained. Nowhere is that more evident than at Abbotsleigh, where Eurocentrism reigned. The school made it clear by social rules, curriculum, and the example of its leaders that England was the standard by which all people and practices were to be measured. In the formality of the dinner table (where the girls, wearing green velvet dresses, were seated in descending order of age and class), in the absence of references to Australian art and literature in their classes, and in virtually all practices at Abbotsleigh, it was British culture that was imitated and admired. For example, Conway notes that in the study of literature, she and her classmates "might have been in Sussex," because their reading consisted of Shakespeare and Shelley, not of the writers of their own country. Australia, then, was defined by default, by what it was not. The girls were left to conclude that because its countryside did not look like the Cotswolds and the Lake Country, it must be ugly; and because its paintings were not mentioned, there must not be any. History pointed out that people of any importance lived somewhere else. The teachers dutifully corrected the girls' speech so that it would conform to standard British pronunciation, unmarred by Australian patterns. In short, "The best standards were derived from Great Britain, and should be emulated unquestioningly." And just in case the message was not clear, geography lessons featured maps with the holdings of the British Empire colored bright red. Obviously, the closest an Australian could come to being judged superior was by mimicry, by being British, even if only partly so.

The subjects and themes of postcolonial literature can be found by asking the following questions:

- Does the narrative look to the past, examine the present, or hypothesize a possible future?
- Where is imitation of the cultural standard depicted, and what is the effect of mimicry on those who are expected to practice it?
- How do specific characters struggle to develop a personal identity by reconciling the two cultures in which they live?

Context Every work has a context, and studying context lies at the heart of postcolonial literary study. Whereas interpreters of a culture sometimes derive insights about it by reading its literature, a postcolonialist critic will look to almost every aspect of a culture to illuminate a text. Significant elements may be social or material; they may be drawn from the culture that produced the text or the culture of its interpreters. For the reader interested in deepening his or her understanding of a work, the process means examining the interaction of the two, which can be a time-consuming business if for no other reason than that it is difficult to know when one has done enough. The complex relationship between text and context, each a product and creator of the other, is called **negotiation**.

The context of Conway's story and the context of its telling are not the same. That is, it is told from the distance of another country, personal independence, and intellectual growth. She has written it from the perspective of one who has moved far enough away from a place and a personal history to achieve insight that is not often found while immersed in them. It is interesting to speculate, for example, whether Conway would have been moved to write about growing up entrenched in colonialist mentality if she had not left it behind. Then, too, the changing social attitudes of the 1960s and later must have influenced her, as they did others, to question the traditional ways of evaluating what is good and what should be, a process that is important to her story. The times and her changing place have allowed her to see her past with greater clarity, and her remembrances shed light on the times, past and present.

The text and its contexts can be examined by asking the following questions:

- Are the context of the story and the context of its telling the same or different? If different, how do they affect each other?
- Where do you observe negotiation—that is, the impact of the context on the text and of the text on its context?
- What significant public events in the writer's life can be said to have contributed to his or her views?

Minor Characters As in the analysis of *Jane Eyre* mentioned earlier, previously unnoticed assumptions in a work can sometimes be detected by paying attention to the characters who do not hold center stage. By noting their treatment and the language used to describe them, attitudes about colonizers and colonized peoples that have gone unnoticed, especially in canonical works, may become evident.

Conway's classmates at the public school she briefly attended are never mentioned by name, and perhaps they were never even known as individuals. In the full scope of the autobiography, they play bit parts. Nevertheless, her brief encounter with them speaks volumes about the class structure of postwar Australia. For example, the superior attitude that she naturally assumed toward them, on the basis of the stereotypes and judgments given to her by her family and their friends, is symptomatic of the elitism common to her class. The jeering schoolmates are well aware of the social gulf between them, and they reflect an authentic Australian culture that is scorned by those who have assumed the colonizers' consciousness of class.

Minor characters can become significant when a reader asks the following questions:

- Which minor characters typify major cultural attitudes?
- How does the principal character view specific minor characters?
- Where do minor characters embody cultural conflict?

Political Statement and Innuendo The question here is whether and how a work promotes resistance to colonialism. Does the text make ideological statements or support a particular course of political, economic, or social action? Does it take up the case for or against a particular group of people? Or does it attempt to present the complexity of the situation without taking a stand on it?

When Jill Ker Conway promotes resistance to colonialism, she does so quietly. Her book is not driven by a desire to rally crowds to march in the streets for a particular cause. Instead, it is a thoughtful recollection of how she came to recognize her own girlhood acceptance of a limited point of view that created in her, as an Australian, a sense of always being less than someone else. It was a sense of self that was derived both from her colonialist background and from growing up female. Although she names no villains or conspirators, there is no mistaking her criticism of institutionalized social practices designed to ensure an inferior status for certain groups. It is clear that she regrets the negative sense of self that was imposed on both children and adults by comparing Australia with the revered Great Britain. Her escape from such smallness of vision came with her move to the United States for graduate study and her subsequent marriage to a Canadian. Her cultural identity has continued to grow—in one sense, making for greater complexity of definition, but in another making for deeper understanding of what it means to reject the colonial mentality as one works out an individual identity. In the end, her own liberation from colonialist boundaries and definitions and her assumption of an identity that has been enriched by numerous cultures make her a model of what citizens of a shrinking world are likely to become. In that way, her autobiography provides a quiet but powerful ideological statement.

The political stance of a literary work may be obvious or subtle. The reader can identify it by asking the following questions:

- Does the text make overt political statements? Does it openly promote a particular social or economic agenda?
- Does it admire characters who stand for a stated cause?
- Does it criticize those who represent a specific ideology?

Similarities Homi Bhabha notes the possibilities for studying world literature not in terms of national traditions but in terms of postcolonial themes that cut across national boundaries. The reader would look, for example, at whether native populations from different countries have commonalities as a result of their experience of having been colonized. This study could take a number of different forms, depending on which groups the reader chose to study.

Conway could easily be the subject of such a study, as she is not the only writer to address the issues named here. Undoubtedly, interesting comparisons could be made between her remembrances and those of others who grew up as natives in a homeland not entirely their own. Did they experience the same sense of double consciousness? Did they have the same knowledge of hybridity? Were they, too, expected to practice mimicry? For example, what correspondences and differences are to be found between *The Road from Coorain* and V. S. Naipaul's novel *A Bend in the River*, the story of a young Indian man who moves to an isolated African town and finds himself dangerously caught up in the clash of an old regime and the new one?

To make such comparisons requires a wide acquaintance with postcolonial literature. For the reader interested in following Bhabha's suggestion, it may be necessary to consult bibliographies of postcolonial literature to find potentially comparable works.

U.S. MULTICULTURALISM

Since the 1960s, U.S. society has undergone radical changes in how it conceives of social structures. School desegregation, new laws barring discrimination, and the demise of old laws that promoted discrimination have opened the door to opportunity for people who had traditionally been shut out. Within such marginalized groups, the renaissance of valued traditions that differ from those of the dominant group has served to enhance self-esteem and reassert distinct identities. In turn, the richness of cultures that had heretofore been ignored or reviled has come to the attention not only of those who belong to them but of a wider public as well. The arts, crafts, rituals, and religion of American Indians, Hispanics, African Americans, and other historically overlooked groups are now generating increasing interest in the many strands that make up U.S. society, allowing people to be less confined by a single way of seeing their lives. Of all such groups, African American culture, burdened with problems from the moment of its introduction to the New World, has probably received more attention than any others. For that reason, it will be discussed here as a model of how cultural studies of other marginalized groups can be made.

African American Literature

Although literature produced by African Americans dates from their earliest presence in North America, notice by the mainstream was a long time coming to those writers who explored their own traditions and forms. Jupiter Hammon and Phyllis Wheatley, the first black man and woman to be published in colonial America, both practiced the literary traditions of white culture. Beginning in 1760, Hammon, the slave of several generations of the Lloyd family of Queen's Village, Long Island, published poems and prose that reflected his resignation to a life of obedience to his earthly master and to God. Wheatley, purchased as a young girl in 1761 by John Wheatley of Boston, was taught to read and write and quickly began to compose poems. Eventually she became the best-known American poet in England. Writing in the neoclassical style of Alexander Pope, she composed verses that reflected her privileged status, not a slave mentality. Expressing love for the Wheatleys, who provided her with an education and tended to her health, and also decrying the cruelty of the slavers who brought Africans to this country, she was clearly a conflicted being. Her situation has led some, but not all, contemporary scholars to reject as genuine her expressions of gratitude for the grace of

God that brought her to America and, instead, to see her as a trickster figure who is writing ironically about (or *signifying* on) white culture. The theme of freedom was dominant, however, in the writing of other African Americans during the slave period (1619–1865) and the period dedicated to readjustment and progress (1866–1917).

It was many decades before black writers would again attract major attention from mainstream American culture. Not until the Harlem Renaissance of the 1920s would their work be celebrated by those outside their own circle. In that postwar decade, the work of black writers shared the popularity that black music and dance found with whites, partly because it represented a departure from traditional forms. The culture that most of America had almost forgotten now seemed new and exciting, though attention waned again when the Depression and World War II demanded the country's attentions, returning only in the 1940s with the appearance of social protest novels such as Richard Wright's *Black Boy*. By mid-century, there was also interest in the black folk tradition, which was in danger of being lost. J. Mason Brewer, for example, collected and called on others to document a long and varied group of verbal artifacts, including religious tales; slave tales; "professor" stories; rich-soil tales (of Louisiana) and poor-land tales (of Alabama); the court story cycle of tales of the Arkansas Negro; humorous Mexican-Negro anecdotes; stories of Uncle Mose, the carefree Negro, the clever Negro, and the Mississippi delta; narratives of Georgia racial prejudice; and ghost stories (Gayle 1969, p. 21). In the 1960s, black writers again claimed notice, but this time with a difference. Writing more consciously out of the African American experience, they no longer asked for white approval of their works but wrote intentionally for black audiences. They no longer tried to conceal faults that might earn white criticism but instead turned to condemning the shortcomings of the dominant culture. Pity and mourning were replaced by an assertion of worth. The success of black writers over the past three decades has been astounding, with far too many prizewinning poets, essayists, playwrights, and fiction writers to begin to name here.

Although the literature of black culture had been part of American history from the eighteenth century on—sometimes appearing in print, sometimes being passed on as an oral tradition—critics who understood the work were not. In the 1920s, anthologies of black literature such as James Weldon Johnson's *The Book of American Negro Poetry* (1922), followed by Alain Locke's *The New Negro* (1925) and Countee Cullen's *Caroling Dusk* (1927), were compiled. A second explosion of collections followed the appearance of Rosey Pool's *Beyond the Blues* in 1962. Obviously, the readers were there, but where were the critics?

Clearly it was time for critical approaches that incorporated an understanding of the purposes of black artists and the forms and styles in which they worked. The standards held up as exemplary in the poetry and fiction of white writers were not always suitable for what African American writers produced; sometimes they did not fit. Needed were readers who could understand the forms and styles of black artists and interpret their works in ways that were valid, finding their uniqueness as well as discovering similarities and differences with the literatures of other cultures. Such interpretations would be based not on white standards but on what came to be known as the **black aesthetic**.

For African American artists, a black aesthetic would ease their struggle to find an identity in a world that was not theirs. It would encourage them to honor their own experience, not remake it in the image of white culture. By asserting a racial identity that was separate from and not dependent on white attitudes, principles, and practices, it would renounce the assumption that because the white experience is the model to follow, its rules and standards of judgment must be adopted. For the world at large, it would counter what Carolyn Gerald called the black community's "zero image," caused sometimes by the absence of visibility and sometimes by negative portraits that appeared in white films, literature, and art. In its most assertive form, a black aesthetic would be a protest against white critics, editors, and publishers and their power to control what is written and published. More pragmatically, it would be the basis of a system of evaluating African American art in terms of the special character of the black experience.

The problem lay in defining what that special character is. To arrive at a consensus about such a complex topic required thinking and talking about the function of black writers, examining their literary techniques, establishing the qualifications of black critics, and devising critical terminology. Although such discussions are still in progress, it is possible to specify some major points of interest. Like the aesthetic of all artists, the black aesthetic is concerned with the materials its artists work with, the purpose of their work, and how they go about doing it.

For black artists, the material is black history, which is unlike that of any other group in America. Their unique past includes Africa, the Middle Passage, slavery, emancipation, northward migration, and racism, as well as the civil rights, Black Power, and Black Arts movements. It also lacks some of the history that other Americans have enjoyed, such as the vision of this country as a land of rights, freedom, and opportunity. The result is a dual identity, one that both partakes of America and doesn't, one that shares the American experience but is denied it. Even today, the sense of belonging and being separate provides material not duplicated in any other American group. W. E. B. DuBois called the sensation of perceiving oneself through the eyes of others **double consciousness**. As he explained in "Of Our Spiritual Strivings," published in his collection of essays *The Souls of Black Folk*, "One ever feels his twoness,—an American, a Negro; two warring souls, two thoughts, two unreconciled strivings; two warring ideals in one dark body, whose dogged strength alone keeps it from being torn asunder."

Henry Louis Gates finds traces of this feeling of separateness but belonging in literature in what he calls **double-voicedness**. In his book *The Signifying Monkey*, he identifies double-voicedness as the source of the uniqueness of black literature, for no other group can lay claim to having its roots in both black and white cultures. (Some readers take his assertion to be overstated, because the work of white artists has certainly been influenced by black culture.)

The purpose of black art, like that of all art, varies with the artist. Nevertheless, African American artists have a strong imperative to reclaim their culture by defining what is of value to them. Such a reclamation takes place by remembering history, defining identity, gaining recognition, and celebrating blackness. It requires that African American literature announce itself as itself, not as a copy of other art. By so doing, it legitimizes the community it comes from and to some degree can be seen as revolutionary.

Black artists generally go about their work in the same way their white counterparts do. However, African American writers are also noted for drawing on **folk traditions** that express their beliefs, values, and social mores. Their written narratives and poetry often come from an oral tradition that features folktales, common expressions, exaggeration, a notable lack of self-consciousness, and a closeness to nature. This influence of the folk tradition is found not only in literature; it is also present in African American music, such as the blues and work songs.

Black artists are not limited to folk materials and techniques, however. Other traditions have also influenced how they do their work. Writing for *The Negro Digest* in 1968, Ron Karenga, for example, cited three characteristics of African art that can be found in the work of African Americans. Artists in both camps, he said, produce art that is functional, collective, and committing or committed. The function of African American art, according to Karenga, is to make revolution. Its collective nature is evident in its presentation of real life and real people, and it is committed to permanent revolution.

Reading as a Multiculturalist

To understand the discussion that follows, you will need to read an excerpt from The Eatonville Anthology, *a remembrance by Zora Neale Hurston, which begins on page 318.*

To approach a text from a multicultural perspective, a reader must look for more than material, purpose, and method. In the case of African American writers, the reader needs to anticipate specific characteristics that distinguish their work. Don Lee stated that such qualities can be most clearly recognized in music, because music is the black art form least affected by European American culture. Actually, these qualities are found in all aspects of African American life—in the ways black people eat, speak, dance, dress, and walk. Such attributes are apparent, too, in written and spoken texts. When dealing with fiction, three topics to think about are narrative forms, diction, and style.

Narrative Forms As mentioned earlier, many of the stories written by African American authors are derived from the folk tradition. Although these stories have been adapted to serve modern audiences, they retain many of the elements of those earlier oral performances. Some of the most recognizable narrative forms include the following:

- *Folktales:* Usually comic stories told to entertain and to pass time.
- *Tall tales:* Narratives that include exaggerated, unbelievable events and people.

- *Fables:* Animal stories, many with African roots, that make a moral point. They typically feature the hare, tortoise, fox, or spider.
- *Trickster stories:* Tales of John (or Jack), an unruly, disruptive character who manipulates people to make fools of them, then tries to clear himself by his wit when he is caught in a misdeed. His creative, inventive nature makes him seem bigger than life. One of the oldest mythical characters, the Trickster appears in folktales of many cultures. In African American stories, he often outwits the slave owner or, later, the police officer or landlord.
- *Why stories:* Narratives that humorously account for the origins of almost everything, from creation to the ways of women.
- *Preacher tales:* Entertaining stories told from the pulpit and stories told about preachers.
- *Blues:* Earthy, honest commentaries on life's difficulties—some spiritual, some material—that offer no apology or defense but never admit defeat or ask for pity.
- *Satire:* Ridicule of folly or stupidity. It is often humorous.
- *The dirty dozens:* Jeers directed at that which is held to be uplifting, holy, and decent. Although they are generated by loss of respect for a world that claims to honor such abstractions but crushes black people, they are often criticized for being obscene and disgusting.
- *Jokes:* Satirical anecdotes told at the expense of others, frequently white people, or to ridicule unfair social practices and stereotypes.

It is not surprising to find several of these narrative approaches in Zora Neale Hurston's *The Eatonville Anthology*. She was well prepared to draw on African American literary traditions to describe the vibrant characters of her childhood. She was, first of all, a natural storyteller who, among members of the Harlem Renaissance and even beyond that group, gained a reputation as a witty and skillful performer of oral narratives. In early childhood, she was steeped in black culture. Until her mother's death when Hurston was eleven, she lived in Eatonville, Florida, an all-black town where she knew no white people. After migrating to New York City, she enrolled at Columbia University, where she studied anthropology under the renowned Franz Boas, generating in her a lifelong interest in Negro folk traditions.

The vignettes of *The Eatonville Anthology* are clearly cast in the oral tradition but are so skillfully managed in written form that the reader is not initially aware of the sophistication of the storyteller. On the one hand, the narrator is a wise and witty observer, recording people and their behavior in a standard dialect. On the other, she tells the stories by taking on the voices of the various characters: the pleading woman, Daisy the town vamp, even Mr. Dog and Miss Nancy Coon. She manages to recreate an oral narrative in a written text, maintaining throughout the dual roles of observer and participant. The simplicity and directness with which she does so obscure the difficulty of the task.

Most of the remembrances are comic stories that make the reader laugh at human foibles. Old Man Anderson, for example, is so careful to protect his wagon from the train that he destroys it himself. And he never sees the train. And he never will. Even the troublemakers are drawn with a smile. Coon Taylor's forays into Joe Clarke's melon patch and sugarcane field are not depicted as "real stealing." Even those who are troubled affirm their situations. Mrs. Laura Crooms, much put upon by the vamp Daisy, talks a great deal about "leaving things in the hands of God." Then she fells Daisy with an ax handle and leaves her in a muddy ditch. The eighth entry, about Sewell, a man who lives by himself, is little more than a joke or two jokes in four sentences about the same man.

Some of the stories approach the tall-tale tradition. In "Village Fiction," men vie for the distinction of being the biggest liar, the evidence being unbelievable assertions about who they are and what they have seen. The final story picks up elements of the fable, using animals as characters. In the end, however, instead of making a moral point, it becomes a why story, for it explains how the dog's tongue got its crease down the middle. There is no preacher tale as such, but the final verse of the song found in "Double-Shuffle" takes a stab at that figure:

Would not marry uh preacher
Tell yuh de reason why
Every time he comes tuh town
He makes de chicken fly.

The blues are usually sung, but their commentary on life's difficulties is verbal. Mrs. Tony Roberts, the pleading woman in the opening selection, certainly moans the blues: "Lawd a mussy, Mis' Pierson, you ain't gonna gimme dat lil' eye-full uh greens fuh me an' mah chillen, is you? Don't be so graspin'; Gawd won't bless yuh. Gimme uh han'full mo'. Lawd, some folks is got everything, an' theys jes' as gripin' an stingy!" Although it is probably going too far to call Mrs. Roberts a Trickster figure, she is clearly a scam artist, but one who is not immune to being tricked herself. In the end, Mr. Clarke, the butcher, charges the slab of salt pork to her husband's account.

Each story is built around a gentle satire that recognizes the foolishness of human beings. The characters may be flawed individuals, and the narrator enjoys exploiting their shortcomings, but they are not mean, unlikable individuals. They have their troubles, and they cause some of them too, but, like other comic characters, they manage to survive their difficulties and go on with their lives.

Folk elements are usually not difficult to identify. You can look for them by asking the following questions:

- Does the story include any of the standard folk characters, such as the trickster or the preacher?
- Does the narrative fall into the category of a traditional folk form, such as the folk tale, tall tale, fable, or why story?
- Does the story satirize or rehearse grievances and injustices?

Diction The language used by African American writers varies all the way from strong dialect to standard American English. It appears in no single form. Nevertheless, some of the following characteristics commonly appear:

- Terse, pointed expressions that say much using few words. They sometimes take the form of proverbs or **aphorisms**.
- Informal language, sometimes labeled obscene, profane, or vulgar. It is the dialect of the street—alive and authentic.
- Language games that provide the user with ways of coping and surviving. They include jiving, sounding (delivering a direct insult), playing the dozens (sexually insulting a parent, usually the mother), and rapping.
- **Signifying** (or "signifyin'," as Henry Louis Gates uses the term, to indicate its pronunciation), a particularly clever, playful way of giving an opinion about another person. Indirect and ironic, it is used to insult or ridicule another person or to pay someone a compliment. Gates uses the **Signifying Monkey**, the master Trickster of African American folktales, as the embodiment of this process. For example, a person may pay a backhanded compliment to a friend, or one black writer may signify on another by making a **parody** of her literary structures.

Because of the several roles that the storyteller assumes in Hurston's vignettes, the language of *The Eatonville Anthology* is highly varied. Although the narrator speaks in standard forms, Hurston is not averse to using informal expressions from time to time, as in the description of the double-shuffle. "Everybody happy, shining eyes, gleaming teeth. Feet dragged 'shhlap, shhlap! to beat out the time. No orchestra needed. Round and round! Back again, parse-me-la! shlap! shlap! Strut! Strut! Seaboard! Shlap! Shlap! Tiddy bumm! Mr. Clarke in the lead with Mrs. Moseley." Neither is Hurston reluctant to give her characters intense dialects. In addition to the dialogue of Mrs. Tony Roberts, there is the conversation Daisy has with the men in front of the store–post office on Saturday night. As she says, "Who? Me! Ah don't keer whut Laura Crooms think. If she ain't a heavy hip-ted Mama enough to keep him, she don't need to come crying to me."

Though the language is informal, it does not approach anything that could be described as vulgar or obscene. Partly because of the age in which it was published, and probably because the author was female, some of the language games that are likely to be found in contemporary black writing are not present in this text. The dialogue is, nevertheless, alive and real. It is believable language that Hurston took from the conversations she heard and knew.

In a few instances, expressions seem compressed and pointed, meaning more than they actually say. When Mrs. McDuffy, for example, is asked why she won't quit shouting in church, even though her husband takes it as a personal affront and beats her for it, she simply replies that she can't "squinch the sperrit." No more need be said.

Many of the linguistic devices mentioned here, and more that are not, are covered by the term *signifying* (or signifyin'). Although signifying in the hands of a particularly clever user can be extraordinarily subtle, its appearance in *The Eatonville Anthology* is fairly apparent and understandable. In the description of Becky Moore, for example, the narrator seems to excuse Becky for any fault in the absence of a father for her children. We are told, "She has never stopped any of the fathers of her children from proposing, so if she has no father for her children it's not her fault. The men round about are entirely to blame." And Becky is thereby criticized. The other mothers are equally chided by the comment that they will not allow their children to play with hers because they think her condition is catching. The **irony** implicit in such statements provides a sense of play and fun for both the speaker and the audience.

Using the definitions of various kinds of diction given above, you can make some inferences about language use in African American works by asking the following questions:

- Where do you find instances of signifying in the text?
- Does the work contain aphorisms?
- What language games are included?

Style The narrative forms, characters, and typical language just described cause certain stylistic characteristics to recur with some regularity in the works of African American writers. The following are likely to be encountered.

- *Exaggeration:* Found particularly in those stories that fall into the tall-tale tradition.
- *Irony:* The indirection of signifying is created by saying one thing and meaning another, resulting in an ironic statement.
- *Rhymes:* Skillful repetition of vowels and consonants that makes a text lend itself to oral presentation.
- *Parody:* An effort to mock the work of another through repetition and variation.
- *Satire:* The ridicule of folly or stupidity. **Satire** is often humorous. The term can refer to an entire work but can also appear as a stylistic device that occurs now and then in a piece of writing. (See "Narrative Forms," discussed earlier.)
- *Sardonic comedy:* **Sardonic comedy** is the practice of making fun of adversity, as in jokes.
- *Superstitions:* Nonrational explanations of unusual occurrences.
- *Indirection:* Making a point without explicitly stating it. This technique allows the speaker to be subversive.

Such stylistic devices are easily noted in Hurston's work. Some have already been mentioned. The use of exaggeration, for example, abounds, giving the reader memorable portraits of the village liars—even of Tippy, the village dog, which has cheerfully survived his owners' dozens of attempts to get rid of him. Although *The*

Eatonville Anthology is a prose work, the language is highly musical, breaking into rhyme only in the song recorded in "The Double-Shuffle" and in the concluding comment: "Stepped on a tin, mah story ends." Nevertheless, the recurrence of sound and the rhythm of the syntax enhance the stories and the characters in them. For example, listen to the courting dialogue of Mr. Dog and Mr. Rabbit as they seek to win Miss Coon's affection in the final selection. "'Miss Coon,' he says, 'Ma'am, also Ma'am which would you rather be—a lark flyin' or a dove a settin'?'" And in his turn, Mr. Rabbit is equally eloquent. "'Oh, Miss Nancy,' he says, 'Ma'am, also Ma'am, if you'd see me settin' straddle of a mud-cat leadin' a minnow, what would you think? Ma'am, also Ma'am?'" Aside from the images used in the proposals, a subtle music—typical of all the pieces of the anthology—is created by the repeated short *a* sounds in *Nancy, Ma'am, straddle,* and *cat*; the initial *m* in *Miss, Ma'am, mud,* and *minnow*; and the *s* of *settin'* and *straddle*; and by rhythmic passages, such as "a lark flyin'" or "a dove a settin'."

It is difficult to separate Hurston's use of irony, satire, and sardonic comedy into distinctive devices, because they work together throughout the *Anthology* to present a picture of a life that is not easy but that is to be celebrated. It is a portrait of a village filled with the good and the bad, the strong and the weak, the troublemakers and those who would make things right. The storytelling is at once simple and complex, just as the presentation is direct and uncluttered. However, the ironic statements and satirical viewpoint deepen what seems on the surface to be a series of naive portraits of village life. The underlying implication throughout is that life can be hard as well as good. In "Turpentine Love," for example, we are told that Jim Merchant fell in love with his wife when a dose of turpentine was accidentally spilled in her eye and she thereupon quit having fits. They have kept each other in good humor throughout a long marriage, even though she has had all her teeth pulled out. This brief portrait of a marriage contains a combination of the grotesque, the comic, and the beautiful. The narrator's implicit comment is that people's lives can be irrational, difficult, and wonderful, but that view is never directly stated; it is only implied through irony and satire that make *The Eatonville Anthology* as a whole a dark, if not sardonic, comedy.

Narrative has been a central means of black expression, probably because of the influence of the oral folk tradition. Thus the poetry of African Americans shares many of the folk tradition's characteristics, particularly stylistic ones. Nevertheless, African American poetry has distinctive elements that distinguish it as a separate genre, though these elements are hard to pin down because they continue to evolve and develop. Undoubtedly, further analysis of that body of work will yield new understandings of it, but some generalizations are available for critical use.

Don Lee, examining the writing of black poets, found seven common characteristics in their poems:

1. **polyrhythms**, uneven, short, and explosive lines
2. intensity; depth, yet simplicity; spirituality, yet flexibility
3. irony; humor; signifying

4. sarcasm—a new comedy
5. direction; positive movement; teaching nation-building
6. subject matter—concrete; reflects a collective and personal lifestyle
7. music: the unique use of vowels and consonants with the developed rap demands that the poetry be real, and read out loud (Gayle 1971, p. 240)

Carolyn Rodgers has also attempted to establish poetic categories, naming ten major ones with twenty-three subdivisions. The chief categories she calls "signifying, teachin/rappin, coversoff, spaced, bein, love, shoutin, jazz, du-wah, and pyramid." Some of the subdivisions include "rundown, hipto, digup, and coatpull" (see Gayle 1971, p. 214). Although Rodgers's terminology would seem to stress content, all of the forms call upon the poet to be innovative and performative.

Although the stylistic elements characteristic of African American stories and poems are widely varied, it is sometimes helpful to identify a few of those that appear with the greatest frequency. The reader can do so by asking the following questions:

- What elements in the text lend themselves to performance?
- Where is the language indirect or ironic, and what does it suggest?
- What occurrences or explanations appear to be nonrational?

WRITING A CULTURAL STUDIES ANALYSIS

Because of the diversity of cultural studies, outlining a single approach to writing such criticism is not possible. The variety of questions that can be asked is likely to lead the writer in so many different directions that providing a single set of guidelines is not possible. However, some of the suggestions for composing introductions, organizing discussions, and making closing statements offered in the earlier chapters can be adapted and applied to postcolonial analyses and multicultural criticism. Because the principles of analytical writing do not change with the topics, you may find it profitable to look back at the preceding discussions about writing analyses to see what is applicable here as well.

SUGGESTED READING

Ashcroft, Bill, Gareth Griffiths, and Helen Tiffin. *The Empire Writes Back: Theory and Practice in Post-colonial Literatures.* New York: Routledge, 2002.

———. *The Post-colonial Studies Reader.* New York: Routledge, 2006.

Awkward, Michael. *Inspiriting Influences: Tradition, Revision, and Afro-American Literature.* New York: Columbia University Press, 1989.

Baker, Houston. *Blues, Ideology, and Afro-American Literature: A Vernacular Theory.* Chicago: University of Chicago Press, 1984.

Bennett, Andrew, and Nicholas Royle. *Introduction to Literature, Criticism, and Theory.* New York: Pearson Longman, 2005.

Bhabha, Homi K. *The Location of Culture.* New York: Routledge, 1994.

Gates, Henry Louis. *The Signifying Monkey: A Theory of African-American Literary Criticism.* New York: Oxford University Press, 1988.

Gayle, Addison, Jr., ed. *Black Expression: Essays by and About Black Americans in the Creative Arts.* New York: Weybright and Talley, 1969.

———. *The Black Aesthetic.* Garden City, NY: Doubleday, 1971.

Loomba, Ania. *Colonialism/Postcolonialism.* New York: Routledge, 2005.

———. *Postcolonial Studies and Beyond.* Durham, NC: Duke University Press, 2005.

Mitchell, Angelyn, ed. *Within the Circle: An Anthology of African American Literary Criticism from the Harlem Renaissance to the Present.* Durham, NC: Duke University Press, 1994.

Morrison, Toni. *Playing in the Dark: Whiteness and the Literary Imagination.* New York: Vintage Books, 1993.

Olson, Gary A., and Lynn Worsham, eds. *Race, Rhetoric, and the Postcolonial.* Albany: State University of New York Press, 1999.

Said, Edward. *Orientalism.* New York: Pantheon, 1978.

———. *Culture and Imperialism.* New York: Vintage Books, 1994.

Tiffin, Helen. "Post-colonial Literatures and Counter-discourse." *Kunapipi* 9, no. 3 (1987): 17–34.

Williams, Patrick, and Laura Chrisman, eds. *Colonial Discourse and Post-colonial Theory: A Reader.* New York: Columbia University Press, 1994.

Young, Robert. *Colonial Desire: Hybridity in Theory, Culture, and Race.* New York: Routledge, 1995.

For up-to-date information on the many Web sites addressing cultural studies approaches, visit www.cengagebrain.com.

Model Student Analyses

Victims Already: Violence and Threat in Nadine Gordimer's "Once upon a Time"

RIC JOHNA

The past few decades have seen a growing interest in literature characterized as postcolonial, works that interrogate the dynamic between imperial settler cultures and the displaced and subordinated native inhabitants. This complicated dynamic can include not only the experience of direct colonization but also the neocolonial influence that persists even after official colonial rule has ended. In the influential *The Empire Writes Back* (1989), Ashcroft, Griffiths, and Tiffin suggest that what is distinct about postcolonial literatures is that they "emerged in their present form out of the experience of colonization and asserted themselves by foregrounding the tension with the imperial power, and by emphasizing their differences from the assumptions of the imperial center" (2). These criteria remain relevant today for most of what is considered postcolonial literature. Increasingly, however, literature produced from within the white settler population is being viewed through a postcolonial lens—not only as an example of the cultural assumptions of the elite that make subordination of native populations possible, but also as a form of postcolonial critique offered from within the dominant group, a critique of the center culture, from the center itself. Such is the case in much of the writing of South African writer and Nobel laureate Nadine Gordimer, an author whose fervent opposition to South African apartheid has spanned several decades.

As a white South African, Gordimer occupies a complicated place within the colonial dynamic. Although her Jewish parents immigrated to South Africa long after the initiation of European colonialism in that country, as a white citizen, Gordimer enjoys the benefits allotted to the country's privileged "race" and hence could be seen to share complicity in the legacy of inequity drawn along color lines. Gordimer, however, has consistently served as a vocal critic of the very system that codifies this privilege, identifying herself with her South African identity and not her European roots. Her short story "Once upon a Time" illustrates the author's capacity to interrogate the sometimes violent tensions brought on by a legislated system of discrimination, in this case South African apartheid.

Historically, tensions between native and settler cultures have often been characterized by violent encounters. Frantz Fanon, the Martinique-born colonial analyst, argued in *The Wretched of the Earth* that the relationship between settler and native cultures is inherently one of violence. "Their first encounter was marked by violence," he wrote, "and their existence together—that is to say the exploitation of the native by the settler—was carried on by dint of a great array of bayonets and cannons" (36). Indeed, in Gordimer's tale, violence, both perceived and realized, permeates the narrative. She evokes this inherent violence not simply as one group acting on the other but rather as a phenomenon fundamental to the social dynamic perpetrated by apartheid. In "Once upon a Time," Nadine Gordimer makes ironic use of the fairy-tale genre, foregrounding the violence at the heart of the colonial dynamic and illustrating the destructive forces the system visits on both settler and native populations.

Rather than launching directly into her fictional tale, Gordimer begins "Once upon a Time" with an introduction that accounts for the story's origin. This portion of the narrative is significant, for it sets the context for the tale to follow. Readers are grounded first in a very real world where the author herself steps forth, noting that "someone has written to ask me to contribute to an anthology of stories for children." This is an invitation that she plans to decline, until one late night she wakes in her home, frightened by an unidentified sound—"A creaking of the kind made by the weight carried by one foot after another along a wooden floor." It is soon made clear that fears for one's personal safety were not unreasonable in South Africa at this time. "I have no burglar bars," Gordimer writes, "no gun under the pillow, but I have the same fears as people who do take these precautions, and my windowpanes are thin as rime, could shatter like a wineglass." Significantly, while Gordimer distinguishes herself from those who take more extreme measures for personal safety, she simultaneously identifies with their fears. She is at once positioned against other privileged white South Africans and, feeling herself "a victim already," located within this same culture of fear. The author draws on existing evidence that gives further validity to such fears: "A woman was murdered (how do they put it) in broad daylight in a house two blocks away, last year, and the fierce dogs who guarded an old widower and his collection of antique clocks were strangled before he was knifed by a casual laborer he had dismissed without pay." In her fear, Gordimer explains, "the arrhythmia of my heart was fleeing, knocking this way and that against its body-cage." Although not explicitly stated, Gordimer's fear and that of her fellow whites is the fear of the Other, the dread of intrusion by the jealous outsider, who transgresses into the tenuous safety of the white world. Fanon explained that this fear of a "terrifying future" in the minds of the white settler grows as the discontent of the native population rises and seeks out what it has long been denied (35–36).

Luckily for Gordimer, the potential menace is revealed as the "buckling" of her own home, a house that, she explains, rests on a relatively unstable tract of earth:

> The house that surrounds me while I sleep is built on undermined ground; far beneath my bed, the floor, the house's foundations, the slopes and passages of gold mines have hollowed the rock, and when some face trembles, detaches and falls, three thousand feet below, the whole house shifts slightly, bringing uneasy strain to the balance and

> counterbalance of brick, cement, wood and glass that hold it as a structure around me.

It is difficult to overlook the significance of Gordimer's description of her house, the condition of which mirrors the instability of the political situation of her country. Of further import is the fact that the source of the house's buckling instability stems from the gold mining industry. The discovery of gold in the region was a primary force in attracting the initial wave of whites to South Africa. These white Europeans were to reap the benefits of this discovery while the natives and immigrants of color were exploited for their labor in the most dangerous jobs, receiving relatively small economic reward. Even now, Gordimer imagines "the Chopi and Tsonga migrant workers who might have been down there, under me in the earth at that moment." Her home rests, as she puts it, on "an epicenter of stress," serving as a correlative to the political volatility that was always threatening to break forth violently in South Africa at that time. This situation sets the context for the "bedtime story" that she is to tell.

The title, "Once upon a Time," immediately calls upon one of the most familiar tropes of the fairy tale and makes use of the associations that go along with this form. The story's first lines further evoke the genre, but begin to introduce an element of irony: "In a house, in a suburb, in a city, there were a man and his wife who loved each other very much and were living happily ever after." Gordimer evokes a contemporary setting and picks up the story where most fairy tales end, forcing the reader to question the direction of the narrative. The happy couple has a young son and two pets, along with "a car and a caravan trailer for holidays, and a swimming-pool which was fenced in so that the little boy and his playmates would not fall in and drown." Here are the familiar trappings of modern suburbia, which carry with them their own cultural associations: insularity, safety, plenty, affluence, middle-class decorum, racial homogeneity. Such a world echoes Fanon's characterization of the colonists' town:

> The settlers' town is a strongly built town, all made of stone and steel. It is a brightly lit town; the streets are covered with asphalt, and the garbage cans swallow up all the leavings, unseen, unknown and hardly thought about. [...] The settler's town is a well-fed town, an easygoing town; its belly is always full of good things. The settlers' town is a town of white people, of foreigners. (39)

Indeed, the suburb of Gordimer's tale is one where threat and danger are kept at bay. Any lurking menace such as the swimming pool is safely quartered off. All is well within the insular world of the family compound, with all the accoutrements of the upper-middle-class dream. The couple allows only natives who are "absolutely trustworthy" into their sphere as servants, heeding the advice of the husband's mother, "the wise old witch," who warns "not to take on anyone off the street." Here, the street represents a departure from the safety of the family compound. The street is a nether region where the potential for intrusion exists as illustrated by the admonitory plaque, reading "YOU HAVE

BEEN WARNED." Hence, even within the apparent domestic bliss of the nuclear suburban family, Gordimer introduces the possibility of outside threat.

Deeper into Gordimer's tale, it is made clear that the safety of the family is contingent upon a political organization that attempts to maintain separate spheres for black and white. "There were riots," it is learned, "but these were outside the city, where people of another color were quartered." The difference in color designates a person as "another," or an Other, a class of individuals prohibited from entering the suburb. Such rigid demarcations recall Fanon's description of the colonial world as "a world cut in two." These rigidly maintained boundaries, however, are always suspect and in danger of breach, as the wife's fears illustrate. She worries "that some day such people might come up the street and tear off the plaque YOU HAVE BEEN WARNED and open the gates and stream in [...]." The husband, in response, reassures his wife that all is safe and that they are protected by "police and soldiers and tear-gas and guns to keep them away." Indeed, Fanon writes, "In colonial countries [...] the policeman and the soldier, by their immediate presence and their frequent and direct action, maintain contact with the native and advise him by means of rifle butts and napalm not to budge" (39). The instability increases in the story as "buses were being burned, cars stoned, and schoolchildren shot by the police in those quarters out of sight and hearing of the suburb." Despite the husband's assurances that there is "nothing to fear," it is fear that drives the narrative, a fear that progresses and intensifies until the family must suffer its consequences.

In response to the growing concerns for their personal safety, the couple turns to the available resources to mitigate the outside threat. Electronically controlled gates are installed, along with a speaker system, which the child, in his innocence, "used [...] as a walkie-talkie in cops and robbers play with his small friends." As the threats remain in the form of violent burglaries, the family installs an alarm system and burglar bars so that "from every window and door in the house where they were living happily ever after they now saw the trees and sky through bars [...]." These efforts, however, are not sufficient to restrain the growing force of the outside:

> [I]ntruders sawed the iron bars and broke into homes, taking away hi-fi equipment, television sets, cassette players, cameras and radios, jewelry and clothing, and sometimes were hungry enough to devour everything in the refrigerator or paused audaciously to drink the whisky in the cabinets or patio bars. Insurance companies paid no compensation for single malt, a loss made keener by the property owner's knowledge that the thieves wouldn't even have been able to appreciate what it was they were drinking.

The brazenness of the colonized Other inserting themselves in the context of the colonizer's home threatens to subvert the already tenuous stability maintained through this system of inequity. This seeming moment of ironic levity is important in establishing the assumptions of superiority held by the suburban settlers of Gordimer's tale and is a fundamental underpinning to the entire colonial enterprise. It is not merely the loss of the fine whisky that troubles the settlers but that it is lost upon a subject unworthy of and ignorant about its quality. These are not frightened thieves in the night but invaders who—if only temporarily making themselves at home—supplant the settlers themselves. Such impulses in any form could prove dangerous to the established system and threaten the stability of its oppression. Further, the inclusion of this passage suggests a fundamental preoccupation of the native when faced with the inequity of the colonial system. As Fanon explained,

> The look that the native turns on the settler's town is a look of lust, a look of envy; it expresses his dreams of possession—all manner of possession: to sit at the settler's table, to sleep in the settler's bed. [...] It is true, for there is no native who does not dream at least once a day of setting himself up in the settler's place. (39)

Determined to offset this threat to their home and to the political structure, the couple resolves to fortify their family compound with a seven-foot wall. Still, the outside threat persists: "But every week there were more reports of intrusion: in broad daylight and the dead of night, in the early hours of the morning, and even in the lovely summer twilight—a certain family was at dinner while the bedrooms were being ransacked upstairs." The Other seemingly uncontainable, the couple is eventually driven to what seems the only solution, an embellishment to the wall that is sure to suffice: "Placed the length of walls, it consisted of a continuous coil of stiff and shining metal serrated into jagged blades, so that there would be no way of climbing over it and no way through its tunnel without getting tangled in its fangs." In their efforts to isolate themselves from the threat of a perceived demonic Other, the family has literally and ironically transformed their own home into a prison. They must view the outside world through bars and are further separated by "concentration-camp style" razor wire. Through their efforts to avoid becoming victimized, Gordimer reveals that they are victims already.

The story's most profound irony, however, is yet to come. After his mother reads him a story from a book of fairy tales, the young boy, pretending to be the prince of the story, attempts to overcome the wall's razor wire, imagining it to be "the terrible thicket of thorns" that must be passed in order "to enter the palace and kiss the Sleeping Beauty back to life [...]." In this attempt to enact an archetypal action typical of fairy tales, it is the son who is consumed by the protective precaution: "[H]e dragged a ladder to the wall, the shining coiled tunnel was just wide enough for his little body to creep in, and with the first fixing of its razor-teeth in his knees and hands and head he screamed and struggled deeper into its tangle." It is the trusted servants who first come to the boy's aid, the gardener cutting his own hands in the process of freeing the boy, who, mutilated and dehumanized, has now become "the bleeding mass." Gordimer's tale indeed does become a children's story. The child, representative of the coming generation, is violently consumed by the fear of his predecessors. "[T]hey carried it—the man, the wife, the hysterical trusted housemaid and the weeping gardener—into the house." Both black and white alike mourn the demise of the child and, by extension, a future ruled by an untenable political system whose destructive forces make victims of both settler and native alike.

WORKS CITED

Ashcroft, Bill, Gareth Griffiths, and Helen Tiffin. *The Empire Writes Back: Theory and Practice in Post-colonial Literatures*. New York: Routledge, 1989.

Fanon, Frantz. *The Wretched of the Earth*. New York: Grove, 1963.

Langston Hughes and the Dream of America

WILEY CASH

Langston Hughes embarked upon his literary career at a very precarious time in American history. Born in Missouri in 1902, Hughes suffered constant minority status during his youth, and he was made aware of the effects racism wrought upon African Americans after the collapse of Reconstruction in the South. Because he lived until 1967, he watched as the nation again wrestled itself during the civil rights movement. In his literature, Hughes chronicled many of the cultural, political, and racial tensions that marked the first half of the twentieth century, and his poems and characters carried readers from the plantations of the post–Civil War South to the smoky jazz clubs of Harlem, and all the way to the inner cities of urban centers like Chicago.

Although Hughes's body of work connected some of the most defining eras in America's struggle to become an equal, multicultural society, it is as the preeminent poet of the Harlem Renaissance that he is best known. As its name denotes, the Harlem Renaissance was an artistic movement that took place in New York City's predominately African American community of Harlem in the 1920s and early 1930s. Although many literary texts are considered highlights of the Harlem Renaissance, it is commonly held that editor Alain Locke's *The New Negro* (1925) exemplified the spirit of the Harlem Renaissance in that the anthology's poetry, prose, and visual art combined the literary promise of contemporary African American writers with a newfound sense of racial pride and self-awareness that was yet to be fully realized in America.

It was Locke's hope that the term "New Negro" would symbolize the African American artists, especially writers, who shunned folk art and dialect poetry and prose in favor of classical and contemporary forms, all the while forging an identity that represented the best of African American artistic excellence. He felt that although African Americans were forced to suffer second-class citizenship in America, that should not keep them from exploring and mastering all the literary and artistic expressions available to whites.

As an African American poet who relied heavily on elements of blues music and African folklore in his work, Langston Hughes found himself caught between a movement that often disregarded any expression that it considered inarticulate or folksy and a white literary world that still questioned the merit of African American literature. This burden of being excluded from mainstream America because of his race and artistic influences manifested itself in Hughes's work throughout his lifetime. His poetry is often narrated by personas who face the task of living in two societies: the black society that struggles against oppression and the white society that sustains it. This task of attempting to realize the benefits and promises enjoyed by white America while staying true and dedicated to an African American identity was the focus of much of Hughes's work.

The phenomenon that forced African Americans to reside in two separate worlds was most eloquently explained by W. E. B. DuBois in his study of African American life titled *The Souls of Black Folk* (1903). DuBois termed this struggle "double consciousness" and defined it as follows:

It is a peculiar sensation, this double consciousness, this sense of always looking at one's self through the eyes of others, of measuring one's soul by the tape of a world that looks on in amused contempt and pity. One ever feels his twoness,—an American, a Negro; two souls, two thoughts, two unreconciled strivings; two warring ideals in one dark body, whose dogged strength alone keeps it from being torn asunder. (694)

As an African American, Langston Hughes understood firsthand the challenge and necessity of double consciousness, and a close reading of his poems "I, Too" (1925) and "Theme for English B" (1949) shows them to exemplify the struggles America and its minorities faced while forging a multicultural nation.

The theme of two Americas—one black and oppressed, the other white and oppressive—runs throughout "I, Too." In the poem, the persona proclaims that although he is the "darker brother," he also sings of the promise of equality and freedom inherent to American citizenship, an idea symbolized here by the invoking of familial relations. However, the fact that the persona is forced to "eat in the kitchen / When company comes" hints at a forced segregation that is similar to the unwritten codes of plantation life in the South and the rule of Jim Crow law in the first half of the twentieth century.

Before the Civil War and in the decades that followed, it was customary for African Americans in the South, whether slaves or, later, employees, to enter through the back doors of white-owned residences and to relegate themselves to eating meals in the kitchen while their white owners or employers would take their meals in a more formal dining room. This domestic segregation carried over into restaurants and public spaces like libraries, theaters, schools, churches, and other places where segregation was enforceable and desirable by whites.

This white-enforced separation of the two races, which was not limited to the South, came to be known as Jim Crow law, an unwritten social code that was similar in design to apartheid in South Africa. This unofficial code gained power and legal status in 1896, when the Supreme Court of the United States upheld the state of Louisiana's ruling in *Plessy v. Ferguson*, a case that argued that a Louisiana railroad company was not legally required to grant the African American Homer Adolph Plessy equal access to the "white only" car on a passenger train. This ruling cemented segregation in America and was used to force African Americans into second-class citizenship for decades to come.

At the time of the authorship of "I, Too" in 1925, African Americans were still segregated from whites in many of the country's public places. Considering this, the forced segregation suffered by the persona symbolizes the way African Americans were treated in the United States. Interestingly, the persona seems to have an ironic attitude about being cloistered in the kitchen away from company. This attitude is apparent as he states, "But I laugh, / And eat well, / And grow strong." He is implying that although he is oppressed, he is still able to feed his physical hunger and gain strength, a feeding and growth that could metaphorically imply educational and intellectual development or the spiritual and emotional sustenance that will allow him to cope with his challenges and one day overcome them.

This willingness to face adversity and the persona's hope for equality is expressed in the second stanza as the persona predicts that "Tomorrow, / I'll be at the table / When company comes." He imagines his long overdue inclusion and knows that "Nobody'll dare / Say to me, / 'Eat in the kitchen,' / Then." This dream also stirs a sense of racial pride in the persona that was not fully realized in the African American community until the civil rights movement. Tapping into this newfound sense of self-actualization, the persona contends that his oppressors will see the error of their ways and predicts, "They'll see how beautiful I am / And be ashamed." Finally, the persona hopes that even though his skin color is different from that of his oppressors', they will realize that "I, too, am America."

This hoped-for inclusion and necessary recognition of African Americans as worthy of full equality recalls DuBois's idea of double consciousness in that the persona must view America through his own eyes as well as through the eyes of his oppressors in order to ascertain the nature of their racism and desire for segregation. African Americans were required to use this "second sight" to successfully navigate a world in which they were not in full control of their own destiny, but could merely hope, plan, and work for a future in which they would realize and enjoy the rights and privileges offered white America.

Hughes's focus on segregation and the ways it attempted to homogenize the two Americas is considered again in his 1949 poem "Theme for English B." The poem is the narrative of an African American student attempting to write a page about himself for a homework assignment. Although he explains, "I am the only colored student in my class," the persona in this poem, unlike the one in "I, Too," is granted equal access to the educational system and is not segregated from the white students. However, because the assignment asks the students to write a page about themselves, the persona begins to consider the differences *and* similarities that are apparent between him and his white peers and the white instructor. Again, DuBois's idea of double consciousness is apparent as the persona's "second sight" allows him to view himself as the "other," an American whose race keeps him from being considered and represented as an easily defined part of mainstream culture.

After the assignment is given, the persona considers how he would explain himself and his background on a single page, and he asks, "I wonder if it's that simple?" This question uncovers the difficult task of unraveling African American identity in a predominately white culture. Because this persona is afflicted with the "twoness" outlined by DuBois, he must consider his role as an American who is also black and therefore somewhat estranged from the full experience of America.

He begins his journey of self-awareness and introspection by chronicling the most obvious attributes of his physical character and geographical background. He acknowledges, "I am twenty-two, colored, born in Winston-Salem." He then recalls that his pursuit of education led him from school in nearby Durham, North Carolina, all the way "to this college on the hill above Harlem." This statement is interesting because it indicates that the persona moved north to pursue higher education, a move that reflects the Great Migration north that many African Americans took in the years after the Civil War to pursue the greater political, educational, and financial opportunities that were not available to them in the South due to the lingering effects of slavery and the rise of the white supremacy movement. This statement is also interesting because the college, which symbolizes the many positive attributes of education, rests on the hill *above* Harlem, a predominately African American area closely associated with the lifestyles of jazz musicians and bohemian artists, making it culturally different from the rest of New York City. The fact that the narrator acknowledges that the college stands above Harlem could lend insight to his own double consciousness, especially considering that he again mentions the location of Harlem by stating, "The steps from the hill lead down into Harlem." The stairs signify the descent the persona must make into a type of netherworld that is looked down upon by the whites who pursue better lives in the college on the top of the hill. This image of the college could also be seen as representing a beacon of hope for the residents of Harlem, who dream of one day pursuing their education.

Yet, the persona is not quite "at home" in Harlem, a fact made apparent by his taking a rented room in the "Harlem Branch Y." Here, the persona is seen as unable to find a permanent residence in either world. Although he is able to take class at a white college where he is the only African American student in the class, he must leave that world at the end of the day and descend into the African American world of Harlem; however, because he is pursuing his education, he cannot possess a permanent residence in Harlem and is required to seek temporary lodging at the Y.

This duality is again referenced as he states, "But I guess I'm what / I feel and see and hear, Harlem, I hear you." And then, two lines later, he admits, "(I hear New York too.)." The straddling of the two worlds is explained in the "twoness" of DuBois, who argued that African Americans continually locate themselves as struggling to find a footing between these two separate but definable worlds. It is in this constant state of flux that the persona must attempt to define himself for his homework assignment.

Although he straddles these two worlds, he must admit that he enjoys many of the things that are enjoyed by everyday Americans. He lists these things, stating, "Well, I like to eat, sleep, drink, and be in love./I like to work, read, learn, and understand life." Although these things are common to many Americans, insight into the persona's sense of double consciousness is apparent when he states, "I like a pipe for a Christmas present,/or records—Bessie, bop, or Bach." Johann Sebastian Bach was an eighteenth-century German composer of classical music, a type of music that is historically associated with intellectual and professional people, whereas on the other hand, Bessie Smith was a twentieth-century African American blues singer whose lyrics often focused on hardship, love, infidelity, and the more lascivious aspects of private life. These two types of music seem to stand in stark opposition to one another, yet they are linked in this line by the inclusion of bop, a type of music popularized in the 1940s and 1950s that borrowed from all musical traditions and blended them into a progressive new form of music that relied heavily on instrumentation and improvisation. This new type of music is similar to the identity that is being forged by the narrator of "Theme for English B" in that he is straddling two worlds and borrowing from two cultures while forging a new identity as one of Alain Locke's New Negroes. The persona recognizes this blending of cultures in himself, and he remarks, as if he is speaking to his instructor, "You are white—/yet a part of me, as I am a part of you./That's American." However, regardless of this intermixture, the persona recognizes a line of demarcation between himself and his instructor and acknowledges, "Sometimes perhaps you don't want to be a part of me./Nor do I often want to be a part of you./But we are, that's true!"

The persona realizes that regardless of his or his instructor's skin color, they are both Americans and are both desirous and capable of the same things, provided that they are given the same opportunities. Unfortunately, for the persona, he realizes that this type of fairness, at least in 1949, is simply a dream. He resignedly admits this unfairness in the poem's closing lines when he states, "As I learn from you,/I guess you learn from me—/although you're older—and white—/and somewhat more free." Here, the same idea of the two Americas that is defined by W. E. B. DuBois and alluded to in "I, Too" is crystallized.

In both of these poems, Hughes's narrators eventually come to terms with the fact that they are living in a country that allows them to live as Americans but also as African Americans who must always work harder and strive longer for equal rights under very unequal laws and social prejudices. However, these poems are not without hope. Both hint at a brighter future of hope and possibility; yet both understand that this America must be dreamed before it can be realized.

WORKS CITED

DuBois, W. E. B. *The Souls of Black Folk. The Norton Anthology of African American Literature*. 2nd ed. Ed. Henry Louis Gates Jr. et al. New York: W. W. Norton, 1994. 692–766.

Hughes, Langston. " I, Too." *The Norton Anthology of African American Literature*. 2nd ed. Ed. Henry Louis Gates Jr. et al. New York: W. W. Norton, 1994. 1295.

———. "Theme for English B." *The Norton Anthology of African American Literature*. 2nd ed. Ed. Henry Louis Gates Jr. et al. New York: W. W. Norton, 1994. 1309–10.

11

Ecocriticism: Literature Goes Green

To me the meanest flower that blows can give
Thoughts that do often lie too deep for tears.
WILLIAM WORDSWORTH, *Intimations of Immortality*

The world of literary theory in the latter part of the twentieth century and through the opening years of this one has been marked by the appearance of numerous innovative approaches to reading and studying works old and new. One of the most recent critical perspectives to gain substantial interest goes by many names. You may have heard it referred to as literary ecology, the term Joseph Meeker used to designate "the study of biological themes and relationships which appear in literary works." Or you may have met it as ecopoetics, environmental literary criticism, green cultural studies, or even compoststructuralists (to mockingly distinguish its theories from those of the poststructuralists). More commonly, it is called **ecocriticism**, a term first used by William Rueckert in his 1978 essay "Literature and Ecology: An Experiment in Ecocriticism" in reference to "the application of ecology and ecological concepts to the study of literature."

WHAT IS IT?

Ecocriticism is still evolving as a school of criticism, but it is possible to form some definitions about what it is and what it tries to do. As in the case of its many labels, the term does not suffer from a shortage of definitions, either. It seems that everyone interested in the field has a favorite, running from a slightly satirical one that says it is "the work of scholars who 'would rather be hiking,'" to Cheryll Glotfelty's succinct statement that it is "the study of the relationship between literature and the physical **environment**," to more complex explanations, such as Lawrence Buell's assertion that "ecocriticism is the study of literature and environment from an interdisciplinary point of view where all sciences come together to analyze the environment and brainstorm possible solutions for the correction of the contemporary environmental situation." Despite their various points of view, its practitioners seem to agree on some things that ecocriticism is not. For example, they hold that it is not simply a celebration of the pastoral or the sublime, nor is it a travelogue or an inspirational address.

Several scholars have built on Glotfelty's fundamental definition by adding an extra-literary purpose to it. Buell, for example, points out that any study of the relationship between literature and the physical environment should be "conducted in a spirit of commitment to environmentalist praxis." Simon C. Estok extends Buell's comment by saying that ecocriticism "takes a stand by its commitment to the natural world as an important thing rather than simply as an object of thematic study and by its commitment to making connections." Camilo Gomides, too, recognizes its social purpose when he speaks of "motivating audiences to live within a limit that will be binding over generations." Finally, in "Shakespeare and Ecocriticism," Estok broadens ecocriticism to include the study of "any theory that is committed to effecting change by analyzing the function—thematic, artistic, social, historical, ideological, theoretical, or otherwise—of the natural environment, or aspects of it, represented in documents (literary or other) that contribute to material practices in material worlds."

What all these perspectives on the field have in common is that they are interested in examining the relationship of literature and **nature** as a way to renew a reader's awareness of the nonhuman world and his or her responsibility to sustain it. Sharing the fundamental premise that all things are interrelated, they are actively concerned about the impact of human actions on the environment. According to Gotfelty, consciousness raising is ecocriticism's most important task.

The formation of Poets for Living Waters in response to the British Petroleum oil spill in the Gulf of Mexico in April 2010 is a recent instance of such consciousness raising. Describing itself as a poetry action group, the organization invited writers to submit works about the disaster to poetsforlivingwaters@yahoo.com for possible publication in its online journal. Basing their actions on the recognition that "the first law of ecology" is that everything is connected to everything else, its founders turned to poetry as a means of offering a meaningful response to the spill. Plans for subsequent action included poetry readings at venues across this country as well as in Canada and Ireland on World Ocean Day, June 8, 2010, along with a published anthology of submitted works. As Brian Spears, poet and instructor at Florida Atlantic University, noted on his blog,

> Poets for Living Waters won't stop oil from gushing into the Gulf of Mexico, nor will it clean the wings of pelicans or make fish able to breathe. It won't even cost Tony Hayward [Chief Executive Officer of BP] his job. When it comes to real-world effectiveness, poetry is down there with shaking a fist at the tide. But we write it anyway, perhaps

> because we feel that if our words can't change the world, maybe they can chronicle it in some small way. And maybe, if they're powerful enough words, they can convince people to take some real world action.

Clearly this movement is an example of a literary-ecosystem partnership that sees its mission to be the creation of poems and prose to make the public aware of the need to limit humankind's impact on the natural world. It is ecocritical.

It is helpful to note some of the ways in which ecocriticism differs from other critical approaches. For example, its social purpose establishes it as a direct contrast to the Formalists, who tried to separate a text from the world. Instead, ecocritics want to use texts as a way to get at the world itself. They also differ from postmodernists by rejecting the idea that everything is socially and/or linguistically constructed. To them, nature really exists as a force that affects human beings and which human beings can affect. (Some scholars have suggested that the interest in ecocriticism is fueled in part by public frustration with complex postmodern theories that seem to have little relevance to life as people experience it.) It can be said that ecocriticism stands apart from literary theory in general because instead of focusing on writers, texts, and the world, as most critical approaches do, ecocriticism attempts to examine writers, texts, and the entire ecosphere.

HISTORICAL BACKGROUND

The practice of ecocriticism had its nascence in the environmentalist movement of the late 1960s and 1970s, but the work of its early practitioners was slow to come together as a recognizable school of criticism. Instead, its welter of different labels suggested that it was splintered into numerous schools that might or might not share commonalities. Some of the titles, like "human ecology" or "science and literature," were new and innovative; others carried traditional names, such as American Studies, and assumed new interests. Unlike the feminists and Marxists, who united behind a relatively solid front, the ecocritics were so scattered that they often did not even know each other's work.

In the early stages of development, ecocriticism focused primarily on what was known as "nature writing." In 1973, for example, British Marxist critic Raymond Williams wrote a critique of pastoral literature, *The Country and the City*, in which he argued that the pastoral had traditionally overlooked the work of rural labor. The scope broadened rapidly, however, to accommodate interest in the depiction of nature in Romantic poetry, canonical literature, and later even in film, theater, animal stories, television, and scientific narratives.

In this country the concept of studying the relationship of literature and nature surfaced in the late 1970s at meetings of the Western Literature Association (WLA). Twenty years later its academic respectability was evident in the appointment of Cheryll Glotfelty as professor of Literature and the Environment at the University of Nevada in Reno. Acceptance by the larger academic community was apparent when special sessions on nature writing or environmental literature began to appear on programs of annual literary conferences—for example, the 1991 MLA special session "Ecocriticism: The Greening of Literary Studies."

Interest in the intersection of literature and nature quickly spread to universities across the country, where it has been received with substantial student interest. Courses are often offered in English departments, but can also be found in environmental studies programs. They are sometimes organized around specific writers or by regions, historical periods, or genres. Their popularity is attributed partly to the popularity of the readings that usually comprise such courses—for example, the writings of Rachel Carson, Annie Dillard, and Wendell Berry, as well as to their potential to bridge the gulf that often exists between the sciences and the humanities. The number of doctoral dissertations addressing concerns about nature and literature seems to be growing steadily; several university presses have brought out ecocritical monographs; and literary and academic journals are increasingly running articles that focus on the natural world.

Another indication of the interest in ecocriticism was the formation of a professional organization dedicated to its development. The Association for the Study of Literature and Environment (ASLE) was established at the 1992 meeting of the Western Literature Association. By 1995, when it held its first conference in Ft. Collins, Colorado, it had 750 members. Composed of teachers, writers, students, artists, and environmentalists who are interested in the natural world and how it appears in language and culture, the organization supports and encourages interdisciplinary and innovative approaches to the study of nature and culture. It holds biennial meetings and, since 1993, has issued a journal, *Interdisciplinary Studies in Literature and Environment* (ISLE), that publishes current scholarship dealing with environmental matters in literature. It also issues *The American Nature Writing Newsletter* (renamed the *ASLE News*). Through all these venues it shares facts, ideas, and texts concerning the study of literature and the environment. Its readership extends well beyond the United States to include Europe, the Far East, India, and Taiwan.

Despite the growing interest in ecocriticism in academia and beyond, the field is not without its disagreements. One issue cited by Michael P. Cohen is that some ecocritics seem to be "nature endorsing" and some to be "nature skeptical." The skeptics are concerned about the tendency to use nature to legitimize what are taken to be gender, sexual, and racial norms; they resist assumptions that a given need not, and perhaps cannot, be redressed or amended. A less serious charge is that nature writers and ecocritics take themselves too seriously. Whether they do or not, they are certainly easy to satirize.

Nevertheless, the future of ecocriticism looks promising, though it is difficult to know what shape it will take as it continues to evolve. Nobody knows if ecocritics will fulfill their goals to reorder the canon and reform curricula so that the genre of nature writing is returned to a position of respect, or whether they will manage to forge new links between the humanities and natural sciences. It is probably safe to say at this point that in the future ecocritical scholarship will be more interdisciplinary, multicultural, and international.

GETTING STARTED AS AN ECOCRITIC

To understand the discussion that follows, you will need to read "Stopping by Woods on a Snowy Evening," by Robert Frost, which begins on page 281.

Selecting a Text

The first step in becoming an ecocritic involves choosing what you want to read. Ecocritics are often drawn to what has traditionally been known as nature writing, and the works of the American transcendentalists have been deeply influential on the direction the movement has taken. Nonfiction prose pieces such as Emerson's *Nature*, Margaret Fuller's *Summer on the Lakes, During 1843*, and Thoreau's *Walden* remain popular favorites. Some readers, however, like to resurrect less well known texts of nature writing that have over the years been virtually forgotten, and literature that is not explicitly about nature is also a frequent choice. Canonical texts in which the presentation of nature has been overlooked provide rich opportunities for a reader to discover new dimensions of works long thought to have been thoroughly dissected.

Choosing an Approach

Your second decision deals with the approach you will take to the text you have selected. Many strategies are open to you, but at the outset you may find the easiest way to proceed is to follow one of the three patterns Cheryll Glotfelty notes that other ecocritics have found useful. She sees the development of ecocriticism to have been similar to that of feminist criticism, whose readers turned their attention to minor characters and forgotten texts in an effort to find new perspectives about the portrayal of women in literature. In fact, Glotfelty has adapted Elaine Showalter's three developmental stages of feminist criticism (see Chapter 6) to explain how ecocritics have moved through similar phases of interest. According to Showalter, the first stage of feminist criticism involved "representations." By concentrating on how women are portrayed as well as where they are inaccurately depicted or not depicted at all in canonical literature, feminist critics raised readers' consciousness of attitudes toward women. The second phase involved the study of literature by women, much of it forgotten or undervalued. The third produced theories about construction of gender and sexuality in literature.

Ecocriticism, according to Glotfelty, is following an analogous pattern, beginning with an interest in "representations," an examination of how nature is depicted in literature, thereby raising public awareness of attitudes toward the natural world. Practitioners look at how stereotypes warp reality and note where nature is absent, simply ignored. Sometimes they narrow the focus to look carefully at a particular aspect of nature such as a geographical region or the wilderness or the mountains. An effort to rediscover and reconsider the genre of nature writing, which had fallen into neglect, constitutes the second phase. The attention that has been paid to this endeavor is apparent in the growing publication of anthologies of nature writing and works that have an ecological awareness. The third stage, the theoretical one, draws upon science, history, and philosophy to ask a wide range of questions about such topics as the consequences of anthropomorphism, the relationship of nature and culture, and more.

A more detailed explanation of how an ecocritic can work through each of these approaches follows.

Questioning the Representation of Nature Addressing the first category of interest, the representation of nature, means taking an earth-centered approach to literary study by looking at the role nature plays in a given work. It should be noted that among ecocritics *nature* is not synonymous with *environment*. Nature refers to the environment before it was impacted by technology: the land, its flora and fauna, its waterways, living creatures, and the ecosystem that nourishes them. Environment, on the other hand, is the surrounding landscape. Environmentalists, who support conservation and limits, are sometimes referred to as "**light greens**"; "**dark greens**" are deep ecologists who advocate a complete return to nature. Although a physical return is not feasible for most people, a reader can experience the preindustrialized world through literature that recreates it.

If you choose to study a text from this perspective, the following questions can help you to be aware of the elements deemed to be important. You can ask ...

- Does the setting function simply as background, or does it play an active role in the narrative?
- If it plays an active role, how important is it in working out the narrative?
- If the physical setting were a character in the text, how would you describe him or her?
- How is nature affected by human beings in the text?
- How are the human beings affected by nature?
- How responsible are the human beings for the environment?
- What questions does the text raise about human interactions with nature?
- Does the text direct the reader's interest to nature, or only to the human characters?
- Does the text raise the reader's awareness of the natural world and his or her connections to it?

If we apply the questions to Robert Frost's poem "Stopping by Woods on a Snowy Evening," for example, we realize that the setting is integral to this vignette in which a man pauses to watch snow falling on the dark woods of his neighbor's land. It can even be said to function as the major character in the poem, for it is clearly more than simply background scenery. The darkness and quietude, the freezing conditions, the "easy wind and downy flake" have an impact on the speaker, who sits alone to hear and feel the presence of nature. It acts upon him, pushing him to respond. In fact, the man is the passive figure in the poem, the recipient of impressions and actions initiated by the elements around him. In this poem nature affects the man more than the man affects nature.

The role the natural world plays here is more complex than it might initially seem to be, because its effects on the speaker are multiple, in some cases pulling him in different directions. He is struck by the beauty of the scene, for instance, but he is also nudged along by his horse (a nonhuman element) that shakes his harness bells to remind the man that the night is cold and dark. Some elements of the nonhuman world urge him to stay and some to continue his journey, leaving him conflicted and non-active.

The complexity of the relationship between man and nature in this poem deepens as the dark woods reach out to the speaker, clashing with the cultural obligations that emanate from the village. He experiences the curious condition of human beings who exist as a part of nature and at the same time as cultural beings. He feels himself pulled to join with nature, to enter the woods that are "lovely, dark, and deep," and simultaneously drawn to return to the village, leaving the woods behind. He wants to stay; he needs to go.

As the opening questions have revealed, reading as an ecocritic basically involves being attentive to nonhuman issues that have traditionally been pushed to the background. Those usually marginal elements, in this case the wind, the horse, the snow, are brought to the center, and what was central, usually humankind, as exemplified by the speaker, is moved to the edges, in effect turning the text inside out. Where a traditional reading is usually anthropocentric, with human characters drawing our attention to them, in an ecocritic's perusal, what would usually be viewed as merely background becomes an active player in the working out of a narrative.

Looking at Nature Writing If you are drawn to exploring the second developmental phase of the ecocritical movement, the one that seeks to make the genre of nature writing more visible, you will need to make a case for the importance of studying a novel, play, poem, or writer that is not widely read and discussed, or in some cases a work that has not been read or studied for its environmental relevance. To begin, you can ask some of the following questions about it.

- Why is this text not widely known, or not well known for its depiction of nature?
- Why should it be?
- What insights about the natural world does this text (or writer) have to offer?
- Does it raise questions or issues about nature or the environment that readers should be concerned with?
- What has been overlooked in traditional readings that can enrich public awareness of humankind's impact on the natural world?
- How does this text qualify as belonging to the genre of nature writing?
- Does this work deal with environmental issues that are addressed in the study of history, philosophy, psychology, art, or ethics?

- How is a new reading of the work now possible because of developments in ecological research?
- What public attitudes toward nature does the text depict?
- What is the stance of the narrator toward nature? Why should readers be aware of it?

When such questions are asked about "Stopping by Woods," the reader is reminded that because Robert Frost often used the New England landscape as the setting of his poems, he is sometimes said to be a nature writer. The opening of his well-known poem "Birches," for example, is a detailed description of a boy swinging to bend the trees' supple trunks and of their icy branches glittering in winter sunlight. Of course, by the end the poem has developed into a commentary on life's experiences, but it begins, as nature poems do, with literal description. "Stopping by Woods," however, is not traditionally read as a poem about nature, but as a poem about a man who confronts a choice, viewed by some as a choice between isolation and community or even between life and death (see Chapter 8). An ecocritical reading, as the earlier questions demonstrate, shows that it can reasonably (and profitably) be read as a poem about nature itself.

As a poem about nature, "Stopping by Woods" presents valuable insights and reminders for the reader. For one, it depicts nature as an instrument of solace and peace. It has the power to comfort, console, and even reassure human beings whose lives are filled with complexities and problems. It poses no threat. The "sweep/ Of easy wind and downy flake" is not menacing. As the reader follows the thoughts of the speaker, he or she is made aware of how the natural world serves to counterbalance the noise and chaos of daily life. The reader becomes conscious once again that the natural world has value not only because of its visual beauty, but also because it has the power to calm the soul.

The poem also reminds the reader that nature is a thing of mystery, "dark and deep." Its power to relieve emotional distress is significant, but the reference to its inscrutability suggests that through it the individual can connect with a spiritual power that exceeds the human capability to understand it. Because an ecocritical perspective of the poem offers a reader a positive, comforting dimension beyond himself, it justifies the use of such an approach to provide yet another reading of this well-known work.

Examining Ecocritical Issues and Questions For readers who want to explore more global issues that are of interest to ecocritics, those involved with the third stage of the field's development, the consideration of theoretical issues, Cheryll Glotfelty has provided a set of questions that address aspects of genre, ecology, gender, institutional attitudes toward nature, and more. She suggests asking the following questions:

- Are the values expressed in a given literary work consistent with ecological wisdom?
- How do our metaphors of the land influence the way we treat it?

- Do men write about nature differently than women do?
- In what ways has literacy itself affected humankind's relationship to the natural world?
- How has the concept of wilderness changed over time?
- In what ways and to what effect is the environmental crisis seeping into contemporary literature and popular culture?
- What view of nature informs U.S. Government reports, corporate advertising, and televised nature documentaries, and to what rhetorical effect?
- What bearing might the science of ecology have on literary studies? How is science itself open to literary analysis?
- How is wilderness constructed?
- How is urban nature contrasted with rural or wild nature?
- What role does science or natural history play in a text?
- What are the links between gender and landscape?
- How does your attitude toward environmental ethics or deep ecology inform your reading?
- Is landscape a metaphor?

Other ecocritics have supplied additional areas of inquiry. They question topics such as the following:

- What, exactly, is meant by the word *nature*, and where is it? Is it found only in rural areas, or does it have an urban presence as well?
- Should the examination of "place" be a distinctive literary category, much as class, gender, or race have become?
- What is nature writing? Is it limited to the nonfiction essay, or does it include poetry and fiction?
- Are nature writing and ecocriticism practiced only by those who have the time and money to indulge them? Are they elitist?

Obviously not all of these questions are readily applicable to any given piece of writing, but keeping them in mind as you read can sensitize you to challenges, concerns, and issues that connect literature with your daily life. Some of them are pertinent to "Stopping by Woods." For example, the question that asks if the work is consistent with ecological wisdom points to one of the most significant aspects of the poem—the harmony that exists between the speaker and the world of nature he has paused to experience. He makes no claims upon it, does no damage to it. He simply values its existence. The question that asks if landscape is a metaphor leads to further interesting ideas. Although the scene is rendered in meticulous detail, affording the reader a clear, literal picture of the man, the horse, the winter night, and more, by the end of the final quatrain, the literal description has moved to a metaphorical level. The poem has been steadily moving in that direction since the beginning, but the closing repetition of the penultimate line ("And miles to go before I sleep") inevitably takes the poem away from the concrete and toward the abstract, and all elements of nature become not only what they are but something more as well.

Ecocritics do not lack for interesting areas of study. The ecofeminists who are combining postmodern approaches with ecological issues, for example, are interested in the way representations of nature are influenced by gender. They also see similarities in the oppression of women and efforts to dominate nature. That their concerns are receiving notice is evident in the publication of a special issue of ISLE that featured their concerns and by the growing publication of anthologies of women nature writers.

WRITING ECOCRITICISM

Prewriting

If you have chosen to make an ecocritical literary analysis, your intent will be to examine how nature is represented (or not represented) in the work or works you have chosen to analyze. You will have a head start if you formulated answers to the opening questions that were applied earlier to Robert Frost's poem "Stopping by Woods on a Snowy Evening." If you did so, you can now return to them and expand them by doing some freewriting. If you did not entertain the questions during your initial readings of the work, now is the time to work your way through them. You will find the process to be more effective if you write your answers out rather than simply muse about them. Something happens when you put your thoughts into specific words. Sometimes you even surprise yourself by setting down ideas you didn't know you had.

If, however, you would prefer to explore the genre of nature writing, you have several ways to do so. Of course, if you have access to forgotten texts of nature writing, you can work to bring them back to public notice, but it is more likely that you will choose to look at a canonical text generally considered to belong to another genre, pointing out how it possesses evidence of ecological awareness. Writers of all genres produce nature writing, although they are not always recognized for doing so. This approach can be particularly effective when canonical works are examined as nature writing by applying the principles of some of the new critical approaches, such as feminist, Bakhtinian, and psychoanalytic theories. You may even want to look at the impact of environment and nature on a particular author, questioning how "place" shaped his view of the world—where he grew up, where he traveled, where he wrote.

If you chose to reflect on some issue being discussed by ecocritics, working in the third phase of ecocritical development, you will need to do some reading and research on the topic. Before you can form an opinion, you must be well informed. To speak authoritatively, you have to be an authority. The available issues are many and complex, as the topics listed earlier indicate, but reading about them and reflecting on them can be a gratifying intellectual endeavor. If you choose to work in this vein, you will be categorized with ecofeminists, scholars working in ecological poetics (using ecological principles regarding interconnections and energy flow to demonstrate how poetry functions in society), and the school of philosophy known as deep ecology (which examines how criticism of anthropocentrism can impact the study of literature).

Drafting and Revising

The Introduction Because ecocriticism is committed to raising the awareness of the reading public regarding its responsibility to nature, you will want to show in the opening of your essay why the work or issue you have chosen to discuss serves that end. How does it call the reader's attention to the importance of minimizing humankind's impact on nature and maximizing his effort to sustain it? If you are working with a literary work, some information about its content or source will be helpful to the reader. If you are writing about an ecological issue or question, an overview of the various opinions about it can be helpful.

The Body The organization of the body of your paper will depend on your purpose. If you are dealing with representations, a generalization about how nature is depicted in the work can be stated, followed by examples that support the claim. Here is where the thinking you did to answer the "getting started" questions will be used. You will want to ask yourself how all the information that you inferred fits together so that you can provide the reader with an overview of how nature appears (or fails to appear) in the text.

If you choose to show how a text qualifies to be categorized as nature writing, you will need to identify the characteristics of the genre, then show where they appear in the text. When working from this perspective you may find it helpful to draw comparisons between the text you are analyzing and some other well-established piece of nature writing, pointing out traits and concerns the two works have in common.

The third option, that of reflecting on one of the "hot topics" in ecocriticism, will probably follow the conventional form of an argumentative essay. After presenting a survey of relevant scholarship that will introduce the reader to the major opinions regarding the issue, you will try to convince the reader of some conclusion you have reached while reading and thinking about the issue. The usual rhetorical strategies for persuading a reader to your point of view are appropriate to use here. For example, you can appeal to logic, emotion, or ethics. You will want to pay close attention to word choice and sentence formation, always looking to find strategies that will convince your audience of what you have to say.

The Conclusion As always, the ending of your paper is your last opportunity to make your major point to the reader. It is literally the final word and should be used to leave a lasting impression on the reader.

SUGGESTED READING

Bate, Jonathan. *Romantic Ecology: Wordsworth and the Environmental Tradition.* New York: Routledge, 1991.

Buell, Lawrence. *The Future of Environmental Criticism: The Environmental Crisis and Literary Imagination.* Malden, MA: Blackwell Publishers, 2005.

Clough, Wilson O. *The Necessary Earth: Nature and Solitude in American Literature.* Austin: University of Texas Press, 1964.

Elder, John. *Imagining the Earth: Poetry and the Vision of Nature.* Athens: University of Georgia Press, 1996.

Finch, Robert and John Elder, eds. *Nature Writing: The Tradition in English.* New York: Norton, 2002.

Glotfelty, Cheryll and Harold Fromm, eds. *The Ecocriticism Reader.* Athens: University of Georgia Press, 1996.

Knowles, Karen, ed. *Celebrating the Land: Women's Nature Writings, 1850–1991.* Flagstaff, AZ: Northland, 1992.

Kolodny, Annette. *The Lay of the Land: Metaphor as Experience and History in American Life and Letters.* Chapel Hill: University of North Carolina Press, 1975.

Meeker, Joseph. *The Comedy of Survival: Studies in Literary Ecology.* New York: Scribner's, 1974.

Slovic, Scott H. and Terrell F. Dixon, eds. *Being in the World: An Environmental Reader for Writers.* New York: Macmillan, 1993.

Snyder, Gary. *The Practice of the Wild.* Washington, D.C.: Shoemaker and Hoard, 2004.

Worster, Donald. *Nature's Economy: A History of Ecological Ideas.* 2nd ed. Cambridge, UK: Cambridge University Press, 1994.

For up-to-date information on the many Web sites addressing ecocriticism, visit www.cengagebrain.com.

Model Student Analysis

The Function of Nature in Keats's "To Autumn"

ROXIE JAMES

Ecocritical scholars heartily assert that nature is important in the study of literature. They argue that it should be regarded as a functioning part of the world that literary critics investigate. In the introduction to her *Ecocritical Reader*, for example, Cheryll Glotfelty defines ecocriticism as "the study of the relationship between literature and the physical environment" (xvii). In her terms such study involves an examination that renews readers' awareness of the nonhuman world and their duty to limit their destructive impact on it. To look at literature through this new lens means asking questions about how nature is depicted in a given text and about the role it plays in it.

In 1819, a few days after Keats wrote his ode "To Autumn," he sent a letter to his friend J. H. Reynolds stating, "I never liked stubble-fields so much as now—Aye, better than the chilly green of the spring. Somehow, a stubble plain looks warm—in the same way that some pictures look warm—this struck me so much in my Sunday's walk that I composed upon it" (Abrams 841). Clearly, he is drawn to ponder and to celebrate nature's impact on humankind. The tendency is evident also in the fact that this is not the only poem in which he reflects on its powerful beauty. In fact, written after some of Keats's other famous odes, "To Autumn" makes allusions to some of their lines. For example, when in the second stanza he describes autumn as "drows'd with the fume of poppies," he echoes his "Ode to Psyche" in which he gives a description of Psyche and Cupid as they "lay calm-breathing on the bedded grass." Nature is not an infrequent presence in his work.

Looking in particular at "To Autumn," it is evident that the poet has made that season the chief character in the poem by focusing on its impact on the world rather than on any effect human beings have had on it. By doing so, he raises the reader's awareness of the complexity and importance of the natural world, particularly that of autumn. More specifically, the poem depicts the season as a force that is powerful, productive, and progressive.

In this ode the speaker is deeply moved by the power of autumn. He observes its effects on crops and flowers and animals. He recognizes that it exercises authority over the cycles of blooming and harvesting, maturation and decline. At one point it is in partnership with the sun to "fill all fruit with ripeness to the core," and at another it brings all things to a quiet rest. It affects all living things, including the speaker who observes and honors its beauty.

Keats also gives the season agency. That is, he notes that it uses its power to do something, to fulfill a function. That function is the production of life. The opening stanza of the poem illustrates the process. The speaker notes that the season conspires with the sun on "how to load and bless / With fruit the vines that round the thatch-eves run." He continues the observation by saying that the season further conspires "To bend with apples the moss'd cottage-trees, / And fill all fruit with ripeness to the core." It is a productive force that nurtures the growth of other elements of nature. It is depicted as being almost maternal in its care of life in its many forms.

The most important characteristic of autumn in this poem is that it is a season of change. It does not remain static but progressively moves from the warmth and ripeness of late summer to the stubble plains that anticipate the barrenness of winter, from fullness to harvest. In the opening stanza, for example, autumn conspires with the sun on "how to load and bless," how to "bend with apples," how to "swell the ground and plump the hazel shells," and how to "set budding more/And still more, later flowers for the bees/Until they think warm days will never cease,/ For Summer has o'er-brimm'd their clammy cells." The second stanza moves on to illustrate the middle of autumn, a time untroubled by the busy growth and productivity of summer, or by the upcoming harshness of winter. It is a time of quietude and plenty spent on the "granary floor," touched by the "winnowing wind," drowsing "with the fume of poppies," and watching the "last oozing [of the cider press] hours by hours" as the season passes. It is a time of peace. In the final stanza the season fulfills its cycle and comes to a close. The "clouds bloom the soft-dying day, / And touch the stubble plains with rosy hue" as the evening approaches and autumn comes to its end. Despite the lush visual image of the sunset, it is principally in the sounds of evening, its music, that the speaker recognizes the beauty of the season. He notes that as the end of autumn approaches, the "wailful choir" of "small gnats mourn," "lambs loud bleat," "hedge-crickets sing," "the red-breast whistles," and "gathering swallows twitter." Such songs impart a mournful, melancholy aura to the scene that is intensified by the wind that "lives or dies." There is beauty, but there is sadness, too.

An ecocritical look at John Keats's "To Autumn" shows it to be an admiring tribute to one part of nature's cycle of birth, growth, fulfillment, and death. The season has beauty equal to that of its more celebrated cousin, the spring, a beauty born of its power to rule other natural elements and beings, of its productivity that furnishes sustenance for all things, and of its progressive nature that mirrors the cycle of human life itself. The opening stanza illustrates the beginning of autumn and its power to produce life. The second describes the quiet contentment of the mature middle of the season, and the final one suggests the sadness that accompanies its end. Throughout all three stanzas the poem gently reminds the reader of the interrelatedness of all life and the consequent necessity for human beings to respect, even honor, the natural world.

WORKS CITED

Glotfelty, Cheryll. *The Ecocriticism Reader: Landmarks in Literary Ecology*. Cheryll Glotfelty and Harold Fromm, eds. Athens: University of Georgia Press, 1996.

Keats, John. "Ode to Psyche." *The Norton Anthology of English Literature*. 7th ed. M. H. Abrams et al., eds. New York: W.W. Norton and Company, 2001.

Keats, John. "To Autumn." *The Norton Anthology of English Literature*. 7th ed. M. H. Abrams et al., eds. New York: W.W. Norton and Company, 2001.

Literary Selections

Chapter 6

Letters of Abigail and John Adams

Abigail Adams

March 31, 1776

I wish you would ever write me a letter half as long as I write you, and tell me, if you may, where your fleet are gone; what sort of defense Virginia can make against our common enemy; whether it is so situated as to make an able defense. Are not the gentry lords, and the common people vassals? Are they not like the uncivilized vassals Britain represents us to be? I hope their riflemen, who have shown themselves very savage and even blood-thirsty, are not a specimen of the generality of the people. I am willing to allow the colony great merit for having produced a Washington; but they have been shamefully duped by a Dunmore.

I have sometimes been ready to think that the passion for liberty cannot be equally strong in the breasts of those who have been accustomed to deprive their fellow-creatures of theirs. Of this I am certain, that it is not founded upon that generous and Christian principle of doing to others as we would that others should do unto us.

Do not you want to see Boston? I am fearful of the small-pox, or I should have been in before this time. I got Mr. Crane to go to our house and see what state it was in. I find it has been occupied by one of the doctors of a regiment; very dirty, but no other damage has been done to it. The few things which were left in it are all gone. I look upon it as a new acquisition of property—a property which one month ago I did not value at a single shilling, and would with pleasure have seen it in flames.

The town in general is left in a better state than we expected; more owing to a precipitate flight than any regard to the inhabitants; though some individuals discovered a sense of honor and justice, and have left the rent of the houses in which they were, for the owners, and the furniture unhurt, or, if damaged, sufficient to make it good. Others have committed abominable ravages. The mansion-house of your President is safe, and the furniture unhurt; while the house and furniture of the Solicitor General have fallen a prey to their own merciless party. Surely the very fiends feel a reverential awe for virtue and patriotism, whilst they detest the parricide and traitor.

I feel very differently at the approach of spring from what I did a month ago. We knew not then whether we could plant or sow with safety, whether where we had tilled we could reap the fruits of our own industry, whether we could rest in our own cottages or whether we should be driven from the seacoast to seek shelter in the wilderness; but now we feel a temporary peace, and the poor fugitives are returning to their deserted habitations.

Though we felicitate ourselves, we sympathize with those who are trembling lest the lot of Boston should be theirs. But they cannot be in similar circumstances unless pusillanimity and cowardice should take possession of them. They have time and warning given them to see the evil and shun it.

I long to hear that you have declared an independency. And, by the way, in the new code of laws which I suppose it will be necessary for you to make, I desire you would remember the ladies and be more generous and favorable to them than your ancestors. Do not put such unlimited power into the hands of the husbands. Remember, all men would be tyrants if they could. If particular care and attention is not paid to the ladies, we are determined to foment a rebellion, and will not hold ourselves bound by any laws in which we have no voice or representation.

That your sex are naturally tyrannical is a truth so thoroughly established as to admit of no dispute; but such of you as wish to be happy willingly give up the harsh title of master for the more tender and endearing one of friend. Why, then, not put it out of the power of the vicious and the lawless to use us with cruelty and indignity with impunity? Men of sense in all ages abhor those customs which treat us only as the vassals of your sex; regard us then as beings placed by Providence under your protection, and in imitation of the Supreme Being make use of that power only for our happiness.

Abigail Adams

April 5, 1776

I want to hear much oftener from you than I do. March 8th was the last date of any that I have yet had. You inquire of me whether I am making saltpetre. I have not yet attempted it, but after soap-making believe I shall make the experiment. I find as much as I can do to manufacture clothing for my family, which would else be naked. I know of but one person in this part of the town who has made any. That is Mr. Tertius Bass, as he is called, who has got very near a hundred-weight which has been found to be very good. I have heard of some others in the other parishes. Mr. Reed, of Weymouth, has been applied to, to go to Andover to the mills which are now at work, and he has gone.

I have lately seen a small manuscript describing the proportions of the various sorts of powder fit for cannon, small-arms, and pistols. If it would be of any service your way I will get it transcribed and send it to you. Every one of your friends sends regards, and all the little ones. Adieu.

John Adams

April 14, 1776

You justly complain of my short letters, but the critical state of things and the multiplicity of avocations must plead my excuse. You ask where the fleet is? The enclosed papers will inform you. You ask what sort of defense Virginia can make? I believe they will make an able defense. Their militia and minute-men have been some time employed in training themselves, and they have nine battalions of regulars, as they call them, maintained among them, under good officers, at the Continental expense. They have set up a number of manufactories of firearms, which are busily employed. They are tolerably supplied with powder, and are successful and assiduous in making saltpetre. Their neighboring sister, or rather daughter colony of North Carolina, which is a warlike colony, and has several battalions at the Continental expense, as well as a pretty good militia, are ready to assist them, and they are in very good spirits and seem determined to make a brave resistance. The gentry are very rich, and the common people very poor. This inequality of property gives an aristocratical turn to all their proceedings, and occasions a strong aversion in their patricians to "Common Sense." But the spirit of these Barons is coming down, and it must submit. It is very true, as you observe, they have been duped by Dunmore. But this is a common case. All the colonies are duped, more or less, at one time and another. A more egregious bubble was never blown up than the story of Commissioners coming to treat with the Congress, yet it has gained credit like a charm, not only with, but against the clearest evidence. I never shall forget the delusion which seized our best and most sagacious friends, the dear inhabitants of Boston, the winter before last. Credulity and the want of foresight are imperfections in the human character, that no politician can sufficiently guard against.

You give me some pleasure by your account of a certain house in Queen Street. I had burned it long ago in imagination. It rises now to my view like a phoenix. What shall I say of the Solicitor General? I pity his pretty children. I pity his father and his sisters. I wish I could be clear that it is no moral evil to pity him and his lady. Upon repentance, they will certainly have a large share in the compassions of many. But let us take warning, and give it to our children. Whenever vanity and gayety, a love of pomp and dress, furniture, equipage, buildings, great company, expensive diversions, and elegant entertainments get the better of the principles and judgments of men or women, there is no knowing where they will stop, nor into what evils, natural, moral, or political, they will lead us.

Your description of your own *gaieté de coeur* charms me. Thanks be to God, you have just cause to rejoice, and may the bright prospect be obscured by no cloud. As to declarations of independency, be patient. Read our privateering laws and our commercial laws. What signifies a word?

As to your extraordinary code of laws, I cannot but laugh. We have been told that our struggle has loosened the bonds of government everywhere; that children and apprentices were disobedient; that schools and colleges were grown turbulent; that Indians slighted their guardians, and negroes grew insolent to their masters. But your letter was the first intimation that another tribe, more numerous and powerful than all the rest, were grown discontented. This is rather too coarse a compliment, but you are so saucy, I won't blot it out. Depend upon it, we know better than to repeal our masculine systems. Although they are in full force, you know they are little more than theory. We dare not exert our power in its full latitude. We are obliged to go fair and softly, and, in practice, you know we are the subjects. We have only the name of masters, and rather than give up this, which would completely subject us to the despotism of the petticoat, I hope General Washington and all our brave heroes would fight; I am sure every good politician would plot, as long as he would against despotism, empire, monarchy, aristocracy, oligarchy, or ochlocracy. A fine story, indeed! I begin to think the ministry as deep as they are wicked. After stirring up Tories, land-jobbers, trimmers, bigots, Canadians, Indians, negroes, Hanoverians, Hessians, Russians, Irish Roman Catholics, Scotch renegadoes, at last they have stimulated the ——— to demand new privileges and threaten to rebel.

Chapter 10

Jill Ker Conway

Excerpt from *The Road from Coorain**

From The Road from Coorain *by Jill Ker Conway, copyright © 1989 by Jill Ker Conway. Used by permission of Alfred A. Knopf, a division of Random House, Inc.*

Because Christmas recalled our father's death, it was a difficult feast for us. Nevertheless, we had one of my mother's succulent roast turkeys and her ambrosial plum puddings before the boys left to spend the rest of the summer at Coorain. During January, we began to talk seriously about where I would attend school. My mother was daunted by the prospect of more private school fees as our debts grew and our assets dwindled. Did I think I would like the local state school? she asked me. We could see it each time we took a train—it was right beside the railway station, empty at present, surrounded by an acre of unkempt ground. I was startled. I had taken on my parents' values sufficiently to see this proposal

*This selection is also featured in the model student essay in Chapter 6.

as a distinct coming down in the world. Recognizing the worry in my mother's eyes, I said I would.

The first day of school in February was hot, 105 degrees. The school, a brick building with an iron roof, was like a furnace, and its inhabitants, teachers and students, wilted as the day wore on. I hated it from the moment I walked in the door. I was a snob, and I knew the accents of the teachers and most of the students were wrong by the exacting standards we'd had drummed into us at home. Worse still was the unruly behavior of everyone of every age. Boys pulled my hair when I refused to answer questions I took as rude or impudent; girls stuck out their tongues and used bad language. Teachers lost their tempers and caned pupils in front of the class. Few books were opened as the staff waged a losing battle to establish order. Recess and lunchtime were purgatorial. Crowds, or so it seemed to me, of jeering boys and a few girls gathered around to taunt me about my accent. "Stuck up, ain't you," they yelled, as I faced them in stubborn silence.

They were right. Now I was in a more diverse social universe than I had known at Coorain. I had no idea how to behave or what the rules were for managing social boundaries. I had been friends, one could say special friends, with Shorty, or with Ron Kelly, but that was in a simple world where we each knew our respective places. Here, I knew only that the old rules could not possibly apply. Everyone around me spoke broad Australian, a kind of speech my parents' discipline had ruthlessly eliminated. My interrogators could unquestionably be described by that word my mother used as a blanket condemnation of lower-class people, customs, and forms of behavior. They were "common." My encounter was a classic confrontation for the Australia of my generation. I, the carefully respectable copier of British manners, was being called to raucous and high-spirited account by the more vital and unquestionably authentic Australian popular culture. I was too uncertain to cope. I faced them in silence till the bell rang and we returned to the pandemonium of the unruly classroom.

After school, the same group assembled to escort me home to the accompaniment of catcalls and vivid commentaries on my parentage. I knew these city children could not outlast someone who was used to walking ten or twelve miles a day behind a herd of sheep, so our comic crocodile set out. I, stalking in front in frozen indignation, my attendant chorus gradually wilting as I led them along hot pavements and across streets where the heat had begun to melt the tarmac. After the last one had tired and dropped away, I made my way home where my mother was ostentatiously doing nothing in the front garden, on the watch for my arrival.

We had our afternoon tea in blissful silence. Finally she asked me how the day had gone. "It was all right," I said, determined not to complain. She studied my face thoughtfully. "You don't have to go back," she said. "I made a mistake. That's not the right school for you." Years later, I asked how she guessed what my day had been like. "I didn't have to ask," she said. "You were a child whose face was always alight with curiosity. When you came home that day, your face was closed. I knew you wouldn't learn anything there."

In fact, had I persevered I would have learned a great deal, though little of it from the harassed and overworked teachers in the ill-equipped classrooms. I'd have been obliged to come to terms with the Australian class system, and to see my family's world from the irreverent and often hilarious perspective of the Australian working class. It would have been invaluable knowledge, and my vision of Australia would have been the better for it. It was to take me another fifteen years to see the world from my own Australian perspective, rather than from the British definition taught to my kind of colonial. On the other hand, had I learned that earthy irreverence in my schooldays, it would have ruled out the appreciation of high culture in any form. My mother had no training for that appreciation, but she knew instinctively to seek it for her children. She did not reflect much about the underlying conflicts in Australian culture. She was simply determined that I would be brought up to abhor anything "common," and that, despite her financial worries, I would have the best education available in the Australia she knew.

The next day, my mother acted decisively. By some wizardry peculiarly hers, she persuaded the headmistress of Abbotsleigh, one of the most academically demanding of the private schools for girls in Sydney, to accept me as a pupil in the last year of the Junior School. Although there were long waiting lists for admission to the school, I was to begin at once, as a day girl, and become a boarder the next term.

Before being formally enrolled, I was taken for an interview with Miss Everett, the headmistress. To me she seemed like a benevolent being from another planet. She was over six feet tall, with the carriage and gait of a splendid athlete. Her dress was new to me. She wore a tweed suit of soft colors and battered elegance. She spoke in the plummy tones of a woman educated in England, and her intelligent face beamed with humor and curiosity. When she spoke, the habit of long years of teaching French made her articulate her words clearly and so forcefully that the unwary who stood too close were in danger of being sprayed like the audience too close to the footlights of a vaudeville show. "She looks strapping," she cheerfully commented to my mother, after talking to me for a few minutes alone. "She can begin tomorrow." Thereafter, no matter how I misbehaved, or what events brought me into her presence, I felt real benevolence radiating from Miss Everett.

The sight of her upright figure, forever striding across the school grounds, automatically caused her charges to straighten their backs. Those who slouched were often startled to have her appear suddenly behind them and seize their shoulders to correct their posture. Perhaps because she liked my stiff back we began a friendship that mattered greatly in my future. I never ceased to wonder at her, for Miss Everett was the first really free spirit I had ever met. She was impatient with bourgeois Australian culture, concerned about ideas, restless with the constraints of a Board of Trustees dominated by the low church evangelical Anglican archdiocese of Sydney, and she never bothered to conceal her feelings. She had been a highly successful amateur athlete, and had earned her first degree in French literature at the Sorbonne. After Paris, she had studied modern literature in Germany. To me and to many others, she was a true bearer of European cultural ideals in Australia. She loved learning for itself, and this made her a most unusual schoolteacher. The academic mentality in the Australia of my childhood focused on knowledge as a credential, a body of information one had to use as a mechanic would his tools. With her French training, she saw her academic task as one of conveying to her charges the kinds of disciplines which released the mind for creativity and speculation. This, to many of her peers, was a subversive goal. She was a successful headmistress because she was also an astute politician, bending before the winds of provincial prejudice whenever they blew strongly over issues of discipline and behavior. But it was characteristic of her that she made her mind up about flouting the waiting lists of daughters of old girls because she'd been struck during our ten minutes together by the range of my vocabulary. My mother and I had had a hard few years, she had remarked to get us started. "Yes," I said, "we have lived through a great natural catastrophe." She wanted eleven-year-olds who thought that way in her school and cheerfully ignored the admission rules.

Thereafter, I hurried quickly past the desert of the local state school to the railway station and rode the seven minutes south to Wahroonga, the suburb of my new school. On my path homeward, I only once saw my former attendant chorus ranging restlessly about the local state school grounds. Seeing me, they took flight like a flock of birds, alighting by the fence as I strode past. I was prepared for hostility, but they were remarkably genial. "We don't blame you for leaving this fucking school, Jill," the ringleader shouted cheerfully. "It's no bloody good." I was too young and insecure to wonder what a good school might have made of such high-spirited pupils, and I had as yet no sense of injustice that the difference between our chances for education were as night and day. At Abbotsleigh, even though I was immediately ushered into a classroom of thirty-six total strangers, it seemed as though I had already arrived in paradise. Many students were boarders from distant country areas who had also had to overcome their shyness and become social beings. At breaks between classes they understood my tongue-tied silence. I was placed at a desk next to one of the kindest and most helpful members of the class, and two girls were deputed to see to it that I was not lonely my first day. I could scarcely believe my good fortune. Better still, the teacher, Miss Webb, a woman in her late twenties, knew exactly when to put the class to work, and when to relax and allow high spirits to run relatively free. Our classroom was an orderly and harmonious place where the subjects were taught well and the students encouraged to learn. Even the strange ritual of the gymnasium was less puzzling. The teachers were used to bush children and took the time to explain what the exercises were for, or to tell me that I would soon learn the eye–hand coordination I lacked.

Our curriculum was inherited from Great Britain, and consequently it was utterly untouched by progressive notions in education. We took English grammar, complete with parsing and analysis, we were drilled in spelling and punctuation, we read English poetry and were tested in scansion, we read English fiction, novels, and short stories and analyzed the style. Each year, we studied a Shakespeare play, committing much of it to memory, and performing scenes from it on April 23 in honor of Shakespeare's birthday.

We might have been in Sussex for all the attention we paid to Australian poetry and prose. It did not count. We, for our part, dutifully learned Shakespeare's imagery drawn from the English landscape and from English horticulture. We memorized Keats's "Ode to Autumn" or Shelley on the skylark without ever having seen the progression of seasons and the natural world they referred to. This gave us the impression that great poetry and fiction were written by and about people and places far distant from Australia. Palgrave's *Golden Treasury* or the Oxford collection of romantic poetry we read were so beautiful it didn't seem to matter, though to us poetry was more like incantation than related to the rhythms of our own speech. As for landscape, we learned by implication that ours was ugly, because it deviated totally from the landscape of the Cotswolds and the Lake Country, or the romantic hills and valleys of Constable.

After English (eight classes a week) came history (five times a week). We learned about Roman Britain and memorized a wonderful jumble of Angles, Saxons, Picts, and Boadiçea. In geography (three times a week), we studied the great rivers of the world. They were the Ganges, the Indus, the Amazon, the Plate, the Rhine, the Danube, the Nile, the Congo, the St. Lawrence, and the Mississippi. When the question was raised, Australia was defined once again by default. Our vast continent had no great river system; its watercourses flowed inland to Lake Eyre, an anomaly which was quickly dismissed as a distraction from the business at hand. Once a week, we read scripture, sticking to the Old Testament and learning its geography as a distraction from its bloodthirsty tribal battles. Nothing in the instruction suggested that this sacred subject bore any relation to our daily lives, although because we read the Bible, we were supposed to be particularly well behaved during this class.

In mathematics, we studied arithmetic and simple geometry, five times a week. The textbooks were English, and the problems to be solved assumed another natural environment. It was possible to do them all as a form of drill without realizing that the mathematical imagination helped one explore and analyze the continuities and discontinuities of the order which lay within and beneath natural phenomena. We learned to treat language as magical, but not numbers and their relationships. Somehow we knew that mathematics was important, as a form of intellectual discipline. However, our problems to solve had to do with shopping and making change, pumping water from one receptacle to another at constant volumes, or measuring the areas of things. These did not encourage the visualizing of shapes and relationships, let alone hint at the wonders of physics.

Once a week we had choir lessons, lessons in painting and drawing, and in sewing. The sewing was of the nonutilitarian type, embroidery or crewel work. The art concerned lessons in perspective, conveyed with no historical context describing the development of Western ideas about the representation of objects. Choir was group instruction in singing and the reading of music. All these practical subjects assumed some previous background which I did not possess, so that I fiddled away the hour and a half appearing busy enough to escape rebuke, but never really undertaking any project. In choir, I soon learned that I could not carry a tune and that it was better to move my mouth soundlessly and look interested. My imagination might have been fired by reproductions of great painting and sculpture, but we did not look at them. Nor did our classes ever hint at the great body of Australian painting which already existed, or the vitality of the artistic efflorescence taking place in our own city even as we studied. As with our study of art, we were not taught what music *was*. It was enough that a lady knew how to carry a tune and to read music. Those who were talented mastered performance, but the rest of us were left to learn about music and dance as forms of expression on our own.

Although our curriculum ignored our presence in Australia, the school itself demonstrated how the Australian landscape could be enhanced by a discerning eye. Its ample grounds were a far cry from the barren setting of my local state school with its hot dusty building and gritty yard. It stood on twenty or so acres rising up a hillside toward one of the highest points of the gentle hills which made up the terrain between Sydney Harbor and the entrance to the Hawkesbury River, to the north of the Harbor. The school's residential buildings clustered along the main highway running north from Sydney, the Pacific Highway. Behind them, close to the main entrance, two groups of classroom buildings formed a quadrangle with a residence and the administration buildings. Patches of bush had been manicured a little to control steep grades down to two levels of playing fields. Paths led to more dispersed dormitories, and around them were plantings which created places for day students to sit outside at lunch, and for boarders to enjoy during the weekend. Rose gardens, jacarandas, jasmine, honeysuckle, mock-orange, peach, plum, and quince trees perfumed the air in spring, and the planting pulled out the contours of the land without interrupting the sense of the wildness of the pockets of bush skillfully left to separate different grades and functional areas. Tucked away at the northern end were banks of tennis courts and closer to the main buildings were basketball courts and a sunken court with a high cement wall at which budding tennis stars honed their backhand and leapt to smash their forehand drive.

In this setting thronged some three hundred pupils in the Junior School, and another eight hundred or so students in high school grades. Much about our way of life symbolized the colonial mentality. Its signs were visible in the maps on our classroom walls, extended depictions of the globe with much of Africa, all of the Indian subcontinent, parts of Southeast Asia, half of North America, colored the bright red of the British Empire. Our uniforms, copies of those of English schools, indicated that we were only partially at home in our environment. In winter, we wore pine green tunics, cream blouses, green flannel blazers, dark brown cotton stockings, green velour hats, and brown cotton gloves. In summer, we wore starched green linen dresses with cream collars, the same blazer, beige socks, a cream panama hat, and the same brown gloves. Woe betide the student caught shedding the blazer or the gloves in public, even when the thermometer was over 100 degrees. She was letting down the school, behaving unbecomingly, and betraying the code involved in being a lady. Ladies, we learned, did not consider comfort more important than propriety in dress or manners. Disciplinary action was taken instantly when it was learned that an Abbotsleigh student had not leapt to her feet in train or bus to offer her seat to an older person, male or female. Speaking loudly, sitting in public in any fashion except bolt upright with a ramrod-straight back, were likewise sorts of behavior which let down the school. When the more rebellious asked why this was so, the answer was clear and unequivocal. We were an elite. We were privileged girls and young women who had an obligation to represent the best standards of behavior to the world at large. The best standards were derived from Great Britain, and should be emulated unquestioningly. Those were the standards which had led to such a sizable part of the map of the globe being colored red, and we let them slip at our peril. No one paused to think that gloves and blazers had a function in damp English springs which they lacked entirely in our blazing summers.

Speech was another important aspect of deportment. One's voice must be well modulated and purged of all ubiquitous Australian diphthongs. Teachers were tireless in pointing them out and stopping the class until the offender got the word right. Drills of "how now brown cow" might have us all scarlet in the face with choked schoolgirl laughter, but they were serious matters for our instructors, ever on guard against the diphthongs that heralded cultural decline.

The disciplinary system also modeled the British heritage. We were an elite. Ergo we were born to be leaders. However, the precise nature of the leadership was by no means clear. For some of our mentors, excelling meant a fashionable marriage and leadership in philanthropy. For others, it meant intellectual achievement and the aspiration to a university education. Since the great majority of the parents supporting the school favored the first definition, the question of the social values which should inform leadership was carefully glossed over. Eminence in the school's hierarchy could come from being a lively and cheerful volunteer, a leader in athletics, or from intellectual achievement. The head girl was always carefully chosen to offend no particular camp aligned behind the competing definitions. She was always a good-natured all-rounder.

The discipline code and the manner of its administration might well have been designed to prepare us to be subalterns in the Indian army, or district officers in some remote jungle colony. The routine running of the school was managed by class captains and prefects selected by the headmistress. Prefects administered the rules of behavior and imposed penalties without there being any recourse to a higher authority. Cheating or letting down the side were far more serious offenses than failures of sensitivity. Theft was the ultimate sin. It being Australia, prowess at sports excused most breaches of the rules or failures of decorum. Bookishness and dislike for physical activity, on the other hand, aroused dark suspicions and warranted disciplinary action for the slightest infringement of the rules.

Hardiness was deemed more important than imagination. Indeed, an observer might have believed that the school's founders had been inspired by John Locke and Mistress Masham. Boarders rose at 6:30 a.m. to take cold showers even in midwinter. The aim was to encourage everyone to run at least a mile before breakfast, although slugabeds and poor planners could manage a frantic dash for breakfast without too frequent rebukes.

While this regimen might be seen as a precursor of later obsessions with health and fitness, our diet undid whatever benefits our routine of exercise conferred. We lived on starch, over-cooked meat, and endless eggs and bacon. Fruit appeared in one's diet only if parents intervened and arranged for special supplies to be made available outside meal hours. Slabs of bread and butter accompanied every meal, so that the slimmest figures thickened and susceptible complexions became blotchy.

What meals lacked in culinary style they made up for in formality. A mistress or a sixth-form boarder sat at the head of each long rectangular table. The rest of us, bathed and changed into a required green velvet dress for evenings, sat in descending order of age and class until the youngest and most recently arrived sat at the distant foot of the table. Food was served by the teacher or sixth former at the head of the table, and the rules of conduct decreed that one might not ask for more or less, and that one must endure in silence until someone farther up the table noticed that one needed salt, pepper, butter, tea, or whatever seasonings made our tasteless dishes palatable. Foibles in food were not tolerated. If a student refused to eat the main dish and the teacher in charge noticed, it would be served to her again at subsequent meals until it was deemed that a satisfactory amount had been consumed. The youngest were required to wait to be spoken to before starting a conversation, as though those seated higher up the table were royalty. People who made too much noise or displayed unseemly manners were sent from the room and left hungry until the next meal.

All these rules might have made for stilted behavior, but in fact, they barely subdued the roar of conversation in the boarders' dining room, and only modestly curtailed the animal spirits of the younger students intent at one and the same time on getting more than their share of food, and on whatever form of mischief might disconcert the figure of authority seated at the head of the table.

After I became a boarder in my second term, I looked forward to the two hours which followed dinner, hours when the whole boarding population gathered for carefully supervised preparation for the next day's classes. I could usually finish what was required in short order, and then I could relish the quiet. The day of classes and the afternoon of games seemed to my bush consciousness to be too full of voices. I liked to sit and read poetry, to race ahead in the history book and ponder the events described. I also liked occasionally to manage some feat of wickedness in total silence, such as to wriggle undetected from one end of the "prep" room to the other to deliver some innocuous note or message. Ron Kelly's training in hunting had given me the patience required to move silently, and the satisfaction of going about my own business rather than following orders appealed to me deeply.

Much of my time during the first year or so of my schooling at Abbotsleigh was taken up with the pleasure of defying adult authority and systematically flouting the rules. Lights out in the evening was merely a license to begin to roam about the school, to climb out the window and appear as a somewhat dusty apparition in someone else's dormitory. Restrictions on what one could bring back to school in the way of food were an invitation to figure out the multifarious opportunities for concealing forbidden chocolates, sponge cakes, fruit cakes, soft drinks, and other bulky items as one returned to school from weekly trips to the dentist or weekends of freedom at midterm. Locks on the door of the tuck-shop were no barrier to country children used to dismantling doors and reassembling them.

These escapades were natural reactions to regimentation. They were also my first opportunity to rebel without the danger of doing psychological damage to adults of whom I was prematurely the care giver. It was a delicious and heady feeling undimmed even when my mother was told of my misbehavior. She took it that I was keeping bad company, although this was hardly reflected in my academic performance. I knew that I was being perversely carefree and irresponsible for the first time in my life. I could not articulate a criticism of my mother yet, but I could see the pretenses behind many of the school's rules, and I enjoyed being hypercritical of the people who tried to make me sleep and wake to a schedule, always wear clean socks on Sundays, and never forget my gloves when leaving the school.

After one rebellious scrape led to my being gated over the Easter break, my mother called on Miss Everett and began to apologize for my bad conduct. Miss Everett, with an imperious wave of the hand, interrupted her in mid-sentence. "My dear Mrs. Ker, don't fuss. There's nothing to worry about. I've yet to see Jill's mind fully extended, and I look forward to the day when I do. When she's really interested, she'll forget about breaking rules." These comments, duly reported to my brothers, led to much teasing, and examinations of my head to detect signs of stretching, but they also gave me some freedom from my mother's pressure for perfect conduct, freedom which I badly needed.

I was not a popular student. No one could call me pretty. I had ballooned on the school's starchy diet, developed a poor complexion, and I looked the embodiment of adolescent ungainliness. Moreover, my pride prevented me from seizing opportunities to correct my lack of coordination. I could not bear to begin tennis lessons with the seven-year-old beginners, but could not pretend to play like my classmates, who had been coached for years. A month after arriving as a boarder, I purchased a magnifying glass, found a quiet spot in the sun, and burned the carefully inscribed name off my tennis racket. Once I was satisfied with the job, I turned the racket in at the school's lost property office and escaped further lessons by bewailing the loss of my racket. Basketball was different. Everyone was beginning that game more or less as I began. With diligence my height could be turned to advantage and I earned a place on a team. Thereafter, afternoons could be filled with basketball practice, and Saturday mornings with competition. I liked the excitement of the game, although I never learned to treat a game as a game, and not to care about losing.

I was as intellectually precocious as I was socially inept. I never understood the unspoken rule which required that one display false modesty and hang back when there was a task to be done, waiting to be asked to undertake it. I also took a long time to learn the social hierarchies of the place: whose parents were very rich, whose family had titled relatives in England, whose mother dressed in the height of fashion, which families owned the most stylish holiday retreats. My boarder friends were mainly the daughters of the real backcountry, people who were homesick for the bush and their families and accepted the school as a term which must be served uncomplainingly.

I liked getting out from under the pressure of my mother's company, but at the same time, I was burdened by the sense that she had taken on two jobs, a secretarial one by day and a nursing one at night, in order to pay my fees. As soon as she had delivered me to Abbotsleigh as a boarder, my mother moved back to my grandmother's house, settled Bob in a rented room down the road, and began to work in earnest. Once she had satisfied herself that she could earn enough to pay Barry's and my school fees and pay the rent for herself and my older brother, she began to concentrate her energies on the kind of investment which would be needed to make Coorain profitable again. She had no thought of selling it, but planned to revive it as a sheep-raising venture once it rained. She had a sure instinct for the economics of a small business, and long before others in our drought-stricken district began to think about restocking, she had realized that if she waited for the rain to fall before buying sheep, the price would be so high it would be years before she paid off the cost of the purchase. Once the drought had broken in areas two to three hundred miles from Coorain, she began to look for suitable sale sheep to form the basis for rebuilding the Coorain flock. She planned to hire a drover to walk her purchases through the stock routes in country where the rains had come until the drought broke at Coorain. On the day she borrowed sixteen hundred pounds from her woolbroker and signed the papers to purchase twelve hundred Merino ewes, she arrived home to learn that there had been two and a half inches of rain at Coorain. The value of her purchase had doubled within a matter of hours and she was rightly jubilant. Two weeks later, there was another inch and a half of rain and by the time the new sheep were delivered by their drover to Coorain, it was producing luxuriant pasture. From that day on our finances were assured, thanks to her inspired gamble.

None of the new earnings were frittered away on improving our style of life. Instead, every penny went back into building up the property, replacing buried fences, repairing the stockyards, buying new equipment. My mother kept on at one of her jobs, found us an inexpensive house to rent in an unfashionable, lower-middle-class suburb to the west of the city, and gradually began to reunite the family.

The reunion at the end of my second term as a boarder at Abbotsleigh brought together a group of young people on the edge of major life changes. Bob, at nineteen, was a young man impatient to savor life, and in search of the adventure he had once expected to find in wartime. Barry, at seventeen, was intent on leaving the King's School before completing high school. He had by then been in boarding school for seven years, and he was convinced that he would learn more from work experience and evening study than during an eighth year of routine in the closed world of the school he no longer enjoyed. I, approaching thirteen years old, looked and felt an awkward adolescent. Our mother, now in her forty-ninth year, looked her years, but she had regained some of her old vitality. Release from stress, and the chance to recoup the family fortunes at Coorain, had restored some of her beautiful coloring and brought back a sparkle to her eyes.

Although many men friends, including our favorite, Angus Waugh, tried to persuade her to marry again, she rebuffed them all. She had loved our father deeply, and she clearly did not want to share the raising of their children with anyone else. She still found herself swept by waves of anger and grief at his loss. Strangers who sat opposite her in the train or the local bus would occasionally be startled by the gaze of hatred she turned on them. She would literally be possessed by rage that other men were alive while her husband was dead.

The intensity of her feelings did not bode well for anyone's peace of mind as we children moved at various paces toward adulthood. She was out of touch with the mood of the postwar world we were entering. She now found it hard to imagine vocations for her sons except the land and the life of a grazier. The boys, understandably, given our recent experiences, did not want to embark on that path. I, for my part, was teetering on the edge of a more mature awareness of the people in my world. I found my brothers entrancing, developed romantic crushes on their friends, and tagged along as often as possible on their diversions.

These were mainly concerned with music, music being the one sociable activity at home my mother approved of and encouraged. Bob began to study the trumpet, Barry the clarinet, while their circle of friends revolved around jazz concerts, listening to recordings of the great jazz musicians, and studying music theory. Our tiny rented house was often crammed with young men participating in or listening to the latest jazz session. When the small living room could not contain the noise of the excited improvisation, I would be dispatched to sit on the curb across the street to listen and report how it really sounded. Doubtless, had we lived in a stuffier neighborhood there would have been complaints about the noise. Our kindly neighbors approved of a widowed mother keeping her sons at home and away from the Australian obsession with pubs and gambling.

My mother's code of thrift, sobriety, and industry had served her well growing up in a simpler Australian society, but it had little appeal for her children, hungry for excitement and experience, and made aware of a more complex society by their urban schooling. Postwar Australia was a society transformed by the economic stimulus of the Second World War. In contrast to the cautious mentality inherited by the generation shaped by the Depression, we were agog with the excitement of prosperity, and the questions raised by Australia's wartime contact with American culture. We went to American movies, used American slang, and listened to American music.

The boys, reluctant to remain dependent on their widowed mother, seized the best jobs they could find, unaware that it was in their long-term interest to attend university and acquire professional training. In my mother's generation, higher education was a luxury available to a tiny elite. In ours, it would become a necessary doorway to opportunity. The choice of early employment meant that Bob and Barry did not find excitement and challenge in the fairly routine tasks which made up their jobs with woolbrokers. They sought excitement instead in music, and later in the world of fast cars and road racing. By reason of my gender, I was not marked out for a career connected with the land. Moreover, as our finances improved it was possible for my mother to dream that I would fulfill her ambition: attend university and become a doctor. So the stereotypes of gender worked in my favor. Unlike my brothers, I grew up knowing that my life would be lived in peacetime, and that it was an unspoken expectation that I would finish high school and attend the University of Sydney.

Chapter 2

William Faulkner

Barn Burning*

The store in which the Justice of the Peace's court was sitting smelled of cheese. The boy, crouched on his nail keg at the back of the crowded room, knew he smelled cheese, and more: from where he sat he could see the ranked shelves close-packed with the solid, squat, dynamic shapes of tin cans whose labels his stomach read, not from the lettering which meant nothing to his mind but from the scarlet devils and the silver curve of fish—this, the cheese which he knew he smelled and the hermetic meat which his intestines believed he smelled coming in intermittent gusts momentary and brief between the other constant one, the smell and sense just a little of fear because mostly of despair and grief, the old fierce pull of blood. He could not see the table where the Justice sat and before which his father and his father's enemy (*our enemy* he thought in that despair; *ours! mine and his both! He's my father!*) stood, but he could hear them, the two of them that is, because his father had said no word yet:

"But what proof have you, Mr. Harris?"

"I told you. The hog got into my corn. I caught it up and sent it back to him. He had no fence that would hold it. I told him so, warned him. The next time I put the hog in my pen. When he came to get it I gave him enough wire to patch up his pen. The next time I put the hog up and kept it. I rode down to his house and saw the wire I gave him still rolled on to the spool in his yard. I told him he could have the hog when he paid me a dollar pound fee. That evening a nigger came with the dollar and got the hog. He was a strange nigger. He said, 'He say to tell you wood and hay kin burn.' I said, 'What?' 'That whut he say to tell you,' the nigger said. 'Wood and hay kin burn.' That night my barn burned. I got the stock out but I lost the barn."

"Where is the nigger? Have you got him?"

"He was a strange nigger, I tell you. I don't know what became of him."

"But that's not proof. Don't you see that's not proof?"

"Get that boy up here. He knows." For a moment the boy thought too that the man meant his older brother until Harris said, "Not him. The little one. The boy," and, crouching, small for his age, small and wiry like his father, in patched and faded jeans even too small for him, with straight, uncombed, brown hair and eyes gray and wild as storm scud, he saw the men between himself and the table part and become a lane of grim faces, at the end of which he saw the Justice, a

*This selection is also featured in the model student essay in Chapter 5.

shabby, collarless, graying man in spectacles, beckoning him. He felt no floor under his bare feet; he seemed to walk beneath the palpable weight of the grim turning faces. His father, stiff in his black Sunday coat donned not for the trial but for the moving, did not even look at him. *He aims for me to lie,* he thought, again with that frantic grief and despair. *And I will have to do hit.*

"What's your name, boy?" the Justice said.

"Colonel Sartoris Snopes," the boy whispered.

"Hey?" the Justice said. "Talk louder. Colonel Sartoris? I reckon anybody named for Colonel Sartoris in this country can't help but tell the truth, can they?" The boy said nothing. *Enemy! Enemy!* he thought; for a moment he could not even see, could not see that the Justice's face was kindly nor discern that his voice was troubled when he spoke to the man named Harris: "Do you want me to question this boy?" But he could hear, and during those subsequent long seconds while there was absolutely no sound in the crowded little room save that of quiet and intent breathing it was as if he had swung outward at the end of a grape vine, over a ravine, and at the top of the swing had been caught in a prolonged instant of mesmerized gravity, weightless in time.

"No!" Harris said violently, explosively. "Damnation! Send him out of here!" Now time, the fluid world, rushed beneath him again, the voices coming to him again through the smell of cheese and sealed meat, the fear and despair and the old grief of blood:

"This case is closed. I can't find against you, Snopes, but I can give you advice. Leave this country and don't come back to it."

His father spoke for the first time, his voice cold and harsh, level, without emphasis: "I aim to. I don't figure to stay in a country among people who ..." he said something unprintable and vile, addressed to no one.

"That'll do," the Justice said. "Take your wagon and get out of this country before dark. Case dismissed."

His father turned, and he followed the stiff black coat, the wiry figure walking a little stiffly from where a Confederate provost's man's musket ball had taken him in the heel on a stolen horse thirty years ago, followed the two backs now, since his older brother had appeared from somewhere in the crowd, no taller than the father but thicker, chewing tobacco steadily, between the two lines of grim-faced men and out of the store and across the worn gallery and down the sagging steps and among the dogs and half-grown boys in the mild May dust, where as he passed a voice hissed:

"Barn burner!"

Again he could not see, whirling; there was a face in a red haze, moonlike, bigger than the full moon, the owner of it half again his size, he leaping in the red haze toward the face, feeling no blow, feeling no shock when his head struck the earth, scrabbling up and leaping again, feeling no blow this time either and tasting no blood, scrabbling up to see the other boy in full flight and himself already leaping into pursuit as his father's hand jerked him back, the harsh, cold voice speaking above him: "Go get in the wagon."

It stood in a grove of locusts and mulberries across the road. His two hulking sisters in their Sunday dresses and his mother and her sister in calico and sunbonnets were already in it, sitting on and among the sorry residue of the dozen and more movings which even the boy could remember—the battered stove, the broken beds and chairs, the clock inlaid with mother-of-pearl, which would not run, stopped at some fourteen minutes past two o'clock of a dead and forgotten day and time, which had been his mother's dowry. She was crying, though when she saw him she drew her sleeve across her face and began to descend from the wagon. "Get back," the father said.

"He's hurt. I got to get some water and wash his ..."

"Get back in the wagon," his father said. He got in too, over the tail-gate. His father mounted to the seat where the older brother already sat and struck the gaunt mules two savage blows with the peeled willow, but without heat. It was not even sadistic; it was exactly that same quality which in later years would cause his descendants to over-run the engine before putting a motor car into motion, striking and reining back in the same movement. The wagon went on, the store with its quiet crowd of grimly watching men dropped behind; a curve in the road hid it. *Forever* he thought. *Maybe he's done satisfied now, now that he has* ... stopping himself, not to say it aloud even to himself. His mother's hand touched his shoulder.

"Does hit hurt?" she said.

"Naw," he said. "Hit don't hurt. Lemme be."

"Can't you wipe some of the blood off before hit dries?" "I'll wash to-night," he said. "Lemme be, I tell you."

The wagon went on. He did not know where they were going. None of them ever did or ever asked, because it was always somewhere, always a house of sorts waiting for them a day or two days or even three days away. Likely his father had already arranged to make a crop on another farm before he ... Again he had to stop himself. He (the father) always did. There was something about his wolflike independence and even courage when the advantage was at least neutral which impressed strangers, as if they got from his latent ravening ferocity not so much a sense of dependability as a feeling that his ferocious conviction in the rightness of his own actions would be of advantage to all whose interest lay with his.

That night they camped, in a grove of oaks and beeches where a spring ran. The nights were still cool and they had a fire against it, of a rail lifted from a nearby fence and cut into lengths—a small fire, neat, niggard almost, a shrewd fire; such fires were his father's habit and custom always, even in freezing weather. Older, the boy might have remarked this and wondered why not a big one; why should not a man who had not only seen the waste and extravagance of war, but who had in his blood an inherent voracious prodigality with material not his own, have burned everything in sight? Then he might have gone a step farther and thought that that was the reason: that niggard blaze was the living fruit of nights passed during those four years in the woods hiding from all men, blue or gray, with his strings of horses (captured horses, he called them). And older still, he might have divined the true reason: that the element of fire spoke to some deep mainspring of his father's being, as the element of steel or of powder spoke to other men, as the one weapon for the preservation of integrity, else breath were not worth the breathing, and hence to be regarded with respect and used with discretion.

But he did not think this now and he had seen those same niggard blazes all his life. He merely ate his supper beside it and was already half asleep over his iron plate when his father called him, and once more he followed the stiff back, the stiff and ruthless limp, up the slope and on to the starlit road where, turning, he could see his father against the stars but without face or depth—a shape black, flat, and bloodless as though cut from tin in the iron folds of the frockcoat which had not been made for him, the voice harsh like tin and without heat like tin:

"You were fixing to tell them. You would have told him." He didn't answer. His father struck him with the flat of his hand on the side of the head, hard but without heat, exactly as he had struck the two mules at the store, exactly as he would strike either of them with any stick in order to kill a horse fly, his voice still without heat or anger: "You're getting to be a man. You got to learn. You got to learn to stick to your own blood or you ain't going to have any blood to stick to you. Do you think either of them, any man there this morning, would? Don't you know all they wanted was a chance to get at me because they knew I had them beat? Eh?" Later, twenty years later, he was to tell himself, "If I had said they wanted only truth, justice, he would have hit me again." But now he said nothing. He was not crying. He just stood there. "Answer me," his father said.

"Yes," he whispered. His father turned. "Get on to bed. We'll be there tomorrow."

Tomorrow they were there. In the early afternoon the wagon stopped before a paintless two-room house identical almost with the dozen others it had stopped before even in the boy's ten years, and again, as on the other dozen occasions, his mother and aunt got down and began to unload the wagon, although his two sisters and his father and brother had not moved.

"Likely hit ain't fitten for hawgs," one of the sisters said.

"Nevertheless, fit it will and you'll hog it and like it," his father said. "Get out of them chairs and help your Ma unload."

The two sisters got down, big, bovine, in a flutter of cheap ribbons; one of them drew from the jumbled wagon bed a battered lantern, the other a worn broom. His father handed the reins to the older son and began to climb stiffly over the wheel. "When they get unloaded, take the team to the barn and feed them." Then he said, and at first the boy thought he was still speaking to his brother: "Come with me." "Me?" he said.

"Yes," his father said. "You."

"Abner," his mother said. His father paused and looked back—the harsh level stare beneath the shaggy, graying, irascible brows.

"I reckon I'll have a word with the man that aims to begin tomorrow owning me body and soul for the next eight months."

They went back up the road. A week ago—or before last night, that is—he would have asked where they were going, but not now. His father had struck him before last night but never before had he paused afterward to explain why;

it was as if the blow and the following calm, outrageous voice still rang, repercussed, divulging nothing to him save the terrible handicap of being young, the light weight of his few years, just heavy enough to prevent his soaring free of the world as it seemed to be ordered but not heavy enough to keep him footed solid in it, to resist it and try to change the course of its events.

Presently he could see the grove of oaks and cedars and the other flowering trees and shrubs where the house would be, though not the house yet. They walked beside a fence massed with honey-suckle and Cherokee roses and came to a gate swinging open between two brick pillars, and now, beyond a sweep of drive, he saw the house for the first time and at that instant he forgot his father and the terror and despair both, and even when he remembered his father again (who had not stopped) the terror and despair did not return. Because, for all the twelve movings, they had sojourned until now in a poor country, a land of small farms and fields and houses, and he had never seen a house like this before. *Hit's big as a courthouse* he thought quietly, with a surge of peace and joy whose reason he could not have thought into words, being too young for that: *They are safe from him. People whose lives are a part of this peace and dignity are beyond his touch, he no more to them than a buzzing wasp: capable of stinging for a little moment but that's all; the spell of this peace and dignity rendering even the barns and stable and cribs which belong to it impervious to the puny flames he might contrive* ... this, the peace and joy, ebbing for an instant as he looked again at the stiff black back, the stiff and implacable limp of the figure which was not dwarfed by the house, for the reason that it had never looked big anywhere and which now, against the serene columned backdrop, had more than ever that impervious quality of something cut ruthlessly from tin, depthless, as though, sidewise to the sun, it would cast no shadow. Watching him, the boy remarked the absolutely undeviating course which his father held and saw the stiff foot come squarely down in a pile of fresh droppings where a horse had stood in the drive and which his father could have avoided by a simple change of stride. But it ebbed only for a moment, though he could not have thought this into words either, walking on in the spell of the house, which he could even want but without envy, without sorrow, certainly never with that ravening and jealous rage which unknown to him walked in the ironlike black coat before him: *Maybe he will feel it too. Maybe it will even change him now from what maybe he couldn't help but be.*

They crossed the portico. Now he could hear his father's stiff foot as it came down on the boards with clocklike finality, a sound out of all proportion to the displacement of the body it bore and which was not dwarfed either by the white door before it, as though it had attained to a sort of vicious and ravening minimum not to be dwarfed by anything—the flat, wide, black hat, the formal coat of broadcloth which had once been black but which had now that friction-glazed greenish cast of the bodies of old house flies, the lifted sleeve which was too large, the lifted hand like a curled claw. The door opened so promptly that the boy knew the Negro must have been watching them all the time, an old man with neat grizzled hair, in a linen jacket, who stood barring the door with his body, saying, "Wipe yo foots, white man, fo you come in here. Major ain't home nohow."

"Get out of my way, nigger," his father said, without heat too, flinging the door back and the Negro also and entering, his hat still on his head. And now the boy saw the prints of the stiff foot on the doorjamb and saw them appear on the pale rug behind the machinelike deliberation of the foot which seemed to bear (or transmit) twice the weight which the body compassed. The Negro was shouting "Miss Lula! Miss Lula!" somewhere behind them, then the boy, deluged as though by a warm wave by a suave turn of carpeted stair and a pendant glitter of chandeliers and a mute gleam of gold frames, heard the swift feet and saw her too, a lady—perhaps he had never seen her like before either—in a gray, smooth gown with lace at the throat and an apron tied at the waist and the sleeves turned back, wiping cake or biscuit dough from her hands with a towel as she came up the hall, looking not at his father at all but at the tracks on the blond rug with an expression of incredulous amazement.

"I tried," the Negro cried. "I tole him to ..."

"Will you please go away?" she said in a shaking voice. "Major de Spain is not at home. Will you please go away?"

His father had not spoken again. He did not speak again. He did not even look at her. He just stood stiff in the center of the rug, in his hat, the shaggy iron-gray brows twitching slightly above the pebble-colored eyes as he appeared to examine the house with brief deliberation. Then with the same deliberation he turned; the boy watched him pivot on the good leg and saw the stiff foot drag round the arc of the turning, leaving a final long and fading smear. His father never looked at it, he never once looked down at the rug. The Negro held the door. It closed behind them, upon the hysteric and indistinguishable woman-wail. His father stopped at the top of the steps and scraped his boot clean on the edge of it. At the gate he stopped again. He stood for a moment, planted stiffly on the stiff foot, looking back at the house. "Pretty and white, ain't it?" he said. "That's sweat. Nigger sweat. Maybe it ain't white enough yet to suit him. Maybe he wants to mix some white sweat with it."

Two hours later the boy was chopping wood behind the house within which his mother and aunt and the two sisters (the mother and aunt, not the two girls, he knew that; even at this distance and muffled by walls the flat loud voices of the two girls emanated an incorrigible idle inertia) were setting up the stove to prepare a meal, when he heard the hooves and saw the linen-clad man on a fine sorrel mare, whom he recognized even before he saw the rolled rug in front of the Negro youth following on a fat bay carriage horse—a suffused, angry face vanishing, still at full gallop, beyond the corner of the house where his father and brother were sitting in the two tilted chairs; and a moment later, almost before he could have put the axe down, he heard the hooves again and watched the sorrel mare go back out of the yard, already galloping again. Then his father began to shout one of the sisters' names, who presently emerged backward from the kitchen door dragging the rolled rug along the ground by one end while the other sister walked behind it.

"If you ain't going to tote, go on and set up the wash pot," the first said.

"You, Sarty!" the second shouted. "Set up the wash pot!" His father appeared at the door, framed against that shabbiness, as he had been against that other bland perfection, impervious to either, the mother's anxious face at his shoulder.

"Go on," the father said. "Pick it up." The two sisters stooped, broad, lethargic; stooping, they presented an incredible expanse of pale cloth and a flutter of tawdry ribbons.

"If I thought enough of a rug to have to git hit all the way from France I wouldn't keep hit where folks coming in would have to tromp on hit," the first said. They raised the rug.

"Abner," the mother said. "Let me do it."

"You go back and git dinner," his father said. "I'll tend to this."

From the woodpile through the rest of the afternoon the boy watched them, the rug spread flat in the dust beside the bubbling wash-pot, the two sisters stooping over it with that profound and lethargic reluctance, while the father stood over them in turn, implacable and grim, driving them though never raising his voice again. He could smell the harsh homemade lye they were using; he saw his mother come to the door once and look toward them with an expression not anxious now but very like despair; he saw his father turn, and he fell to with the axe and saw from the corner of his eye his father raise from the ground a flattish fragment of field stone and examine it and return to the pot, and this time his mother actually spoke: "Abner. Abner. Please don't. Please, Abner."

Then he was done too. It was dusk; the whippoorwills had already begun. He could smell coffee from the room where they would presently eat the cold food remaining from the mid-afternoon meal, though when he entered the house he realized they were having coffee again probably because there was a fire on the hearth, before which the rug now lay spread over the backs of the two chairs. The tracks of his father's foot were gone. Where they had been were now long, water-cloudy scoriations resembling the sporadic course of a lilliputian mowing machine.

It still hung there while they ate the cold food and then went to bed, scattered without order or claim up and down the two rooms, his mother in one bed, where his father would later lie, the older brother in the other, himself, the aunt, and the two sisters on pallets on the floor. But his father was not in bed yet. The last thing the boy remembered was the depthless, harsh silhouette of the hat and coat bending over the rug and it seemed to him that he had not even closed his eyes when the silhouette was standing over him, the fire almost dead behind it, the stiff foot prodding him awake. "Catch up the mule," his father said.

When he returned with the mule his father was standing in the black door, the rolled rug over his shoulder. "Ain't you going to ride?" he said.

"No. Give me your foot."

He bent his knee into his father's hand, the wiry, surprising power flowed smoothly, rising, he rising with it, on to the mule's bare back (they had owned a saddle once; the boy could remember it though not when or where) and with the same effortlessness his father swung the rug up in front of him. Now in the starlight they retraced the afternoon's path, up the dusty road rife with honeysuckle, through the gate and up the black tunnel of the drive to the lightless house, where he sat on the mule and felt the rough warp of the rug drag across his thighs and vanish.

"Don't you want me to help?" he whispered. His father did not answer and now he heard again that stiff foot striking the hollow portico with that wooden and clock-like deliberation, that outrageous overstatement of the weight it carried. The rug, hunched, not flung (the boy could tell that even in the darkness) from his father's shoulder struck the angle of wall and floor with a sound unbelievably loud, thunderous, then the foot again, unhurried and enormous; a light came on in the house and the boy sat, tense, breathing steadily and quietly and just a little fast, though the foot itself did not increase its beat at all, descending the steps now; now the boy could see him.

"Don't you want to ride now?" he whispered. "We kin both ride now," the light within the house altering now, flaring up and sinking. *He's coming down the stairs now,* he thought. He had already ridden the mule up beside the horse block; presently his father was up behind him and he doubled the reins over and slashed the mule across the neck, but before the animal could begin to trot the hard, thin arm came round him, the hard, knotted hand jerking the mule back to a walk.

In the first red rays of the sun they were in the lot, putting plow gear on the mules. This time the sorrel mare was in the lot before he heard it at all, the rider collarless and even bareheaded, trembling, speaking in a shaking voice as the woman in the house had done, his father merely looking up once before stooping again to the hame he was buckling, so that the man on the mare spoke to his stooping back:

"You must realize you have ruined that rug. Wasn't there anybody here, any of your women ..." he ceased, shaking, the boy watching him, the older brother leaning now in the stable door, chewing, blinking slowly and steadily at nothing apparently. "It cost a hundred dollars. But you never had a hundred dollars. You never will. So I'm going to charge you twenty bushels of corn against your crop. I'll add it in your contract and when you come to the commissary you can sign it. That won't keep Mrs. de Spain quiet but maybe it will teach you to wipe your feet off before you enter her house again."

Then he was gone. The boy looked at his father, who still had not spoken or even looked up again, who was now adjusting the logger-head in the hame.

"Pap," he said. His father looked at him—the inscrutable face, the shaggy brows beneath which the gray eyes glinted coldly. Suddenly the boy went toward him, fast, stopping as suddenly. "You done the best you could!" he cried. "If he wanted hit done different why didn't he wait and tell you how? He won't git no twenty bushels! He won't git none! We'll gether hit and hide hit! I kin watch ..." "Did you put the cutter back in that straight stock like I told you?"

"No, sir," he said.

"Then go do it."

That was Wednesday. During the rest of that week he worked steadily, at what was within his scope and some which was beyond it, with an industry that did not need to be driven nor even commanded twice; he had this from his mother, with the difference that some at least of what he did he liked to do, such as splitting wood with the half-size axe which his mother and aunt had earned, or saved money somehow, to present him with at Christmas. In company with the two older women (and on one afternoon, even one of the sisters), he built pens for the shoat and the cow which were a part of his father's contract with the landlord, and one afternoon, his father being absent, gone somewhere on one of the mules, he went to the field.

They were running a middle buster now, his brother holding the plow straight while he handled the reins, and walking beside the straining mule, the rich black soil shearing cool and damp against his bare ankles, he thought *Maybe this is the end of it. Maybe even that twenty bushels that seems hard to have to pay for just a rug will be a cheap price for him to stop forever and always from being what he used to be;* thinking, dreaming now, so that his brother had to speak sharply to him to mind the mule: *Maybe he even won't collect the twenty bushels. Maybe it will all add up and balance and vanish—corn, rug, fire; the terror and grief, the being pulled two ways like between two teams of horses—gone, done with for ever and ever.*

Then it was Saturday; he looked up from beneath the mule he was harnessing and saw his father in the black coat and hat. "Not that," his father said. "The wagon gear." And then, two hours later, sitting in the wagon bed behind his father and brother on the seat, the wagon accomplished a final curve, and he saw the weathered paintless store with its tattered tobacco- and patent-medicine posters and the tethered wagons and saddle animals below the gallery. He mounted the gnawed steps behind his father and brother, and there again was the lane of quiet, watching faces for the three of them to walk through. He saw the man in spectacles sitting at the plank table and he did not need to be told this was a Justice of the Peace; he sent one glare of fierce, exultant, partisan defiance at the man in collar and cravat now, whom he had seen but twice before in his life, and that on a galloping horse, who now wore on his face an expression not of rage but of amazed unbelief which the boy could not have known was at the incredible circumstance of being sued by one of his own tenants, and came and stood against his father and cried at the Justice: "He ain't done it! He ain't burnt ..."

"Go back to the wagon," his father said.

"Burnt?" the Justice said. "Do I understand this rug was burned too?"

"Does anybody here claim it was?" his father said. "Go back to the wagon." But he did not, he merely retreated to the rear of the room, crowded as that other had been, but not to sit down this time, instead, to stand pressing among the motionless bodies, listening to the voices:

"And you claim twenty bushels of corn is too high for the damage you did to the rug?"

"He brought the rug to me and said he wanted the tracks washed out of it. I washed the tracks out and took the rug back to him."

"But you didn't carry the rug back to him in the same condition it was in before you made the tracks on it."

His father did not answer, and now for perhaps half a minute there was no sound at all save that of breathing, the faint, steady suspiration of complete and intent listening.

"You decline to answer that, Mr. Snopes?" Again his father did not answer: "I'm going to find against you, Mr. Snopes. I'm going to find that you were responsible for the injury to Major de Spain's rug and hold you liable for it. But twenty bushels of corn seems a little high for a man in your circumstances to have to pay. Major de Spain claims it cost a hundred dollars. October corn will be worth about fifty cents. I figure that if Major de Spain can stand a ninety-five dollar loss on something he paid cash for, you can stand a five-dollar loss you haven't earned yet. I hold you in damages to Major de Spain to the amount of ten bushels of corn over and above your contract with him, to be paid to him out of your crop at gathering time. Court adjourned."

It had taken no time hardly, the morning was but half begun. He thought they would return home and perhaps back to the field, since they were late, far behind all other farmers. But instead his father passed on behind the wagon, merely indicating with his hand for the older brother to follow with it, and crossed the road toward the blacksmith shop opposite, pressing on after his father, overtaking him, speaking, whispering up at the harsh, calm face beneath the weathered hat: "He won't git no ten bushels neither. He won't git one. We'll . . ." until his father glanced for an instant down at him, the face absolutely calm, the grizzled eyebrows tangled above the cold eyes, the voice almost pleasant, almost gentle:

"You think so? Well, we'll wait till October anyway."

The matter of the wagon—the setting of a spoke or two and the tightening of the tires—did not take long either, the business of the tires accomplished by driving the wagon into the spring branch behind the shop and letting it stand there, the mules nuzzling into the water from time to time, and the boy on the seat with the idle reins, looking up the slope and through the sooty tunnel of the shed where the slow hammer rang and where his father sat on an upended cypress bolt, easily, either talking or listening, still sitting there when the boy brought the dripping wagon up out of the branch and halted it before the door.

"Take them on to the shade and hitch," his father said. He did so and returned. His father and the smith and a third man squatting on his heels inside the door were talking, about crops and animals; the boy, squatting too in the ammoniac dust and hoof-parings and scales of rust, heard his father tell a long and unhurried story out of the time before the birth of the older brother even when he had been a professional horsetrader. And then his father came up beside him where he stood before a tattered last year's circus poster on the other side of the store, gazing rapt and quiet at the scarlet horses, the incredible poisings and convolutions of tulle and tights and the painted leers of comedians, and said, "It's time to eat."

But not at home. Squatting beside his brother against the front wall, he watched his father emerge from the store and produce from a paper sack a segment of cheese and divide it carefully and deliberately into three with his pocket knife and produce crackers from the same sack. They all three squatted on the gallery and ate, slowly, without talking; then in the store again, they drank from a tin dipper tepid water smelling of the cedar bucket and of living beech trees.

And still they did not go home. It was a horse lot this time, a tall rail fence upon and along which men stood and sat and out of which one by one horses were led, to be walked and trotted and then cantered back and forth along the road while the slow swapping and buying went on and the sun began to slant westward, they—the three of them—watching and listening, the older brother with his muddy eyes and his steady, inevitable tobacco, the father commenting now and then on certain of the animals, to no one in particular.

It was after sundown when they reached home. They ate supper by lamplight, then, sitting on the doorstep, the boy watched the night fully accomplish, listening to the whippoorwills and the frogs, when he heard his mother's voice: "Abner! No! No! Oh, God. Oh, God. Abner!" and he rose, whirled, and saw the altered light through the door where a candle stub now burned in a bottle neck on the table and his father, still in the hat and coat, at once formal and burlesque as though dressed carefully for some shabby and ceremonial violence, emptying the reservoir of the lamp back into the five-gallon kerosene can from which it had been filled, while the mother tugged at his arm until he shifted the lamp to the other hand and flung her back, not savagely or viciously, just hard, into the wall, her hands flung out against the wall for balance, her mouth open and in her face the same quality of hopeless despair as had been in her voice. Then his father saw him standing in the door.

"Go to the barn and get that can of oil we were oiling the wagon with," he said. The boy did not move. Then he could speak.

"What ..." he cried. "What are you ..."

"Go get that oil," his father said. "Go."

Then he was moving, running, outside the house, toward the stable: this the old habit, the old blood which he had not been permitted to choose for himself, which had been bequeathed him willy nilly and which had run for so long (and who knew where, battening on what of outrage and savagery and lust) before it came to him. *I could keep on,* he thought. *I could run on and on and never look back, never need to see his face again. Only I can't. I can't,* the rusted can in his hand now, the liquid sploshing in it as he ran back to the house and into it, into the sound of his mother's weeping in the next room, and handed the can to his father.

"Ain't you going to even send a nigger?" he cried. "At least you sent a nigger before!"

This time his father didn't strike him. The hand came even faster than the blow had, the same hand which had set the can on the table with almost excruciating care flashing from the can toward him too quick for him to follow it, gripping him by the back of his shirt and on to tiptoe before he had seen it quit the can, the face stooping at him in breathless and frozen ferocity, the cold, dead voice speaking over him to the older brother who leaned against the table, chewing with that steady, curious, sidewise motion of cows:

"Empty the can into the big one and go on. I'll catch up with you."

"Better tie him up to the bedpost," the brother said.

"Do like I told you," the father said. Then the boy was moving, his bunched shirt and the hard, bony hand between his shoulder-blades, his toes just touching the floor, across the room and into the other one, past the sisters sitting with spread heavy thighs in the two chairs over the cold hearth, and to where his mother and aunt sat side by side on the bed, the aunt's arms about his mother's shoulders.

"Hold him," the father said. The aunt made a startled movement. "Not you," the father said. "Lennie. Take hold of him. I want to see you do it." His mother took him by the wrist. "You'll hold him better than that. If he gets loose don't you know what he is going to do? He will go up yonder." He jerked his head toward the road. "Maybe I'd better tie him."

"I'll hold him," his mother whispered.

"See you do then." Then his father was gone, the stiff foot heavy and measured upon the boards, ceasing at last.

Then he began to struggle. His mother caught him in both arms, he jerking and wrenching at them. He would be stronger in the end, he knew that. But he had no time to wait for it. "Lemme go!" he cried. "I don't want to have to hit you!"

"Let him go!" the aunt said. "If he don't go, before God, I am going up there myself!"

"Don't you see I can't?" his mother cried. "Sarty! Sarty! No! No! Help me, Lizzie!"

Then he was free. His aunt grasped at him but it was too late. He whirled, running, his mother stumbled forward on to her knees behind him, crying to the nearer sister: "Catch him, Net! Catch him!" But that was too late too, the sister (the sisters were twins, born at the same time, yet either of them now gave the impression of being, encompassing as much living meat and volume and weight as any other two of the family) not yet having begun to rise from the chair, her head, face, alone merely turned, presenting to him in the flying instant an astonishing expanse of young female features untroubled by any surprise even, wearing only an expression of bovine interest. Then he was out of the room, out of the house, in the mild dust of the starlit road and the heavy rifeness of honey-suckle, the pale ribbon unspooling with terrific slowness under his running feet, reaching the gate at last and turning in, running, his heart and lungs drumming, on up the drive toward the lighted house, the lighted door. He did not knock, he burst in, sobbing for breath, incapable for the moment of speech; he saw the astonished face of the Negro in the linen jacket without knowing when the Negro had appeared.

"De Spain!" he cried, panted. "Where's ..." then he saw the white man too emerging from a white door down the hall. "Barn!" he cried. "Barn!"

"What?" the white man said. "Barn?"

"Yes!" the boy cried. "Barn!"

"Catch him!" the white man shouted.

But it was too late this time too. The Negro grasped his shirt, but the entire sleeve, rotten with washing, carried away, and he was out that door too and in the drive again, and had actually never ceased to run even while he was screaming into the white man's face.

Behind him the white man was shouting, "My horse! Fetch my horse!" and he thought for an instant of cutting across the park and climbing the fence into the road, but he did not know the park nor how high the vine-massed fence might be and he dared not risk it. So he ran on down the drive, blood and breath roaring; presently he was in the road again though he could not see it. He could not hear either: the galloping mare was almost upon him before he heard her, and even then he held his course, as if the very urgency of his wild grief and need must in a moment more find him wings, waiting until the ultimate instant to hurl himself aside and into the weed-choked roadside ditch as the horse thundered past and on, for an instant in furious silhouette against the stars, the tranquil early summer night sky which, even before the shape of the horse and rider vanished, stained abruptly and violently upward: a long, swirling roar incredible and soundless, blotting the stars, and he springing up and into the road again, running again, knowing it was too late yet still running even after he heard the shot and, an instant later, two shots, pausing now without knowing he had ceased to run, crying "Pap! Pap!", running again before he knew he had begun to run, stumbling, tripping over something and scrabbling up again without ceasing to run, looking backward over his shoulder at the glare as he got up, running on among the invisible trees, panting, sobbing, "Father! Father!"

At midnight he was sitting on the crest of a hill. He did not know it was midnight and he did not know how far he had come. But there was no glare behind him now and he sat now, his back toward what he had called home for four days anyhow, his face toward the dark woods which he would enter when breath was strong again, small, shaking steadily in the chill darkness, hugging himself into the remainder of his thin, rotten shirt, the grief and despair now no longer terror and fear but just grief and despair. *Father. My father,* he thought. "He was brave!" he cried suddenly, aloud but not loud, no more than a whisper: "He was! He was in the war! He was in Colonel Sartoris' cav'ry!" not knowing that his father had gone to that war a private in the fine old European sense, wearing no uniform, admitting the authority of and giving fidelity to no man or army or flag, going to war as Malbrouck himself did: for booty—it meant nothing and less than nothing to him if it were enemy booty or his own.

The slow constellations wheeled on. It would be dawn and then sun-up after a while and he would be hungry. But that would be tomorrow and now he was only cold, and walking would cure that. His breathing was easier now and he decided to get up and go on, and then he found that he had been asleep because he knew it was almost dawn, the night almost over. He could tell that from the whippoorwills. They were everywhere now among the dark trees below him, constant and inflectioned and ceaseless, so that, as the instant for giving over to the day birds drew nearer and nearer, there was no interval at all between them. He got up. He was a little stiff, but walking would cure that too as it would the cold, and soon there would be the sun. He went on down the hill, toward the dark woods within which the liquid silver voices of the birds called unceasing—the rapid and urgent beating of the urgent and quiring heart of the late spring night. He did not look back.

Chapter 8 and Chapter 11

Robert Frost

Stopping by Woods on a Snowy Evening

Whose woods these are I think I know.
His house is in the village, though;
He will not see me stopping here
To watch his woods fill up with snow.

My little horse must think it queer
To stop without a farmhouse near
Between the woods and frozen lake
The darkest evening of the year.

He gives his harness bells a shake
To ask if there is some mistake.
The only other sound's the sweep
Of easy wind and downy flake.

The woods are lovely, dark, and deep,
But I have promises to keep,
And miles to go before I sleep,
And miles to go before I sleep.

Chapter 9

Ernest J. Gaines

The Sky Is Gray*

1

Go'n be coming in a few minutes. Coming round that bend down there full speed. And I'm go'n get out my handkerchief and wave it down, and we go'n get on it and go.

---

*This selection is also featured in the model student essay in Chapter 4.

I keep on looking for it, but Mama don't look that way no more. She's looking down the road where we just come from. It's a long old road, and far's you can see you don't see nothing but gravel. You got dry weeds on both sides, and you got trees on both sides, and fences on both sides, too. And you got cows in the pastures and they standing close together. And when we was coming out here to catch the bus I seen the smoke coming out of the cows's noses.

I look at my mama and I know what she's thinking. I been with Mama so much, just me and her, I know what she's thinking all the time. Right now it's home—Auntie and them. She's thinking if they got enough wood—if she left enough there to keep them warm till we get back. She's thinking if it go'n rain and if any of them go'n have to go out in the rain. She's thinking 'bout the hog—if he go'n get out, and if Ty and Val be able to get him back in. She always worry like that when she leaves the house. She don't worry too much if she leave me there with the smaller ones, 'cause she know I'm go'n look after them and look after Auntie and everything else. I'm the oldest and she say I'm the man.

I look at my mama and I love my mama. She's wearing that black coat and that black hat and she's looking sad. I love my mama and I want put my arm round her and tell her. But I'm not supposed to do that. She say that's weakness and that's cry-baby stuff, and she don't want no crybaby round her. She don't want you to be scared, either. 'Cause Ty's scared of ghosts and she's always whipping him. I'm scared of the dark, too, but I make 'tend I ain't. I make 'tend I ain't 'cause I'm the oldest, and I got to set a good sample for the rest. I can't ever be scared and I can't ever cry. And that's why I never said nothing 'bout my teeth. It's been hurting me and hurting me close to a month now, but I never said it. I didn't say it 'cause I didn't want act like a crybaby, and 'cause I know we didn't have enough money to go have it pulled. But, Lord, it been hurting me. And look like it wouldn't start till at night when you was trying to get yourself little sleep. Then soon 's you shut your eyes—ummm-ummm, Lord, look like it go right down to your heartstring.

"Hurting, hanh?" Ty'd say.

I'd shake my head, but I wouldn't open my mouth for nothing. You open your mouth and let that wind in, and it almost kill you.

I'd just lay there and listen to them snore. Ty there, right 'side me, and Auntie and Val over by the fireplace. Val younger than me and Ty, and he sleeps with Auntie. Mama sleeps round the other side with Louis and Walker.

I'd just lay there and listen to them, and listen to that wind out there, and listen to that fire in the fireplace. Sometimes it'd stop long enough to let me get little rest. Sometimes it just hurt, hurt, hurt. Lord, have mercy.

2

Auntie knowed it was hurting me. I didn't tell nobody but Ty, 'cause we buddies and he ain't go'n tell nobody. But some kind of way Auntie found out. When she asked me, I told her no, nothing was wrong. But she knowed it all the time. She told me to mash up a piece of aspirin and wrap it in some cotton and jugg it down in that hole. I did it, but it didn't do no good. It stopped for a little while, and started right back again. Auntie wanted to tell Mama, but I told her, "Uh-uh." 'Cause I knowed we didn't have any money, and it just was go'n make her mad again. So Auntie told Monsieur Bayonne, and Monsieur Bayonne came over to the house and told me to kneel down 'side him on the fireplace. He put his finger in his mouth and made the Sign of the Cross on my jaw. The tip of Monsieur Bayonne's finger is some hard, 'cause he's always playing on that guitar. If we sit outside at night we can always hear Monsieur Bayonne playing on his guitar. Sometimes we leave him out there playing on the guitar.

Monsieur Bayonne made the Sign of the Cross over and over on my jaw, but that didn't do no good. Even when he prayed and told me to pray some, too, that tooth still hurt me.

"How you feeling?" he say.

"Same," I say.

He kept on praying and making the Sign of the Cross and I kept on praying, too.

"Still hurting?" he say. "Yes, sir."

Monsieur Bayonne mashed harder and harder on my jaw. He mashed so hard he almost pushed me over on Ty. But then he stopped.

"What kind of prayers you praying, boy?" he say. "Baptist," I say.

"Well, I'll be—no wonder that tooth still killing him. I'm going one way and he pulling the other. Boy, don't you know any Catholic prayers?"

"I know 'Hail Mary,'" I say.

"Then you better start saying it."

"Yes, sir."

He started mashing on my jaw again, and I could hear him praying at the same time. And, sure enough, after while it stopped hurting me.

Me and Ty went outside where Monsieur Bayonne's two hounds was and we started playing with them. "Let's go hunting," Ty say. "All right," I say; and we went on back in the pasture. Soon the hounds got on a trail, and me and Ty followed them all 'cross the pasture and then back in the woods, too. And then they cornered this little old rabbit and killed him, and me and Ty made them get back, and we picked up the rabbit and started on back home. But my tooth had started hurting me again. It was hurting me plenty now, but I wouldn't tell Monsieur Bayonne. That night I didn't sleep a bit, and first thing in the morning Auntie told me to go back and let Monsieur Bayonne pray over me some more. Monsieur Bayonne was in his kitchen making coffee when I got there. Soon's he seen me he knowed what was wrong.

"All right, kneel down there 'side that stove," he say. "And this time make sure you pray Catholic. I don't know nothing 'bout that Baptist, and I don't want know nothing 'bout him."

3

Last night Mama say, "Tomorrow we going to town."

"It ain't hurting me no more," I say. "I can eat anything on it."

"Tomorrow we going to town," she say.

And after she finished eating, she got up and went to bed. She always go to bed early now. 'Fore Daddy went in the Army, she used to stay up late. All of us sitting out on the gallery or round the fire. But now, look like soon's she finish eating she go to bed.

This morning when I woke up, her and Auntie was standing 'fore the fireplace. She say: "Enough to get there and get back. Dollar and a half to have it pulled. Twenty-five for me to go, twenty-five for him. Twenty-five for me to come back, twenty-five for him. Fifty cents left. Guess I get little piece of salt meat with that." "Sure can use it," Auntie say. "White beans and no salt meat ain't white beans."

"I do the best I can," Mama say.

They was quiet after that, and I made 'tend I was still sleep.

"James, hit the floor," Auntie say.

I still made 'tend I was asleep. I didn't want them to know I was listening.

"All right," Auntie say, shaking me by the shoulder. "Come on. Today's the day."

I pushed the cover down to get out, and Ty grabbed it and pulled it back.

"You, too, Ty," Auntie say.

"I ain't getting no teef pulled," Ty say.

"Don't mean it ain't time to get up," Auntie say. "Hit it, Ty."

Ty got up grumbling.

"James, you hurry up and get in your clothes and eat your food," Auntie say. "What time y'all coming back?" she say to Mama.

"That 'leven o'clock bus," Mama say. "Got to get back in that field this evening."

"Get a move on you, James," Auntie say.

I went in the kitchen and washed my face, then I ate my breakfast. I was having bread and syrup. The bread was warm and hard and tasted good. And I tried to make it last a long time.

Ty came back there grumbling and mad at me.

"Got to get up," he say. "I ain't having no teefes pulled. What I got to be getting up for?"

Ty poured some syrup in his pan and got a piece of bread. He didn't wash his hands, neither his face, and I could see that white stuff in his eyes.

"You the one getting your teef pulled," he say. "What I got to get up for. I bet if I was getting a teef pulled, you wouldn't be getting up. Shucks; syrup again. I'm getting tired of this old syrup. Syrup, syrup, syrup. I'm go'n take with the sugar diabetes. I want me some bacon sometime."

"Go out in the field and work and you can have your bacon," Auntie say. She stood in the middle door looking at Ty. "You better be glad you got syrup. Some people ain't got that—hard's time is."

"Shucks," Ty say. "How can I be strong."

"I don't know too much 'bout your strength," Auntie say; "but I know where you go'n be hot at, you keep that grumbling up. James, get a move on you; your mama waiting."

I ate my last piece of bread and went in the front room. Mama was standing 'fore the fireplace warming her hands. I put on my coat and my cap, and we left the house.

4

I look down there again, but it still ain't coming. I almost say, "It ain't coming yet," but I keep my mouth shut. 'Cause that's something else she don't like. She don't like for you to say something just for nothing. She can see it ain't coming, I can see it ain't coming, so why say it ain't coming. I don't say it, I turn and look at the river that's back of us. It's so cold the smoke's just raising up from the water. I see a bunch of pool-doos not too far out—just on the other side the lilies. I'm wondering if you can eat pool-doos. I ain't too sure, 'cause I ain't never ate none. But I done ate owls and blackbirds, and I done ate redbirds, too. I didn't want kill the redbirds, but she made me kill them. They had two of them back there. One in my trap, one in Ty's trap. Me and Ty was go'n play with them and let them go, but she made me kill them 'cause we needed the food.

"I can't," I say. "I can't."

"Here," she say. "Take it."

"I can't," I say. "I can't. I can't kill him, Mama, please."

"Here," she say. "Take this fork, James."

"Please, Mama, I can't kill him," I say.

I could tell she was go'n hit me. I jerked back, but I didn't jerk back soon enough.

"Take it," she say.

I took it and reached in for him, but he kept on hopping to the back.

"I can't, Mama," I say. The water just kept on running down my face. "I can't," I say.

"Get him out of there," she say.

I reached in for him and he kept on hopping to the back. Then I reached in farther, and he pecked me on the hand.

"I can't, Mama," I say.

She slapped me again.

I reached in again, but he kept on hopping out my way. Then he hopped to one side and I reached there. The fork got him on the leg and I heard his leg pop. I pulled my hand but 'cause I had hurt him.

"Give it here," she say, and jerked the fork out my hand.

She reached in and got the little bird right in the neck. I heard the fork go in his neck, and I heard it go in the ground. She brought him out and helt him right in front of me.

"That's one," she say. She shook him off and gived me the fork. "Get the other one."

"I can't, Mama," I say. "I'll do anything, but don't make me do that."

She went to the corner of the fence and broke the biggest switch over there she could find. I knelt 'side the trap, crying.

"Get him out of there," she say.

"I can't, Mama."

She started hitting me 'cross the back. I went down on the ground, crying.

"Get him," she say.

"Octavia?" Auntie say.

'Cause she had come out of the house and she was standing by the tree looking at us.

"Get him out of there," Mama say.

"Octavia," Auntie say, "explain to him. Explain to him. Just don't beat him. Explain to him."

But she hit me and hit me and hit me.

I'm still young—I ain't no more than eight; but I know now; I know why I had to do it. (They was so little, though. They was so little. I 'member how I picked the feathers off them and cleaned them and helt them over the fire. Then we all ate them. Ain't had but a little bitty piece each, but we all had a little bitty piece, and everybody just looked at me 'cause they was so proud.) Suppose she had to go away? That's why I had to do it. Suppose she had to go away like Daddy went away? Then who was go'n look after us? They had to be somebody left to carry on. I didn't know it then, but I know it now. Auntie and Monsieur Bayonne talked to me and made me see.

5

Time I see it I get out my handkerchief and start waving. It's still 'way down there, but I keep waving anyhow. Then it come up and stop and me and Mama get on. Mama tell me go sit in the back while she pay. I do like she say, and the people look at me. When I pass the little sign that say "White" and "Colored," I start looking for a seat. I just see one of them back there, but I don't take it, 'cause I want my mama to sit down herself. She comes in the back and sit down, and I lean on the seat. They got seats in the front, but I know I can't sit there, 'cause I have to sit back of the sign. Anyhow, I don't want sit there if my mama go'n sit back here.

They got a lady sitting 'side my mama and she looks at me and smiles little bit. I smile back, but I don't open my mouth, 'cause the wind'll get in and make that tooth ache. The lady take out a pack of gum and reach me a slice, but I shake my head. The lady just can't understand why a little boy'll turn down gum, and she reach me a slice again. This time I point to my jaw. The lady understands and smiles little bit, and I smile little bit, but I don't open my mouth, though.

They got a girl sitting 'cross from me. She got on a red overcoat and her hair's plaited in one big plait. First, I make 'tend I don't see her over there, but then I start looking at her little bit. She make 'tend she don't see me, either, but I catch her looking that way. She got a cold, and every now and then she h'ist that little handkerchief to her nose. She ought to blow it, but she don't. Must think she's too much a lady or something.

Every time she h'ist that little handkerchief, the lady 'side her say something in her ear. She shakes her head and lays her hands in her lap again. Then I catch her kind of looking where I'm at. I smile at her little bit. But think she'll smile back? Uh-uh. She just turn up her little old nose and turn her head. Well, I show her both of us can turn us head. I turn mine too and look out at the river.

The river is gray. The sky is gray. They have pool-doos on the water. The water is wavy, and the pool-doos go up and down. The bus go round a turn, and you got plenty trees hiding the river. Then the bus go round another turn, and I can see the river again.

I look toward the front where all the white people sitting. Then I look at that little old gal again. I don't look right at her, 'cause I don't want all them people to know I love her. I just look at her little bit, like I'm looking out that window over there. But she knows I'm looking that way, and she kind of look at me, too. The lady sitting 'side her catch her this time, and she leans over and says something in her ear.

"I don't love him nothing," that little old gal says out loud.

Everybody back there hear her mouth, and all of them look at us and laugh.

"I don't love you, either," I say. "So you don't have to turn up your nose, Miss."

"You the one looking," she say.

"I wasn't looking at you," I say. "I was looking out that window, there."

"Out that window, my foot," she say. "I seen you. Everytime I turned round you was looking at me."

"You must of been looking yourself if you seen me all them times," I say.

"Shucks," she say, "I got me all kind of boyfriends."

"I got girlfriends, too," I say.

"Well, I just don't want you getting your hopes up," she say.

I don't say no more to that little old gal 'cause I don't want have to bust her in the mouth. I lean on the seat where Mama sitting, and I don't even look that way no more. When we get to Bayonne, she jugg her little old tongue out at me. I make 'tend I'm go'n hit her, and she duck down 'side her mama. And all the people laugh at us again.

6

Me and Mama get off and start walking in town. Bayonne is a little bitty town. Baton Rouge is a hundred times bigger than Bayonne. I went to Baton Rouge once—me, Ty, Mama, and Daddy. But that was 'way back yonder, 'fore Daddy went in the Army. I wonder when we go'n see him again. I wonder when. Look like he ain't ever coming back home.... Even the pavement all cracked in Bayonne. Got grass shooting right out the sidewalk. Got weeds in the ditch, too; just like they got at home.

It's some cold in Bayonne. Look like it's colder than it is home. The wind blows in my face, and I feel that stuff running down my nose. I sniff. Mama says use that handkerchief. I blow my nose and put it back.

We pass a school and I see them white children playing in the yard. Big old red school, and them children just running and playing. Then we pass a café, and

I see a bunch of people in there eating. I wish I was in there 'cause I'm cold. Mama tells me keep my eyes in front where they belong.

We pass stores that's got dummies, and we pass another café, and then we pass a shoe shop, and that bald-head man in there fixing on a shoe. I look at him and I butt into that white lady, and Mama jerks me in front and tells me stay there.

We come up to the courthouse, and I see the flag waving there. This flag ain't like the one we got at school. This one here ain't got but a handful of stars. One at school got a big pile of stars—one for every state. We pass it and we turn and there it is—the dentist office. Me and Mama go in, and they got people sitting everywhere you look. They even got a little boy in there younger than me.

Me and Mama sit on that bench, and a white lady come in there and ask me what my name is. Mama tells her and the white lady goes on back. Then I hear somebody hollering in there. Soon's that little boy hear him hollering, he starts hollering, too. His mama pats him and pats him, trying to make him hush up, but he ain't thinking 'bout his mama.

The man that was hollering in there comes out holding his jaw. He is a big old man and he's wearing overalls and a jumper.

"Got it, hanh?" another man asks him.

The man shakes his head—don't want open his mouth.

"Man, I thought they was killing you in there," the other man says. "Hollering like a pig under a gate."

The man don't say nothing. He just heads for the door, and the other man follows him.

"John Lee," the white lady says. "John Lee Williams."

The little boy juggs his head down in his mama's lap and holler more now. His mama tells him go with the nurse, but he ain't thinking 'bout his mama. His mama tells him again, but he don't even hear her. His mama picks him up and takes him in there, and even when the white lady shuts the door I can still hear little old John Lee.

"I often wonder why the Lord let a child like that suffer," a lady says to my mama. The lady's sitting right in front of us on another bench. She's got on a white dress and a black sweater. She must be a nurse or something herself, I reckon.

"Not us to question," a man says.

"Sometimes I don't know if we shouldn't," the lady says.

"I know definitely we shouldn't," the man says. The man looks like a preacher. He's big and fat and he's got on a black suit. He's got a gold chain, too.

"Why?" the lady says.

"Why anything?" the preacher says.

"Yes," the lady says. "Why anything?"

"Not us to question," the preacher says.

The lady looks at the preacher a little while and looks at Mama again.

"And look like it's the poor who suffers the most," she says. "I don't understand it."

"Best not to even try," the preacher says. "He works in mysterious ways—wonders to perform."

Right then little John Lee bust out hollering, and everybody turn they head to listen.

"He's not a good dentist," the lady says. "Dr. Robillard is much better. But more expensive. That's why most of the colored people come here. The white people go to Dr. Robillard. Y'all from Bayonne?"

"Down the river," my mama says. And that's all she go'n say, 'cause she don't talk much. But the lady keeps on looking at her, and so she says, "Near Morgan."

"I see," the lady says.

7

"That's the trouble with the black people in this country today," somebody else says. This one here's sitting on the same side me and Mama's sitting, and he is kind of sitting in front of that preacher. He looks like a teacher or somebody that goes to college. He's got on a suit, and he's got a book that he's been reading. "We don't question is exactly our problem," he says. "We should question and question and question—question everything."

The preacher just looks at him a long time. He done put a toothpick or something in his mouth, and he just keeps on turning it and turning it. You can see he don't like that boy with that book.

"Maybe you can explain what you mean," he says.

"I said what I meant," the boy says. "Question everything. Every stripe, every star, every word spoken. Everything."

"It 'pears to me that this young lady and I was talking 'bout God, young man," the preacher says.

"Question Him, too," the boy says.

"Wait," the preacher says. "Wait now."

"You heard me right," the boy says. "His existence as well as everything else. Everything."

The preacher just looks across the room at the boy. You can see he's getting madder and madder. But mad or no mad, the boy ain't thinking 'bout him. He looks at that preacher just's hard's the preacher looks at him.

"Is this what they coming to?" the preacher says. "Is this what we educating them for?"

"You're not educating me," the boy says. "I wash dishes at night so that I can go to school in the day. So even the words you spoke need questioning."

The preacher just looks at him and shakes his head.

"When I come in this room and seen you there with your book, I said to myself, 'There's an intelligent man.' How wrong a person can be."

"Show me one reason to believe in the existence of a God," the boys says.

"My heart tells me," the preacher says.

"'My heart tells me,'" the boys says. "'My heart tells me.' Sure, 'My heart tells me.' And as long as you listen to what your heart tells you, you will have only what the white man gives you and nothing more. Me, I don't listen to my heart. The purpose of the heart is to pump blood throughout the body, and nothing else."

"Who's your paw, boy?" the preacher says.

"Why?"

"Who is he?"

"He's dead."

"And your mon?"

"She's in Charity Hospital with pneumonia. Half killed herself, working for nothing."

"And 'cause he's dead and she's sick, you mad at the world?"

"I'm not mad at the world. I'm questioning the world. I'm questioning it with cold logic, sir. What do words like Freedom, Liberty, God, White, Colored mean? I want to know. That's why *you* are sending us to school, to read and to ask questions. And because we ask these questions, you call us mad. No sir, it is not us who are mad."

"You keep saying 'us'?"

"'Us.' Yes—us. I'm not alone."

The preacher just shakes his head. Then he looks at everybody in the room—everybody. Some of the people look down at the floor, keep from looking at him. I kind of look 'way myself, but soon's I know he done turn his head, I look that way again.

"I'm sorry for you," he says to the boy.

"Why?" the boy says. "Why not be sorry for yourself? Why are you so much better off than I am? Why aren't you sorry for these other people in here? Why not be sorry for the lady who had to drag her child into the dentist office? Why not be sorry for the lady sitting on that bench over there? Be sorry for them. Not for me. Some way or the other I'm going to make it."

"No, I'm sorry for you," the preacher says.

"Of course, of course," the boy says, nodding his head. "You're sorry for me because I rock that pillar you're leaning on."

"You can't ever rock the pillar I'm leaning on, young man. It's stronger than anything man can ever do." "You believe in God because a man told you to believe in God," the boy says. "A white man told you to believe in God. And why? To keep you ignorant so he can keep his feet on your neck."

"So now we the ignorant?" the preacher says.

"Yes," the boy says. "Yes." And he opens his book again.

The preacher just looks at him sitting there. The boy done forgot all about him. Everybody else make 'tend they done forgot the squabble, too.

Then I see that preacher getting up real slow. Preacher's a great big old man and he got to brace himself to get up. He comes over where the boy is sitting. He just stands there a little while looking down at him, but the boy don't raise his head.

"Get up, boy," preacher says.

The boy looks up at him, then he shuts his book real slow and stands up. Preacher just hauls back and hit him in the face. The boy falls back 'gainst the wall, but he straightens himself up and looks right back at that preacher.

"You forgot the other cheek," he says.

The preacher hauls back and hit him again on the other side. But this time the boy braces himself and don't fall.

"That hasn't changed a thing," he says.

The preacher just looks at the boy. The preacher's breathing real hard like he just run up a big hill. The boy sits down and opens his book again.

"I feel sorry for you," the preacher says. "I never felt so sorry for a man before."

The boy makes 'tend he don't even hear that preacher. He keeps on reading his book. The preacher goes back and gets his hat off the chair.

"Excuse me," he says to us. "I'll come back some other time. Y'all, please excuse me."

And he looks at the boy and goes out the room. The boy h'ist his hand up to his mouth one time to wipe 'way some blood. All the rest of the time he keeps on reading. And nobody else in there say a word.

8

Little John Lee and his mama come out the dentist office, and the nurse calls somebody else in. Then little bit later they come out, and the nurse calls another name. But fast's she calls somebody in there, somebody else comes in the place where we sitting, and the room stays full.

The people coming in now, all of them wearing big coats. One of them says something 'bout sleeting, another one says he hope not. Another one says he think it ain't nothing but rain. 'Cause, he says, rain can get awful cold this time of year.

All round the room they talking. Some of them talking to people right by them, some of them talking to people clear 'cross the room, some of them talking to anybody'll listen. It's a little bitty room, no bigger than us kitchen, and I can see everybody in there. The little old room's full of smoke, 'cause you got two old men smoking pipes over by that side door. I think I feel my tooth thumping me some, and I hold my breath and wait. I wait and wait, but it don't thump me no more. Thank God for that.

I feel like going to sleep, and I lean back 'gainst the wall. But I'm scared to go to sleep. Scared 'cause the nurse might call my name and I won't hear her. And Mama might go to sleep, too, and she'll be mad if neither one of us heard the nurse.

I look up at Mama. I love my mama. I love my mama. And when cotton come I'm go'n get her a new coat. And I ain't go'n get a black one, either. I think I'm go'n get her a red one.

"They got some books over there," I say. "Want read one of them?"

Mama looks at the books, but she don't answer me.

"You got yourself a little man there," the lady says.

Mama don't say nothing to the lady, but she must've smiled, 'cause I seen the lady smiling back. The lady looks at me a little while, like she's feeling sorry for me.

"You sure got that preacher out here in a hurry," she says to that boy.

The boy looks up at her and looks in his book again. When I grow up I want be just like him. I want clothes like that and I want keep a book with me, too.

"You really don't believe in God?" the lady says.

"No," he says.

"But why?" the lady says.

"Because the wind is pink," he says.

"What?" the lady says.

The boy don't answer her no more. He just reads in his book.

"Talking 'bout the wind is pink," that old lady says. She's sitting on the same bench with the boy and she's trying to look in his face. The boy makes 'tend the old lady ain't even there. He just keeps on reading. "Wind is pink," she says again. "Eh, Lord, what children go'n be saying next?"

The lady 'cross from us bust out laughing.

"That's a good one," she says. "The wind is pink. Yes sir, that's a good one."

"Don't you believe the wind is pink?" the boy says. He keeps his head down in the book.

"Course I believe it, honey," the lady says. "Course I do." She looks at us and winks her eye. "And what color is grass, honey?"

"Grass? Grass is black."

She bust out laughing again. The boy looks at her.

"Don't you believe grass is black?" he says.

The lady quits her laughing and looks at him. Everybody else looking at him, too. The place quiet, quiet.

"Grass is green, honey," the lady says. "It was green yesterday, it's green today, and it's go'n be green tomorrow."

"How do you know it's green?"

"I know because I know."

"You don't know it's green," the boy says. "You believe it's green because someone told you it was green. If someone had told you it was black you'd believe it was black."

"It's green," the lady says. "I know green when I see green."

"Prove it's green," the boy says.

"Sure, now," the lady says. "Don't tell me it's coming to that."

"It's coming to just that," the boy says. "Words mean nothing. One means no more than the other."

"That's what it all coming to?" that old lady says. That old lady got on a turban and she got on two sweaters. She got a green sweater under a black sweater. I can see the green sweater 'cause some of the buttons on the other sweater's missing.

"Yes ma'am," the boy says. "Words mean nothing. Action is the only thing. Doing. That's the only thing." "Other words, you want the Lord to come down here and show Hisself to you?" she says.

"Exactly, ma'am," he says.

"You don't mean that, I'm sure?" she says.

"I do, ma'am," he says.

"Done, Jesus," the old lady says, shaking her head.

"I didn't go 'long with that preacher at first," the other lady says; "but now—I don't know. When a person say the grass is black, he's either a lunatic or something's wrong."

"Prove to me that it's green," the boy says.

"It's green because the people say it's green."

"Those same people say we're citizens of these United States," the boy says.

"I think I'm a citizen," the lady says.

"Citizens have certain rights," the boy says. "Name me one right that you have. One right, granted by the Constitution, that you can exercise in Bayonne."

The lady don't answer him. She just looks at him like she don't know what he's talking 'bout. I know I don't.

"Things changing," she says.

"Things are changing because some black men have begun to think with their brains and not their hearts," the boy says.

"You trying to say these people don't believe in God?"

"I'm sure some of them do. Maybe most of them do. But they don't believe that God is going to touch these white people's hearts and change things tomorrow. Things change through action. By no other way."

Everybody sit quiet and look at the boy. Nobody says a thing. Then the lady 'cross the room from me and Mama just shakes her head.

"Let's hope that not all your generation feel the same way you do," she says.

"Think what you please, it doesn't matter," the boy says. "But it will be men who listen to their heads and not their hearts who will see that your children have a better chance than you had."

"Let's hope they ain't all like you, though," the old lady says. "Done forgot the heart absolutely."

"Yes ma'am, I hope they aren't all like me," the boy says. "Unfortunately, I was born too late to believe in your God. Let's hope that the ones who come after will have your faith—if not in your God, then in something else, something definitely that they can lean on. I haven't anything. For me, the wind is pink, the grass is black."

9

The nurse comes in the room where we all sitting and waiting and says the doctor won't take no more patients till one o'clock this evening. My mama jumps up off the bench and goes up to the white lady.

"Nurse, I have to go back in the field this evening," she says.

"The doctor is treating his last patient now," the nurse says. "One o'clock this evening." "Can I at least speak to the doctor?" my mama asks.

"I'm his nurse," the lady says.

"My little boy's sick," my mama says. "Right now his tooth almost killing him."

The nurse looks at me. She's trying to make up her mind if to let me come in. I look at her real pitiful. The tooth ain't hurting me at all, but Mama say it is, so I make 'tend for her sake.

"This evening," the nurse says, and goes on back in the office.

"Don't feel 'jected, honey," the lady says to Mama. "I been round them a long time—they take you when they want to. If you was white, that's something else; but we the wrong color."

Mama don't say nothing to the lady, and me and her go outside and stand 'gainst the wall. It's cold out there. I can feel that wind going through my coat. Some of the other people come out of the room and go up the street. Me and Mama stand there a little while and we start walking. I don't know where we going. When we come to the other street we just stand there.

"You don't have to make water, do you?" Mama says.

"No, ma'am," I say.

We go on up the street. Walking real slow. I can tell Mama don't know where she's going. When we come to a store we stand there and look at the dummies. I look at a little boy wearing a brown overcoat. He's got on brown shoes, too. I look at my old shoes and look at his'n again. You wait till summer, I say.

Me and Mama walk away. We come up to another store and we stop and look at them dummies, too. Then we go on again. We pass a café where the white people in there eating. Mama tells me keep my eyes in front where they belong, but I can't help from seeing them people eat. My stomach starts to growling 'cause I'm hungry. When I see people eating, I get hungry; when I see a coat, I get cold.

A man whistles at my mama when we go by a filling station. She makes 'tend she don't even see him. I look back and I feel like hitting him in the mouth. If I was bigger, I say; if I was bigger, you'd see.

We keep on going. I'm getting colder and colder, but I don't say nothing. I feel that stuff running down my nose and I sniff.

"That rag," Mama says.

I get it out and wipe my nose. I'm getting cold all over now—my face, my hands, my feet, everything. We pass another little café, but this'n for white people, too, and we can't go in there, either. So we just walk. I'm so cold now I'm 'bout ready to say it. If I knowed where we was going I wouldn't be so cold, but I don't know where we going. We go, we go, we go. We walk clean out of Bayonne. Then we cross the street and we come back. Same thing I seen when I got off the bus this morning. Same old trees, same old walk, same old weeds, same old cracked pave—same old everything.

I sniff again.

"That rag," Mama says.

I wipe my nose real fast and jugg that handkerchief back in my pocket 'fore my hand gets too cold. I raise my head and I can see David's hardware store. When we come up to it, we go in. I don't know why, but I'm glad.

It's warm in there. It's so warm in there you don't ever want to leave. I look for the heater, and I see it over by them barrels. Three white men standing round the heater talking in Creole. One of them comes over to see what my mama want.

"Got any axe handles?" she says.

Me, Mama and the white man start to the back, but Mama stops me when we come up to the heater. She and the white man go on. I hold my hands over the heater and look at them. They go all the way to the back, and I see the white man pointing to the axe handles 'gainst the wall. Mama takes one of them and shakes it like she's trying to figure how much it weighs. Then she rubs her hand over it from one end to the other end. She turns it over and looks at the other side, then she shakes it again, and shakes her head and puts it back. She gets another one and she does it just like she did the first one, then she shakes her head. Then she gets a brown one and do it that, too. But she don't like this one, either. Then she gets another one, but 'fore she shakes it or anything, she looks at me. Look like she's trying to say something to me, but I don't know what it is. All I know is I done got warm now and I'm feeling right smart better. Mama shakes this axe handle just like she did the others, and shakes her head and says something to the white man. The white man just looks at his pile of axe handles, and when Mama pass him to come to the front, the white man just scratch his head and follows her. She tells me come on and we go on out and start walking again.

We walk and walk, and no time at all I'm cold again. Look like I'm colder now 'cause I can still remember how good it was back there. My stomach growls and I suck it in to keep Mama from hearing it. She's walking right 'side me, and it growls so loud you can hear it a mile. But Mama don't say a word.

10

When we come up to the courthouse, I look at the clock. It's got quarter to twelve. Mean we got another hour and a quarter to be out here in the cold. We go and stand 'side a building. Something hits my cap and I look up at the sky. Sleet's falling.

I look at Mama standing there. I want stand close 'side her, but she don't like that. She say that's crybaby stuff. She say you got to stand for yourself, by yourself.

"Let's go back to that office," she says.

We cross the street. When we get to the dentist office I try to open the door, but I can't. I twist and twist, but I can't. Mama pushes me to the side and she twist the knob, but she can't open the door, either. She turns 'way from the door. I look at her, but I don't move and I don't say nothing. I done seen her like this before and I'm scared of her.

"You hungry?" she says. She says it like she's mad at me, like I'm the cause of everything.

"No, ma'am," I say.

"You want eat and walk back, or you rather don't eat and ride?"

"I ain't hungry," I say.

I ain't just hungry, but I'm cold, too. I'm so hungry and cold I want to cry. And look like I'm getting colder and colder. My feet done got numb. I try to work my toes, but I don't even feel them. Look like I'm go'n die. Look like I'm go'n stand right here and freeze to death. I think 'bout home. I think 'bout Val and Auntie and Ty and Louis and Walker. It's 'bout twelve o'clock and I know they eating dinner now. I can hear Ty making jokes. He done forgot 'bout getting up early this morning and right now he's probably making jokes. Always trying to make somebody laugh. I wish I was right there listening to him. Give anything in the world if I was home round the fire.

"Come on," Mama says.

We start walking again. My feet so numb I can't hardly feel them. We turn the corner and go on back up the street. The clock on the courthouse starts hitting for twelve.

The sleet's coming down plenty now. They hit the pave and bounce like rice. Oh, Lord; oh, Lord, I pray. Don't let me die, don't let me die, don't let me die, Lord.

11

Now I know where we going. We going back of town where the colored people eat. I don't care if I don't eat. I been hungry before. I can stand it. But I can't stand the cold.

I can see we go'n have a long walk. It's 'bout a mile down there. But I don't mind. I know when I get there I'm go'n warm myself. I think I can hold out. My hands numb in my pockets and my feet numb, too, but if I keep moving I can hold out. Just don't stop no more, that's all.

The sky's gray. The sleet keeps on falling. Falling like rain now—plenty, plenty. You can hear it hitting the pave. You can see it bouncing. Sometimes it bounces two times 'fore it settles.

We keep on going. We don't say nothing. We just keep on going, keep on going.

I wonder what Mama's thinking. I hope she ain't mad at me. When summer come I'm go'n pick plenty cotton and get her a coat. I'm go'n get her a red one.

I hope they'd make it summer all the time. I'd be glad if it was summer all the time—but it ain't. We got to have winter, too. Lord, I hate the winter. I guess everybody hate the winter.

I don't sniff this time. I get out my handkerchief and wipe my nose. My hands's so cold I can hardly hold the handkerchief.

I think we getting close, but we ain't there yet. I wonder where everybody is. Can't see a soul but us. Look like we the only two people moving round today. Must be too cold for the rest of the people to move round in.

I can hear my teeth. I hope they don't knock together too hard and make that bad one hurt. Lord, that's all I need, for that bad one to start off.

I hear a church bell somewhere. But today ain't Sunday. They must be ringing for a funeral or something.

I wonder what they doing at home. They must be eating. Monsieur Bayonne might be there with his guitar. One day Ty played with Monsieur Bayonne's guitar and broke one of the strings. Monsieur Bayonne was some mad with Ty. He say Ty wasn't go'n ever 'mount to nothing. Ty can go just like Monsieur Bayonne when he ain't there. Ty can make everybody laugh when he starts to mocking Monsieur Bayonne.

I used to like to be with Mama and Daddy. We used to be happy. But they took him in the Army. Now, nobody happy no more.... I be glad when Daddy comes home.

Monsieur Bayonne say it wasn't fair for them to take Daddy and give Mama nothing and give us nothing. Auntie say, "Shhh, Etienne. Don't let them hear you talk like that." Monsieur Bayonne say, "It's God truth. What they giving his children? They have to walk three and a half miles to school hot or cold. That's anything to give for a paw? She's got to work in the field rain or shine just to make ends meet. That's anything to give for a husband?" Auntie say, "Shhh, Etienne, shhh." "Yes, you right," Monsieur Bayonne say. "Best don't say it in front of them now. But one day they go'n find out. One day." "Yes, I suppose so," Auntie say. "Then what, Rose Mary?" Monsieur Bayonne say. "I don't know, Etienne," Auntie say. "All we can do is us job, and leave everything else in His hand ..."

We getting closer, now. We getting closer. I can even see the railroad tracks.

We cross the tracks, and now I see the café. Just to get in there, I say. Just to get in there. Already I'm starting to feel little better.

12

We go in. Ahh, it's good. I look for the heater; there 'gainst the wall. One of them little brown ones. I just stand there and hold my hands over it. I can't open my hands too wide 'cause they almost froze.

Mama's standing right 'side me. She done unbuttoned her coat. Smoke rises out of the coat, and the coat smells like a wet dog.

I move to the side so Mama can have more room. She opens out her hands and rubs them together. I rub mine together, too, 'cause this keep them from hurting. If you let them warm too fast, they hurt you sure. But if you let them warm just little bit at a time, and you keep rubbing them, they be all right every time.

They got just two more people in the café. A lady back of the counter, and a man on this side the counter. They been watching us ever since we come in.

Mama gets out the handkerchief and count up the money. Both of us know how much money she's got there. Three dollars. No, she ain't got three dollars, 'cause she had to pay us way up here. She ain't got but two dollars and a half left. Dollar and a half to get my tooth pulled, and fifty cents for us to go back on, and fifty cents worth of salt meat.

She stirs the money round with her finger. Most of the money is change 'cause I can hear it rubbing together. She stirs it and stirs it. Then she looks at the door. It's still sleeting. I can hear it hitting 'gainst the wall like rice.

"I ain't hungry, Mama," I say.

"Got to pay them something for they heat," she says.

She takes a quarter out the handkerchief and ties the handkerchief up again. She looks over her shoulder at the people, but she still don't move. I hope she don't spend the money. I don't want her spending it on me. I'm hungry, I'm almost starving I'm so hungry, but I don't want her spending the money on me.

She flips the quarter over like she's thinking. She's must be thinking 'bout us walking back home. Lord, I sure don't want walk home. If I thought it'd do any good to say something, I'd say it. But Mama makes up her own mind 'bout things.

She turns 'way from the heater right fast, like she better hurry up and spend the quarter 'fore she change her mind. I watch her go toward the counter. The man and the lady look at her, too. She tells the lady something and the lady walks away. The man keeps on looking at her. Her back's turned to the man, and she don't even know he's standing there.

The lady puts some cakes and a glass of milk on the counter. Then she pours up a cup of coffee and sets it 'side the other stuff. Mama pays her for the things and comes on back where I'm standing. She tells me sit down at the table 'gainst the wall.

The milk and the cakes's for me; the coffee's for Mama. I eat slow and I look at her. She's looking outside at the sleet. She's looking real sad. I say to myself, I'm go'n make all this up one day. You see, one day, I'm go'n make all this up. I want say it now; I want tell her how I feel right now; but Mama don't like for us to talk like that.

"I can't eat all this," I say.

They ain't got but just three little old cakes there. I'm so hungry right now, the Lord knows I can eat a hundred times three, but I want my mama to have one.

Mama don't even look my way. She knows I'm hungry, she knows I want it. I let it stay there a little while, then I get it and eat it. I eat just on my front teeth, though, 'cause if cake touch that back tooth I know what'll happen. Thank God it ain't hurt me at all today.

After I finish eating I see the man go to the juke box. He drops a nickel in it, then he just stand there a little while looking at the record. Mama tells me keep my eyes in front where they belong. I turn my head like she say, but then I hear the man coming toward us.

"Dance, pretty?" he says.

Mama gets up to dance with him. But 'fore you know it, she done grabbed the little man in the collar and done heaved him 'side the wall. He hit the wall so hard he stop the juke box from playing.

"Some pimp," the lady back of the counter says. "Some pimp."

The little man jumps up off the floor and starts toward my mama. 'Fore you know it, Mama done sprung open her knife and she's waiting for him.

"Come on," she says. "Come on. I'll gut you from your neighbo to your throat. Come on."

I go up to the little man to hit him, but Mama makes me come and stand 'side her. The little man looks at me and Mama and goes on back to the counter.

"Some pimp," the lady back of the counter says. "Some pimp." She starts laughing and pointing at the little man. Yes sir, you a pimp, all right. Yes sir-ree."

13

"Fasten that coat, let's go," Mama says.

"You don't have to leave," the lady says.

Mama don't answer the lady, and we right out in the cold gain. I'm warm right now—my hands, my ears, my feet—but know this ain't go'n last too long. It done sleet so much now you got ice everywhere you look.

We cross the railroad tracks, and soon's we do, I get cold. That wind goes through this little old coat like it ain't even there. I got on a shirt and a sweater under the coat, but that wind don't pay them no mind. I look up and I can see we got a long way to go. I wonder if we go'n make it 'fore I get too cold.

We cross over to walk on the sidewalk. They got just one sidewalk back here, and it's over there.

After we go just a little piece, I smell bread cooking. I look, then I see a baker shop. When we get closer, I can smell it more better. I shut my eyes and make 'tend I'm eating. But I keep them shut too long and I butt up 'gainst a telephone post. Mama grabs me and see if I'm hurt. I ain't bleeding or nothing and she turns me loose.

I can feel I'm getting colder and colder, and I look up to see how far we still got to go. Uptown is 'way up yonder. A half mile more, I reckon. I try to think of something. They say think and you won't get cold. I think of that poem, "Annabel Lee." I ain't been to school in so long—this bad weather—I reckon they done passed "Annabel Lee" by now. But passed it or not, I'm sure Miss Walker go'n make me recite it when I get there. That woman don't never forget nothing. I ain't never seen nobody like that in my life.

I'm still getting cold. "Annabel Lee" or no "Annabel Lee," I'm still getting cold. But I can see we getting closer. We getting there gradually.

Soon's we turn the corner, I see a little old white lady up in front of us. She's the only lady on the street. She's all in black and she's got a long black rag over her head.

"Stop," she says.

Me and Mama stop and look at her. She must be crazy to be out in all this bad weather. Ain't got but a few other people out there, and all of them's men.

"Y'all done ate?" she says.

"Just finish," Mama says.

"Y'all must be cold then?" she says.

"We headed for the dentist," Mama says. "We'll warm up when we get there."

"What dentist?" the old lady says. "Mr. Bassett?"

"Yes, ma'am," Mama says.

"Come on in," the old lady says. "I'll telephone him and tell him y'all coming."

Me and Mama follow the old lady in the store. It's a little bitty store, and it don't have much in there. The old lady takes off her head rag and folds it up.

"Helena?" somebody calls from the back.

"Yes, Alnest?" the old lady says.

"Did you see them?"

"They're here. Standing beside me."

"Good. Now you can stay inside."

The old lady looks at Mama. Mama's waiting to hear what she brought us in here for. I'm waiting for that, too.

"I saw y'all each time you went by," she says. "I came out to catch you, but you were gone."

"We went back of town," Mama says.

"Did you eat?"

"Yes, ma'am."

The old lady looks at Mama a long time, like she's thinking Mama might be just saying that. Mama looks right back at her. The old lady looks at me to see what I have to say. I don't say nothing. I sure ain't going 'gainst my mama.

"There's food in the kitchen," she says to Mama. "I've been keeping it warm."

Mama turns right around and starts for the door.

"Just a minute," the old lady says. Mama stops. "The boy'll have to work for it. It isn't free."

"We don't take no handout," Mama says.

"I'm not handing out anything," the old lady says. "I need my garbage moved to the front. Ernest has a bad cold and can't go out there."

"James'll move it for you," Mama says.

"Not unless you eat," the old lady says. "I'm old, but I have my pride, too, you know."

Mama can see she ain't go'n beat this old lady down, so she just shakes her head.

"All right," the old lady says. "Come into the kitchen."

She leads the way with that rag in her hand. The kitchen is a little bitty little old thing, too. The table and the stove just 'bout fill it up. They got a little room to the side. Somebody in there laying 'cross the bed—'cause I can see one of his feet. Must be the person she was talking to: Ernest or Alnest—something like that.

"Sit down," the old lady says to Mama. "Not you," she says to me. "You have to move the cans." "Helena?" the man says in the other room.

"Yes, Alnest?" the old lady says.

"Are you going out there again?"

"I must show the boy where the garbage is, Alnest," the old lady says.

"Keep that shawl over your head," the old man says.

"You don't have to remind me, Alnest. Come, boy," the old lady says.

We go out in the yard. Little old back yard ain't no bigger than the store or the kitchen. But it can sleet here just like it can sleet in any big back yard. And 'fore you know it, I'm trembling.

"There," the old lady says, pointing to the cans. I pick up one of the cans and set it right back down. The can's so light, I'm go'n see what's inside of it.

"Here," the old lady says. "Leave that can alone."

I look back at her standing there in the door. She's got that black rag wrapped round her shoulders, and she's pointing one of her little old fingers at me.

"Pick it up and carry it to the front," she says. I go by her with the can, and she's looking at me all the time. I'm sure the can's empty. I'm sure she could've carried it herself—maybe both of them at the same time. "Set it on the sidewalk by the door and come back for the other one," she says.

I go and come back, and Mama looks at me when I pass her. I get the other can and take it to the front. It don't feel a bit heavier than that first one. I tell myself I ain't go'n be nobody's fool, and I'm go'n look inside this can to see just what I been hauling. First, I look up the street, then down the street. Nobody coming. Then I look over my shoulder toward the door. That little old lady done slipped up there quiet 's mouse, watching me again. Look like she knowed what I was go'n do.

"Ehh, Lord," she says. "Children, children. Come in here, boy, and go wash your hands."

I follow her in the kitchen. She points toward the bathroom, and I go in there and wash up. Little bitty old bathroom, but it's clean, clean. I don't use any of her towels; I wipe my hands on my pants legs.

When I come back in the kitchen, the old lady done dished up the food. Rice, gravy, meat—and she even got some lettuce and tomato in a saucer. She even got a glass of milk and a piece of cake there, too. It looks so good, I almost start eating 'fore I say my blessing.

"Helena?" the old man says.

"Yes, Alnest?"

"Are they eating?"

"Yes," she says.

"Good," he says. "Now you'll stay inside."

The old lady goes in there where he is and I can hear them talking. I look at Mama. She's eating slow like she's thinking. I wonder what's the matter now. I reckon she's thinking 'bout home.

The old lady comes back in the kitchen.

"I talked to Dr. Bassett's nurse," she says. "Dr. Bassett will take you as soon as you get there."

"Thank you, ma'am," Mama says.

"Perfectly all right," the old lady says. "Which one is it?"

Mama nods toward me. The old lady looks at me real sad. I look sad, too.

"You're not afraid, are you?" she says.

"No, ma'am," I say.

"That's a good boy," the old lady says. "Nothing to be afraid of. Dr. Bassett will not hurt you."

When me and Mama get through eating, we thank the old lady again.

"Helena, are they leaving?" the old man says.

"Yes, Alnest."

"Tell them I say good-bye."

"They can hear you, Alnest."

"Good-bye both mother and son," the old man says. "And may God be with you."

Me and Mama tell the old man good-bye, and we follow the old lady in the front room. Mama opens the door to go out, but she stops and comes back in the store.

"You sell salt meat?" she says.

"Yes."

"Give me two bits worth."

"That isn't very much salt meat," the old lady says.

"That's all I have," Mama says.

The old lady goes back of the counter and cuts a big piece off the chunk. Then she wraps it up and puts it in a paper bag.

"Two bits," she says.

"That looks like awful lot of meat for a quarter," Mama says.

"Two bits," the old lady says. "I've been selling salt meat behind this counter twenty-five years. I think I know what I'm doing."

"You got a scale there," Mama says.

"What?" the old lady says.

"Weigh it," Mama says.

"What?" the old lady says. "Are you telling me how to run my business?"

"Thanks very much for the food," Mama says.

"Just a minute," the old lady says.

"James," Mama says to me. I move toward the door.

"Just one minute, I said," the old lady says.

Me and Mama stop again and look at her. The old lady takes the meat out of the bag and unwraps it and cuts 'bout half of it off. Then she wraps it up again and juggs it back in the bag and gives the bag to Mama. Mama lays the quarter on the counter.

"Your kindness will never be forgotten," she says. "James," she says to me.

We go out, and the old lady comes to the door to look at us. After we go a little piece I look back, and she's still there watching us.

The sleet's coming down heavy, heavy now, and I turn up my coat collar to keep my neck warm. My mama tells me turn it right back down.

"You not a bum," she says. "You a man."

Nadine Gordimer

Once upon a Time*

*This selection is featured in the model student essay in Chapter 9 and Chapter 10.

Someone has written to ask me to contribute to an anthology of stories for children. I reply that I don't write children's stories; and he writes back that at a recent congress/book fair/seminar a certain novelist said every writer ought to write at least one story for children. I think of sending a postcard saying I don't accept that I "ought" to write anything.

And then last night I woke up—or rather was awakened without knowing what had roused me.

A voice in the echo-chamber of the subconscious?

A sound.

A creaking of the kind made by the weight carried by one foot after another along a wooden floor. I listened. I felt the apertures of my ears distend with concentration. Again: the creaking. I was waiting for it; waiting to hear if it indicated that feet were moving from room to room, coming up the passage—to my door. I have no burglar bars, no gun under the pillow, but I have the same fears as people who do take these precautions, and my windowpanes are thin as rime, could shatter like a wineglass. A woman was murdered (how do they put it) in broad daylight in a house two blocks away, last year, and the fierce dogs who guarded an old widower and his collection of antique clocks were strangled before he was knifed by a casual laborer he had dismissed without pay.

I was staring at the door, making it out in my mind rather than seeing it, in the dark. I lay quite still—a victim already—the arrhythmia of my heart was fleeing, knocking this way and that against its body-cage. How finely tuned the senses are, just out of rest, sleep! I could never listen intently as that in the distractions of the day; I was reading every faintest sound, identifying and classifying its possible threat.

But I learned that I was to be neither threatened nor spared. There was no human weight pressing on the boards, the creaking was a buckling, an epicenter of stress. I was in it. The house that surrounds me while I sleep is built on undermined ground; far beneath my bed, the floor, the house's foundations, the stopes and passages of gold mines have hollowed the rock, and when some face trembles, detaches and falls, three thousand feet below, the whole house shifts slightly, bringing uneasy strain to the balance and counterbalance of brick, cement, wood and glass that hold it as a structure around me. The misbeats of my heart tailed off like the last muffled flourishes on one of the wooden xylophones made by the Chopi and Tsonga* migrant miners who might have been down there, under me in the earth at that moment. The stope where the fall was could have been disused, dripping water from its ruptured veins; or men might now be interred there in the most profound of tombs.

I couldn't find a position in which my mind would let go of my body—release me to sleep again. So I began to tell myself a story; a bedtime story.

In a house, in a suburb, in a city, there were a man and his wife who loved each other very much and were living happily ever after. They had a little boy, and they loved him very much. They had a cat and a dog that the little boy

*Chopi and Tsonga: two peoples from Mozambique, northeast of South Africa.

loved very much. They had a car and a caravan trailer for holidays, and a swimming-pool which was fenced so that the little boy and his playmates would not fall in and drown. They had a housemaid who was absolutely trustworthy and an itinerant gardener who was highly recommended by the neighbors. For when they began to live happily ever after they were warned, by that wise old witch, the husband's mother, not to take on anyone off the street. They were inscribed in a medical benefit society, their pet dog was licensed, they were insured against fire, flood damage and theft, and subscribed to the local Neighborhood Watch, which supplied them with a plaque for their gates lettered YOU HAVE BEEN WARNED over the silhouette of a would-be intruder. He was masked; it could not be said if he was black or white, and therefore proved the property owner was no racist.

It was not possible to insure the house, the swimming-pool or the car against riot damage. There were riots, but these were outside the city, where people of another color were quartered. These people were not allowed into the suburb except as reliable housemaids and gardeners, so there was nothing to fear, the husband told the wife. Yet she was afraid that some day such people might come up the street and tear off the plaque YOU HAVE BEEN WARNED and open the gates and stream in ... Nonsense, my dear, said the husband, there are police and soldiers and tear-gas and guns to keep them away. But to please her—for he loved her very much and buses were being burned, cars stoned, and schoolchildren shot by the police in those quarters out of sight and hearing of the suburb—he had electronically controlled gates fitted. Anyone who pulled off the sign YOU HAVE BEEN WARNED and tried to open the gates would have to announce his intentions by pressing a button and speaking into a receiver relayed to the house. The little boy was fascinated by the device and used it as a walkie-talkie in cops and robbers play with his small friends.

The riots were suppressed, but there were many burglaries in the suburb and somebody's trusted housemaid was tied up and shut in a cupboard by thieves while she was in charge of her employers' house. The trusted housemaid of the man and wife and little boy was so upset by this misfortune befalling a friend left, as she herself often was, with responsibility for the possessions of the man and his wife and the little boy that she implored her employers to have burglar bars attached to the doors and windows of the house, and an alarm system installed. The wife said, She is right, let us take heed of her advice. So from every window and door in the house where they were living happily ever after they now saw the trees and sky through bars, and when the little boy's pet cat tried to climb in by the fanlight to keep him company in his little bed at night, as it customarily had done, it set off the alarm keening through the house.

The alarm was often answered—it seemed—by other burglar alarms, in other houses, that had been triggered by pet cats or nibbling mice. The alarms called to one another across the gardens in shrills and bleats and wails that everyone soon became accustomed to, so that the din roused the inhabitants of the suburb no more than the croak of frogs and musical grating of cicadas' legs. Under cover of the electronic harpies' discourse intruders sawed the iron bars and broke into homes, taking away hi-fi equipment, television sets, cassette players, cameras and radios, jewelry and clothing, and sometimes were hungry enough to devour everything in the refrigerator or paused audaciously to drink the whiskey in the cabinets or patio bars. Insurance companies paid no compensation for single malt,* a loss made keener by the property owner's knowledge that the thieves wouldn't even have been able to appreciate what it was they were drinking.

Then the time came when many of the people who were not trusted housemaids and gardeners hung about the suburb because they were unemployed. Some importuned for a job: weeding or painting a roof; anything, *baas,** madam. But the man and his wife remembered the warning about taking on anyone off the street. Some drank liquor and fouled the street with discarded bottles. Some begged, waiting for the man or his wife to drive the car out of the electronically operated gates. They sat about with their feet in the gutters, under the jacaranda trees that made a green tunnel of the street—for it was a beautiful suburb, spoilt only by their presence—and sometimes they fell asleep lying right before the gates in the midday sun. The wife could never see anyone go hungry. She sent the trusted housemaid out with bread and tea, but the trusted housemaid said these were loafers and *tsotsis,** who would come and tie her and shut her in a cupboard. The husband said, She's right. Take heed of her advice. You only encourage them with your bread and tea. They are looking for their chance ... And he brought the little boy's tricycle from the garden into the house every night, because if the house was surely secure, once locked and with the alarm set, someone might still be able to climb over the wall or the electronically closed gates into the garden.

You are right, said the wife, then the wall should be higher. And the wise old witch, the husband's mother, paid for the extra bricks as her Christmas present to her son and his wife—the little boy got a Space Man outfit and a book of fairy tales.

But every week there were more reports of intrusion: in broad daylight and the dead of night, in the early hours of the morning, and even in the lovely summer twilight—a certain family was at dinner while the bedrooms were being ransacked upstairs. The man and his wife, talking of the latest armed robbery in the suburb, were distracted by the sight of the little boy's pet cat effortlessly arriving over the seven-foot wall, descending first with a rapid bracing of extended forepaws down on the sheer vertical surface, and then a graceful launch, landing with swishing tail within the property. The whitewashed wall was marked with the cat's comings and goings; and on the street side of the wall there were larger red-earth smudges that could have been made by the kind of broken running shoes, seen on the feet of unemployed loiterers, that had no innocent destination.

---

* ***Single malt:*** an expensive Scotch whiskey

* ***baas:*** boss

* ***tsotis:*** hooligans

When the man and wife and little boy took the pet dog for its walk round the neighborhood streets they no longer paused to admire this show of roses or that perfect lawn; these were hidden behind an array of different varieties of security fences, walls and devices. The man, wife, little boy and dog passed a remarkable choice: there was the low-cost option of pieces of broken glass embedded in cement along the top of walls, there were iron grilles ending in lance-points, there were attempts at reconciling the aesthetics of prison architecture with the Spanish Villa style (spikes painted pink) and with the plaster urns of neoclassical façades (twelve-inch pikes finned like zigzags of lightning and painted pure white). Some walls had a small board affixed, giving the name and telephone number of the firm responsible for the installation of the devices. While the little boy and the pet dog raced ahead, the husband and wife found themselves comparing the possible effectiveness of each style against its appearance; and after several weeks when they paused before this barricade or that without needing to speak, both came out with the conclusion that only one was worth considering. It was the ugliest but the most honest in its suggestion of the pure concentration-camp style, no frills, all evident efficacy. Placed the length of walls, it consisted of a continuous coil of stiff and shining metal serrated into jagged blades, so that there would be no way of climbing over it and no way through its tunnel without getting entangled in its fangs. There would be no way out, only a struggle getting bloodier and bloodier, a deeper and sharper hooking and tearing of flesh. The wife shuddered to look at it. You're right, said the husband, anyone would think twice … And they took heed of the advice on a small board fixed to the wall: Consult DRAGON'S TEETH The People For Total Security.

Next day a gang of workmen came and stretched the razor-bladed coils all round the walls of the house where the husband and wife and little boy and pet dog and cat were living happily ever after. The sunlight flashed and slashed, off the serrations, the cornice of razor thorns encircled the home, shining. The husband said, Never mind. It will weather. The wife said, You're wrong. They guarantee it's rust-proof. And she waited until the little boy had run off to play before she said, I hope the cat will take heed … The husband said, Don't worry, my dear, cats always look before they leap. And it was true that from that day on the cat slept in the little boy's bed and kept to the garden, never risking a try at breaching security.

One evening, the mother read the little boy to sleep with a fairy story from the book the wise old witch had given him at Christmas. Next day he pretended to be the Prince who braves the terrible thicket of thorns to enter the palace and kiss the Sleeping Beauty back to life: he dragged a ladder to the wall, the shining coiled tunnel was just wide enough for his little body to creep in, and with the first fixing of its razor-teeth in his knees and hands and head he screamed and struggled deeper into its tangle. The trusted housemaid and the itinerant gardener, whose "day" it was, came running, the first to see and to scream with him, and the itinerant gardener tore his hands trying to get at the little boy. Then the man and his wife burst wildly into the garden and for some reason (the cat, probably) the alarm set up wailing against the screams while the bleeding mass of the little boy was hacked out of the security coil with saws, wire-cutters, choppers, and they carried it—the man, the wife, the hysterical trusted housemaid and the weeping gardener—into the house.

Chapter 4

Nathaniel Hawthorne

Young Goodman Brown*

From The Complete Novels and Selected Tales of Nathaniel Hawthorne, *ed. Norman Holmes Pierson (New York: Random House, Modern Library, 1937), pp. 1033–42.*

Young Goodman Brown came forth at sunset into the street at Salem village; but put his head back, after crossing the threshold, to exchange a parting kiss with his young wife. And Faith, as the wife was aptly named, thrust her own pretty head into the street, letting the wind play with the pink ribbons of her cap while she called to Goodman Brown.

"Dearest heart," whispered she, softly and rather sadly, when her lips were close to his ear, "prithee put off your journey until sunrise and sleep in your own bed to-night. A lone woman is troubled with such dreams and such thoughts that she's afeard of herself sometimes. Pray tarry with me this night, dear husband, of all nights in the year."

"My love and my Faith," replied young Goodman Brown, "of all nights in the year, this one night must I tarry away from thee. My journey, as thou callest it, forth and back again, must needs be done 'twixt now and sunrise. What, my sweet, pretty wife, dost thou doubt me already, and we but three months married?"

"Then God bless you!" said Faith, with the pink ribbons; "and may you find all well when you come back."

"Amen!" cried Goodman Brown. "Say thy prayers, dear Faith, and go to bed at dusk, and no harm will come to thee."

So they parted; and the young man pursued his way until, being about to turn the corner by the meeting-house, he looked back and saw the head of Faith still peeping after him with a melancholy air, in spite of her pink ribbons.

"Poor little Faith!" thought he, for his heart smote him. "What a wretch am I to leave her on such an errand! She talks of dreams, too. Me-thought as she spoke there was trouble in her face, as if a dream had warned her what work is to be done tonight. But no, no; 't would kill her to think it. Well, she's a blessed angel on earth; and after this one night I'll cling to her skirts and follow her to heaven."

---

*This selection is also featured in the model student essay in Chapter 2.

With this excellent resolve for the future, Goodman Brown felt himself justified in making more haste on his present evil purpose. He had taken a dreary road, darkened by all the gloomiest trees of the forest, which barely stood aside to let the narrow path creep through, and closed immediately behind. It was all as lonely as could be; and there is this peculiarity in such a solitude, that the traveller knows not who may be concealed by the innumerable trunks and the thick boughs overhead; so that with lonely footsteps he may yet be passing through an unseen multitude.

"There may be a devilish Indian behind every tree," said Goodman Brown to himself; and he glanced fearfully behind him as he added, "What if the devil himself should be at my very elbow!" His head being turned back, he passed a crook of the road, and, looking forward again, beheld the figure of a man, in grave and decent attire, seated at the foot of an old tree. He arose at Goodman Brown's approach and walked onward side by side with him.

"You are late, Goodman Brown," said he. "The clock of the Old South was striking as I came through Boston, and that is full fifteen minutes agone."

"Faith kept me back a while," replied the young man, with a tremor in his voice, caused by the sudden appearance of his companion, though not wholly unexpected.

It was now deep dusk in the forest, and deepest in that part of it where these two were journeying. As nearly as could be discerned, the second traveller was about fifty years old, apparently in the same rank of life as Goodman Brown, and bearing a considerable resemblance to him, though perhaps more in expression than features. Still they might have been taken for father and son. And yet, though the elder person was as simply clad as the younger, and as simple in manner too, he had an indescribable air of one who knew the world, and who would not have felt abashed at the governor's dinner table or in King William's court, were it possible that his affairs should call him thither. But the only thing about him that could be fixed upon as remarkable was his staff, which bore the likeness of a great black snake, so curiously wrought that it might almost be seen to twist and wriggle itself like a living serpent. This, of course, must have been an ocular deception, assisted by the uncertain light.

"Come, Goodman Brown," cried his fellow-traveller, "this is a dull pace for the beginning of a journey. Take my staff, if you are so soon weary."

"Friend," said the other, exchanging his slow pace for a full stop, "having kept covenant by meeting thee here, it is my purpose now to return whence I came. I have scruples touching the matter thou wot'st of."

"Sayest thou so?" replied he of the serpent, smiling apart. "Let us walk on, nevertheless, reasoning as we go; and if I convince thee not thou shalt turn back. We are but a little way in the forest yet."

"Too far! too far!" exclaimed the goodman, unconsciously resuming his walk. "My father never went into the woods on such an errand, nor his father before him. We have been a race of honest men and good Christians since the days of the martyrs; and shall I be the first of the name of Brown that ever took this path and kept"—

"Such company, thou wouldst say," observed the elder person, interpreting his pause. "Well said, Goodman Brown! I have been as well acquainted with your family as with ever a one among the Puritans; and that's no trifle to say. I helped your grandfather, the constable, when he lashed the Quaker woman so smartly through the streets of Salem; and it was I that brought your father a pitch-pine knot, kindled at my own hearth, to set fire to an Indian village, in King Philip's war. They were my good friends, both; and many a pleasant walk have we had along this path, and returned merrily after midnight. I would fain be friends with you for their sake."

"If it be as thou sayest," replied Goodman Brown, "I marvel they never spoke of these matters; or, verily, I marvel not, seeing that the least rumor of the sort would have driven them from New England. We are a people of prayer, and good works to boot, and abide no such wickedness."

"Wickedness or not," said the traveller with the twisted staff, "I have a very general acquaintance here in New England. The deacons of many a church have drunk the communion wine with me; the selectmen of divers towns make me their chairman; and a majority of the Great and General Court are firm supporters of my interest. The governor and I, too—But these are state secrets."

"Can this be so?" cried Goodman Brown, with a stare of amazement at his undisturbed companion. "Howbeit, I have nothing to do with the governor and council; they have their own ways, and are no rule for a simple husbandman like me. But, were I to go on with thee, how should I meet the eye of that good old man, our minister, at Salem village? Oh, his voice would make me tremble both Sabbath day and lecture day."

Thus far the elder traveller had listened with due gravity; but now burst into a fit of irrepressible mirth, shaking himself so violently that his snake-like staff actually seemed to wriggle in sympathy.

"Ha! ha! ha!" shouted he again and again; then composing himself, "Well, go on, Goodman Brown, go on; but, prithee, don't kill me with laughing."

"Well, then, to end the matter at once," said Goodman Brown, considerably nettled, "there is my wife, Faith. It would break her dear little heart; and I'd rather break my own."

"Nay, if that be the case," answered the other, "e'en go thy ways, Goodman Brown. I would not for twenty old women like the one hobbling before us that Faith should come to any harm."

As he spoke he pointed his staff at a female figure on the path, in whom Goodman Brown recognized a very pious and exemplary dame, who had taught him his catechism in youth, and was still his moral and spiritual adviser, jointly with the minister and Deacon Gookin.

"A marvel, truly, that Goody Cloyse should be so far in the wilderness at nightfall," said he. "But with your leave, friend, I shall take a cut through the woods until we have left this Christian woman behind. Being a stranger to you, she might ask whom I was consorting with and whither I was going."

"Be it so," said his fellow-traveller. "Betake you to the woods, and let me keep the path."

Accordingly the young man turned aside, but took care to watch his companion, who advanced softly along the road until he had come within a staff's length of the old dame. She, meanwhile, was making the best of her way, with singular speed for so aged a woman, and mumbling some indistinct words—a prayer, doubtless—as she went. The traveller put forth his staff and touched her withered neck with what seemed the serpent's tail.

"The devil!" screamed the pious old lady.

"Then Goody Cloyse knows her old friend?" observed the traveller, confronting her and leaning on his writhing stick.

"Ah, forsooth, and is it your worship indeed?" cried the good dame. "Yea, truly is it, and in the very image of my old gossip, Goodman Brown, the grandfather of the silly fellow that now is. But—would your worship believe it?—my broomstick hath strangely disappeared, stolen, as I suspect, by that unhanged witch, Goody Cory, and that, too, when I was all anointed with the juice of smallage, and cinquefoil, and wolf's bane"—

"Mingled with fine wheat and the fat of a new-born babe," said the shape of old Goodman Brown.

"Ah, your worship knows the recipe," cried the old lady, cackling aloud. "So, as I was saying, being all ready for the meeting, and no horse to ride on, I made up my mind to foot it; for they tell me there is a nice young man to be taken into communion to-night. But now your good worship will lend me your arm, and we shall be there in a twinkling."

"That can hardly be," answered her friend. "I may not spare you my arm, Goody Cloyse; but here is my staff, if you will."

So saying, he threw it down at her feet, where, perhaps, it assumed life, being one of the rods which its owner had formerly lent to the Egyptian magi. Of this fact, however, Goodman Brown could not take cognizance. He had cast up his eyes in astonishment, and, looking down again, beheld neither Goody Cloyse nor the serpentine staff, but his fellow-traveller alone, who waited for him as calmly as if nothing had happened.

"That old woman taught me my catechism," said the young man; and there was a world of meaning in this simple comment.

They continued to walk onward, while the elder traveller exhorted his companion to make good speed and persevere in the path, discoursing so aptly that his arguments seemed rather to spring up in the bosom of his auditor than to be suggested by himself. As they went, he plucked a branch of maple to serve for a walking stick, and began to strip it of the twigs and little boughs, which were wet with evening dew. The moment his fingers touched them they became strangely withered and dried up as with a week's sunshine. Thus the pair proceeded, at a good free pace, until suddenly, in a gloomy hollow of the road, Goodman Brown sat himself down on the stump of a tree and refused to go any farther.

"Friend," said he, stubbornly, "my mind is made up. Not another step will I budge on this errand. What if a wretched old woman do choose to go to the devil when I thought she was going to heaven: is that any reason why I should quit my dear Faith and go after her?"

"You will think better of this by and by," said his acquaintance, composedly. "Sit here and rest yourself a while; and when you feel like moving again, there is my staff to help you along."

Without more words, he threw his companion the maple stick, and was as speedily out of sight as if he had vanished into the deepening gloom. The young man sat a few moments by the roadside, applauding himself greatly, and thinking with how clear a conscience he should meet the minister in his morning walk, nor shrink from the eye of good old Deacon Gookin. And what calm sleep would be his that very night, which was to have been spent so wickedly, but so purely and sweetly now, in the arms of Faith! Amidst these pleasant and praiseworthy meditations, Goodman Brown heard the tramp of horses along the road, and deemed it advisable to conceal himself within the verge of the forest, conscious of the guilty purpose that had brought him thither, though now so happily turned from it.

On came the hoof tramps and the voices of the riders, two grave old voices, conversing soberly as they drew near. These mingled sounds appeared to pass along the road, within a few yards of the young man's hiding-place; but, owing doubtless to the depth of the gloom at that particular spot, neither the travellers nor their steeds were visible. Though their figures brushed the small boughs by the wayside, it could not be seen that they intercepted, even for a moment, the faint gleam from the strip of bright sky athwart which they must have passed. Goodman Brown alternately crouched and stood on tiptoe, pulling aside the branches and thrusting forth his head as far as he durst without discerning so much as a shadow. It vexed him the more, because he could have sworn, were such a thing possible, that he recognized the voices of the minister and Deacon Gookin, jogging along quietly, as they were wont to do, when bound to some ordination or ecclesiastical council. While yet within hearing, one of the riders stopped to pluck a switch.

"Of the two, reverend sir," said the voice like the deacon's, "I had rather miss an ordination dinner than to-night's meeting. They tell me that some of our community are to be here from Falmouth and beyond, and others from Connecticut and Rhode Island, besides several of the Indian powwows, who, after their fashion, know almost as much deviltry as the best of us. Moreover, there is a goodly young woman to be taken into communion."

"Mighty well, Deacon Gookin!" replied the solemn old tones of the minister. "Spur up, or we shall be late. Nothing can be done, you know, until I get on the ground."

The hoofs clattered again; and the voices, talking so strangely in the empty air, passed on through the forest, where no church had ever been gathered or solitary Christian prayed. Whither, then, could these holy men be journeying so deep into the heathen wilderness? Young Goodman Brown caught hold of a tree for support, being ready to sink down on the ground, faint and overburdened with the heavy sickness of his heart. He looked up to the sky, doubting whether there really was a heaven above him. Yet there was the blue arch, and the stars brightening in it.

"With heaven above and Faith below, I will yet stand firm against the devil!" cried Goodman Brown.

While he still gazed upward into the deep arch of the firmament and had lifted his hands to pray, a cloud, though no wind was stirring, hurried across the zenith and hid the brightening stars. The blue sky was still visible, except directly overhead, where this black mass of cloud was sweeping swiftly northward. Aloft in the air, as if from the depths of the cloud, came a confused and doubtful sound of voices. Once the listener fancied that he could distinguish the accents of towns-people of his own, men and women, both pious and ungodly, many of whom he had met at the communion table, and had seen others rioting at the tavern. The next moment, so indistinct were the sounds, he doubted whether he had heard aught but the murmur of the old forest, whispering without a wind. Then came a stronger swell of those familiar tones, heard daily in the sunshine at Salem village, but never until now from a cloud of night. There was one voice of a young woman, uttering lamentations, yet with an uncertain sorrow, and entreating for some favor, which, perhaps, it would grieve her to obtain; and all the unseen multitude, both saints and sinners, seemed to encourage her onward.

"Faith!" shouted Goodman Brown, in a voice of agony and desperation; and the echoes of the forest mocked him, crying, "Faith! Faith!" as if bewildered wretches were seeking her all through the wilderness.

The cry of grief, rage, and terror was yet piercing the night, when the unhappy husband held his breath for a response. There was a scream, drowned immediately in a louder murmur of voices, fading into far-off laughter, as the dark cloud swept away, leaving the clear and silent sky above Goodman Brown. But something fluttered lightly down through the air and caught on the branch of a tree. The young man seized it, and beheld a pink ribbon.

"My Faith is gone!" cried he, after one stupefied moment. "There is no good on earth; and sin is but a name. Come, devil; for to thee is this world given."

And, maddened with despair, so that he laughed loud and long, did Goodman Brown grasp his staff and set forth again, at such a rate that he seemed to fly along the forest path rather than to walk or run. The road grew wilder and drearier and more faintly traced, and vanished at length, leaving him in the heart of the dark wilderness, still rushing onward with the instinct that guides mortal man to evil. The whole forest was peopled with frightful sounds—the creaking of the trees, the howling of wild beasts, and the yell of Indians; while sometimes the wind tolled like a distant church bell, and sometimes gave a broad roar around the traveller, as if all Nature were laughing him to scorn. But he was himself the chief horror of the scene, and shrank not from its other horrors.

"Ha! ha! ha!" roared Goodman Brown when the wind laughed at him. "Let us hear which will laugh loudest. Think not to frighten me with your deviltry. Come witch, come wizard, come Indian powwow, come devil himself, and here comes Goodman Brown. You may as well fear him as he fear you."

In truth, all through the haunted forest there could be nothing more frightful than the figure of Goodman Brown. On he flew among the black pines, brandishing his staff with frenzied gestures, now giving vent to an inspiration of horrid blasphemy, and now shouting forth such laughter as set all the echoes of the forest laughing like demons around him. The fiend in his own shape is less hideous than when he rages in the breast of man. Thus sped the demoniac on his course, until, quivering among the trees, he saw a red light before him, as when the felled trunks and branches of a clearing have been set on fire, and throw up their lurid blaze against the sky, at the hour of midnight. He paused, in a lull of the tempest that had driven him onward, and heard the swell of what seemed a hymn, rolling solemnly from a distance with the weight of many voices. He knew the tune; it was a familiar one in the choir of the village meeting-house. The verse died heavily away, and was lengthened by a chorus, not of human voices, but of all the sounds of the benighted wilderness pealing in awful harmony together. Goodman Brown cried out, and his cry was lost to his own ear by its unison with the cry of the desert.

In the interval of silence he stole forward until the light glared full upon his eyes. At one extremity of an open space, hemmed in by the dark wall of the forest, arose a rock, bearing some rude, natural resemblance either to an altar or a pulpit, and surrounded by four blazing pines, their tops aflame, their stems untouched, like candles at an evening meeting. The mass of foliage that had overgrown the summit of the rock was all on fire, blazing high into the night and fitfully illuminating the whole field. Each pendent twig and leafy festoon was in a blaze. As the red light arose and fell, a numerous congregation alternately shone forth, then disappeared in shadow, and again grew, as it were, out of the darkness, peopling the heart of the solitary woods at once.

"A grave and dark-clad company," quoth Goodman Brown.

In truth they were such. Among them, quivering to and fro between gloom and splendor, appeared faces that would be seen next day at the council board of the province, and others which, Sabbath after Sabbath, looked devoutly heavenward, and benignantly over the crowded pews, from the holiest pulpits in the land. Some affirm that the lady of the governor was there. At least there were high dames well known to her, and wives of honored husbands, and widows, a great multitude, and ancient maidens, all of excellent repute, and fair young girls, who trembled lest their mothers should espy them. Either the sudden gleams of light flashing over the obscure field bedazzled Goodman Brown, or he recognized a score of the church members of Salem village famous for their especial sanctity. Good old Deacon Gookin had arrived, and waited at the skirts of that venerable saint, his revered pastor. But, irreverently consorting with these grave, reputable, and pious people, these elders of the church, these chaste dames and dewy virgins, there were men of dissolute lives and women of spotted fame, wretches given over to all mean and filthy vice, and suspected even of horrid crimes. It was strange to see that the good shrank not from the wicked, nor were the sinners abashed by the saints. Scattered also among their pale-faced enemies were the Indian priests, or powwows, who had often scared their native forest with more hideous incantations than any known to English witchcraft.

"But where is Faith?" thought Goodman Brown; and, as hope came into his heart, he trembled.

Another verse of the hymn arose, a slow and mournful strain, such as the pious love, but joined to words which expressed all that our nature can conceive of sin, and darkly hinted at far more. Unfathomable to mere mortals is the lore of fiends. Verse after verse was sung; and still the chorus of the desert swelled between like the deepest tone of a mighty organ; and with the final peal of that dreadful anthem there came a sound, as if the roaring wind, the rushing streams, the howling beasts, and every other voice of the unconcerted wilderness were mingling and according with the voice of guilty man in homage to the prince of all. The four blazing pines threw up a loftier flame, and obscurely discovered shapes and visages of horror on the smoke wreaths above the impious assembly. At the same moment the fire on the rock shot redly forth and formed a glowing arch above its base, where now appeared a figure. With reverence be it spoken, the figure bore no slight similitude, both in garb and manner, to some grave divine of the New England churches.

"Bring forth the converts!" cried a voice that echoed through the field and rolled into the forest.

At the word, Goodman Brown stepped forth from the shadow of the trees and approached the congregation, with whom he felt a loathful brotherhood by the sympathy of all that was wicked in his heart. He could have well-nigh sworn that the shape of his own dead father beckoned him to advance, looking downward from a smoke wreath, while a woman, with dim features of despair, threw out her hand to warn him back. Was it his mother? But he had no power to retreat one step, not to resist, even in thought, when the minister and good old Deacon Gookin seized his arms and led him to the blazing rock. Thither came also the slender form of a veiled female, led between Goody Cloyse, that pious teacher of the catechism, and Martha Carrier, who had received the devil's promise to be queen of hell. A rampant hag was she. And there stood the proselytes beneath the canopy of fire.

"Welcome, my children," said the dark figure, "to the communion of your race. Ye have found thus young your nature and your destiny. My children, look behind you!" They turned; and flashing forth, as it were, in a sheet of flame, the fiend worshippers were seen; the smile of welcome gleamed darkly on every visage.

"There," resumed the sable form, "are all whom ye have reverenced from youth. Ye deemed them holier than yourselves, and shrank from your own sin, contrasting it with their lives of righteousness and prayerful aspirations heavenward. Yet here are they all in my worshipping assembly. This night it shall be granted you to know their secret deeds: how hoary-bearded elders of the church have whispered wanton words to the young maids of their households; how many a woman, eager for widows' weeds, has given her husband a drink at bedtime and let him sleep his last sleep in her bosom; how beardless youths have made haste to inherit their fathers' wealth; and how fair damsels—blush not, sweet ones—have dug little graves in the garden, and bidden me, the sole guest to an infant's funeral. By the sympathy of your human hearts for sin ye shall scent out all the places—whether in church, bedchamber, street, field, or forest—where crime has been committed, and shall exult to behold the whole earth one stain of guilt, one mighty blood spot. Far more than this. It shall be yours to penetrate, in every bosom, the deep mystery of sin, the fountain of all wicked arts, and which inexhaustibly supplies more evil impulses than human power—than my power at its utmost—can make manifest in deeds. And now, my children, look upon each other."

They did so; and, by the blaze of the hell-kindled torches, the wretched man beheld his Faith, and the wife her husband, trembling before that unhallowed altar.

"Lo, there ye stand, my children," said the figure, in a deep and solemn tone, almost sad with its despairing awfulness, as if his once angelic nature could yet mourn for our miserable race. "Depending upon one another's hearts, ye had still hoped that virtue were not all a dream. Now are ye undeceived. Evil is the nature of mankind. Evil must be your only happiness. Welcome again, my children, to the communion of your race."

"Welcome," repeated the fiend worshippers, in one cry of despair and triumph.

And there they stood, the only pair, as it seemed, who were yet hesitating on the verge of wickedness in this dark world. A basin was hollowed, naturally, in the rock. Did it contain water, reddened by the lurid light? or was it blood? or, perchance, a liquid flame? Herein did the shape of evil dip his hand and prepare to lay the mark of baptism upon their foreheads, that they might be partakers of the mystery of sin, more conscious of the secret guilt of others, both in deed and thought, than they could now be of their own. The husband cast one look at his pale wife, and Faith at him. What polluted wretches would the next glance show them to each other, shuddering alike at what they disclosed and what they saw!

"Faith! Faith!" cried the husband, "look up to heaven, and resist the wicked one."

Whether Faith obeyed he knew not. Hardly had he spoken when he found himself amid calm night and solitude, listening to a roar of the wind which died heavily away through the forest. He staggered against the rock, and felt it chill and damp; while a hanging twig, that had been all on fire, besprinkled his cheek with the coldest dew.

The next morning young Goodman Brown came slowly into the street of Salem village, staring around him like a bewildered man. The good old minister was taking a walk along the graveyard to get an appetite for breakfast and meditate his sermon, and bestowed a blessing, as he passed, on Goodman Brown. He shrank from the venerable saint as if to avoid an anathema. Old Deacon Gookin was at domestic worship, and the holy words of his prayer were heard through the open window. "What God doth the wizard pray to?" quoth Goodman Brown. Goody Cloyse, that excellent old Christian, stood in the early sunshine at her own lattice, catechizing a little girl who had brought her a pint of morning's milk. Goodman Brown snatched away the child as from the grasp of the fiend himself. Turning the corner by the meeting-house, he spied the head of Faith, with the pink ribbons, gazing anxiously forth, and bursting into such joy at sight of him that she skipped along the street and almost kissed her husband before the whole village. But Goodman Brown looked sternly and sadly into her face, and passed on without a greeting.

Had Goodman Brown fallen asleep in the forest and only dreamed a wild dream of a witch-meeting?

Be it so if you will; but, alas! it was a dream of evil omen for young Goodman Brown. A stern, a sad, a darkly meditative, a distrustful, if not a desperate man did he become from the night of that fearful dream. On the Sabbath day, when the congregation were singing a holy psalm, he could not listen because an anthem of sin rushed loudly upon his ear and drowned all the blessed strain. When the minister spoke from the pulpit with power and fervid eloquence, and, with his hand on the open Bible, of the sacred truths of our religion, and of saint-like lives and triumphant deaths, and of future bliss or misery unutterable, then did Goodman Brown turn pale, dreading lest the roof should thunder down upon the gray blasphemer and his hearers. Often, waking suddenly at midnight, he shrank from the bosom of Faith; and at morning or eventide, when the family knelt down at prayer, he scowled and muttered to himself, and gazed sternly at his wife, and turned away. And when he had lived long, and was borne to his grave a hoary corpse, followed by Faith, an aged woman, and children and grandchildren, a goodly procession, besides neighbors not a few, they carved no hopeful verse upon his tombstone, for his dying hour was gloom.

Langston Hughes

I, Too*

I, too, sing America.
I am the darker brother.
They send me to eat in the kitchen
When company comes,
But I laugh,
And eat well,
And grow strong.

Tomorrow,
I'll be at the table
When company comes.
Nobody'll dare
Say to me,
"Eat in the kitchen,"
Then.

Besides,
They'll see how beautiful I am
And be ashamed—

I, too, am America.

---

*This selection is featured in the model student essay in Chapter 10.

Langston Hughes

Theme for English B*

The instructor said,
Go home, and write a page tonight.
And let that page come out of you—
Then, it will be true.

I wonder if it's that simple?
I am twenty-two, colored, born in Winston-Salem.
I went to school there, then Durham, then here
to this college on the hill above Harlem.
I am the only colored student in my class.
The steps from the hill lead down into Harlem,
through a park, then I cross St. Nicholas,
Eighth Avenue, Seventh, and I come to the Y,
the Harlem Branch Y, where I take the elevator
up to my room, sit down, and write this page:

It's not easy to know what is true for you or me
at twenty-two, my age. But I guess I'm what
I feel and see and hear, Harlem, I hear you:
hear you, hear me—we two—you, me, talk on this page.
(I hear New York, too.) Me—who?
Well, I like to eat, sleep, drink, and be in love.
I like to work, read, learn, and understand life.
I like a pipe for a Christmas present,
or records—Bessie,* bop, or Bach.
I guess being colored doesn't make me *not* like
the same things other folks like who are other races.
So will my page be colored that I write?
Being me, it will not be white.
But it will be a part of you, instructor.
You are white—
yet a part of me, as I am a part of you.
That's American.
Sometimes perhaps you don't want to be a part of me.

---

*This selection is featured in the model student essay in Chapter 10.

*Biessie Smith: African-American blues singer (1898–1937).

Nor do I often want to be a part of you.
But we are, that's true!
As I learn from you,
I guess you learn from me—
although you're older—and white—
and somewhat more free.

This is my page for English B.

Chapter 10

Zora Neale Hurston

Excerpt from *The Eatonville Anthology*

From I Love Myself When I Am Laughing ... and Then Again When I Am Looking Mean and Impressive *by Zora Neale Hurston, edited by Alice Walker. New York: HarperCollins Publishers, 1979.*

1
The Pleading Woman

Mrs. Tony Roberts is the pleading woman. She just loves to ask for things. Her husband gives her all he can rake and scrape, which is considerably more than most wives get for their housekeeping, but she goes from door to door begging for things.

She starts at the store. "Mist' Clarke," she sing-songs in a high keening voice, "gimme lil' piece uh meat tuh boil a pot uh greens wid. Lawd knows me an' mah chillen is so hongry! Hits uh shame! Tony don't fee-ee-eee-ed me!"

Mr. Clarke knows that she has money and that her larder is well stocked, for Tony Roberts is the best provider on his list. But her keening annoys him and he rises heavily. The pleader at his elbow shows all the joy of a starving man being seated at a feast.

"Thass right Mist' Clarke. De Lawd loveth de cheerful giver. Gimme jes' a lil' piece 'bout dis big (indicating the width of her hand) an' de Lawd'll bless yuh."

She follows this angel-on-earth to his meat tub and superintends the cutting, crying out in pain when he refuses to move the knife over just a teeny bit mo'.

Finally, meat in hand, she departs, remarking on the meanness of some people who give a piece of salt meat only two-fingers wide when they were plainly asked for a hand-wide piece. Clarke puts it down to Tony's account and resumes his reading.

With the slab of salt pork as a foundation, she visits various homes until she has collected all she wants for the day. At the Piersons, for instance: "Sister Pierson, plee-ee-ease gimme uh han'ful uh collard greens fuh me an' mah po' chillen! 'Deed, me an' mah chillen is so hongry. Tony doan' fee-ee-eed me!"

Mrs. Pierson picks a bunch of greens for her, but she springs away from them as if they were poison. "Lawd a mussy, Mis' Pierson, you ain't gonna gimme dat lil' eye-full uh greens fuh me an' mah chillen, is you? Don't be so graspin'; Gawd won't bless yuh. Gimme uh han'full mo'. Lawd, some folks is got everything, an' theys jes' as gripin' an' stingy!"

Mrs. Pierson raises the ante, and the pleading woman moves on to the next place, and on and on. The next day, it commences all over.

2
Turpentine Love

JIM MERCHANT is always in good humor—even with his wife. He says he fell in love with her at first sight. That was some years ago. She has had all her teeth pulled out, but they still get along splendidly.

He says the first time he called on her he found out that she was subject to fits. This didn't cool his love, however. She had several in his presence.

One Sunday, while he was there, she had one, and her mother tried to give her a dose of turpentine to stop it. Accidentally, she spilled it in her eye and it cured her. She never had another fit, so they got married and have kept each other in good humor ever since.

3

BECKY MOORE has eleven children of assorted colors and sizes. She has never been married, but that is not her fault. She has never stopped any of the fathers of her children from proposing, so if she has no father for her children it's not her fault. The men round about are entirely to blame.

The other mothers of the town are afraid that it is catching. They won't let their children play with hers.

4
Tippy

SYKES JONES' FAMILY all shoot craps. The most interesting member of the family—also fond of bones, but of another kind—is Tippy, the Jones' dog.

He is so thin, that it amazes one that he lives at all. He sneaks into village kitchens if the housewives are careless about the doors and steals meats, even off the stoves. He also sucks eggs.

For these offenses he has been sentenced to death dozens of times, and the sentences executed upon him, only they didn't work. He has been fed bluestone, strychnine, nux vomica, even an entire Peruna bottle beaten up. It didn't fatten him, but it didn't kill him. So Eatonville has resigned itself to the plague of Tippy, reflecting that it has erred in certain matters and is being chastened.

In spite of all the attempts upon his life, Tippy is still willing to be friendly with anyone who will let him.

5
The Way of a Man with a Train

OLD MAN ANDERSON lived seven or eight miles out in the country from Eatonville. Over by Lake Apopka. He raised feed-corn and cassava and went to market with it two or three times a year. He bought all of his victuals wholesale so he wouldn't have to come to town for several months more.

He was different from citybred folks. He had never seen a train. Everybody laughed at him for even the smallest child in Eatonville had either been to Maitland or Orlando and watched a train go by. On Sunday afternoons all of the young people of the village would go over to Maitland, a mile away, to see Number 35 whizz southward on its way to Tampa and wave at the passengers. So we looked down on him a little. Even we children felt superior in the presence of a person so lacking in wordly knowledge.

The grown-ups kept telling him he ought to go see a train. He always said he didn't have time to wait so long. Only two trains a day passed through Maitland. But patronage and ridicule finally had its effect and Old Man Anderson drove in one morning early. Number 78 went north to Jacksonville at 10:20. He drove his light wagon over in the woods beside the railroad below Maitland, and sat down to wait. He began to fear that his horse would get frightened and run away with the wagon. So he took him out and led him deeper into the grove and tied him securely. Then he returned to his wagon and waited some more. Then he remembered that some of the train-wise villagers had said the engine belched fire and smoke. He had better move his wagon out of danger. It might catch fire. He climbed down from the seat and placed himself between the shafts to draw it away. Just then 78 came thundering over the trestle spouting smoke, and suddenly began blowing for Maitland. Old Man Anderson became so frightened he ran away with the wagon through the woods and tore it up worse than the horse ever could have done. He doesn't know yet what a train looks like, and says he doesn't care.

6
Coon Taylor

COON TAYLOR never did any real stealing. Of course, if he saw a chicken or a watermelon he'd take it. The people used to get mad but they never could catch him. He took so many melons from Joe Clarke that he set up in the melon patch one night with his shotgun loaded with rock salt. He was going to fix Coon. But he was tired. It is hard work being a mayor, postmaster, storekeeper and everything. He dropped asleep sitting on a stump in the middle of the patch. So he didn't see Coon when he came. Coon didn't see him either, that is, not at first. He knew the stump was there, however. He had opened many of Clarke's juicy Florida Favorite on it. He selected his fruit, walked over to the stump and burst the melon on it. That is, he thought it was the stump until it fell over with a yell. Then he knew it was no stump and departed hastily from those parts. He had cleared the fence when Clarke came to, as it were. So the charge of rock-salt was wasted on the desert air.

During the sugar-cane season, he found he couldn't resist Clarke's soft green cane, but Clarke did not go to sleep this time. So after he had cut six of eight stalks by the moonlight, Clarke rose up out of the cane strippings with his shotgun and made Coon sit right down and chew up the last one of them on the spot. And the next day he made Coon leave his town for three months.

7
Village Fiction

JOE LINDSAY is said by Lum Boger to be the largest manufacturer of prevarications in Eatonville; Brazzle (late owner of the world's leanest and meanest mule) contends that his business is the largest in the state and his wife holds that he is the biggest liar in the world.

Exhibit A—He claims that while he was in Orlando one day he saw a doctor cut open a woman, remove everything—liver, lights and heart included—clean each of them separately; the doctor then washed out the empty woman, dried her out neatly with a towel and replaced the organs so expertly that she was up and about her work in a couple of weeks.

8

SEWELL is a man who lives all to himself. He moves a great deal. So often, that 'Lige Moseley says his chickens are so used to moving that every time he comes out into his backyard the chickens lie down and cross their legs, ready to be tied up again.

He is baldheaded; but he says he doesn't mind that, because he wants as little as possible between him and God.

9

MRS. CLARKE is Joe Clarke's wife. She is a soft-looking, middle-aged woman, whose bust and stomach are always holding a get-together.

She waits on the store sometimes and cries every time he yells at her which he does every time she makes a mistake, which is quite often. She calls her husband "Jody." They say he used to beat her in the store when he was a young man, but he is not so impatient now. He can wait until he goes home.

She shouts in Church every Sunday and shakes the hand of fellowship with everybody in the Church with her eyes closed, but somehow always misses her husband.

10

MRS. MCDUFFY goes to Church every Sunday and always shouts and tells her "determination." Her husband always sits in the back row and beats her soon as they get home. He says there's no sense in her shouting, as big a devil as she is. She just does it to slur him. Elijah Moseley asked her why she didn't stop shouting, seeing she always got a beating about it. She says she can't "squinch the sperrit." Then Elijah asked Mr. McDuffy to stop beating her, seeing that she was going to shout anyway.

He answered that she just did it for spite and that his fist was just as hard as her head. He could last just as long as she. So the village let the matter rest.

11
Double-Shuffle

BACK IN THE GOOD OLD DAYS before the World War, things were very simple in Eatonville. People didn't fox-trot. When the town wanted to put on its Sunday clothes and wash behind the ears, it put on a "breakdown." The daring younger set would two-step and waltz, but the good church members and the elders stuck to the grand march. By rural canons dancing is wicked, but one is not held to have danced until the feet have been crossed. Feet don't get crossed when one grand marches.

At elaborate affairs the organ from the Methodist church was moved up to the hall and Lizzimore, the blind man presided. When informal gatherings were held, he merely played his guitar assisted by any volunteer with mouth organs or accordions.

Among white people the march is as mild as if it had been passed on by Volstead. But it still has a kick in Eatonville. Everybody happy, shining eyes, gleaming teeth. Feet dragged 'shhlap, shhlap! to beat out the time. No orchestra needed. Round and round! Back again, parse-me-la! shlap! shlap! Strut! Strut! Seaboard! Shlap! Shlap! Tiddy bumm! Mr. Clarke in the lead with Mrs. Moseley.

It's too much for some of the young folks. Double shuffling commences. Buck and wing. Lizzimore about to break his guitar. Accordion doing contortions. People fall back against the walls, and let the soloist have it, shouting as they clap the old, old double shuffle songs.

"Me an' mah honey got two mo' days
Two mo' days tuh do de buck"

Sweating bodies, laughing mouths, grotesque faces, feet drumming fiercely. Deacons clapping as hard as the rest.

"Great big nigger, black as tar
Trying tuh git tuh hebben on uh 'lectric car."

"Some love cabbage, some love kale
But I love a gal wid a short skirt tail."

"Long tall angel—steppin' down,
Long white robe an' starry crown."

"Ah would not marry uh black gal (bumm bumm!)
Tell yuh de reason why
Every time she comb her hair
She make de goo-goo eye.

Would not marry a yaller gal (bumm bumm!)
Tell yuh de reason why
Her neck so long an' stringy
Ahm 'fraid she'd never die.

Would not marry uh preacher
Tell yuh de reason why
Every time he comes tuh town
He makes de chicken fly."

When the buck dance was over, the boys would give the floor to the girls and they would parse-me-la with a slye eye out of the corner to see if anybody was looking who might "have them up in church" on conference night. Then there would be more dancing. Then Mr. Clarke would call for everybody's best attention and announce that *'freshments was served! Every gent'man would please take his lady by the arm and scorch her right up to de table fur a treat!*

Then the men would stick their arms out with a flourish and ask their ladies: "You lak chicken? Well, then, take a wing." And the ladies would take the proffered "wings" and parade up to the long table and be served. Of course most of them had brought baskets in which were heaps of jointed and fried chicken, two or three kinds of pies, cakes, potato pone and chicken purlo. The hall would separate into happy groups about the baskets until time for more dancing.

But the boys and girls got scattered about during the war, and now they dance the fox-trot by a brand new piano. They do waltz and two-step still, but no one now considers it good form to lock his chin over his partner's shoulder and stick out behind. One night just for fun and to humor the old folks, they danced, that is, they grand marched, but everyone picked up their feet. *Bah!!*

12
The Head of the Nail

DAISY TAYLOR was the town vamp. Not that she was pretty. But sirens were all but non-existent in the town. Perhaps she was forced to it by circumstances. She was quite dark, with little bushy patches of hair squatting over her head. These were held down by shingle-nails often. No one knows whether she did this for artistic effect or for lack of hairpins, but there they were shining in the little patches of hair when she got all dressed for the afternoon and came up to Clarke's store to see if there was any mail for her.

It was seldom that anyone wrote to Daisy, but she knew that the men of the town would be assembled there by five o'clock, and some one could usually be induced to buy her some soda-water or peanuts.

Daisy flirted with married men. There were only two single men in town. Lum Boger, who was engaged to the assistant school-teacher, and Hiram Lester, who had been off to school at Tuskegee and wouldn't look at a person like Daisy. In addition to other drawbacks, she was pigeon-toed and her petticoat was always showing so perhaps he was justified. There was nothing else to do except flirt with married men.

This went on for a long time. First one wife and then another complained of her, or drove her from the preserves by threat.

But the affair with Crooms was the most prolonged and serious. He was even known to have bought her a pair of shoes.

Mrs. Laura Crooms was a meek little woman who took all of her troubles crying, and talked a great deal of leaving things in the hands of God.

The affair came to a head one night in orange picking time. Crooms was over at Oneido picking oranges. Many fruit pickers move from one town to the other during the season.

The *town* was collected at the store-postoffice as is customary on Saturday nights. The *town* has had its bath and with its week's pay in pocket fares forth to be merry. The men tell stories and treat the ladies to soda-water, peanuts and peppermint candy.

Daisy was trying to get treats, but the porch was cold to her that night.

"Ah don't keer if you don't treat me. What's a dirty lil nickel?" She flung this at Walter Thomas. "The everloving Mister Crooms will gimme anything atall Ah wants."

"You better shet up yo' mouf talking 'bout Albert Crooms. Heah his wife comes right now."

Daisy went akimbo. "Who? Me! Ah don't keer whut Laura Crooms think. If she ain't a heavy hip-ted Mama enough to keep him, she don't need to come crying to me."

She stood making goo-goo eyes as Mrs. Crooms walked upon the porch. Daisy laughed loud, made several references to Albert Crooms, and when she saw the mail-bag come in from Maitland she said, "Ah better go in an' see if Ah ain't got a letter from Oneido."

The more Daisy played the game of getting Mrs. Crooms' goat, the better she liked it. She ran in and out of the store laughing until she could scarcely stand. Some of the people present began to talk to Mrs. Crooms—to egg her on to halt Daisy's boasting, but she was for leaving it all in the hands of God. Walter Thomas kept on after Mrs. Crooms until she stiffened and resolved to fight. Daisy was inside when she came to this resolve and never dreamed anything of the kind could happen. She had gotten hold of an envelope and came laughing and shouting, "Oh, Ah can't stand to see Oneido lose!"

There was a box of ax-handles on display on the porch, propped up against the door jamb. As Daisy stepped upon the porch, Mrs. Crooms leaned the heavy end of one of those handles heavily upon her head. She staggered from the porch to the ground and the timid Laura, fearful of a counter-attack, struck again and Daisy toppled into the town ditch. There was not enough water in there to do more than muss her up. Every time she tried to rise, down would come that ax-handle again. Laura was fighting a scared fight. With Daisy thoroughly licked, she retired to the store porch and left her fallen enemy in the ditch. But Elijah Moseley, who was some distance down the street when the trouble began arrived as the victor was withdrawing. He rushed up and picked Daisy out of the mud and began feeling her head.

"Is she hurt much?" Joe Clarke asked from the doorway.

"I don't know," Elijah answered, "I was just looking to see if Laura had been lucky enough to hit one of those nails on the head and drive it in."

Before a week was up, Daisy moved to Orlando. There in a wider sphere, perhaps, her talents as a vamp were appreciated.

13
Pants and Cal'line

SISTER CAL'LINE POTTS was a silent woman. Did all of her laughing down inside, but did the thing that kept the town in an uproar of laughter. It was the general opinion of the village that Cal'line would do anything she had a mind to. And she had a mind to do several things.

Mitchell Potts, her husband, had a weakness for women. No one ever believed that she was jealous. She did things to the women, surely. But most any townsman would have said that she did them because she liked the novel situation and the queer things she could bring out of it.

Once he took up with Delphine—called Mis' Pheeny by the town. She lived on the outskirts on the edge of the piney woods. The town winked and talked. People don't make secrets of such things in villages. Cal'line went about her business with her thin black lips pursed tight as ever, and her shiny black eyes unchanged.

"Dat devil of a Cal'line's got somethin' up her sleeve!" The town smiled in anticipation.

"Delphine is too big a cigar for her to smoke. She ain't crazy," said some as the weeks went on and nothing happened. Even Pheeny herself would give an extra flirt to her over-starched petticoats as she rustled into church past her of Sundays.

Mitch Potts said furthermore, that he was tired of Cal'line's foolishness. She had to stay where he put her. His African soup-bone (arm) was too strong to let a woman run over him. 'Nough was 'nough. And he did some fancy cussing, and he was the fanciest cusser in the county.

So the town waited and the longer it waited, the odds changed slowly from the wife to the husband.

One Saturday, Mitch knocked off work at two o'clock and went over to Maitland. He came back with a rectangular box under his arm and kept straight on out to the barn to put it away. He ducked around the corner of the house quickly, but even so, his wife glimpsed the package. Very much like a shoe-box. So!

He put on the kettle and took a bath. She stood in her bare feet at the ironing board and kept on ironing. He dressed. It was about five o'clock but still very light. He fiddled around outside. She kept on with her ironing. As soon as the sun got red, he sauntered out to the barn, got the parcel and walked away down the road, past the store and into the piney woods. As soon as he left the house, Cal'line slipped on her shoes without taking time to don stockings, put on one of her husband's old Stetsons, worn and floppy, slung the axe over her shoulder and followed in his wake. He was hailed cheerily as he passed the sitters on the store porch and answered smiling sheepishly and passed on. Two minutes later passed his wife, silently, unsmilingly, and set the porch to giggling and betting.

An hour passed perhaps. It was dark. Clarke had long ago lighted the swinging kerosene lamp inside.

14

ONCE 'WAY BACK YONDER before the stars fell all the animals used to talk just like people. In them days dogs and rabbits was the best of friends—even tho' both of them was stuck on the same gal—which was Miss Nancy Coon. She had the sweetest smile and the prettiest striped and bushy tail to be found anywhere.

They both run their legs nigh off trying to win her for themselves—fetching nice ripe persimmons and such. But she never give one or the other no satisfaction.

Finally one night Mr. Dog popped the question right out. "Miss Coon," he says, "Ma'am, also Ma'am which would you ruther be—a lark flyin' or a dove a settin'?"

Course Miss Nancy she blushed and laughed a little and hid her face behind her bushy tail for a spell. Then she said sorter shy like, "I does love yo' sweet voice, brother dawg—but—I ain't jes' exactly set my mind yit."

Her and Mr. Dog set on a spell, when up comes hopping Mr. Rabbit wid his tail fresh washed and his whiskers shining. He got right down to business and asked Miss Coon to marry him, too.

"Oh, Miss Nancy," he says, "Ma'am, also Ma'am, if you'd see me settin' straddle of a mud-cat leadin' a minnow, what would you think? Ma'am also Ma'am?" Which is a out and out proposal as everybody knows.

"Youse awful nice, Brother Rabbit and a beautiful dancer, but you cannot sing like Brother Dog. Both you uns come back next week to gimme time for to decide."

They both left arm-in-arm. Finally Mr. Rabbit says to Mr. Dog. "Taint no use in me going back—she ain't gwinter have me. So I mought as well give up. She loves singing, and I ain't got nothing but a squeak."

"Oh, don't talk that a way," says Mr. Dog, tho' he is glad Mr. Rabbit can't sing none.

"Thass all right, Brer Dog. But if I had a sweet voice like you got, I'd have it worked on and make it sweeter."

"How! How! How!" Mr. Dog cried, jumping up and down.

"Lemme fix it for you, like I do for Sister Lark and Sister Mocking-bird."

"When? Where?" asked Mr. Dog, all excited. He was figuring that if he could sing just a little better Miss Coon would be bound to have him.

"Just you meet me t'morrer in de huckleberry patch," says the rabbit and off they both goes to bed.

The dog is there on time next day and after a while the rabbit comes loping up.

"Mawnin', Brer Dawg," he says kinder chippy like. "Ready to git yo' voice sweetened?"

"Sholy, sholy, Brer Rabbit. Let's we all hurry about it. I wants tuh serenade Miss Nancy from the piney woods tuh night."

"Well, den, open yo' mouf and poke out yo' tongue," says the rabbit.

No sooner did Mr. Dog poke out his tongue than Mr. Rabbit split it with a knife and ran for all he was worth to a hollow stump and hid hisself.

The dog has been mad at the rabbit ever since.

Anybody who don't believe it happened, just look at the dog's tongue and he can see for himself where the rabbit slit it right up the middle.

Stepped on a tin, mah story ends.

Chapter 3

James Joyce

Araby*

North Richmond Street, being blind, was a quiet street except at the hour when the Christian Brothers' School set the boys free. An uninhabited house of two storeys stood at the blind end, detached from its neighbours in a square ground. The other houses of the street, conscious of decent lives within them, gazed at one another with brown imperturbable faces.

The former tenant of our house, a priest, had died in the back drawingroom. Air, musty from having been long enclosed, hung in all the rooms and the waste room behind the kitchen was littered with old useless papers. Among these I found a few papercovered books, the pages of which were curled and damp: *The Abbot* by Walter Scott, *The Devout Communicant* and *The Memoirs of Vidocq*. I liked the last best because its leaves were yellow. The wild garden behind the house contained a central apple tree and a few straggling bushes under one of which I found the late tenant's rusty bicycle pump. He had been a very charitable priest; in his will he had left all his money to institutions and the furniture of his house to his sister.

When the short days of winter came dusk fell before we had well eaten our dinners. When we met in the street the houses had grown sombre. The space of sky above us was the colour of everchanging violet and towards it the lamps of the street lifted their feeble lanterns. The cold air stung us and we played till our bodies glowed. Our shouts echoed in the silent street. The career of our play brought us through the dark muddy lanes behind the houses where we ran the gantlet of the rough tribes from the cottages, to the back doors of the dark dripping gardens where odours arose from the ashpits, to the dark odorous stables where a coachman smoothed and combed the horse or shook music from the

---

*This selection is also featured in the model student essay in Chapter 7.

buckled harness. When we returned to the street light from the kitchen windows had filled the areas. If my uncle was seen turning the corner we hid in the shadow until we had seen him safely housed. Or if Mangan's sister came out on the doorstep to call her brother in to his tea we watched her from our shadow peer up and down the street. We waited to see whether she would remain or go in and if she remained we left our shadow and walked up to Mangan's steps resignedly. She was waiting for us, her figure defined by the light from the half-opened door. Her brother always teased her before he obeyed and I stood by the railings looking at her. Her dress swung as she moved her body and the soft rope of her hair tossed from side to side.

Every morning I lay on the floor in the front parlour watching her door. The blind was pulled down to within an inch of the sash so that I could not be seen. When she came out on the doorstep my heart leaped. I ran to the hall, seized my books and followed her. I kept her brown figure always in my eye and when we came near the point at which our ways diverged I quickened my pace and passed her. This happened morning after morning. I had never spoken to her except for a few casual words and yet her name was like a summons to all my foolish blood.

Her image accompanied me even in places the most hostile to romance. On Saturday evenings when my aunt went marketing I had to go to carry some of the parcels. We walked through the flaring streets, jostled by drunken men and bargaining women, amid the curses of labourers, the shrill litanies of shop boys who stood on guard by the barrels of pigs' cheeks, the nasal chanting of street singers who sang a *come-all-you* about O'Donovan Rossa or a ballad about the troubles in our native land. These noises converged in a single sensation of life for me: I imagined that I bore my chalice safely through a throng of foes. Her name sprang to my lips at moments in strange prayers and praises which I myself did not understand. My eyes were often full of tears (I could not tell why) and at times a flood from my heart seemed to pour itself out into my bosom. I thought little of the future. I did not know whether I would ever speak to her or not or, if I spoke to her, how I could tell her of my confused adoration. But my body was like a harp and her words and gestures were like fingers running upon the wires.

One evening I went into the back drawingroom in which the priest had died. It was a dark rainy evening and there was no sound in the house. Through one of the broken panes I heard the rain impinge upon the earth, the fine incessant needles of water playing in the sodden beds. Some distant lamp or lighted window gleamed below me. I was thankful that I could see so little. All my senses seemed to desire to veil themselves and, feeling that I was about to slip from them, I pressed the palms of my hands together until they trembled, murmuring: *O love! O love!* many times.

At last she spoke to me. When she addressed the first words to me I was so confused that I did not know what to answer. She asked me was I going to *Araby*. I forget whether I answered yes or no. It would be a splendid bazaar, she said; she would love to go.

—And why can't you? I asked.

While she spoke she turned a silver bracelet round and round her wrist. She could not go, she said, because there would be a retreat that week in her convent. Her brother and two other boys were fighting for their caps and I was alone at the railings. She held one of the spikes, bowing her head towards me. The light from the lamp opposite our door caught the white curve of her neck, lit up the hair that rested there and, falling, lit up the hand upon the railing. It fell over one side of her dress and caught the white border of a petticoat, just visible as she stood at ease.

—It's well for you, she said.
—If I go, I said, I will bring you something.

What innumerable follies laid waste my waking and sleeping thoughts after that evening! I wished to annihilate the tedious intervening days. I chafed against the work of school. At night in my bedroom and by day in the classroom her image came between me and the page I strove to read. The syllables of the word *Araby* were called to me through the silence in which my soul luxuriated and cast an eastern enchantment over me. I asked for leave to go to the bazaar on Saturday night. My aunt was surprised and hoped it was not some freemason affair. I answered few questions in class. I watched my master's face pass from amiability to sternness; he hoped I was not beginning to idle. I could not call my wandering thoughts together. I had hardly any patience with the serious work of life which, now that it stood between me and my desire, seemed to me child's play, ugly monotonous child's play.

On Saturday morning I reminded my uncle that I wished to go to the bazaar in the evening. He was fussing at the hallstand, looking for the hatbrush, and answered me curtly:

—Yes, boy, I know.

As he was in the hall I could not go into the front parlour and lie at the window. I left the house in bad humour and walked slowly towards the school. The air was pitilessly raw and already my heart misgave me.

When I came home to dinner my uncle had not yet been home. Still it was early. I sat staring at the clock for some time and when its ticking began to irritate me I left the room. I mounted the staircase and gained the upper part of the house. The high cold empty gloomy rooms liberated me and I went from room to room singing. From the front window I saw my companions playing below in the street. Their cries reached me weakened and indistinct and, leaning my forehead against the cool glass, I looked over at the dark house where she lived. I may have stood there for an hour seeing nothing but the brownclad figure cast by my imagination, touched discreetly by the lamplight at the curved neck, at the hand upon the railings and at the border below the dress.

When I came downstairs again I found Mrs Mercer sitting at the fire. She was an old garrulous woman, a pawnbroker's widow who collected used stamps for some pious purpose. I had to endure the gossip of the teatable. The meal was prolonged beyond an hour and still my uncle did not come. Mrs Mercer stood up to go: she was sorry she couldn't wait any longer but it was after eight o'clock and she did not like to be out late as the night air was bad for her. When she had gone I began to walk up and down the room, clenching my fists. My aunt said:

—I'm afraid you may put off your bazaar for this night of Our Lord.

At nine o'clock I heard my uncle's latchkey in the halldoor. I heard him talking to himself and heard the hallstand rocking when it had received the weight of his overcoat. I could interpret these signs. When he was midway through his dinner I asked him to give me the money to go to the bazaar. He had forgotten.

—The people are in bed and after their first sleep now, he said.

I did not smile. My aunt said to him energetically:

— Can't you give him the money and let him go? You've kept him late enough as it is.

My uncle said he was very sorry he had forgotten. He said he believed in the old saying: *All work and no play makes Jack a dull boy.* He asked me where I was going and when I had told him a second time he asked me did I know *The Arab's Farewell to His Steed.* When I left the kitchen he was about to recite the opening lines of the piece to my aunt.

I held a florin tightly in my hand as I strode down Buckingham Street towards the station. The sight of the streets thronged with buyers and glaring with gas recalled to me the purpose of my journey. I took my seat in a third class carriage of a deserted train. After an intolerable delay the train moved out of the station slowly. It crept onward among ruinous houses and over the twinkling river. At Westland Row Station a crowd of people pressed at the carriage doors; but the porters moved them back, saying that it was a special train for the bazaar. I remained alone in the bare carriage. In a few minutes the train drew up beside an improvised wooden platform. I passed out on to the road and saw by the lighted dial of a clock that it was ten minutes to ten. In front of me was a large building which displayed the magical name.

I could not find any sixpenny entrance and, fearing that the bazaar would be closed, I passed in quickly through a turnstile, handing a shilling to a wearylooking man. I found myself in a big hall girdled at half its height by a gallery. Nearly all the stalls were closed and the greater part of the hall was in darkness. I recognised a silence like that which pervades a church after a service. I walked into the centre of the bazaar timidly. A few people were gathered about the stalls which were still open. Before a curtain over which the words *Café Chantant* were written in coloured lamps two men were counting money on a salver. I listened to the fall of the coins.

Remembering with difficulty why I had come I went over to one of the stalls and examined porcelain vases and flowered teasets. At the door of the stall a young lady was talking and laughing with two young gentlemen. I remarked their English accents and listened vaguely to their conversation.

—O, I never said such a thing!

—O, but you did!
—O, but I didn't!
—Didn't she say that? —She did. I heard her.
—O, there's a … fib!

Observing me the young lady came over and asked me did I wish to buy anything. The tone of her voice was not encouraging: she seemed to have spoken to me out of a sense of duty. I looked humbly at the great jars that stood like eastern guards at either side of the dark entrance to her stall and murmured:

—No, thank you.

The young lady changed the position of one of the vases and went back to the two young men. They began to talk of the same subject. Once or twice the young lady glanced at me over her shoulder.

I lingered before her stall, though I knew my stay was useless, to make my interest in her wares seem the more real. Then I turned away slowly and walked down the middle of the bazaar. I allowed the two pennies to fall against the sixpence in my pocket. I heard a voice call from one end of the gallery that the light was out. The upper part of the hall was now completely dark.

Gazing up into the darkness I saw myself as a creature driven and derided by vanity: and my eyes burned with anguish and anger.

John Keats

To Autumn*

1

SEASON of mists and mellow fruitfulness,
  Close bosom-friend of the maturing sun;
Conspiring with him how to load and bless
  With fruit the vines that round the thatch-eaves run;
To bend with apples the mossed cottage-trees,
  And fill all fruit with ripeness to the core;
    To swell the gourd, and plump the hazel shells
  With a sweet kernel; to set budding more,
And still more, later flowers for the bees,
Until they think warm days will never cease,
  For Summer has o'er-brimmed their clammy cells.

2

Who hath not seen thee oft amid thy store?
  Sometimes whoever seeks abroad may find

*This selection is featured in the model student essay in Chapter 11.

Thee sitting careless on a granary floor,
  Thy hair soft-lifted by the winnowing wind;
Or on a half-reaped furrow sound asleep,
  Drowsed with the fume of poppies, while thy hook
    Spares the next swath and all its twinèd flowers;
And sometimes like a gleaner thou dost keep
  Steady thy laden head across a brook;
  Or by a cider-press, with patient look,
    Thou watchest the last oozings hours by hours.

3

Where are the songs of spring? Ay, where are they?
  Think not of them, thou hast thy music too,—
While barred clouds bloom the soft-dying day,
  And touch the stubble-plains with rosy hue;
Then in a wailful choir the small gnats mourn
  Among the river sallows, borne aloft
    Or sinking as the light wind lives or dies;
And full-grown lambs loud bleat from hilly bourn;
  Hedge-crickets sing; and now with treble soft
  The redbreast whistles from a garden-croft;
    And gathering swallows twitter in the skies.

Chapter 5

Guy De Maupassant

The Diamond Necklace*

From Selected Tales of Guy de Maupassant, *ed. Faye Commins (New York: Random House, 1950), pp. 137–44.*

She was one of those pretty, charming young ladies, born, as if through an error of destiny, into a family of clerks. She had no dowry, no hopes, no means of becoming known, appreciated, loved, and married by a man either rich or distinguished; and she allowed herself to marry a petty clerk in the office of the Board of Education.

She was simple, not being able to adorn herself; but she was unhappy, as one out of her class; for women belong to no caste, no race; their grace, their beauty, and their charm serving them in the place of birth and family. Their inborn

*This selection is also featured in the model student essay in Chapter 8.

finesse, their instinctive elegance, their suppleness of wit are their only aristocracy, making some daughters of the people the equal of great ladies.

She suffered incessantly, feeling herself born for all delicacies and luxuries. She suffered from the poverty of her apartment, the shabby walls, the worn chairs, and the faded stuffs. All these things, which another woman of her station would not have noticed, tortured and angered her. The sight of the little Breton, who made this humble home, awoke in her sad regrets and desperate dreams. She thought of quiet antechambers, with their Oriental hangings, lighted by high, bronze torches, and of the two great footmen in short trousers who sleep in the large armchairs, made sleepy by the heavy air from the heating apparatus. She thought of large drawing-rooms, hung in old silks, of graceful pieces of furniture carrying bric-à-brac of inestimable value, and of the little perfumed coquettish apartments, made for five o'clock chats with most intimate friends, men known and sought after, whose attention all women envied and desired.

When she seated herself for dinner, before the round table where the tablecloth had been used three days, opposite her husband who uncovered the tureen with a delighted air, saying: "Oh! the good potpie! I know nothing better than that—" she would think of the elegant dinners, of the shining silver, of the tapestries peopling the walls with ancient personages and rare birds in the midst of fairy forests; she thought of the exquisite food served on marvelous dishes, of the whispered gallantries, listened to with the smile of the sphinx, while eating the rose-colored flesh of the trout or a chicken's wing.

She had neither frocks nor jewels, nothing. And she loved only those things. She felt that she was made for them. She had such a desire to please, to be sought after, to be clever, and courted.

She had a rich friend, a schoolmate at the convent, whom she did not like to visit, she suffered so much when she returned. And she wept for whole days from chagrin, from regret, from despair, and disappointment.

One evening her husband returned, elated, bearing in his hand a large envelope. "Here," said he, "here is something for you." She quickly tore open the wrapper and drew out a printed card on which were inscribed these words:

"The Minister of Public Instruction and Madame George Ramponneau
ask the honor of Mr. and Mrs. Loisel's company Monday evening,
January 18, at the Minister's residence."

Instead of being delighted, as her husband had hoped, she threw the invitation spitefully upon the table murmuring:

"What do you suppose I want with that?"

"But, my dearie, I thought it would make you happy. You never go out, and this is an occasion, and a fine one! I had a great deal of trouble to get it. Everybody wishes one, and it is very select; not many are given to employees. You will see the whole official world there."

She looked at him with an irritated eye and declared impatiently:

"What do you suppose I have to wear to such a thing as that?"

He had not thought of that; he stammered:

"Why, the dress you wear when we go to the theater. It seems very pretty to me—" He was silent, stupefied, in dismay, at the sight of his wife weeping. Two great tears fell slowly from the corners of his eyes toward the corners of his mouth; he stammered:

"What is the matter? What is the matter?"

By a violent effort, she had controlled her vexation and responded in a calm voice, wiping her moist cheeks:

"Nothing. Only I have no dress and consequently I cannot go to this affair. Give your card to some colleague whose wife is better fitted out than I."

He was grieved, but answered:

"Let us see, Matilda. How much would a suitable costume cost, something that would serve for other occasions, something very simple?"

She reflected for some seconds, making estimates and thinking of a sum that she could ask for without bringing with it an immediate refusal and a frightened exclamation from the economical clerk.

Finally she said, in a hesitating voice:

"I cannot tell exactly, but it seems to me that four hundred francs ought to cover it."

He turned a little pale, for he had saved just this sum to buy a gun that he might be able to join some hunting parties the next summer, on the plains at Nanterre, with some friends who went to shoot larks up there on Sunday. Nevertheless, he answered:

"Very well. I will give you four hundred francs. But try to have a pretty dress."

The day of the ball approached and Mme. Loisel seemed sad, disturbed, anxious. Nevertheless, her dress was nearly ready. Her husband said to her one evening:

"What is the matter with you? You have acted strangely for two or three days."

And she responded: "I am vexed not to have a jewel, not one stone, nothing to adorn myself with. I shall have such a poverty-laden look. I would prefer not to go to this party."

He replied: "You can wear some natural flowers. At this season they look very *chic.* For ten francs you can have two or three magnificent roses."

She was not convinced. "No," she replied, "there is nothing more humiliating than to have a shabby air in the midst of rich women."

Then her husband cried out: "How stupid we are! Go and find your friend Mrs. Forestier and ask her to lend you her jewels. You are well enough acquainted with her to do this."

She uttered a cry of joy: "It is true!" she said. "I had not thought of that."

The next day she took herself to her friend's house and related her story of distress. Mrs. Forestier went to her closet with the glass doors, took out a large jewel-case, brought it, opened it, and said: "Choose, my dear."

She saw at first some bracelets, then a collar of pearls, then a Venetian cross of gold and jewels and of admirable workmanship. She tried the jewels before the glass, hesitated, but could neither decide to take them nor leave them. Then she asked:

"Have you nothing more?"

"Why, yes. Look for yourself. I do not know what will please you."

Suddenly she discovered, in a black satin box, a superb necklace of diamonds, and her heart beat fast with an immoderate desire. Her hands trembled as she took them up. She placed them about her throat against her dress, and remained in ecstasy before them. Then she asked, in a hesitating voice, full of anxiety:

"Could you lend me this? Only this?"

"Why, yes, certainly."

She fell upon the neck of her friend, embraced her with passion, then went away with her treasure.

The day of the ball arrived. Mme. Loisel was a great success. She was the prettiest of all, elegant, gracious, smiling, and full of joy. All the men noticed her, asked her name, and wanted to be presented. All the members of the Cabinet wished to waltz with her. The Minister of Education paid her some attention.

She danced with enthusiasm, with passion, intoxicated with pleasure, thinking of nothing, in the triumph of her beauty, in the glory of her success, in a kind of cloud of happiness that came of all this homage, and all this admiration, of all these awakened desires, and this victory so complete and sweet to the heart of woman.

She went home toward four o'clock in the morning. Her husband had been half asleep in one of the little salons since midnight, with three other gentlemen whose wives were enjoying themselves very much.

He threw around her shoulders the wraps they had carried for the coming home, modest garments of everyday wear, whose poverty clashed with the elegance of the ball costume. She felt this and wished to hurry away in order not to be noticed by the other women who were wrapping themselves in rich furs.

Loisel retained her: "Wait," said he. "You will catch cold out there. I am going to call a cab."

But she would not listen and descended the steps rapidly. When they were in the street, they found no carriage; and they began to seek one, hailing the coachmen whom they saw at a distance.

They walked along toward the Seine, hopeless and shivering. Finally they found on the dock one of those old, nocturnal *coupés* that one sees in Paris after nightfall, as if they were ashamed of their misery by day.

It took them as far as their door in Martyr Street, and they went wearily up to their apartment. It was all over for her. And on his part, he remembered that he would have to be at the office by ten o'clock.

She removed the wraps from her shoulders before the glass, for a final view of herself in her glory. Suddenly she uttered a cry. Her necklace was not around her neck.

Her husband, already half undressed, asked: "What is the matter?"

She turned toward him excitedly:

"I have—I have—I no longer have Mrs. Forestier's necklace."

He arose in dismay: "What! How is that? It is not possible."

And they looked in the folds of the dress, in the folds of the mantle, in the pockets, everywhere. They could not find it.

He asked: "You are sure you still had it when we left the house?"

"Yes, I felt it in the vestibule as we came out."

"But if you had lost it in the street, we should have heard it fall. It must be in the cab."

"Yes. It is probable. Did you take the number?"

"No. And you, did you notice what it was?"

"No."

They looked at each other utterly cast down. Finally, Loisel dressed himself again.

"I am going," said he, "over the track where we went on foot, to see if I can find it."

And he went. She remained in her evening gown, not having the strength to go to bed, stretched upon a chair, without ambition or thoughts.

Toward seven o'clock her husband returned. He had found nothing.

He went to the police and to the cab offices, and put an advertisement in the newspapers, offering a reward; he did everything that afforded them a suspicion of hope.

She waited all day in a state of bewilderment before this frightful disaster. Loisel returned at evening with his face harrowed and pale; he had discovered nothing.

"It will be necessary," said he, "to write to your friend that you have broken the clasp of the necklace and that you will have it repaired. That will give us time to turn around."

She wrote as he dictated.

At the end of a week, they had lost all hope. And Loisel, older by five years, declared:

"We must take measures to replace this jewel."

The next day they took the box which had enclosed it, to the jeweler whose name was on the inside. He consulted his books.

"It is not I, Madame," said he, "who sold this necklace; I only furnished the casket."

Then they went from jeweler to jeweler seeking a necklace like the other one, consulting their memories, and ill, both of them, with chagrin and anxiety.

In a shop of the Palais-Royal, they found a chaplet of diamonds which seemed to them exactly like the one they had lost. It was valued at forty thousand francs. They could get it for thirty-six thousand.

They begged the jeweler not to sell it for three days. And they made an arrangement by which they might return it for thirty-four thousand francs if they found the other one before the end of February.

Loisel possessed eighteen thousand francs which his father had left him. He borrowed the rest.

He borrowed it, asking for a thousand francs of one, five hundred of another, five louis of this one, and three louis of that one. He gave notes, made ruinous promises, took money of usurers and the whole race of lenders. He compromised his whole existence, in fact, risked his signature, without even knowing whether he could make it good or not, and, harassed by anxiety for the future, by the black misery which surrounded him, and by the prospect of all physical privations and moral torture, he went to get the new necklace, depositing on the merchant's counter thirty-six thousand francs.

When Mrs. Loisel took back the jewels to Mrs. Forestier, the latter said to her in a frigid tone:

"You should have returned them to me sooner, for I might have needed them." She did open the jewel-box as her friend feared she would. If she should perceive the substitution, what would she think? What should she say? Would she take her for a robber?

Mrs. Loisel now knew the horrible life of necessity. She did her part, however, completely, heroically. It was necessary to pay this frightful debt. She would pay it. They sent away the maid; they changed their lodgings; they rented some rooms under a mansard roof.

She learned the heavy cares of a household, the odious work of a kitchen. She washed the dishes, using her rosy nails upon the greasy pots and the bottoms of the stewpans. She washed the soiled linen, the chemises and dishcloths, which she hung on the line to dry; she took down the refuse to the street each morning and brought up the water, stopping at each landing to breathe. And, clothed like a woman of the people, she went to the grocer's, the butcher's, and the fruiterer's, with her basket on her arm, shopping, haggling, defending to the last sou her miserable money.

Every month it was necessary to renew some notes, thus obtaining time, and to pay others.

The husband worked evenings, putting the books of some merchants in order, and nights he often did copying at five sous a page.

And this life lasted for ten years.

At the end of ten years, they had restored all, all, with interest of the usurer, and accumulated interest besides.

Mrs. Loisel seemed old now. She had become a strong, hard woman, the crude woman of the poor household. Her hair badly dressed, her skirts awry, her hands red, she spoke in a loud tone, and washed the floors, using large pails of water. But sometimes, when her husband was at the office, she would seat herself before the window and think of that evening party of former times, of that ball where she was so beautiful and so flattered.

How would it have been if she had not lost that necklace? Who knows? Who knows? How singular is life, and how full of changes! How small a thing will ruin or save one!

One Sunday, as she was taking a walk in the Champs-Elysées to rid herself of the cares of the week, she suddenly perceived a woman walking with a child. It was Mrs. Forestier, still young, still pretty, still attractive. Mrs. Loisel was affected. Should she speak to her? Yes, certainly. And now that she had paid, she would tell her all. Why not?

She approached her. "Good morning, Jeanne."

Her friend did not recognize her and was astonished to be so familiarly addressed by this common personage. She stammered:

"But, Madame—I do not know—You must be mistaken—"

"No, I am Matilda Loisel."

Her friend uttered a cry of astonishment: "Oh! my poor Matilda! How you have changed—"

"Yes, I have had some hard days since I saw you; and some miserable ones—and all because of you—"

"Because of me? How is that?"

"You recall the diamond necklace that you loaned me to wear to the Commissioner's ball?"

"Yes, very well."

"Well, I lost it."

"How is that, since you returned it to me?"

"I returned another to you exactly like it. And it has taken us ten years to pay for it. You can understand that it was not easy for us who have nothing. But it is finished and I am decently content."

Madame Forestier stopped short. She said:

"You say that you bought a diamond necklace to replace mine?"

"Yes. You did not perceive it then? They were just alike."

And she smiled with a proud and simple joy. Madame Forestier was touched and took both her hands as she replied:

"Oh! my poor Matilda! Mine were false. They were not worth over five hundred francs!"

Chapter 7

Edgar Allan Poe

The Masque of the Red Death

From The Gold Bug and Other Tales and Poems *(New York: Macmillan, 1945), pp. 164–71.*

The "Red Death" had long devastated the country. No pestilence had ever been so fatal, or so hideous. Blood was its Avatar and its seal—the redness and the horror of blood. There were sharp pains, and sudden dizziness, and then profuse bleeding at the pores, with dissolution. The scarlet stains upon the body and especially upon the face of the victim, were the pest ban which shut him out from the aid and from the sympathy of his fellow-men. And the whole seizure, progress and termination of the disease, were the incidents of half an hour.

But the Prince Prospero was happy and dauntless and sagacious. When his dominions were half depopulated, he summoned to his presence a thousand hale and light-hearted friends from among the knights and dames of his court, and with these retired to the deep seclusion of one of his castellated abbeys. This was an extensive and magnificent structure, the creation of the prince's own eccentric yet august taste. A strong and lofty wall girdled it in. This wall had gates of iron. The courtiers, having entered, brought furnaces and massy hammers and welded the bolts. They resolved to leave means neither of ingress or egress to the sudden impulses of despair or of frenzy from within. The abbey was amply provisioned. With such precautions the courtiers might bid defiance to contagion. The external world could take care of itself. In the meantime it was folly to grieve, or to think. The prince had provided all the appliances of pleasures. There were buffoons, there were improvisatori, there were ballet-dancers, there were musicians, there was Beauty, there was wine. All these and security were within. Without was the "Red Death."

It was toward the close of the fifth or sixth month of his seclusion, and while the pestilence raged most furiously abroad, that the Prince Prospero entertained his thousand friends at a masked ball of the most unusual magnificence.

It was a voluptuous scene, that masquerade. But first let me tell of the rooms in which it was held. There were seven—an imperial suite. In many palaces, however, such suites form a long and straight vista, while the folding doors slide back nearly to the walls on either hand, so that the view of the whole extent is scarcely impeded. Here the case was very different; as might have been expected from the duke's love of the *bizarre.* The apartments were so irregularly disposed that the vision embraced but little more than one at a time. There was a sharp turn at every twenty or thirty yards, and at each turn a novel effect. To the right and left, in the middle of each wall, a tall and narrow Gothic window looked out upon a closed corridor which pursued the windings of the suite. These windows were of stained glass whose color varied in accordance with the prevailing hue of the decorations of the chamber into which it opened. That at the eastern extremity was hung, for example, in blue—and vividly blue were its windows. The second chamber was purple in its ornaments and tapestries, and here the panes were purple. The third was green throughout, and so were the casements. The fourth was furnished and lighted with orange—the fifth with white—the sixth with violet. The seventh apartment was closely shrouded in black velvet tapestries that hung all over the ceiling and down the walls, falling in heavy folds upon a carpet of the same material and hue. But in this chamber only, the color of the windows failed to correspond with the decorations. The panes here were scarlet—a deep blood color. Now in no one of the seven apartments was there any lamp or candelabrum, amid the profusion of golden ornaments that lay scattered to and fro or depended from the roof. There was no light of any kind emanating from lamp or candle within the suite of chambers. But in the corridors that followed the suite, there stood, opposite to each window, a heavy tripod, bearing a brazier of fire that projected its rays through the tinted glass and so glaringly illumined the room. And thus were produced a multitude of gaudy and fantastic appearances. But in the western or black chamber the effect of the firelight that streamed upon the dark hangings through the blood-tinted panes was ghastly in the extreme, and produced so wild a look upon the countenances of those who entered, that there were few of the company bold enough to set foot within its precincts at all.

It was in this apartment, also, that there stood against the western wall, a gigantic clock of ebony. Its pendulum swung to and fro with a dull, heavy, monotonous clang; and when the minute-hand made the circuit of the face, and the hour was to be stricken, there came from the brazen lungs of the clock a sound which was clear and loud and deep and exceedingly musical, but of so peculiar a note and emphasis that, at each lapse of an hour, the musicians of the orchestra were constrained to pause, momentarily, in their performance, to hearken to the sound; and thus the waltzers perforce ceased their evolutions; and there was a brief disconcert of the whole gay company; and, while the chimes of the clock yet rang, it was observed that the giddiest grew pale, and the more aged and sedate passed their hands over their brows as if in confused reverie or meditation. But when the echoes had fully ceased, a light laughter at once pervaded the assembly; the musicians looked at each other and smiled as if at their own nervousness and folly, and made whispering vows, each to the other, that the next chiming of the clock should produce in them no similar emotion; and then, after the lapse of sixty minutes (which embrace three thousand and six hundred seconds of the Time that flies), there came yet another chiming of the clock, and then were the same disconcert and tremulousness and meditation as before.

But, in spite of these things, it was a gay and magnificent revel. The tastes of the duke were peculiar. He had a fine eye for colors and effects. He disregarded the *decora* of mere fashion. His plans were bold and fiery, and his conceptions glowed with barbaric lustre. There are some who would have thought him mad. His followers felt that he was not. It was necessary to hear and see and touch him to be *sure* that he was not.

He had directed, in great part, the movable embellishments of the seven chambers, upon occasion of this great *fête;* and it was his own guiding taste which had given character to the masqueraders. Be sure they were grotesque. There were much glare and glitter and piquancy and phantasm—much of what has been since seen in "Hernani." There were arabesque figures with unsuited limbs and appointments. There were delirious fancies such as the madman fashions. There was much of the beautiful, much of the wanton, much of the *bizarre,* something of the terrible, and not a little of that which might have excited disgust. To and fro in the seven chambers there stalked, in fact, a multitude of dreams. And these—the dreams—writhed in and about, taking hue from the rooms, and causing the wild music of the orchestra to seem as the echo of their steps. And, anon, there strikes the ebony clock which stands in the hall of the velvet. And then, for a moment, all is still, and all is silent save the voice of the clock. The dreams are stiff-frozen as they stand. But the echoes of the chime die away—they have endured but an instant—and a light, half-subdued laughter floats after them as they depart. And now again the music swells, and the dreams live, and writhe to and fro more merrily than ever, taking hue from the many-tinted windows through which stream the rays from the tripods. But to the chamber which lies most westwardly of the seven, there are now none of the maskers who venture; for the night is waning away; and there flows a ruddier light through the blood-colored panes; and the blackness of the sable drapery appals; and to him whose foot falls upon the sable carpet, there comes from the near clock of ebony a muffled peal more solemnly emphatic than any which reaches *their* ears who indulge in the more remote gaieties of the other apartments.

But these other apartments were densely crowded, and in them beat feverishly the heart of life. And the revel went whirlingly on, until at length there commenced the sounding of mid-night upon the clock. And then the music ceased, as I have told; and the evolutions of the waltzers were quieted; and there was an uneasy cessation of all things as before. But now there were twelve strokes to be sounded by the bell of the clock; and thus it happened, perhaps, that more of thought crept, with more of time, into the meditations of the thoughtful among those who revelled. And thus, too, it happened, perhaps, that before the last echoes of the last chime had utterly sunk into silence, there were many individuals in the crowd who had found leisure to become aware of the presence of a masked figure which had arrested the attention of no single individual before. And the rumor of this new presence having spread itself whisperingly around, there arose at length from the whole company a buzz, or murmur, expressive of disapprobation and surprise—then, finally, of terror, of horror, and of disgust.

In an assembly of phantasms such as I have painted, it may well be supposed that no ordinary appearance could have excited such sensation. In truth the masquerade license of the night was nearly unlimited; but the figure in question had out-Heroded Herod, and gone beyond the bounds of even the prince's indefinite decorum. There are chords in the hearts of the most reckless which cannot be touched without emotion. Even with the utterly lost, to whom life and death are equally jests, there are matters of which no jest can be made. The whole company, indeed, seemed now deeply to feel that in the costume and bearing of the stranger neither wit nor propriety existed. The figure was tall and gaunt, and shrouded from head to foot in the habiliments of the grave. The mask which concealed the visage was made so nearly to resemble the countenance of a stiffened corpse that the closest scrutiny must have had difficulty in detecting the cheat. And yet all this might have been endured, if not approved, by the mad revellers around. But the mummer had gone so far as to assume the type of the Red Death. His vesture was dabbled in *blood*—and his broad brow, with all the features of the face, was besprinkled with the scarlet horror.

When the eyes of Prince Prospero fell upon this spectral image (which with a slow and solemn movement, as if more fully to sustain its *rôle,* stalked to and fro among the waltzers) he was seen to be convulsed, in the first moment with a strong shudder either of terror or distaste; but, in the next, his brow reddened with rage.

"Who dares?" he demanded hoarsely of the courtiers who stood near him—"who dares insult us with this blasphemous mockery? Seize him and unmask him—that we may know whom we have to hang at sunrise, from the battlements!" It was in the eastern or blue chamber in which stood the Prince Prospero as he uttered these words. They rang throughout the seven rooms loudly and clearly—for the prince was a bold and robust man, and the music had become hushed at the waving of his hand.

It was in the blue room where stood the prince, with a group of pale courtiers by his side. At first, as he spoke, there was a slight rushing movement of this group in the direction of the intruder, who at the moment was also near at hand, and now, with deliberate and stately step, made closer approach to the speaker. But from a certain nameless awe with which the mad assumptions of the mummer had inspired the whole party, there were found none who put forth hand to seize him; so that, unimpeded, he passed within a yard of the prince's person; and, while the vast assembly, as if with one impulse, shrank from the centres of the rooms to the walls, he made his way uninterruptedly, but with the same solemn and measured step which had distinguished him from the first, through the blue chamber to the purple—through the purple to the green—through the green to the orange—through this again to the white—and even thence to the violet, ere a decided movement had been made to arrest him. It was then, however, that the Prince Prospero, maddening with rage and the shame of his own momentary cowardice, rushed hurriedly through the six chambers, while none followed him on account of a deadly terror that had seized upon all. He bore aloft a drawn dagger, and had approached, in rapid impetuosity, to within three or four feet of the retreating figure, when the latter, having attained the extremity of the velvet apartment, turned suddenly and confronted his pursuer. There was a sharp cry—and the dagger dropped gleaming upon the sable carpet, upon which, instantly afterwards, fell prostrate in death the Prince Prospero. Then, summoning the wild courage of despair, a throng of the revellers at once threw themselves into the black apartment, and, seizing the mummer, whose tall figure stood erect and motionless within the shadow of the ebony clock, gasped in unutterable horror at finding the grave-cerements and corpse-like mask which they handled with so violent a rudeness, untenanted by any tangible form.

And now was acknowledged the presence of the Red Death. He had come like a thief in the night. And one by one dropped the revellers in the blood-bedewed halls of their revel, and died each in the despairing posture of his fall. And the life of the ebony clock went out with that of the last of the gay. And the flames of the tripods expired. And Darkness and Decay and the Red Death held illimitable dominion over all.

Edwin Arlington Robinson

Richard Cory*

Whenever Richard Cory went down town,
We people on the pavement looked at him:
He was a gentleman from sole to crown,
Clean favored, and imperially slim.

*This selection is featured in the model student essay in Chapter 3.

And he was always quietly arrayed,
And he was always human when he talked;
But still he fluttered pulses when he said,
"Good-morning," and he glittered when he walked.

And he was rich—yes, richer than a king—
And admirably schooled in every grace:
In fine, we thought that he was everything
To make us wish that we were in his place.

So on we worked, and waited for the light,
And went without the meat, and cursed the bread;
And Richard Cory, one calm summer night,
Went home and put a bullet through his head.

Information at a Glance

Approach	Purpose(s)	Assumption(s)
Familiar	To understand literature in the context of an author's biography and/or historical period.	Literature reflects the life and world of its author.
Formalist	To value a literary work for its own intrinsic properties.	Literature is an utterance of abstract, absolute truths about reality.
Psychological	To determine meanings that are suggested but not overtly stated.	(1) Literature comes from the unconscious of a writer, expressing meanings that even he or she may not recognize. (2) A character's nature is revealed by more than external actions: dreams, symbols, slips of language. Some literary patterns can be universally recognized.
Archetypal	To identify universal images and patterns of conduct that carry emotional power.	Some literary patterns are universally recognized.
Marxist	To reveal how those in control of the means of production manipulate the rest and thereby change the system.	Economics controls all aspects of a society. The material, not the spiritual, is all important.
Feminist	(1) To read with heightened awareness of the nature, social roles, and treatment of female characters.	(1) Because society is and has been basically patriarchal, the talents and products of women have been undervalued, leaving them without visible power.

(Continued)

Approach	Purpose(s)	Assumption(s)
	(2) To recognize ignored and undervalued female writers. (3) To explore more sexual identities than the traditional male/female binary.	(2) Sexual orientation is central to critical analysis and understanding.
Reader-Response	To include the reader in constructing the meaning of a text.	Whatever a text means is at least partially the product of a reader's interaction with it.
Deconstructionist	To demonstrate the multiplicity of meanings in a given text.	Meaning is always provisional, not stable, united, or unchanging.
New Historicist	To understand a text as a product and maker of complex and sometimes conflicting historical forces.	Because a text is the product of more than a single contributing source, it is not explainable simply as the reflection of a controlling idea of a given period.
Postcolonialist	To examine the literature of colonized peoples and that of the descendants of their colonizers, featuring what happens when one culture is dominated by another.	Physical conquest of a culture leads to loss or serious modification of it, resulting in uncertainty of identity for both the conquered and the colonizers, who live in a mixed culture often marked by contrasts and antagonisms, resentment, and blended practice.
Multiculturalist	To identify and analyze the literatures of racial and ethnic minorities in order to discover their unique characteristics and worldviews.	The literature of historically marginalized groups provides a rich source of works for analysis.
Ecocritical	To examine the relationship of literature and nature as a way to renew a reader's awareness of the nonhuman world and his or her responsibility to sustain it.	Because all life is inter-related, the impact of human activity on the environment should be minimized.

Strategy or Strategies	Strength	Weakness
Read literature as a reflection of major events, figures, and ideas of a period.	Provides a framework for tracing growth and development of literary ideas and styles.	Subordinates literary concerns to nonliterary ones.
Read closely to see how tensions in diction and style are resolved into a unified whole.	Shows how meaning is a product of form.	Looks for a single best interpretation.

(Continued)

Strategy or Strategies	Strength	Weakness
Pay close attention to unconscious motivations and meanings expressed indirectly through dreams, language, and symbols.	Reveals meanings that are not explicitly stated.	Can degenerate into nonliterary jargon or arrive at unjustified interpretations.
Identify characters or behaviors similar to those you have met in other narratives.	Deepens the emotional and thematic impact of a text.	Can overlook meaningful details in the search for universal patterns.
Identify the powerful individuals or groups in the text and show how they create the superstructure that controls the proletariat.	Connects literature with life—that is, with everyday concerns about economics, class, and power.	Is essentially nonliterary—that is, does not take aesthetic matters into account.
(1) Examine the roles and treatment of female characters. (2) Discover (or reintroduce) works by neglected female writers. (3) Look for fluidity of characters' sexual identities.	Gives attention to traditionally overlooked aspects of a text and to heretofore ignored writers.	Can become narrowly focused, leaving out other important aspects of a text.
Connect the life experiences and worldviews of the reader with the text.	Makes the reader an active coparticipant in creating a text, not simply a passive receiver of it.	Can produce idiosyncratic readings.
Identify those places where misstatements, gaps, and inconsistencies in a text undermine what it claims to be saying.	Opens up a text to an unending series of new interpretations.	Uses difficult, specialized vocabulary.
Acknowledge all the social concerns that surround and infuse a text, particularly the power structures of the culture it depicts and that of the author's world.	Accepts any written text as worthy of serious analysis (not just those composed in traditional literary genres).	May neglect literary elements of a text for its political aspects.
Determine the stance of a text regarding colonialism, postcolonialism, and/or neocolonialism.	Generates understanding of cultures as well as texts.	Can be more concerned with social criticism than literary criticism.
Identify materials, purposes, and styles that are characteristic of a racial or ethnic minority.	Liberates the minority from dependence on mainstream standards of performance.	Divides cultural groups from one another.
Pull traditionally disregarded elements of nature into the center of your reading.	Makes the reader aware of his or her obligation to treat nature with respect.	Is more interested in social change than in literary analysis.

Glossary of Terms Used in Literary Criticism

Note that terms found in boldface type throughout the text are defined in the glossary.

Affective fallacy Concern for the effect a work has on the reader. According to the formalists, to use affect as a criterion of judgment is a mistake because doing so judges a poem by what it *does* instead of what it *is*. Aristotle's theory of catharsis as an element of tragic drama is a strong example of the affective fallacy at work.

Allusion A brief reference to a character, person, object, event, or situation outside the work in which it is made. Well-known biblical **allusions** are common in all **genres**, but modern poets sometimes make more obscure references that assume a considerable breadth of learning to understand.

Ambiguity Wording that suggests more than one meaning or interpretation. It is to be avoided in some **genres**, such as nonfiction prose, but can be powerfully suggestive in others, such as poetry. By calling up more than a single meaning, ambiguous wording can add to the thematic complexity in a work.

Androcentric A term used to describe attitudes, practices, or social organizations that are based on the assumption that men are the model of being. Feminists challenge that belief because it ignores or marginalizes the characteristics of female existence.

Anima/animus The life force within an individual. It is both life itself and the creator of life. In the male, it is made up of female elements of the self (the anima), and in the female, it is composed of the male elements of the self (the animus). It belongs to the personal and **collective unconscious**. The term is important in Jungian theory.

Anthropomorphism Attribution of human characteristics to things not human.

Aphorism A short, succinct statement of a principle or piece of wisdom. It is notable more for its wisdom than its wit. It lends itself to frequent quotation.

Aporia A point in a text where contradictions cannot be resolved, causing it to deconstruct itself. Traditionally it refers to a condition of uncertainty or doubt, though Derrida has used it to refer to terms that resist being divided into **binary oppositions**.

Archetypes Inherited ideas or ways of thinking generated by the experiences of the human race that exist in the unconscious of an individual. They are universal and recurring **images**, patterns, or **motifs** representing typical human experience that often appear in literature, art, fairy tales, myths, dreams, and rituals. They unite the conscious and the unconscious, helping to make an individual whole.

Base The methods of production in a given society. Marxist theory argues that the modes of production of material life determine the ideological **superstructure** (composed of state, legal, social, and political forms).

Binary opposition Paired opposites in which the first named is the dominant figure—e.g., male/female, white/black, making the dichotomy an evaluative hierarchy. Such opposing elements are always unstable, however, because they can be inverted. The term is important to **structuralists** and deconstructionists.

Black aesthetic Methods of literary interpretation that are concerned with the materials black artists work with, the purpose of their work, and how they go about doing it.

Bourgeoisie The name given by Marx to the owners of the means of production in a society. It is a term taken from French, used to refer to members of the middle class—i.e., shopkeepers and merchants.

Carnival Mikhail Bakhtin's term for a social practice that mocks authority and reverses hierarchies. It challenges traditional power bases and opens the way to a new social order. He sees the novel as carnivalesque because it has the ability to challenge restrictive social forces, obliterate social hierarchies and blur distinctions among social classes. It can reverse the traditional systems of authority and order.

Collective unconscious The inherited experience of the human race that resides at a deep level of the psyche. Its contents come from recurrent life situations that are common to all human beings. They take the form of **archetypes** and are revealed in **images** and **symbols** that appear in dreams, literature, religions, and mythologies. The concept of the collective unconscious is one of the major differences between the theories of Freud and Jung.

Colonialism The subjection of one **culture** by another. It may involve military conquest but also extends to the imposition of the dominant power's values and customs on those of the conquered peoples. It usually suggests some form of exploitation of the colonized peoples.

Commodification A Marxist term referring to the attitude of valuing things not for their utility but for their power to impress others or for their resale possibilities.

Condensation Freud's term for the workings of the unconscious in which a single word or **image** in a dream represents the intersections of a number of ideas of associations. The term or **image** condenses their unconscious meanings and emotions.

Connotation Secondary meanings and feelings associated with a word in addition to its denotative, or dictionary, meaning. Connotation can be affected by the context in which a word is used, although some words carry fairly universal secondary meanings. For example, to most people the word *home* suggests warm feelings associated with family.

Conspicuous consumption The obvious acquisition of things only for their **sign value** and/or **exchange value**.

Cosmic irony The suggestion that the universe manipulates events so that characters in a narrative are led to anticipate logical outcomes of their actions that do not occur. The novels of Thomas Hardy frequently depict such situations, suggesting that individuals are mocked by whatever power controls their lives.

Cultural colonization The imposition of the beliefs and social practices of a dominant power on a subjugated one, resulting in loss or change of the native **culture**. Cultural colonization often follows political or military colonization.

Cultural materialism The British counterpart of new literary historicism, significantly influenced by Marxist principles.

Cultural studies A broadly inclusive term that refers to the work of literary theorists, philosophers, and critics who focus on the work of marginalized, overlooked, and repressed groups. It seeks to go beyond institutional politics and look at social change from the perspective of **culture** and cultural production as manifested in social life, class relations, institutions, and more. It is interdisciplinary in its approach.

Culture The sum of the social patterns, traits, and products of a particular time or group of people. It includes the ideas, customs, skills, and arts that characterize the era or the community.

Dark greens Deeply committed ecologists who advocate a complete return to nature, a move that is not feasible for most people. They differ from environmentalists known as **light greens**, who are less zealous in their commitment to minimizing humankind's impact on nature.

Defamiliarization A term coined by the **Russian formalists** to refer to the artful aspects of a work that, by making the familiar seem strange, awaken the reader to new experiences and understandings. They change a reader's perception of even an ordinary object so that he seems to be seeing it as if for the first time.

Demonic other The view that those who are different from oneself are not only backward but also savage, even evil. The term is frequently used in postcolonial studies.

Denotation The core or specific meaning of a word, without any associated or suggested meanings.

Diachronic An approach to the study of language that traces how and why words have evolved in meaning or sound over time. Saussure sees it in opposition to a **synchronic** approach that studies the state of a language at one particular stage of its development.

Dialectical materialism The theory that history develops neither in a random fashion nor in a linear one but instead as a struggle between contradictions that ultimately find resolution in a synthesis of the two sides. For example, conflicts of social classes that are defined by economic relations of production lead to new social systems.

Dialogism The belief that language (all forms of speech and writing) is always a dialogue consisting of at least one speaker, one listener/respondent, and a relationship between the two. It opposes the view that language is an utterance that issues from a single speaker or writer—i.e., that it is monologic (see **monologism**). Dialogism is a key concept in Mikhail Bakhtin's theory of language.

Dialogized heteroglossia. A characteristic of prose in general and the novel in particular, according to Mikhail Bakhtin. The novel features a diversity of voices (making it heteroglossic) in ongoing responses to each other (making it dialogic). It recounts multiple experiences and worldviews in frequent interactions, some of them actual and some of them fictive.

Différance The term Jacques Derrida used to indicate that meaning is based on differences and is always postponed. (Its spelling suggests two meanings, both difference and deferral.) If language and meaning have no origin and no end, it is ultimately undecideable.

Discourse Ways of thinking, talking, and writing about the world. The term usually refers to a relatively formal discussion that has a serious purpose. Modern linguistics supports the view that discourse is not subjective, but instead promotes subjectivity by making human beings subjects.

Displacement Like **condensation**, a Freudian reference to the workings of the unconscious. It refers to the process of moving emotions that are related to an idea or person to a less important object.

Double consciousness A term coined by W. E. B. DuBois that refers to the "sense of always looking at one's self through the eyes of others." He describes it as the experience of perceiving oneself to be "an American, a Negro; two souls, two thoughts, two unreconciled strivings; two warring ideals in one dark body, whose dogged strength alone keeps it from being torn asunder."

Double-voicedness A term used by Henry Louis Gates to refer to evidence in literature of the black person's sense of "twoness" that comes from being both an American and a Negro. Gates identifies this quality as the source of the uniqueness of black literature.

Dramatic irony A form of irony in which the audience knows what is about to happen but the characters do not. A famous example is found in *Oedipus Rex*, in which Oedipus seeks to find his father's murderer without knowing that the killer is he himself.

Dyadic pair (dyads) A term used by Claude Lévi-Strauss to refer to basic oppositions in a narrative that hold symbolic and thematic meanings. They interact to form the larger structure to which the narrative belongs.

Ecocriticism A school of literary criticism that studies the relationship between literature and the surrounding environment. It is sometimes referred to as literary ecology, ecopoetics, environmental literary criticism, green cultural studies, or (somewhat mockingly) as compoststructuralism.

Ego In Freudian terms, the central part of the psyche that mediates between the inner self and the external world. It also mediates between the contradictory demands of the **id** and the **superego**, partly by postponing the id's urges or by diverting them into socially acceptable actions.

Environment The surrounding landscape. For ecocritics environment differs from **nature**, which refers to the landscape as it was before it was impacted by technology.

Episteme The system that defines the conditions for how a particular age views its world. Its original meaning in Greek was "knowledge," but in Foucault's use it is not a body of knowledge but the conditions that allow knowledge to exist or to be limited. It underlies the interaction of **discourse**s of the period.

Essentialism The idea that a person's true identity is composed of fixed and unchanging properties. The theory has been challenged by feminists who see references to "an eternal female nature" as pejorative and reductive. On the other hand, some feminists have themselves been accused of being essentialists in their emphasis on specific differences that women embody, thereby suggesting "the eternal feminine" once again.

Eurocentrism The assumption that European ideals and experiences are the standard by which all other **cultures** are to be measured and judged inferior. It is hotly challenged by those who value cultures that exist outside of Europe, particularly those that have been colonized.

Etymology The study of the origins of words or of a specific word.

Exchange value A Marxist term referring to an assessment of the worth of something based on what it can be traded or sold for. The amount of human labor-power contained in it is the basis for establishing the value of a commodity.

Exotic other The view that those who are different from oneself possess an inherent dignity and beauty, perhaps because of their more undeveloped, natural state of being. It is a theme of postcolonial studies.

Explication de texte A detailed analysis of small units that compose a work, including words, meanings, and images, and of how they work together to create meaning. The method originated in France. Its purpose is to discover the structure and meaning of a work. Frequently the simpler term *explication* is used to refer to general interpretation of a text.

False consciousness People's acceptance of an unfavorable social system without protest or questioning. When they assume that the difficult conditions under which they live are simply the logical way for things to be, they are exhibiting false consciousness.

Figure of speech Words used in more than their literal sense. They may appear as similes, metaphors, synecdoches, metonymies, or other forms.

Folk tradition Customs, language, legends, beliefs, and attitudes characteristic of peoples generally regarded as unsophisticated, possibly unlettered. In literature folk traditions are contained in ballads, epics, tall tales, fairy tales, myths, and riddles.

Geneva critic A reader who attempts to identify with the unique consciousness of a writer through his written works. Sometimes referred to as "critics of consciousness," such readers seek to discover how characters, imagery, and style are projections of the author's own awareness and feelings. The purpose is to participate in, perhaps even identify, with the writer's essential being. The Geneva critics sometimes assemble widely disparate examples of a writer's work or even examine the total oeuvre to demonstrate recurring themes and **motifs** that are unique to that author.

Genre An artistic form. The categories are based on commonalities of form, technique, and content. In literature the **genres** are sometimes broadly defined (e.g., as drama, poetry, fiction) and sometimes more narrowly delineated (e.g., as lyric, epic, essay, or novel).

Grammar The system of rules and codes that directs literary interpretation. **Structuralist** A critic who seeks to reveal the grammar of literature.

Gynocriticism A movement that examines the distinctive characteristics of the female experience, in contrast to earlier methods that explained the female by using male models. As applied to literature, gynocriticism is concerned with developing new ways to study the writing of women. The school seeks to make visible a continuous female experience that could easily be ignored by Marxist critics intent on examining class conflicts or by **structuralists** who are interested in diagrams and systems.

Hegemony Dominance of one state or group over another.

Heteroglossia Mikhail Bakhtin's term for the interplay of the numerous forms of social speech that people use as they go about their daily lives. It refers to the manner in which their diverse ways of speaking—their varied vocabularies, accents, expressions, and rhetorical strategies—mix with each other. It can be described as living language because it features multiplicity and variety, as well as suggestions of different professions, age groups, and backgrounds.

Heterosexual privilege The assumption that heterosexuality is the standard by which sexual practice is measured. Objections to it from the gay and lesbian community mirror those of feminists who protested against explanations of female experience that were based on male models.

Historical situation The ideological atmosphere generated by **material circumstances**. According to Marxist theory, to understand social or political events and conditions, one must have a grasp of the material circumstances and the historical situation in which they occur.

Homophobia The fear, dislike, and/or disapproval of homosexuals and homosexuality. It is observable in demeaning

images, casual comments, jokes, and other forms of expression.

Horizon of expectations A term generated by Hans Robert Jauss to refer to the linguistic and aesthetic expectations of a reading public. It is important in the work of the **receptionists**, who look for what readers of a particular era valued and looked for in a literary work.

Hybridity/syncretism A postcolonial term referring to the quality of **culture**s that have characteristics of both the colonizers and the colonized. Marked by conflicts and **tensions**, they are continually changing and evolving. Hybridity challenges traditional identities based on class, race, and gender and offers a release from singular identities.

Id An unconscious part of the psyche that is the source of psychic energy and desires. It operates for the sole purpose of finding pleasure through gratification of its instinctual needs. Part of the **ego** merges with the id, drawing energy from it through sublimation.

Ideology A belief system. It is a set of values and ways of thinking through which people see the world they live in and explain why it exists. Two principal elements of the ideology of Marxist theory are expressed in figurative terms as a **superstructure** and a **base** that generates it.

Image A mental picture created by references to the senses: visual, auditory, tactile, olfactory, gustatory, thermal, and kinesthetic. On occasion an image can appeal to more than one sense, as in "I heard the rainbow sing." Images are often the basis of figurative language because they provide a way to talk in concrete terms about abstract matters.

Imaginary Order A term used by Jacques Lacan to refer to the prelinguistic psychic stage at the beginning of which the infant is unaware of its separateness from the mother or any other object that serves its needs. It includes the **mirror stage**, during which the infant begins to recognize its separateness from other objects and to develop a sense of self, which is actually illusory since it is based on an external reflected image. The other two developmental orders, according to Lacan, are the **Real Order** and the **Symbolic Order**.

Implied reader Wolfgang Iser's term for a reader with the skills and qualities required by a text if it is to have the intended effect. The work itself helps to create that reader by using patterns, points of view, and withheld information to indicate the role he or she is to play as the narrative unfolds. It invites certain responses that, when made, make the real reader the one that is implied by the text.

Individuation A term used by Carl Jung to denote successful discovery, acceptance, and integration of one's own **shadow**, **anima/animus**, and **persona**. It is a psychological maturation.

Intentional fallacy Concern for the author's purpose in writing the work. To formalists, this way of determining the meaning and effectiveness of a work is erroneous, because it is based on information outside the text.

Interpellation A term used by Louis Althusser to refer to the process by which the working class is manipulated to accept the **ideology** of the dominant class.

Interpretive communities Stanley Fish's term for groups of competent, even sophisticated, readers who make meaning based on assumptions and strategies they hold in common. They are agreed as to what constitutes literature and have mastered the practices that allow them to read literary texts.

Irony A statement or situation in which the intended meaning is the opposite of what is literally said, done, or expected. It can take several forms, including **Socratic irony**, **dramatic irony**, and **cosmic irony**. It was prized by the formalists, who recognized the complexity and suggestiveness it brought to a poem. A famous example of irony is Jonathan Swift's *A Modest Proposal*, in which the essayist proposes that the Irish sell their children to the British for food. The indirection of signifying in African American **culture**, created by saying one thing and meaning another, is another practice of irony.

Jouissance Jacques Lacan's term for the sense of being whole. In his earlier work it seems to refer to enjoyment, but from the 1960s onward it carries sexual **connotations**. The French noun can also mean orgasm, and Lacan pushes it to refer to an intense eroticism associated with a death drive that goes well beyond the pleasure principle.

Langue The language that is used by all members of a particular language community. As Saussure conceives of it, it is composed of **signs** that are organized into a system that can be used to express ideas. Since the signs are arbitrary and conventional, it is the differences among them that give them meaning, making *langue* an organized system of differences.

L'Écriture féminine A term used by French critics to designate women's writing. It is sometimes referred to as "writing the body." This experimental form of writing celebrates femininity and reflects on a society that is dominated by the **image** of the **phallus**. It often weaves creative and theoretical texts together by ignoring traditional distinctions between theory and fiction.

Lexies A word coined by Roland Barthes to indicate units of meaning in a narrative. He classified them into five codes that he deemed to constitute the basic structure of all stories.

Libido A Freudian term referring to instinctual energies and desires that are derived from the **id**. Although Freud never defines it clearly, it is commonly used as a synonym for sexual energy.

Light greens Environmentalists who support conservation and limits. They differ from "**dark greens**," the deeply committed ecologists who advocate a complete return to nature, a move that is not feasible for most people.

Logocentrism Belief in an absolute that grounds existence. Based on the Greek word *logos*, it expresses credence in a rational and structured cosmos, providing human beings with an explanation for their origin and their nature. In terms of language, it assumes that the linguistic system is capable of producing a spoken or written utterance that has a fixed, understandable meaning. Derrida's objections to logocentrism are central to his theories of deconstruction.

Material circumstances The economic conditions underlying the society. To understand social events, one must have a grasp of the material circumstances and the **historical situation** in which they occur.

Means, Objects, and Manner Aristotle's classification of literary forms as set forth in his ***Poetics***. The term *means* refers to the medium of the work—for example, music, prose, or verse; *objects* refers to the nature of the situation or characters being imitated; and *manner* is the **point of view**, which can be the voice of a character, the author's own voice, or the voice of an actor.

Metaphysics of presence Beliefs including **binary oppositions**, **logocentrism**, and **phonocentrism** that have been the basis of Western philosophy since Plato. They are grounded in the assumption that conscious, integrated selves are at the center of human activity. Derrida and other deconstructionists raise serious objections to such beliefs.

Mimicry Imitation of the dress, manners, and language of the dominant **culture** by an oppressed one. The term is found in postcolonial criticism.

Mirror stage A term used by Jacques Lacan to refer to an event that occurs between the ages of six and eighteen months involving an infant seeing him- or herself in a mirror and identifying with the **image**

that appears there. The reflection signals a functional unity that the child has not yet developed. Since the child is not an **image** in a mirror, the experience begins a lifelong misrecognition of identity that eventually leads to alienation.

Misogyny The hatred of women, especially by a man. Feminists critics are quick to note its presence in works of literature.

Monologism The assumption that language issues from a single speaker, in contrast to **dialogism**, which involves at least two speakers. It honors a unified discourse cleansed of differences that interrupt one accepted way of using language. According to Mikhail Bakhtin, monologic language operates according to centripetal force, forcing everything into a single form that emanates from one central source. It standardizes language and rhetorical forms, ridding itself of differences in an effort to establish a single way of speaking and writing.

Monomyth Northrop Frye's term for literature, a self-contained universe that incorporates the indifferent world of nature into archetypal forms that serve the needs and desires of human beings. It is composed of four **mythoi**.

Motif A recurring phrase, **image**, scene or theme in a work. Its function is to unify the piece. The term is also applied to musical compositions in which a melody is repeated throughout.

Mytheme Claude Lévi-Stauss's term for the smallest elements used in the analysis of myths. They are used to reveal larger, more universal structures. He chose the name for its reference to phonemes, Saussure's term for the smallest phonological unit. Mythemes are analogous to the functions named by Vladimir Propp in his study of Russian folk tales.

Myth A narrative that purports to explain why something exists or why something happens. Myths often feature acts by supernatural characters and develop according to archetypal patterns. They establish social customs and rules that control a people's behavior. They usually involve ritual observances.

Mythoi Four narrative patterns that, according to Northrop Frye, exhibit the structural principles of the various **genres**. He associated each (comedy, romance, tragedy, and satire) with a season of the world of nature, incorporating that world into a verbal universe that human beings understand because it serves human needs.

Narrative functions Rules that, according to Vladimir Propp, generate narratives. They do not all appear in any one work, but those that do must appear in the order in which he listed them. His work was important in the development of **narratology**.

Narratology The structuralist study of narrative plots. Influential in its development have been Claude Lévi-Strauss's study of myths and Vladimir Propp's study of the morphology of Russian folk tales. It seeks to provide a formal description of narrative possibilities. It is not intended to evaluate a work.

Nature The environment before it was impacted by technology. For ecocritics it is an inclusive term used to refer to the land, its flora and fauna, its waterways, living creatures, and the ecosystem that nourishes them.

Negotiation The relationship between a text and its context, both the one that produced it and those that consume it. The assumption is that each affects the other in significant ways.

Neocolonialism Domination of a developing nation by international corporations attracted by cheap labor and manipulable political and legal systems. It is the modern version of colonization in which militarism has been replaced by economic forces.

Oedipal attachment Sigmund Freud's theory that around the age of five a boy perceives his father to be a rival for the love of his mother. The desire to possess the mother and to be rid of the rival father can be repressed but continue into adulthood, leading to aberrant behavior. The term is drawn from Sophocles's tragedy *Oedipus the King*.

other Jacques Lacan's term (spelled with a lower case "o") to refer to the reflection an infant mistakenly takes to be the self during the **mirror stage** of development. The infant thinks the reflection is real and uses what it sees to create the ego, the sense of "I." It is only an illusion, however, and we are, in actuality, not complete selves. Thus the "self" is always manufactured by the erroneous acceptance of an external image for an internal identity. Lacan refers to it as the "other" because it is not the actual self, only an image outside of the self. The term is used in another sense by postcolonial theorists to refer to the negative view of subjected peoples held by their colonizers. It assumes that those who are different from oneself are inferior beings.

Other Those remaining elements that exist outside the self, objects and people that the infant comes to know before becoming aware of its own "other." When the infant realizes it is not connected to that which serves its needs, when it recognizes the Other and its own "other," he begins to enter the **Symbolic Order**. The term is used in another sense by postcolonial theorists to refer to colonized peoples. It carries with it the negative view of them held by their colonizers, who assume that those who are different from themselves are inferior beings.

Paradox A statement that seems to contradict itself but is actually true. An example is Wordsworth's comment that "the child is father of the man."

Paraphrase A reworded version of a passage or work, usually made by someone other than the original writer. To a formalist, it cannot substitute for what it restates.

Parody An effort to mock a person, an event, or a work of literature through imitation and variation. It uses humor to ridicule and criticize.

Parole Individual verbalizations within the system called ***langue***. According to Saussure, whereas *langue* is the social aspect of language, *parole* consists of particularized speech acts. The dialectic between the two, wherein *parole* can affect *langue*, is responsible for evolution of the language.

Patriarchal A term describing an institution or social system that is headed and directed by a male. It can also refer to someone who approves of such a system. The patriarch, usually an older, venerated person, may be the founder or current ruler of the group. Feminists regard it as being synonymous with "male domination."

Performative A term that refers to a locution that is also the act it names. For example, in a marriage ceremony the words "I take this man to be my lawfully wedded husband" are not just a spoken statement, but also the act of marriage itself. Judith Butler uses the term to refer to the ongoing construction of gender that begins when someone says "It's a girl" at the moment of birth.

Persona Carl Jung's term for the social mask that an individual constructs and wears to face others. It is a blending of what the person is and what society expects him or her to be. It is the being that other people know as one's self.

Personal conscious A state of awareness of the present moment. Once that moment has passed, it moves into the realm of the **personal unconscious**. According to Jung, it is one of the three parts of the human psyche, the other two being the personal unconscious and the **collective unconscious**.

Personal unconscious A storehouse of past personal experience no longer extant in the **personal conscious**. In Jung's theory, it is one of the three parts of the human psyche, the other two being the personal conscious and the **collective unconscious**.

Phallic symbol A masculine **symbol**. It is recognizable because it is convex. That is, its length exceeds its diameter.

Phallus A term used by Jacques Lacan that refers to a privileged **signifier**, the **symbol** of power that gives meaning to other objects. Desired by the mother, it becomes an object of identification for the child, who wants to satisfy the mother's desire and its own desire for the mother. Thus has Lacan reworked Freud's concept of the Oedipus complex.

Phenomenologist One who subscribes to a branch of philosophy that asserts that the perceiver of an object plays a central role in determining meaning. In fact, the person and the object it is aware of are deemed to be inseparable. As applied to literature, a work is created when an author directs his attention toward an object and records the act in a text. A reader, in what is called "active reading," reexperiences the act, but also fills in elements that have not been fully realized, making him or her a co-creator.

Phenomenological critics Critics whose philosophical perspective assumes that a thinking subject and the object of which it is aware are inseparable. The **Geneva critics**, who read a text as the consciousness of an author put into words, are often described as practicing phenomenological criticism.

Phonocentrism The belief that speech is privileged over writing. Derrida argues that the assumption that it is only the acoustic differences between phonemes that give language meaning makes modern linguistics logocentric.

Poetics A general descriptive theory of literature. It does not refer solely to poetry or verse alone. Instead, it tries to define and describe the elements that create a work's "literariness." The earliest such study was Aristotle's *Poetics*. More recently it has been carried on in the work of the **structuralists**. The **Russian formalists** considered poetics to be the proper subject of literary study.

Point of view The perspective from which a narrative is told. If the author chooses to use a character to relate events, he assumes a first-person point of view. The character may be a major participant in the events depicted, or a minor one who sits on the sidelines and observes. If the narrative is told by an anonymous but all-knowing storyteller, the point of view is said to be omniscient.

Polyphonic Mikhail Bakhtin's term for novels that depict a world in which the dialogue goes on ad infinitum without reaching a conclusion or closure. Its structure is not predetermined to demonstrate the author's worldview, nor are the characters drawn to exemplify it. It is typified by the novels of Dostoyevsky, in which the reader hears many voices uttering contradictory and inconsistent statements in the context of a real-life event.

Polyrhythms Short, uneven, explosive lines in a poem. According to Don Lee, they are one of seven characteristics commonly found in the work of black poets.

Postcolonialism The study of the global effects of European colonization. It seeks to analyze **cultures** whose traditional language, laws, religion, and literature have been affected by domination from Europe. There is considerable disagreement about which cultures should be included and some disagreement as to whether it is limited to the period following physical and/or political withdrawal of an oppressive power or whether it includes the entire period of colonization.

Postcolonial literary criticism Analysis that looks to uncover the colonialist or anticolonialist ideologies in a text. It frequently brings marginalized characters and events to the center of a reading or looks at how colonialism initiated pejorative cultural stereotypes.

Postcolonial literature The writings produced by members of the indigenous **culture** or by settlers (and their descendants) who have ties to both the invading culture and the oppressed one. (Agreement about the inclusion of the latter is not universal.) In English-speaking nations, the term usually refers to the literature of former colonies of the British Empire.

Poststructuralism Theories (including deconstruction, new historicism, postcolonial, and neo-Freudian theory) that are based on Ferdinand de Saussure's linguistic concepts but that at the same time undermine them. The term is used loosely, making it difficult to arrive at a succinct definition, but its various manifestations find points of commonality in their acceptance of the instability of meaning, their rejection of belief in metaphysical origins of **discourse**, and their suspicions of scientific systems.

Power The ability or official capacity to exercise control. According to Michel Foucault, knowledge is a form of power, and the search for knowledge manifests a will to exercise power over others. It is not an object, but a group of forces in which power meets with resistance.

Production theory The name given to Louis Althusser's ideas about the ability of literature and art to change a society's **base**. By creating and celebrating its own cultural artifacts, the **proletariat** can produce a revolution that replaces the **hegemony** of the dominant class with its own.

Proletariat The name given by Marx to the workers in a society. Its members have nothing but their labor to sell to survive, and in a capitalist system they are deemed by Marxists to be traditionally exploited.

Psychobiography The use of a psychoanalytic approach to writing the life of an author. A psychobiographer traces the subject's psychological development by examining the events of his life and looking for evidence of himself in his writings. Using Freudian theory principally, the psychobiographer looks for unconscious motivations and desires in an effort to discover the usually overlooked forces in a writer's maturation.

Race, Milieu, et Moment According to Hippolyte Taine, these three major factors determine a work's uniqueness. By *race*, Taine referred to national characteristics that are typically found in works of art produced by the creative artists of a given country. By *milieu*, he meant the artist's environment. He used *moment* to refer to the less personal influences in a writer's life, to those that govern not the individual but the age.

Real Order A term used by Jacques Lacan to refer to the psychic state of the infant in which there is no language, no loss, lack, or absence. As one of the three orders that structure human existence in Lacanian theory, it is characterized by wholeness, fullness, and unity with the mother. It precedes the development of a sense of the self as a being that is separate and apart from others. The other stages of development include the **Imaginary Order** and the **Symbolic Order**.

Reception Theory A historical approach to a work that involves examining the changing responses to it on the part of the general reading public over a period of time. It can be viewed as an historical application of reader response theory, the difference being that instead of focusing on a single reader at one particular time, it looks at how readers in general have responded to a work over a long period of time. The process of revising critical interpretations and evaluations of a text is referred to as a "dialectic" or "dialogue" between a text and an ongoing series of readers.

Reflectionism A theory of Marxist critics that the **superstructure** of a society mirrors its economic base and, by extension, that a text reflects the society that produced it.

Reflectionist A critic who practices **reflectionism** for the purpose of discovering how characters and their relationships typify and reveal class conflict, the socioeconomic system, or the politics of a time and place.

Russian formalism A school of criticism active in Russia and Czechoslovakia in the early part of the twentieth century that worked to establish a scientific basis for explaining how literary devices produce aesthetic effects. Its members advocated examination of the linguistic and structural elements of a work, rejecting methods or knowledge from other fields of study as extraneous to literary scholarship. Its leaders included Viktor Shklovsky and Roman Jakobson. It was abolished by the Soviet government in 1930 when its followers refused to examine literature through the lens of its political ideology. In the 1940s and 1950s it indirectly influenced the development of the New Criticism.

Sardonic comedy The practice of making fun of adversity, as in jokes. The effect can be bitter, sarcastic, or ironic.

Satire A literary work that ridicules the folly or stupidity of a person, a type of person, an institution, nation, or even humankind. It differs from comedy, which generates laughter for its own sake, in that it evokes amusement to point out human vice and foolishness. It can be a potent weapon.

Self-positioning The announcement of one's own political and philosophical leanings. Critics working from a new historicist perspective recognize their inability to be purely objective in their studies, making it important to acknowledge their social stance and biases to their readers. It constitutes an ethical responsibility.

Semiology A science proposed by Saussure that investigates meaning through **signs** observable in cultural phenomena. Sometimes called semiotics, it seeks to discover the laws that govern signs. The field was significantly broadened by Barthes, whose concept of it included all sign-systems in play in a society.

Semiotics Another study of signs, this one pioneered by Charles Sanders Pierce in the United States. It differs little from the work begun by Saussure and Barthes, except that it has continued to grow and develop.

Shadow Carl Jung's term for the dark, unattractive aspects of the self that reside in the **personal unconscious**. An individual's impulse is to reject the shadow and project it onto someone or something else.

Sign The combination of a **signifier** and a **signified**, according to Saussurean linguistics. (It is not a combination of an object and a name for the object.) As there is no logical connection between the signifier and the signified, a sign is simply arbitrary. Signs are distinguished from one another by their phonic differences. It is the basic unit of the analysis of language.

Sign value An assessment of something based on how impressive it makes a person look. Marxists draw distinctions between **sign value**, **use value**, and **exchange value**.

Signified The conceptual meaning indicated by a **signifier**. It is one part of a **sign**.

Signifier A conventional sound utterance or written mark. It is one part of a **sign**.

Signifying/Signifyin' A clever, playful, but indirect way of giving an opinion about another person. It is part of the African-American vernacular and literary practices from the Harlem Renaissance of the 1920s, but it is found in both its musical and oral traditions. The second form of the word is used by Henry Louis Gates to indicate pronunciation.

Signifying Monkey The master Trickster of African-American folktales who embodies the practice of signifying. He outwits his adversaries by using double talk. The signifying monkey is important in the theories of Henry Louis Gates but widely recognized by other African-American artists as well.

Social constructivist One who supports the idea that human identity is formed by the **culture** into which one is born.

Socialist Realism Works of fiction that depict Marxist views of the struggle between social classes. Through the 1930s and for decades thereafter it was the doctrine that governed the work of Soviet writers. Such works typically recount narratives that feature oppressive bourgeois capitalists and virtuous members of the **proletariat**. Life under the Soviet Socialist system is depicted as happy and fulfilling.

Socratic irony A rhetorical device used by Plato in Socrates's *Dialogues*. The narrator, who pretends not to understand the comments of his respondent, asks seemingly innocent questions that eventually demonstrate the opposing point of view to be ill conceived.

Spheres of action Seven character types formulated by Vladimir Propp. They are based on the types of actions they perform.

Structuralism A science that seeks to understand how systems work. It sees any cultural product or activity to be a signifying system with a self-sufficient and self-determining structure of interrelationships. Its practitioners try to describe the underlying (and not necessarily visible) principles by which systems exist.

Structuralist A critic who analyzes literature following principles of modern linguistic theory. Structuralist critics seek to uncover the rules and codes by which a work is written and read and thereby to reveal the **grammar** of literature. They make an analysis by applying linguistic concepts (such as the differences between phonemic and morphemic levels of organization) to a work of literature.

Structure How a work of literature makes a statement. For the Formalist critic the term refers to more than the external order of a poem or story. It is the whole that is produced by various structural elements working together to create a unified whole. Structure is a work's essential, basic meaning.

Subaltern A person of inferior status. The subordinate position of subalterns may be based on gender, class, office, or caste. Subaltern writers seek to make their marginalized **cultures**, which are largely unrecognized by history, known and valued for their past and present. The term figures largely in postcolonial studies.

Subject An ambiguous term that is used by postmodernists to refer to a person. The practice serves to shift the source of meaning away from the individual toward structures and ideologies. It undermines the premise that the individual has a stable sense of self or can be the center of experience.

Superego The part of the psyche that provides discipline and restraint by forcing unacceptable desires back into the unconscious. It is formed early on by parents and later by social institutions and other models.

Superstructure The social, political, and ideological systems and institutions—for example, the values, art, and legal processes of a society—that are generated by the **base**, the socioeconomic system. There is some disagreement among Marxists about the manner and degree of influence the base and superstructure have on each other.

Supplementation An ambiguous term devised by Derrida to refer to the lack existing in speech that must be complemented by writing. It is part of his argument regarding **logocentrism**'s practice of privileging speech over writing.

Symbol Someone or something that is a literal presence but is also a representation of something beyond himself, herself, or itself. The physical object or person usually refers to something abstract. Some symbols are "conventional" or "public," readily recognized by members of a particular **culture**. Others are "personal" or "private," making them more difficult to interpret. Poets are often given to using the latter.

Symbolic Order A term used by Jacques Lacan to refer to the psychic stage of development in which an individual learns language and it shapes his or her identity by taking the place of what is lacking and giving the speaker the capacity to name the self as "I." (During that process it overlaps to some degree with the Imaginary.) The Symbolic also initiates socialization by setting up rules of behavior and putting limits on desire. It is ruled by what Lacan calls the Law of the Father, because it is the father who enforces cultural norms and laws. The other Lacanian orders are the **Real** and the **Imaginary Orders**.

Synchronic An approach to the study of language that searches for the principles that govern its functions by examining a language at one particular point in time. Saussure sees it in opposition to a **diachronic** approach, which traces the changes that have taken place in a language throughout its history. Most schools of modern linguistics are synchronic.

Tension A term devised by Allen Tate and used by other Formalists to refer to the energy created by conflicting elements in a work, usually appearing in the form of **ambiguity**, **irony**, and **paradox**. It occurs when such elements resist coming together easily or comfortably to form a unified whole.

Textual criticism The process of establishing a version of a work that is as close as possible to what the author wrote or intended to be its final form for the purpose of giving the public an authorized version of that work. It involves comparing the various published texts of a work and original manuscripts to discover where they differ, then locating the source of errors and correcting them. The procedure requires the critic to render expert judgment, since during their lifetime authors sometimes approve differing versions of the same work for publication.

Thick description A term used by anthropologist Clifford Geertz to designate the collection of seemingly insignificant details that will reveal a **culture**. It is not a neutral observation but an attempt to discover and understand the layers of meaning that reside in complex cultural structures and stories.

Trace The illusory effect of meaning that is left in a **signifier** by other signifiers—that is, what it is not. It is Derrida's term for all the nonpresent meanings whose differences from the signifier give a statement the effect of having meaning in itself.

Transactional analysis An approach advocated by Louise Rosenblatt in which the critic considers how the reader interprets the text as well as how the text produces a response in him or her. It is a form of reader-response criticism in which meaning is created by the author and the audience.

Transcendental signified A fixed, ultimate center of meaning. It provides human beings stable, unchanging, ongoing meaning that grounds belief and actions. Over the ages it has gone by many names—God, truth, essence. Derrida denies its existence.

Übermensch Nietzsche's strong, independent "superman" of the future who will be freed of all values except those he holds to be valid. The philosopher foresees the development of a higher man who will be joyful and wise, thereby overcoming the decadence and nihilism Nietzsche saw in the society of his day.

Unfinalizability Mikhail Bakhtin's term for ongoing changes that occur in an individual, making it impossible to fully understand him or her. Because it is language that defines a person, and language is dialogic (see **dialogism**), one is always in a process of becoming and can never be completely known.

Unhomeliness The sense of being culturally displaced, of being caught between two **culture**s and not "at home" in either of them. The term was devised by Homi Bhabha to refer to the condition felt by those who lack a clearly defined cultural identity.

Unity The coherence of the elements of a work that creates a sense of an organic whole. It is created when all the various parts of a work (diction, **images**, **point-of-view, symbols**, meter, rhyme and more) interrelate with each other to make a statement. The Formalists look for a work's unifying elements.

Universalism The belief that a great work of literature deals with certain themes and characters whose significance and appeal are not limited by time or place. They are thought to be common to people in all civilizations regardless of geography or era. In actuality, the themes and characters alluded to are common in European literature, making universalism Eurocentric in nature.

Use value An appraisal of something based on what it can do. It evaluates an object according to the degree to which it satisfies a human need. The term is important in Marxist theory, which is centered on the analysis of commodities.

Vulgar Marxism Another name for ***reflectionism***. Those critics who practice it assume that literary works of the last century have been dominated by bourgeois **ideology**. They call for social realism to replace that impetus, a move that in practice can push art to conform to the political strictures of governing authorities.

Weltanschauung The author's worldview. It is a German term that means "manner of looking at the world." As such, it is used to refer to an individual's philosophy or how one views civilization and his or her relationship to it.

Yonic symbol A feminine symbol, particularly significant for Freudian critics. It is recognizable because it is concave—for example, a bowl or a cave.

Index

B

C

D

E

N

T

Y